CLASSICAL SOCIOLOGY

CLASSICAL SOCIOLOGY

Bryan S. Turner

SAGE Publications
London • Thousand Oaks • New Delhi

SAGE Publications Ltd
6 Bonhill Street
London EC2A 4PU

SAGE Publications Inc
2455 Teller Road
Thousand Oaks, California 91320

SAGE Publications India Pvt Ltd
32, M-Block Market
Greater Kailash - I
New Delhi 110 048

British Library Cataloguing in Publication data

A catalogue record for this book is available from the
British Library

ISBN 0 7619 6457 6
ISBN 0 7619 6458 4 (pbk)

Library of Congress catalog card number 99–71432

Typeset by SIVA Math Setters, Chennai, India.
Printed in Great Britain by Cromwell Press Ltd,
Trowbridge, Wiltshire.

Contents

Preface: The Sociological Classics

There is in contemporary social theory a degree of hostility to the study of the sociological classics. It is sometimes argued that the world we live in is so manifestly different from the social context within which the classics of sociology were written that the view of social life of early sociologists can have little relevance to us. For example, the computer on which this manuscript was written would have been unimaginable to Max Weber whose cramped but energetic handwriting has given translators so much difficulty. It is also claimed that the canon which constitutes classical sociology represents a unified view of sociology which can no longer be sustained in our academic world which is fragmented, diverse and contested. Canonical works in literature have been challenged by a process of decolonization which has rejected the hegemony of western literature. Critics also feel uncomfortable with the sociological canon of 'founding fathers'. We know that women in sociology have found it difficult to find a voice and the idea of a definite founding event in the construction of a separate discipline of sociology is controversial. Finally, the construction of a tradition within the discipline of sociology must be somewhat artificial given the fact that most of the principal contributions came from people who would not have self-consciously regarded themselves as sociologists. Despite these difficulties, a hasty and ill-considered rejection of classical sociology is to be avoided for reasons which I try to establish in this study of early sociological theory.

In part, I support existing defences of the classics which suggest that the nature of dispute and development in sociological theory is very different from the pattern of intellectual development in the natural sciences. Analytical difficulties and debates in sociology are not easily resolved, because the issues themselves remain essentially contested. Because there is no obvious theory cumulation or resolution of disputes, one can still learn from and value the classical accounts of sociological theory. The epistemological, theoretical and methodological difficulties which were identified and debated by Max Weber and Emile Durkheim have not been and cannot be easily resolved. In contemporary sociology, we may have a better understanding of the implications of these debates and may have more sophisticated technologies for approaching certain problems in sociology but in essence the arguments for and against the use of ideal types, for example, are largely unchanged In this respect, sociological theory is no different from political theory. One can enjoy and benefit from reading Thomas Hobbes on sovereignty as one can enjoy reading Weber on bureaucracy. Reading the classics is simply a useful aspect of the intellectual education of a social scientist.

The study of classical sociology is therefore a worthwhile exercise provided the following conditions are recognized: the canon remains open to revision; it is not reified into an exclusionary justification of professional membership of sociology departments; it is accepted as in part a retrospective summary of intellectual endeavour and thus remains always a somewhat arbitrary collection of texts; defending the classics cannot be an excuse for neglecting contemporary social theory, and finally it does not stand in the way of contemporary intellectual activity and development. A healthy scepticism should not be a legitimation of or an excuse for ignorance.

While these general principles are useful, it is possible to offer a more robust defence of the sociological canon. My principal argument is that, although rupture and diversity are very obvious features of sociological theory, there are also some hidden points of continuity, and the contemporary student of sociology cannot understand the discipline without such an historical awareness. Let us take an issue which plays a significant part in my understanding of the sociology of Weber. In his approach to power and culture, Weber was heavily influenced by the work of the German philosopher Friedrich Nietzsche (1844–1900). Nietzsche had argued that we can only know the world from some vantage point or perspective, in the current situation these perspectives are in a state of constant conflict, and finally therefore reason has very specific limitations. The authority of these perspectives lies not necessarily in its inherent analytical or moral value, but on the political powers which underpin intellectual authority.

Weber's uncertainty about the ability of sociology ever to know the world unambiguously followed from this lesson of Nietzsche's epistemology and hence his various analyses of sociological method (ideal types, the principles of hermeneutic understanding, the fact-value distinction and so forth) were thoroughly grounded in Nietzsche. In addition, Weber followed Nietzsche in believing that many of our ethical approaches are expressions of psychoanalytical conflicts in the individual and are ultimately expressions of the presence or absence of real power. In this respect, Nietzsche's criticisms of Christianity are well known and they also once more influenced Weber's sociology of religion.

What we can define as Nietzsche's perspectivism also had a profound impact on the philosophy of Martin Heidegger (1889–1976) and through Heidegger's critique of the 'metaphysics of being' Nietzsche's philosophy has fundamentally shaped the modern debate about modernism and postmodernism. For example, the most frequently quoted definition of postmodernism comes from J.-F. Lyotard who claimed that postmodernism is simply a scepticism about grand narratives. In short, perspectivism makes certain large-scale world views untenable. Similarly, Richard Rorty has argued, from the standpoint of what he calls liberal or bourgeois postmodernism, that postmodernism is the realization that there are no 'final vocabularies', that is there is no way of being finally certain that our view of reality is true. In fact as a pragmatist, Rorty argues that it is more profitable to ask whether a philosophy is useful or adequate to certain problems rather than whether it is true.

If we try to put this contemporary debate about postmodernism in its larger historical framework, we can see that the problem about perspectivism has gone through three phases. In the nineteenth century, philosophers and theologians debated the problems of historicism. In the world of Christian belief, the Bible came to be regarded as a somewhat arbitrary collection of the texts and these biblical texts were seen to be an expression of different historical context. How was it possible then to derive some universalistic message from the Christian faith which could be true for all people in their various historical settings? Historicism thus relativized the Christian message by arguing that the prophetic message of Jesus was historically specific. Ernest Renan's comparative philology developed a critique of the sacred texts of the Abrahamic religions by demonstrating the local Semitic quality of their respective sacred languages. His *Vie de Jesus* transformed Christ into a Jewish prophet of a particular time and place. In the first part of the twentieth century, cultural relativism was profoundly shaped by the discoveries of social anthropologists whose work on 'primitive religions' began to provide some interesting comparisons with the 'world religions', especially Christianity. Protestant theologians like William Robertson Smith began to develop an early sociology of religion which translated these specific ethnographic studies into a more coherent and far-reaching sociology of the sacred. But the consequences of their intellectual inquiry were to raise critical responses from ecclesiastical authorities who recognized the corrosive impact of their ideas. This debate about local cultures in relation to world religions and globalization continues today. The final stage of this historical development of relativism is in fact the postmodern debate, which has, along with subaltern studies, feminism and postcolonial theory, brought into question large, universalistic claims about the authority of final vocabularies.

Reading Weber's attempts to come to terms with the legacy of Nietzsche is not only a useful preparation for understanding postmodernism, it is in fact an essential foundation for such an approach. The ironic aspect of postmodernism of course is that it often denies there can be any history of any idea or institution. For postmodernism, history is merely one type of narrative which can be offered for an institution or individual. It is part of the postmodern agenda to undermine historical narratives, including historical accounts of postmodernism itself. Such a closure of history provides postmodernism, however, with some protection from its own relativity.

A grounding in Weber's confrontation with Nietzschean perspectivism is helpful in putting postmodernism in its (historical) place. There is thus a strange parallel between the reconstruction of social consciousness in the 1890s and the postmodernization of social thought in the 1990s.

How does Karl Marx fit into this picture? One argument is that Marx, Nietzsche and Weber produced similar responses to the problem of human existence in industrial society, where the traditional world of the ecclesiastical institutions, agricultural economies, political conventions, traditional moral codes and conventional values was breaking down. Marx's theory of the alienation of human beings from themselves and their social world, Nietzsche's sense of the separation of human beings from their own consciousness by the neurotic character of Prussian Germany and Weber's view of the world as disenchanted (as an iron cage) exhibit certain similarities. In order to illustrate that argument, I have in this collection of writing on classical sociology included an introduction to Karl Löwith's study of *Max Weber and Karl Marx*. Löwith was a student of Heidegger and read Weber and Marx from the perspective of Heideggerian theology. Both Weber and Marx in their respective writing on rationalization and alienation provided an analysis of the human condition which is closely related to Heidegger's sense that modern people have lost their way in the world. Heidegger's classical study of *Being and Time* constantly refers to the importance of discovering a way in the forest, of clearing a space for man to dwell in harmony with Being. By studying Löwith's extended essay on Weber and Marx, we can begin to see this close connection between Nietzsche, Weber and Heidegger, and also appreciate how Marx's philosophical anthropology of human estrangement foreshadowed a profound philosophical and sociological critique of technological civilization and its negative consequences. The sociological classics within this framework become living documents to a tradition of critical reflection and research on the dilemmas of human existence in an industrial and technological civilization.

This book falls into two parts. The first part looks at key thinkers in the growth of early sociology (Karl Marx, Max Weber, Georg Simmel, Emile Durkheim, Karl Mannheim and Talcott Parsons). The second part explores the key institutions which dominated sociological and anthropological inquiry in the late nineteenth and early twentieth centuries. Together these two parts provide the student with a systematic introduction to classical sociology and its development in the twentieth century. The guiding theme of this study is the idea of alienation as an account of human existence in a social world which has been transformed by a process of rationalization.

Thus in Part I, I explore the influence of the legacy of Marx and Marxism on early sociology, and trace the evolution of that Marxist influence through Weber, Simmel, Mannheim and Durkheim. The discussion concludes with the work of Parsons who is recognized as, in many respects, the conclusion of the classical tradition. Part I starts with an essay comparing and contrasting Marx and Weber (from the Heideggerian perspective of the work of Löwith), which sets the scene by comparing the themes of human alienation and social rationalization. The second chapter looks at Weber's sociology as a major sociological response to the legacy of Marx. The following chapters explore Mannheim's work on ideology and culture as responses to Marxist theories of ideology. The chapter on Durkheim considers his analysis of civil society, the state and 'intermediary groups' which demonstrates that the claim that he had no political sociology is a serious misreading. Durkheim, like Marx, was aware of the negative impact of economic individualism on mental life and social harmony. Against the utilitarian view of society, Durkheim developed a theory of the role of the state as a moral agent, which anticipated some features of the contemporary debate about citizenship. The chapter on Simmel examines his philosophy of money as an alternative to Marxist economic sociology. Part I concludes with a study of Parsons as a critic of utilitarian economic thought and treats Parsonian sociology as the end point of the first wave of sociology.

In Part II, I examine key institutions in the development of the socio-logical imagination and the theme of Marxism and its critique is continued into the area of institutional analysis. To some extent, the question of the role of religion in the development of capitalist society preoccupied both Marxism and early sociology. In a comparison of Marxist and Weberian approaches to class analysis, I also explore the debate about social class and consider the emergence of social stratification theory in North American sociology. Other chapters look at the contributions of both Marxists and sociologists to the study of the family in industrial capitalism. The growth of the sociology of the city also illustrates the contested views of the impor-tance of urban social relations in debates about alienation, marginalization and ethnic conflicts. Part II also includes an examination of the sociology of generations which elaborates Mannheim's criticisms of Marxist class analysis and concludes with a chapter exploring the contribution of T.H. Marshall to political sociology. In Marshall's sociology, citizenship is an institution which contributes to the reform of capitalism and mitigates the impact of class conflict through a redistribution of resources.

These essays provide therefore one possible defence of the importance of the legacy of classical sociology for an understanding of the modern world. Early sociology engaged with a range of social issues to do with inequality and power, which remain relevant to contemporary society. More importantly, classical sociology addressed a series of moral questions through the themes of alienation, anomie and rationalization which are useful tools by which to probe the ethical dilemmas of the next century.

Acknowledgements

Chapter 1 is a rewritten version of the introduction to the second edition of *For Weber* London, Sage, 1997. Chapter 2 was originally an introduction to volume one of *Max Weber. Critical Responses* London, Routledge, 1999. It has been modified and developed. Chapter 3 was first published as a new preface to Karl Löwith's classic study of *Max Weber and Karl Marx* London, Routledge, 1993. Chapter 4 was a new preface to Hans Gerth and C. Wright Mills's *From Max Weber* London, Routledge, 1991. Chapter 5 was the preface to the second edition of Emile Durkheim's *Professional Ethics and Civic Morals* London, Routledge, 1992. Chapter 6 was published as a new preface to Karl Mannheim's *Ideology and Utopia* London, Routledge, 1991 and Chapter 7 was a new preface to *Essays on the Sociology of Culture* London, Routledge, 1992. Chapter 8 on Georg Simmel was first published in *The Sociological Review* (1986) vol. 34(1) and Chapter 9 was a new preface to Talcott Parsons's *The Social System* London, Routledge, 1991.

Chapter 10 was an introduction to *The Early Sociology of Religion* London, Thoemmes Press, 1997. Chapter 11 was an introduction to *The Early Sociology of the City* London, Thoemmes Press, 1997. Chapter 12 was an introduction to *Readings on the Sociology of Social Class* London, Thoemmes Press, 1998. Chapter 13 was an introduction to *Readings in the Anthropology and Sociology of Family and Kinship* London, Thoemmes Press, 1998. Chapter 14 was written with Ron Eyerman and published as 'Outline of a theory of generations', *European Journal of Social Theory* (1998) vol. 1(1). Finally Chapter 15 was published as 'Citizenship studies, a general theory', *Citizenship Studies* (1997) vol. 1(1).

I would like to thank Professor Chris Rojek of Nottingham Trent University for his support and encouragement in writing these contributions to classical sociological theory and to Frances Parkes of Routledge for her advice in putting together many of the collections that formed the Thoemmes Press publications on early social theory. Discussions and exchanges with various members of Research Committee 16 of the International Sociological Association, especially Professor Ron Eyerman, formed the intellectual background to this book. Finally, the editorial board of *Theory, Culture & Society* has played an important educative role in my own intellectual and personal development.

PART I

CLASSICAL THEORY

CHAPTER I

THE CENTRAL THEMES OF SOCIOLOGY: AN INTRODUCTION

The Marx–Weber Debate

Although the relationship between Marx and Weber has been the topic of considerable debate and research (Antonio and Glassman, 1985), we need to distinguish carefully between three somewhat separate issues: Weber's relationship to the social theories of Marx, his relation to Marxism as an intellectual tradition and his relation to communism as a revolutionary movement. It is clear that, while Weber was impressed by Marx as a social analyst, he did not know about the entire corpus of Marx's work, he did not fully understand Marx and finally Marx did not make a systematic impact on Weber. There is no simple way in which Weber was involved in a debate with 'the ghost of Marx' (Salomon, 1935). Both supporters and critics of Weber of course welcomed *The Protestant Ethic and the Spirit of Capitalism* as a possible refutation of Marx's analysis of industrial capitalism. In the 1960s and 1970s, in a similar fashion academic sociologists treated Weber's *Economy and Society* as the principal alternative to Marx's *Capital*.

In fact, there is relatively little overt discussion of the work of Marx in Weber's sociology. As many commentators have noted, Weber would not have had access to such crucial texts of Marx as *Economic and Philosophical Manuscripts, Theses on Feuerbach* or *Grundrisse*. For Weber, Marx's work represented a mono-causal explanation of history in terms of economic conditions and therefore Weber believed that Marxist sociology had not adequately confronted the problems raised by neo-Kantianism and in particular by the methodological theories of Wilhelm Dilthey, Heinrich Rickert and Wilhelm Windelband (Sahay, 1971). To some extent, it was left to Austro-Marxism to undertake this confrontation with neo-Kantian epistemology (Bottomore and Goode, 1978).

Although in the formulation of his sociology Weber was not systematically influenced by Marx, this empirical observation does not imply that there was no relationship. For example, it is important for the central argument of this book to note that there is a significant similarity and connection between Marx's concept of alienation and Weber's concept of rationalization (Löwith, 1993). It is also true that Marx and Weber shared similar ambiguities towards an understanding of bureaucracy, markets and science as crucial components of capitalist society and as forces of modernization (Sayer, 1991). However, we cannot argue that during his lifetime an engagement with the work of Marx was constitutive of Weber's sociological arguments. Weber was by contrast very much concerned with the issue of the impact of Marxism as a social ideology on the German working class through the Social Democratic movement. Although Marx developed a revolutionary politics of capitalism, by the 1890s it was obvious that German capitalism would not collapse as a consequence of revolution. If anything, the real incomes and the standard of living of the working class had risen. There had been as a result no polarization or pauperization of society. Weber was critical of the German Social Democratic Party (SPD) which attempted to combine a reformist approach to electoral politics with a faith in the final triumph of socialism. Under the leadership of intellectuals like Eduard Bernstein, the SPD had adopted political reformism, namely the theory that there would be a gradual transformation of capitalism through the electoral participation of the working class. Bernstein and his followers abandoned any commitment to practical revolutionary strategies and tactics, such as the general strike. Weber tended therefore either to despise reformism, because it combined political conservatism with a revolutionary rhetoric, or to regard it as no longer a significant dimension of German politics, and yet paradoxically he was often in agreement with Bernstein who rejected, for example, Marx's doctrine of economic determinism (Breuilly, 1987).

While Weber was interested in the fortunes of the SPD, he was fearful of any further destabilization of the German state, especially after the political defeat of 1918–19. Weber was closely involved with other scholars in political disputes about Germany after the War and, in the debates in 1917 at Lauenstein Castle about the constitutional future, radical students, including Georg Lukács, had anticipated that Weber would announce a new political order (Kadarkay, 1991: 187). Instead Weber welcomed the fact that Russian interference in Germany had been averted, and recognized the inevitability of American hegemony in the emerging world system. Weber's lack of engagement with the radical politics of the student movement was also a function of the fact that he remained consistently anxious about the 'Russian danger'. As a nationalist, Weber was concerned to protect the cohesion of Germany as a strong nation-state. In his essays on the Russian revolutions (Weber, 1995), he attempted to analyse the failures of liberal-bourgeois democracy. The constitutional reforms had been frustrated by the failure of local and provincial governments to gain autonomy, the social and political weakness of the bourgeoisie as a class and the permanent authoritarianism of the Tsarist regime. Weber remained fearful over the persistent threat of eastern authoritarianism, and therefore rejected the views of the radical youth of Munich who sought an end to war through a Russian-style revolution.

Weber, influenced by the work of Robert Michels on 'the iron law of oligarchy', believed that a revolution could not succeed without a loyal bureaucratic staff, but bureaucratization would also limit the scope of revolution (Mommsen, 1989). It was over these issues that he, for example, departed company with Lukács whose views he treated as romantic and utopian. In an important but incomplete passage on revolution in *Economy and Society*, Weber argued that the German bureaucracy had survived the War and thereby demonstrated the durability of modern bureaucracies. He also attributed some of the success of the Russian Revolution to the fact that workers and soldiers were able to take up bureaucratic tasks successfully. He concluded that 'every revolution which has been attempted under modern conditions has failed completely because of the indispensability of trained officials and of the lack of its own organized staff' (Weber, 1978: 266). Lukács and other radicals who regarded revolution as a spiritual transformation of society found it difficult to accept Weber's realism when it came to the assessment of political conditions.

After Weber's death, there was little discussion of his sociology in the English-speaking world and obviously intellectual exchange between Germany and the Allies was very limited. However, from the 1950s until the end of the 1970s, there was a steady stream of translations of Weber's major works, which illustrated the scope of Weber's intellectual achievement. Weber's reception into North American sociology was, however, through the interpretation and perspective of Talcott Parsons, who did not pay much attention to Weber's economic and political sociology. Parsons was primarily concerned with Weber's relationship to the voluntaristic theory of action and to the sociology of religion (Holton and Turner, 1986). Against this perspective, a number of sociologists emphasized the importance of so-called 'conflict sociology' and interpreted Weber as a social theorist whose major contribution had been to the analysis of material interests, group struggle and social conflict (Rex, 1961).

During the cold war period, there was also a huge expansion of undergraduate sociology in European universities. In this context, there emerged a considerable ideological battle around the works of Marx and Weber. With the growth in popularity of so-called structural Marxism, Weber was increasingly defined as a 'bourgeois sociologist', whose commitment to methodological individualism and political liberalism confirmed his membership of the bourgeois class. There were a number of important translations of Marxist works into English which fuelled the debate such as *For Marx* (Althusser, 1969) and *Political Power and Social Classes* (Poulantzas, 1973). In England, sociology became polarized around those who supported Poulantzas's criticisms of individualistic and 'unscientific' sociology and those who by contrast supported the view of Marxism as a scientific theory of social formations.

In both America and continental Europe, these Marxist debates had less impact on the curriculum of sociology in the universities. The May events of 1968 passed without any permanent damage to the governments of western Europe. In the United States, despite the Vietnam War, Marxism made little serious progress and debates about social theory were more likely to be organized around pro-Parsons and anti-Parsons factions (Alexander, 1987), while actual empirical research was quantitative in the tradition of P.F. Lazarsfeld. Radical and critical appraisals of Parsons drew upon both Marx and Weber, because in the American context Weber often appeared as a radical social theorist (Gouldner, 1970; Mills, 1959). We therefore have the paradox that in the communist bloc social theorists took Weber very seriously, but regarded him as a bourgeois sociologist. In western sociology, Weber was often neglected in favour of structural Marxism or neglected because he appeared to be a Machiavellian theorist of power politics.

By the time Parsons died in 1979, functionalism was moribund and has remained so, despite attempts to revive it in the shape of neo-functionalism (Alexander, 1985). A decade later organized communism eventually collapsed and there has been throughout the eastern bloc a significant revival of sociology which has ironically often involved a renewal of interest in Weberian sociology. Althusser committed suicide in 1990, by which time structural Marxism had ceased to be influential. During this period, however, there was also a general decline in sociology within western universities and a new interest in cultural studies with the result that the notion of 'culture' has somewhat replaced 'society' as the key topic of sociological discussion. The sociological reasons for these changes are to be sought in the growth of cultural consumerism, global tourism, the aestheticization of everyday life and the postmodernization of culture (Connor, 1996). As one might expect, therefore, the contemporary interest in Weber tends to emphasize the importance of culture in Weber's sociology, to associate Weber with Nietzsche as a cultural critic and to relate Weber's dispute over values to postmodernism as a cultural theory. The relationship between Marx and Weber in western sociology is understated and other relationships (Weber and Nietzsche, Weber and Simmel) are discussed and promoted (Turner, 1992b). The future of Weberian sociology in the post-communist societies remains an issue of fascinating speculation (Weiss, 1986).

The Unintended Consequences of Action

In *For Weber* (Turner, 1981) I made a direct reply to theories of social structure which had been primarily influenced by structural Marxism, particularly by the writings of the French Marxist philosopher Louis Althusser. Althusser's influential reading of Marx, which had been originally published in France in 1965 as *Pour Marx*, appeared in English in 1969. *For Weber* was intended to be a direct challenge to the influence of structural Marxism by arguing that many of the claims of Althusser were inaccurate when applied to the work of Weber and that there was a structuralist reading of Weber which demonstrated at least some similarities with the work of Marx from a particular vantage point of interpretation. Marxist critics of Weberian sociology often dismissed this legacy as individualistic, subjectivist and unscientific. My study of Weber attempted to show that there was an objective dimension to his sociology which was exhibited in the notion of the unintended consequences of social action, namely consequences which lay outside the consciousness and intention of the social actors involved. The deterministic element in Weber's interpretive sociology was illustrated through a set of historical case studies which showed the fateful consequences of action over which social actors had no significant control, or indeed knowledge. The classical illustration of this fateful view of history was primarily demonstrated in Weber's famous 'Protestant Ethic' thesis (Lehmann and Roth, 1993). The unanticipated consequence of ascetic religious actions had been the creation of a capitalist culture, the secular outcomes of which often denied or undermined their religious callings which had given rise to the capitalist spirit in the seventeenth century. Weber's sociology of religion could be read or interpreted as a series of tragic narratives about the negative and unanticipated consequences of actions directed towards personal salvation. The tragic or fatalistic dimensions of Weber's sociology were in many respects parallel to the narrative structure of the tragic novels of Thomas Mann, particularly in such works as *The Magic Mountain* and *Buddenbrooks* (Marcus, 1987).

Weber's sense of personal tragedy and the fatefulness of western history was in part the cultural product of the transformations of the academic community in Germany where there had been a major decline in the status of the independent scholar and intellectual, a transformation which has been captured by Fritz Ringer in the notion of the decline of the German mandarins (Ringer, 1969). The theme of social tragedy or fate influenced not only the sociology of Weber but also the work of Tönnies, Troeltsch, Simmel and Lukács (Liebersohn, 1988). At a more profound level this *Kulturpessimismus* was a reflection of significant changes in the relationship between culture and social class in the educated middle strata of nineteenth-century Germany. This pessimism about culture was reflected in the debate about *Bildung* and personality which shaped the outlook of the late nineteenth-century educated, middle classes in Germany. This fatalistic view regarded the growth of civilization as a direct challenge to traditional culture and thereby to the status of the intellectual as the guardian of high culture (Elias, 1978; Goldman, 1992). The problems of social change, interpersonal ethics, the self and the demise of traditional rural values shaped the narrative content of the *Bildungsroman* in this period (Moretti, 1987). In a society where the traditional intellectual was being overtaken and bypassed by the technical specialist within an industrial civilization, what was the role of intellectuals in such an environment? Weber's bitter complaint about 'hedonists without a heart and experts without a spirit' (*Genussmenschen ohne Hertz und Fach menschen ohne Geist*) at the conclusion of *The Protestant Ethic and the Spirit of Capitalism* was an expression of this sense of the decline of the fully educated and comprehensive personality of the traditional intellectual. Weber's critique of the bureaucratization of intellectual callings was partly inspired by Friedrich Nietzsche's abhorrence at the growing dominance of the soulless state intellectuals within the emergent Prussian bureaucracy. Against these specialists with their calling to serve the state (the new *Berufsmenschentum*) Nietzsche proposed a revolutionary creation, Overman (*Übermensch*). Here again there was an important relationship between the literary treatment of the intellectual in Mann's novels (such as *Death in Venice* and *Doctor Faustus*) and Weber's particular concentration on the notion of intellectual vocations in science and politics (Lassman and Velody, 1989).

Nietzsche and Weber

For Weber was therefore engaged in a debate with Weber's sociology from the point of view of an interest in a tragic vision of history which was worked out within the context of Weber's highly technical sociology of social action. This pessimistic view of history was a consequence of Weber's direct and specific engagement with the legacy of the philosophy of Nietzsche, particularly with Nietzsche's concept of resentment (Stauth and Turner, 1988). Various aspects of Nietzsche's philosophy impinged upon Weber's formulation of a sociology of action. For example, there is in Nietzsche the contrast between Apollo, the God of Form and Reason, and Dionysus, the God of Emotion and Sexuality. Weber's analysis of the 'Protestant Ethic thesis' can be seen as an account of how the Apollo principle dominated over the emotional life through the formation of vocations in the economic sphere. This conflict between sexuality and civilization played a general role in Weber's analysis of the civilizational functions of religious values, but also in Weber's personality as a struggle between family responsibilities and sexual fulfilment (Green, 1974). Weber's personal values were thoroughly ambiguous, he admired the seriousness of the professional calling in science and politics, while also remaining aware of the destructive consequences of this-worldly asceticism. Secondly, the relationship between Weber's concept of charisma and the superman has also been noted in various aspects of the literature on Weber (Eden, 1983). Certainly the problem of leadership in a bureaucratic social environment remained a significant issue in Weber's political sociology. Thirdly, the central importance of power in Weber's sociology as a whole and Weber's interest in German politics in particular (Mayer, 1944; Mommsen, 1984) has often been associated with Nietzsche's concern for the role of the will to power in the shaping of human societies and human culture. Finally, Weber's ambiguous and critical relationship to religion, particularly the ascetic sects of Christianity, has, as a number of commentators have suggested, a direct relationship to Nietzsche's critical attacks on conventional religiosity in the nineteenth century (Schroeder, 1992).

These conventional commentaries on the relationship between Nietzsche and Weber may however have missed some of the essential features of the legacy of Nietzsche's critical philosophy in Weber's sociology. Nietzsche's philosophy grew out of a cultural critique of late nineteenth-century German society within which a new mentality, the mentality of professional specialists, was beginning to dominate cultural debate and ascetic appreciation. These cultural specialists were in Nietzsche's view closely associated with the dominance of Calvinistic theology and the expansion of the new Prussian state. This dominance of the state specialist was part of a long historical evolution of the relationship between church, state and education in German society. Weber's view of the professionalization of the scientific vocation was part of this Nietzsche critique of state functionaries. Returning to the 'Protestant Ethic' theme, Weber regarded these Calvinistic men of vocations as carriers of an ethic of world mastery which involved the domination of emotions and affectivity as merely irrational passions which stood in the way of rational action. Their social lives were controlled by a commitment to an ethic of mastery which subordinated such sexual emotions in the interests of personal control. Alongside these Protestant figures, Weber also placed the professional men of calling in science and politics, whose social relations were organized by a commitment to a rational plan in the interests of their personal achievement of public status within the new regime. These religious callings, as we know, drove these men beyond what was actually necessary for the satisfaction of their everyday needs and wants. This personal drive was the irrationality of economic rationality. This striving for world mastery did not lead however to a satisfaction with the meaningfulness of everyday life, but rather resulted in a continuing disenchantment with reality which drove out moral significance from everyday life. Weber argued in his sociology of civilizations that the peculiar danger of our period is characterized by expanding rationalization which results ultimately in religious and moral disenchantment. Weber explored various solutions to this dilemma, including for example the ethic of responsibility, the development of new forms of communitarian life, explorations with new patterns of eroticism, a return to the arms of the Church, and a series of vocations in science and politics. This search for a solution to personal disenchantment and meaninglessness provided the central tensions and ambiguities of Weber's sociological perspective. Some aspects of the feminist critique of Weber have dwelt on these issues of ethical heroism and world mastery in Weber's allegedly patriarchal view of power and values (Bologh, 1990).

The core of Nietzsche's social philosophy was an attachment to 'the little things' of everyday life (Stauth and Turner, 1988). Nietzsche thought that the values and practices of everyday life, which were centred on reciprocity and emotion, were being transformed by the rationalistic cultures of a technological civilization driven by industrial needs. For Nietzsche, religion and abstract philosophy were both misapprehensions and distortions of the values of everyday social life. In the terminology of contemporary critical theory, the life-world was being destroyed and rendered inauthentic by the new rationalist culture of the state as the values and morals of the private world were colonized by the rationalistic culture of the public arena. Nietzsche approached this problem of the inauthentication of the life-world via a discussion of the demise of Christian authority, or more generally, religious authority in his famous slogan that 'God is dead'. By this shocking slogan, Nietzsche wanted to indicate that in contemporary society it is no longer possible to identify a moral principle that will give a uniform, coherent and unquestioned authority to some general pattern of life or society. Following Richard Rorty's account of irony, we can say Nietzsche's vision of the death of God indicates that no 'final vocabulary' for justifying belief is possible and hence we are all exposed to the contingency of our own moral positions. In this ironist view, 'there is no such thing as a "natural" order of justification for beliefs or desires' (Rorty, 1989: 83). Weber engaged with this debate through a commentary on the polytheistic character of value conflicts in contemporary society. In short, Nietzsche's so-called 'perspectivism' became a part of Weber's basic epistemology of the social sciences. The 'truths' and empirical findings of sociological research are always the result or product of particular frameworks and methodologies. These partial results are always temporary and contingent. Weber's use of the 'ideal type' was based on the assumption that knowledge is always a biased summary of many possible positions and alternatives.

The End of Organized Marxism

In the 1970s the character of sociology, particularly within the European universities, was shaped and driven by the historic relationship between Marxism and Weber's sociology. Weber's sociology was seen to be a specific response to the challenge of Marxism and Marxist sociology. For example, Weber's treatment of social stratification involving an analysis of status, power and economic classes was often interpreted as a more appropriate interpretation of the social structure of capitalist societies (Aron, 1963) than Marx's dichotomous analysis of class. Weber's notion of social closure as a strategy for the monopolistic control of resources was treated as a fundamental approach to class divisions alongside other fissures in society. Weber's concept of social closure provided a systemic bourgeois critique of Marxist class theory (Parkin, 1979). In other areas, it can be argued that Weber's ontology of human beings provided a radical alternative to Marx's post-Feuerbachian account of the nature of human beings as constituted by social practice (Löwith, 1993). Weber's notion of human beings as creators of meaning through practical action in the world provided an interesting comparison with the varieties of Marxist humanism which have emerged from east European Marxism (Satterwhite, 1992). In addition, one can argue that Weber's comparative historical sociology (Kalberg, 1994), his macro sociological theory (Collins, 1986a) and his sociology of power (Roth, 1987) provide contemporary sociology with a systematic and general view of history and society which is deeper, richer and more systematic than the legacy of Marx's political economy.

Clearly the debate between Marx and Weber is controversial and incomplete (Antonio and Glassman, 1985; Weiss, 1986). The unintended consequence of the controversy between Weber and Marx was that it provided an effective and clear method by which the very nature of sociology could be defined. Sociology was an academic discipline which through the intellectual interaction with Marxism produced a distinctive perspective on the structure of industrial capitalist society, generated a clear view of historical development, embraced a sociological approach to ontology and had a philosophy of social science which provided the philosophical framework for empirical social research. Weber's social theory provided contemporary sociology with a systematic approach to the construction of social theory (Albrow, 1990), an all embracing vision of history (Kalberg, 1994), and a significant body of political theory (Mommsen, 1989). Finally, Weber's analysis of such notions as value neutrality, value relevance and the fact-value distinction offered sociologists a valuable ethical framework for the conduct of practical research; Weber's account of value neutrality has of course been the topic of much philosophical and political dispute (Runciman, 1972).

The social and intellectual context of the debate between Marx and Weber has of course been radically transformed by two significant social changes in the 1980s and 1990s. The first has been the political collapse of communism in eastern Europe and the Soviet Union, and the second is the corrosive effect on modernism of the process of postmodernization. I shall deal with the question of postmodernism towards the end of this introductory chapter and at this stage I am merely concerned to note the collapse of the Marx–Weber debate as a consequence of the institutional catastrophe which hit organized Marxism in the late 1980s. The collapse of organized communism could be taken as some historical validation for Weber's pessimistic view of the iron cage of capitalism, namely that an ethic of socialist solidarity could never triumph over the historical and ineluctable processes of bureaucratization and rationalization. The Soviet Empire was simply another instance of the processes of rationalization in everyday life, which overcame the humanistic values of Marxism as a secular ethic of brotherly love. Weber was fascinated by the social struggles in Russia around 1905 and 1906 as the autocratic government of Tsar Nicholas II tried to reach some compromise with the liberal reform movement. Weber wrote a number of important articles on the provincial and district organizations of local self-government (the zemstvos) which were the conduit for demands for civil liberties. Weber believed that the prospects of significant liberalization in autocratic Russia were socially limited (Weber, 1995) and Weber's scepticism regarding the possibilities of a socialist transformation of capitalism are well known, but the dramatic collapse of communism in the 1980s was not anticipated in academic circles. However, if we accept Weber's critical attitudes towards centralized socialism, we should not forget his equally ambiguous views of the possibilities of liberal democracy within capitalism. Weber was pessimistic about the possibilities of genuine political participation and believed that the needs of leadership in a contemporary political environment required an authoritarian or plebiscitary form of democracy.

The collapse of organized communism has therefore put an end, for the time being, to the historic debate between Marx and Weber. The demise of Marxism has been associated as a result with new lines of interpretation with regard to the significance of Weber's sociology. The erosion of Marxism has been associated with a new emphasis on Weber's relationship to Nietzsche and to the romantic critique of capitalism which had been developed in Germany. Writers like George, Klages and Gundolf specifically adopted a Nietzschean critique of modern rational culture, rejecting the standardization of social and cultural reality. Only a new breed or a new creation of men could overcome this cultural debasement, because the rational intellect threatened to destroy the soul and the body. Weber admired much of the visionary poetry of Stefan George but rejected his romanticism as inadequate for the tasks of contemporary society. These romantic criticisms of industrial capitalism did, however, exercise a covert and indirect influence on the rise and development of early forms of critical theory in Germany.

Before the collapse of organized communism, there had of course been growing disillusionment with and alienation from Marxism as a social movement and with the communist regimes of eastern Europe. Many leading Marxist theorists of the post-war period who attempted to transform Marxist theory subsequently turned to alternative paradigms such as postmodernism. The intellectuals who were associated with the journal *Socialisme ou Barbarie* in France are typical of this situation. For example, J.-F. Lyotard (1988: 63) has complained that behind the facade of the workers' movement 'unions contributed to regulating the exploitation of the labour force; the party served to modulate the alienation of consciousnesses; socialism was a totalitarian regime; and Marxism was no longer anything but a screen of words thrown over real différends'. From within sociology, one might argue that the same anxieties about centralized socialism also drove Weber to a clear appreciation of the dangers of Russian socialism.

With the collapse of communism, there has been a theoretical tendency to resurrect the debate about modernization as an alternative to more traditional contrasts between capitalism and socialism. The view of Weber as a major analyst of capitalism, alongside Marx, Veblen, Schumpeter, and Spencer, has given way to an interpretation of Weber as the primary theorist of rational modernity and modernization. In the 1960s and 1970s Marxist sociologists condemned concepts like modernity and moderniza-tion as false concepts within functionalism which really meant western-ization. In the 1980s and 1990s there has been a revival of concepts of modernity and modernization. Anthony Giddens (1994: 68–9) has recently moved away from an interpretation of Weber as a theorist of capitalism to a theorist of modernity. Thus he asks rhetorically 'What is Weber's discus-sion of the Protestant Ethic if not an analysis of the obsessional nature of modernity?' We might note also that Marx has been restored as an inter-preter of modern culture by writers like Marshall Berman in his *All That is Solid Melts into Air* (1983). Also Derek Sayer in his *Capitalism and Modernity* (1991) regards both Marx and Weber as developing a theory of modernity within which capitalism is simply a specific instance. Sociological debate therefore has swung away from the analysis of the structures of capitalism to an interpretation of culture in modernization and postmodernism. As a result the concept of culture has replaced much of the original debate about ideology and structure within the sociological canon. Because Weber devoted much of his intellectual endeavour to the analysis of cultural soci-ology, we may expect that Weberian notions will play a significant part in the contemporary interest in cultural themes.

Reading Weber

This debate between the legacy of Marx and Weber gave rise to a number of more specific, and possibly more interesting, questions about whether it is possible to discover a coherent organizing theme or principle in the work of Weber which would integrate his rather diverse collection of pub-lications into a systematic whole. This search for a principle of thematic unity in Weberian sociology is also associated with the dispute regarding the validity of the view of Weber as the founding father of contemporary sociology. The quest for an organizing theme in Weber has been compli-cated by the peculiarities with which Weber's work has actually been pub-lished and translated. Weber's academic career was of course disrupted by his severe illness which, from the winter of 1898, prevented Weber con-ducting serious research. Various explanations of this crisis have been offered, such as the conflict between the parental values, sexual repression and the failure to achieve a successful political career (Collins, 1986b). Much of Weber's work subsequently, such as the 'Protestant Ethic thesis', was published as separate and discreet essays. As a result, much of Weber's work was posthumously published by his wife Marianne Weber. For example, the monumental *Economy and Society* (1978) was posthu-mously published by his wife in an attempt to present Weber's work as a systemic outline of interpretive sociology. His *General Economic History* (Weber, 1981) was assembled from students' notes relating to Weber's final lectures. Many of his publications such as *The Agrarian Sociology of Ancient Civilizations* (Weber, 1976) were in fact collections of articles which had been published separately. Weber's work is clearly large, complex and diverse (Käsler, 1988). The complexity of the publishing history of Weber's legacy has provided an ideal and fertile breeding ground for a variety of interpretations of Weber's work.

Much of the debate was centred around the notion of rationalization in Weber's sociology. By rationalization, Weber referred to a set of inter-related social processes by which the modern world had been systematically transformed. In this perspective, the rise of capitalist society can be taken as simply an illustration of this general pattern of rationalization. As a social process rationalization includes the systematic application of scientific reason to the everyday world and the intellectualization of routine activities through the application of systematic knowledge to practice. Rationalization in everyday life was also associated with the disenchantment of reality, that is the secularization of values and attitudes. In institutional terms, this process involved the decline of the authority of the Church and the erosion of the status of the clergy. In religious terms rationalization involved the development of an intellectual stratum of theologians who produced religious thought as a systematic statement about reality. In legal terms, rationalization involved the decline and erosion of *ad hoc* legal decision making based upon arbitrary processes and the creation of a deductive legal system following universalistic laws. Within the political sphere, rationalization was associated with the decline and disappearance of traditional norms of legitimization, such as the dependence upon charismatic leadership. In social terms generally, rationalization was constituted by the spread of bureaucratic control, the establishment of modern systems of surveillance, the dependence on the nation state as a controlling agency and the rise of new forms of administration. Rationalization as a master theme in Weber's sociology has therefore often been compared with the theme of alienation and reification in the work of Marx (Löwith, 1993). The rationalization theme has dominated much contemporary Weberian scholarship (Scaff, 1989; Sica, 1988; Whimster and Lash, 1987). However the argument that rationalization is the key to Max Weber's sociology is most closely associated with the work of Frederich Tenbruck (1975; 1980). It is the debate with Tenbruck which has established the contours of recent Weber scholarship.

Tenbruck's famous essay on 'The problem of thematic unity in the works of Max Weber' has two principal dimensions. The first is to question Marianne Weber's description of *Economy and Society* as Weber's principal work (*Hauptwerk*) and secondly to identify and express the underlying anthropological dimension of Weber's sociology, namely his account of humans as 'cultural beings'. For Tenbruck, there is no particular key to the interpretation of *Economy and Society*, precisely because that text is a conglomerate of disparate elements which do not constitute a recognizable major work. Tenbruck by contrast draws our attention to the central role of the Economic Ethic of World Religions, namely Weber's interest in the sociology of religion with respect to the rationalization process. For Tenbruck, the essays on the Economic Ethic of World Religions are the principal consolidation and elaboration of the arguments begun first in the essays on the 'Protestant Ethic thesis'. The 'Protestant Ethic' was merely a component therefore of the central analysis of religion and economics which occupied the *Gesammelte Aufsätze zur Religions soziologie* (Weber, 1921). In addition, Tenbruck draws our attention to the special importance of the 'Author's introduction' (*Vorbemerkung*) to the sociology of religion as a whole which was included by Parsons in his translation of *The Protestant Ethic and the Spirit of Capitalism*. Weber also wrote an additional introduction in 1913 which was published in 1915 with the title 'Intermediate reflections' (*Zwischenbetrachtung*) which was conceived after the 'Author's introduction' was already in print. The *Zwischenbetrachtung* was translated by Gerth and Mills in *From Max Weber* (Gerth and Mills, 1961: 323–62) as 'religious rejections of the world and their directions'. Tenbruck's argument is therefore that the analysis of the Economic Ethic of World Religions dominated Weber's intellectual activities from around 1904 to 1920. Because his publications on religion occupied this creative period of Weber's life, we should regard these texts on religion and economics as his principal work rather than *Economy and Society*.

Tenbruck then argues that the thematic unity of these sociology of religion texts is the way in which religious orientations towards the world did or did not lead to an ethic of world mastery, that is to a process of rationalization. In the principal essays of his sociology of religion, that is in the 'Introduction', the 'Intermediate reflections' and the 'Author's introduction', Weber came to a universalistic and historical conceptualization of these rationalization processes. It was these dominant world religious views which generated different patterns of rationalism and rationalization in the modern world. This development is completely compatible with Weber's interpretative sociology because it was these meaning systems within religion that generated specific world views that acted as the motivations for action. In particular, it was the problem of theodicy which generated this drive towards world mastery. This interpretation also falls in line with the idea of fatefulness of world images because it was the irrational quest for salvation which generated a rational solution to being in the world. This question of religion and salvation also produced Weber's anthropology of the rules which govern the practical conduct of life (*Lebensführung*). In this anthropology of conduct, Weber distinguished between a theodicy of good fortune (*Glück*) and a theodicy of suffering (*Leid*). In coming to terms with fortune and suffering, human beings extend their conception of their personal experience beyond the everyday material world. It is these experiences of fortune and suffering which destroy the rational or purposive categories of pragmatic orientation to reality.

However it was only within the monotheistic salvational religions that the rationalization of the question of theodicy reached its ultimate fruition. The development of the concept of a universalistic God who organized reality around a quest for personal salvation developed into an intellectual theodicy of reality as such. In short it was the legacy of the Judaeo-Christian world, which included the notions of ethical prophecy and monotheism, which was crucial to the development of a radical solution to the question of theodicy in forms of intellectualized soteriology. For example, the intellectual rationalism of the Protestant churches was critical in pushing European civilization towards a pattern of personal salvation or life regulation.

Tenbruck has provided a radical reinterpretation of Weber's legacy, in particular by raising the problem of 'the world' as a concept in sociology to its proper place (Turner, 1992a). Secondly, he has demonstrated the importance of the concept of theodicy to Weber's cultural sociology generally. Thirdly, Tenbruck has identified the anthropological underpinnings of Weber's sociology. Many of these issues have been taken up and further elaborated by Wilhelm Hennis in his important study of Weber in his essays in reconstruction (1988). For Hennis the central question in Weber's sociology is to do with the issues of personality and life-orders. Hennis rejects the idea of rationalism and rationalization as central questions for Weber and argues instead that it was the development of *Menschentum* which was the central question of Weber's sociology, namely how certain cultural developments produced a particular type of personality and a particular rational conduct of life (*Lebenführung*) particularly in the idea of 'calling' as part of the constitutive question of modern culture. In more precise terms, Weber's sociology is concerned with the historical origins of life regulation as a rational conduct of life in the development of modern vocations in the social world. Weber's analysis of the Protestant ascetic organization of life is therefore simply one dimension of this analysis of *Lebenführung* or the study of the characterological effects of particular kinds of piety. The rationalization theme to which Weber draws attention in the 'Protestant Ethic thesis' was a particular transformation of patterns of discipline and methodology relevant to particular forms of economic life regulation. In this context we can understand the world religions as systems of life regulation producing different personality types and different life-orders. Weber's concern with capitalism was not so much to understand its economic structure and functions but to understand how a capitalist civilization would influence and transform personality, namely what sort of people would a capitalist regulation of life produce. By 'personality' Weber did not have in mind what we would understand within an empirical social psychology, but rather what kind of ontological reality would be produced by different life-orders, that is, Weber asks the question from the standpoint of German cultural values.

Weber and Classical Sociology

Part of the motivation behind the work of Tenbruck, Hennis and Tribe (Tribe, 1989) is to re-establish Weber as a figure in the tradition of classical political philosophy who was concerned to understand the political order of society as the foundation of ethics and ontology. These issues, particularly as they impinge upon questions of liberalism and democracy, have dominated much of the philosophical debate about the implications of Weber's work in contemporary Germany (Gneuss and Kocka, 1988). The cultural and political context of this debate has often been generated by a critical rejection of American sociology and the American reception of Weber. This critical view of American sociology has been specifically directed against Talcott Parsons's interpretation of Weber as one of the founding fathers of the sociology of action. Hennis has been fairly explicit in his view of Weber as contributing to a German tradition of political and philosophical enquiry. First of all 'Weber was a German thinker, from the land of "Dr Faustus"' (Hennis, 1988: 195). It is in the novels of Thomas Mann that we are able to understand the intellectual world of Weber. Secondly, the misunderstanding of the 'Weber thesis' which is so common among followers of Parsons, 'no longer happens among German scholars' (Hennis, 1988: 26). For Hennis, Weber's central question was about the ethical character of human existence and therefore sociologists like Gordon Marshall (1982) are mistaken in continuing to debate the origins of capitalism as the central issue of Weber's sociology. These remarks seem less than generous to Parsons, since it was Parsons in *The Structure of Social Action* (Parsons, 1937) who did much to introduce the work of Weber to an American audience, and it was Parsons who was responsible for translating *The Protestant Ethic and the Spirit of Capitalism* (Weber, 1930) and who drew attention to the importance of the sociology of religion in his introductory essay to Weber's *The Sociology of Religion* (Weber, 1966). Parsons was, given his own interest in religion and ethics, perfectly aware of the central importance of the concept of theodicy in Weber's historical sociology.

One might also question the originality of Tenbruck and Hennis in recent approaches to Weber's anthropology. Much of the recent debate about Weber in fact reproduces the Heideggerian interpretation of Weber by Karl Löwith whose article on Weber and Marx first appeared in *Archiv für Sozialwissenschaft und Sozialpolitik* in 1932, and was subsequently translated into English in 1982 as *Max Weber and Karl Marx* (Löwith, 1993). Löwith sought to demonstrate that, regardless of the very important differences between Marx and Weber, their sociological perspectives were joined by a common philosophical anthropology. That is, they shared a basic interest in the ontological problem of human beings in bourgeois capitalism. From the perspective of this ontology, both Weber and Marx saw capitalism as a destructive economic system, but one which also opened up new possibilities through the transformation of traditional systems.

Weber's sociology was driven by a concern for 'human dignity', but Weber was basically pessimistic about the outcome of capitalism which was fateful in the sense of producing an iron cage within which human beings were trapped. Löwith's interpretation of Weber developed from a philosophical indebtedness to the work of Martin Heidegger (1962). Since human beings live in a condition of existential homelessness (*Heimatlosigkeit*), Heidegger (1977) developed a profound critique of the technological conditions of capitalist society, which result in profound alienation. Löwith was also able to appreciate the importance of Nietzsche's critique of conventional metaphysics as the background to Heidegger's approach to everyday reality. Nietzsche's rejection of traditional religion as a viable orientation to the lifeworld was the background to Heidegger's critique of metaphysics. Weber's anxieties about the problem of cultural slavery in the modern bureaucratic machine were partly generated by Nietzsche's analysis of the problem of modern existence in terms of the death of God.

Löwith's social philosophy was grounded in the view that the decisive characteristic of western culture is to be located in the divorce between the classical view of the world in which there was no real history but merely the harmonious repetition of the same and the Christian world-view in which the birth of Christ created a revolutionary teleological framework for reality. History was now meaningful in terms of the revelation of grace through the advent of Christ, the lives of the saints, and the creation of the Church leading towards a Second Coming (Löwith, 1966; 1970). In a similar fashion, Weber recognized that the problem of theodicy in Christian theology drove the Protestant Reformers to a new perception of history as catastrophic. These philosophical views about the meaning of history within a Christian framework have been replaced in a secular epoch by the idea that history has no meaning and that we are living in a post-historical period (Niethammer, 1992).

We can see in the recent interpretation of Weber's sociology a common theme, namely the profoundly ethical character of Weber's social theory and its underpinning in a particular anthropology of personality and life-orders. Both Tenbruck and Löwith share this interest in the religious theme within Weber's life and work, particularly the focus on questions relating to theodicy. Hennis (1988: 24) is wrong, in my view, to suggest that Löwith, because of the analysis of the relationship of Weber to Marx, was fascinated by the problem of rationality and thereby missed the underlying significance of this question in Weber's sociology. On the contrary, Löwith recognized that the rationalization theme was a product of the existential question of meaning in Weber's sociological framework.

Weber and Postmodernity

We have noted that in the last twenty years there has been a continuing and growing fascination with the sociological work of Weber. How might we explain this fascination and what is the relevance of Weber's work for contemporary cultural and social problems? A number of sociologists of course want to claim that because of some profound transformation of society in recent times that the work of writers like Weber is no longer relevant as a framework for understanding the conditions under which we now live. In particular, Anthony Giddens in *The Consequences of Modernity* (1990) and Ulrich Beck in *Risk Society* (1992) have argued that we must go beyond Weberian sociology to grasp the essential features of modern societies. We might say therefore that contemporary sociology is confronted with two principal issues, namely whether society has gone through a radical transformation which has altered its very character and whether we need an entirely new theoretical framework to understand these transformations. Both Beck and Giddens are attempting to propose that we do live within an entirely transformed social reality which requires a new theoretical paradigm. Because high modernity in Giddens's terms and risk society in Beck's sociology present us with new conditions, we also need to develop new theories for analysing these societies. This new reality is described in terms of the theory of reflexive modernization in Beck, Giddens and Lash (1994) which is presented as an alternative to the idea of postmodernization. In this concluding commentary, I wish to challenge Beck and Giddens, particularly in their interpretation of Weber and defend the idea of postmodernization as a real process in contemporary society. Finally, I argue that Weber's sociology is to some extent compatible with postmodernization because of his dependence on Nietzsche's perspectivism.

In *The Consequences of Modernity*, Giddens argued that Weber equated 'society' with the 'nation state', had no understanding of the processes of globalization and failed to address the issue of reflexive modernity as the real focus of sociology. Thus classical Weberian social theory is too unidimensional to offer us a relevant and informative perspective on our condition. From my perspective, Giddens's position can be questioned by considering Weber's account of personality. Thus Giddens's recent interest in the self in *Modernity and Self Identity* (Giddens, 1991) and sexuality in *The Transformation of Intimacy* (Giddens, 1992) is not far removed from Weber's focus on personality and life orders. Giddens's argument is that self-reflexivity and in particular the notion of the self as a project is a specific feature of high modernity and the outcome of a process of detraditionalization. As we have seen, Weber believed that personality was indeed a project, the outcome of a self-conscious system of discipline and creativity. Indeed, for Weber personality was that rational project of the person or self which distinguished human beings from the non-human world. In Weber's terms personality was not a fact about human beings but something which was produced by culture through a system of lifelong education. Weber thus elaborated the idea of individuality and personality through a concept of singularity. This idea of the rational project and the self was part of a German tradition which emphasized the idea of individuality and individual singularity, particularly amongst the cultured middle class (*Bildungsbürgertum*), as a feature of the debate about the relationship between culture and civilization. Within this tradition personality was the outcome of culture in a struggle against civilization, that is against a materialistic culture which was thought to be typical of the Anglo-Saxon world, especially English materialism. Personality for Weber was thus a calling or vocation whereby a singular individual imposed on him or herself the disciplines and rationality which were necessary to produce a self as an effect of educational training. This aspect of Weber's sociology has been analysed by Harvey Goldman in his *Politics, Death and the Devil. Self and power in Max Weber and Thomas Mann* (1992). Weber's principal concern was that personality within this tradition would be undermined by the growth of scientific rationalization, the growth of the nation state and the bureaucratic domination of the everyday world. Weber's sociological perspective was concerned to understand the cultivation of the self against the constraints of a rational secular order. This anticipated at least some of the current debate about reflexivity, the self, emotionality and the collapse of traditional paradigms of the self. Weber's analysis of personality, particularly in his study of Protestant spirituality influenced a variety of twentieth-century social theorists in their approach to the nature of the modern self. Of particular significance in this group of writers who are influenced by Weber was Benjamin Nelson, whose *On the Roads to Modernity* (Nelson, 1981) is a major historical study of the evolution of the idea of conscience in western cultures, specifically within Weber's historical sociological paradigm. Nelson's task was no less than a history of the self and civilization.

The point of this commentary is basically to indicate that Giddens's analysis of the reflexive self is not necessarily an original contribution to sociology since there are a number of well-known traditions in classical sociology by which the self can be approached and understood as a reflexive and rational project of modernity. The consequence of this critical argument is to claim that there is no automatic justification for abandoning or rejecting traditional sociology as a paradigm since there are well-known traditions by which the idea of reflexive modernity including the reflexive self could be understood. If it is possible to defend Weber's sociology against Giddens, can we defend Weber against current postmodern theory? In discussing postmodernization it is useful to distinguish between postmodernism as a theory of modern society and postmodernization as a social process. Postmodern theory plays upon the importance of irony, simulation, self-referential writing styles, randomness and depthless reading of texts. Postmodern theory is fascinated by the artificial and the facile. Postmodernism rejects the traditional authority of intellectuals, and mixes and combines both high and low culture. It is in this sense a special form of cultural reflexivity about the complexities of modern popular life-styles (Turner, 1990). By postmodernity I am referring to the social condition of modern societies which are experiencing a process of postmodernization.

Social postmodernity involves cultural differentiation, fragmentation and complexity, the demise of the authority of high culture and elite traditions. The growth of ethnic multiculturalism and cultural diversity as a consequence of the processes of globalization, particularly tourism and a global labour market and the prevalence and dominance of certain stylistic devices in culture which use simulation, parody and irony as argumentative styles or rhetoric. This process of postmodernization produces the subjective experience of the artificial and the constructed nature of social and cultural phenomena. In terms of life-style, postmodernization of the life-course involves the disappearance of single career patterns, the emergence of fragmented life-styles, the erosion of traditional patterns of employment and retirement, and the breakup of traditional household structures into more fragmented and diversified forms. The essential argument of postmodernism has been summarized most neatly by Lyotard (1984), namely that the postmodern condition involves scepticism towards grand narratives. The grand narratives of democracy, liberalism, the nation state and religion are specific illustrations. Contemporary societies characterized by the notion that our commitments are contingent and our beliefs only temporary.

Nietzsche has been one of the most influential philosophers in the development of postmodern theory because it was from Nietzsche's philosophy that the whole problem of perspectivism in the slogan that 'God is dead' has been derived. Nietzsche's influence on postmodern philosophy comes to us via Heidegger and more recently from Richard Rorty (1989). It should now be fairly obvious that Weber's perspectivism is in many respects highly compatible with the current postmodern mood. Weber was clearly influenced by Nietzsche's analysis of the polytheistic struggle of values in modern society and Weber's philosophy of social sciences clearly committed to the idea that facts are always observed from a particular perspective and cannot be theory neutral. Weber was in fact profoundly ambiguous about the nature of rationality and modernity, being specifically conscious of the irrational drive behind the growth of rational values.

However it would be a mistake to regard Weber as an ironist in Rorty's terms. I have elsewhere (Turner, 1992b: 18) suggested that Weber departed from Nietzsche on at least three grounds. While Weber feared and deplored the growth of polytheistic values, Nietzsche celebrated this diversity as a necessary framework for undermining monotheistic values and moralities. For Nietzsche, polytheism was a necessary condition for individuality. Secondly, Weber's highly rationalistic analysis of the ethic of responsibility would have been rejected by Nietzsche as a form of resentment, namely as Socratism. Finally Nietzsche rejected the fatalism and nihilism of Schopenhauer, and embraced the idea of the revaluation of values as an escape from the negativity of our period. Obviously, Weber lacked the playfulness and ironic self reflexivity which we find characteristically in postmodernism (Rojek and Turner, 1993). Weber's tragic view of reality as a fateful order is ultimately incompatible with the sense of ironic parody which pervades postmodern analysis. Weber would have rejected or have been bemused by the argumentative style of postmodern theory. However, Weber's sociological attempt to come to terms with the very ambiguities of modern culture, the uncertainties and conflicts of contemporary political life and the erosion and secularization of religious traditions provide us with one of the greatest insights into the problematic condition of the twentieth century.

There is another issue which separates Weber's sociology from the moral and aesthetic mood of postmodernism, which is the question of otherness and difference. Modernization, as Weber recognized, involved standardization and normalization; it precluded any sensitivity to and empathy for personal and social difference. Postmodernism follows liberalism in its responsibility towards otherness, but whereas liberalism tolerates individual differences, postmodernism celebrates, fosters and encourages difference. Weber's tough-minded realism with regard to the inevitable domination of rationalization as a process appears to be far removed from the elevation of concern and care as foundations of postmodern moral orientations. Thus, while Weber's analysis of the iron cage of rational capitalism has a relationship to Foucault's account of panoptic disciplines, Foucault went further to discover that 'our very conceptions of subjectivity are themselves already deepstructured by processes of power. And these processes are inextricably related to the generation of knowledge in the human sciences' (White, 1991: 120). The idea that a vocation in science could be a morally adequate response to a secular and pluralistic society would be foreign to postmodern ethics which turns to concepts such as sublime rather than reason as an approach to authenticity (Lyotard, 1989).

In this chapter I have noted a number of major changes in the way in which Weber's sociology is received in contemporary social theory. There has been a growing recognition of the importance of Nietzsche for Weber's cultural critique of capitalism, his interest in the growth of discipline and new forms of personality, and in his concern for the relationship between power and knowledge. Secondly, there has been an increasing concern for Weber's contribution to cultural sociology in which Weber's analysis of values and meaning is assimilated to an epistemology driven by literary theory. Thirdly, there has been correspondingly a declining interest in Weber's sociology of industrial capitalism, his comparative sociology of industrial societies and his political sociology of the modern state. Fourthly and as a consequence of these tendencies, the contemporary interest in Weber centres on the contrast between traditionalism and modernity, and as a consequence there is an emerging debate about Weber's relationship to postmodern social theory and postmodern society. Fifthly, there has been a debate about Weber's relationship to the classical tradition of sociology, namely to the works of Marx and Durkheim. Writers like Beck, Giddens and Lash have, in their recent work, turned away from any overt concern the question of postmodernization to a focus on reflexive modernization. In this particular approach to Weber, there has been a concern to undermine the notion that Weber has anything particularly important or interesting to say about the contemporary world which has been transformed by various processes of globalization.

The idea that Weber's sociology was shaped by a number of significantly ethical concerns is a welcome development in the analysis of the history of sociology. Clearly Weber's sociology engaged with the problems of a post-Christian reality in which many traditional assumptions about the meaning of life and the significance of the sacred have been challenged by the processes of secularization, industrialization and, in Weber's terms, rationalization. Weber's sociology of religion, while significantly different from Durkheim's contribution to the understanding of the sacred in many respects, nevertheless addressed the problem of the elementary forms of religion in a post-Christian environment. Whereas Durkheim was concerned with the problem of the conditions of social solidarity in a post-religious order, Weber addressed the question of meaning in a world which was disenchanted. As both Löwith and Hennis have noted, Weber was concerned to understand the condition of human beings in an alienated environment where the old certanties of faith had been challenged by secularization. Löwith's introduction of a strongly Heideggerian theme presented a strikingly original interpretation of the underlying anthropology of Weber's sociology.

Reinterpreting Weber and Modern Sociology

This recovery of the significance of Nietzsche and ethical issues in Weber has meant that Weberian sociology can engage significantly with questions of secularization and postmodernization in contemporary social theory. Weber's perspectivism, his concern for the legacy of Nietzsche, his overwhelming conviction about the provisional nature of social inquiry and his anxiety with respect to the limitations of rationality and reason are all themes which have entered directly into the postmodern debate. This evolving paradigm of ethical interpretation has transformed conventional understanding of Weber as the theorist of the fact-value dichotomy. Weber's sociology was ethically engaged with the primary concerns of his time, was sensitive to major theological and moral debates, was driven by a tragic vision of the human condition and was underpinned by a profoundly committed view of the problems of German politics.

While these new developments in Weber interpretations are significant, they nevertheless both exaggerate certain features of Weber's work and understate many important dimensions of his empirical sociology. Against current cultural and ethical interpretation of Weber's sociology, we might start by asking ourselves the question: what are the criteria or conditions which make for the continuity and maintenance of a significant social theory? The successful accumulation of social theory requires an explicit commitment to articulating and developing a set of fundamental concepts and categories by which the nature of the social can be explained. There has to be an overt reflexive commitment to building up theory as an accumulative exercise with the goal of generating a paradigm of some explanatory force. It requires a grounding in a basic research programme of some scope and significance. It requires a public goal or arena within which theoretical concepts and research can engage with contemporary political, or more generally public problems. Finally it requires a strong institutional environment including the existence of journals and associations by which these theories can be developed and elaborated. In presenting this argument I am suggesting that via the sociology of knowledge, we know that a successful social theory needs an institutional climate which can foster and enhance social theory but we also have a philosophical set of concerns about the coherence, significance and empirical relevance of social theory.

To some extent Weber's sociology fits rather well within these criteria. For example, although Weber's work was published often posthumously by his wife, Weber did have access to both journals, institutions and associations by which his work could come to public attention, and in recent years there has been significant institutional support for, for example, publishing the entire works of Weber. Unlike his contemporary Georg Simmel, Weber's academic status was not held back by anti-Semitism or other forms of prejudice or exclusion. However the essence of this conclusion is that Weber's sociology remains of interest to sociologists precisely because it provides us with an ariticulate framework of concepts and theories, a project which is grounded in a research agenda, and a sociology which is relevant to and engaged with contemporary political issues.

Recent interpretations of Weber by, in particular, Hennis and Tribe have understated the richness of Weber's contribution to concept formation in sociology (Albrow, 1990; McKinney, 1966; Sica, 1988). We have seen that the study of social conditions and certain types of personality and their relevant social orders were indeed a central theme of Weber's ethical and sociological concerns. Weber sought to understand the nature of the times in which we live, namely the conditions and dimensions of modernity. This attempt to understand the nature of modernity involved Weber in a series of interconnected research programmes of which the sociology of religion was certainly dominant. However, in his attempt to understand the unique conditions under which we live and the problem of meaning in a disenchanted society, he ultimately condemned the negative consequences of the spirit of capitalism. Essential to his sociological paradigm was a historic investigation about the nature of rational life. Within his sociology of law Weber engaged in a variety of significant debates such as the *Critique of Stammler* (Weber, 1977) which have been neglected in recent discussions. Although Weber was clearly concerned with the economic ethics of the world religions which he pursued through a variety of comparative studies,

Weber was also significantly involved in the understanding of economic history (Weber, 1981).

Weber also engaged in wide-ranging debates about economics and economic institutions (Weber, 1981) but he was also interested in the philosophical and methodological problems of historical economics in his debate with Roscher and Knies (Weber, 1975). It is obvious that recent interpretations of Weber have down-played his substantive interests in law, economics and history but of central importance to Weber was the historical and sociological understandings of the conditions by which liberal politics could operate and within which therefore individuality could flourish and develop. Weber's concern with what we might call 'ethical personality' was thus combined with a profoundly empirical concern with practical day-to-day politics. This concern for the conditions of liberalism underpins his entire political sociology, his comparative study of German, American and British political institutions, and his comparative concern with the understanding of authoritarianism (Turner, 1994). The practical orientation of Weber's political sociology was to understand the peculiar problems of German political leadership within an imperial context where the Anglo-Saxon cultures of North America and Great Britain dominated colonial policies and politics. Weber sought to understand the problem of German leadership against a background of class structures and politics which were dominated by the *Junker* class and which constrained or prohibited more liberal forms of politics. The political failure of the 1848 revolution in Germany, the underdevelopment of socialism and working-class institutions, the legacy of Bismarck's centralized bureaucracy and the dominance of the Prussian state were social conditions which precluded the growth of laissez-faire industrial capitalism and the evolution of a liberal middle class capable of exercising significant political leadership. These general social issues lay behind his analysis of the Russian revolutions (Weber, 1995). Weber believed that the promising start of liberalism in Russia between 1905 and 1906 had collapsed by 1917 into a 'pseudo-democracy'. Weber was concerned to understand the social conditions under which effective political leadership could be achieved in order to secure his particular vision of liberalism against bureacracy and the state with the ethical objective of sustaining individuality and individualism within a rationalized world.

Weber's version of liberalism was not a cosy middle-class notion of pluralism and free speech. Rather Weber's understanding of politics was based upon an acceptance of the inevitability of political struggle and, where necessary, violence. Weber's concept of politics was driven by an acceptance of Nietzsche which often assumed almost Darwinistic characteristics. For example, Weber's concerns about East Germany in terms of Polish migrant settlement was bound up with his commitment to establishing Germany as a dominant political culture and state. The ethical concerns which underlay Weber's interest and individualism were within the broader context of unacceptance of violence as a method of political action. Indeed we could say that two central sociological questions lay behind Weber's research programme, namely who owns the means of (physical) violence, particularly military violence, and who controls the means of symbolic violence especially ecclesiastical or sacred institutions? These two critical questions in Weber's sociology, which derive significantly from both Marx and Nietzsche, are crucial in understanding Weber's substantive sociology, such as the sociology of law, which addressed the problem of how these orders of violence were held together by systems of normative legitimation. The fragmentation of modern cultures presents a significant difficulty for the functioning of these orders of regulation and control. Putting this in rather different terms we could say that Weber was interested in the interaction between the market (economic institutions), the state (political institutions) and the symbolic order (religious institutions), and these institutional relations were expressed through a fundamental dichotomy between rationalized bureaucracy and the individual capacity for action on the part of charismatic leaders. Weber was thus overwhelmingly concerned with the ethical dilemmas of leadership and power against a realistic acceptance of the necessity for both violence and legitimacy in any human society. This set of foundational questions concerning politics and religion was also an important feature of Weber's concern with the impact of technology on human societies, particularly military technology, and it was with the military implications of technology whether in feudal or in capitalist times that Weber's tragic vision of history found a poignant expression. It seems appropriate therefore to conclude this discussion with a somewhat lengthy quotation from Weber's essay on 'Russia's transition to pseudo-constitutionalism' from the recently translated collection of essays on the Russian revolutions (Weber, 1995: 231).

> It is a continuous, unrelenting struggle, with wild deeds of murder and merciless acts of tyranny in such numbers that even these horrors finally become accepted as normal. Modern revolution is like modern warfare, which, robbed of the romantic aura of knightly contest of days gone by, represents itself as a mechanical process caught between the instrumentalized products of the intellectual labour of laboratories and workshops, on the one hand, and the icy power of money on the other, but at the same time actually is a terrible, unending test of nerve both for the leaders and for the hundreds of thousands of the led.

Contemporary culturalist interpretations of Weber should not forget his demonic vision of human history as an endless series of struggles for dominance, the unintended consequences of which can have fateful consequences for both leaders and led. The modern world with its instrumentalized products of intellectual labour can often create an iron cage of tragic proportions within which the scope for individual action is clearly limited.

References

Albrow, M. (1990) *Max Weber's Construction of Social Theory*. London: Macmillan.

Alexander, J.C. (ed.) (1985) *Neofunctionalism*. Beverly Hills, CA: Sage.

Alexander, J.C. (1987) *Twenty Lectures: Sociological theory since World War II*. New York: Columbia University Press.

Althusser, L. (1969) *For Marx*. London: Allen Lane The Penguin Press.

Antonio, R.J. and Glassman, R.M. (eds) (1985) *A Weber–Marx Dialogue*. Lawrence, Kansas: University Press of Kansas.

Aron, R. (1963) *Eighteen Lectures on Industrial Society*. London: Weidenfeld and Nicolson.

Beck, U. (1992) *Risk Society: Towards a new modernity*. London: Sage.

Beck, U., Giddens, A. and Lash, S. (1994) *Reflexive Modernization: Politics, tradition and aesthetics in the modern social order*. Cambridge: Polity Press.

Berman, M. (1983) *All That is Solid Melts into Air. The experience of modernity*. London: Verso.

Bologh, R.W. (1990) *Love or Greatness. Max Weber or masculine thinking: a feminist inquiry*. London: Unwin and Hyman.

Bottomore, T. and Goode, P. (eds) (1978) *Austro-Marxism*. Oxford: Oxford University Press.

Breuilly, J. (1987) 'Eduard Bernstein and Max Weber', in W.J. Mommsen and J.Osterhammel (eds), *Max Weber and his Contemporaries*. London: Allen & Unwin. pp. 345–54.

Collins, R. (1986a) *Weberian Sociological Theory*. Cambridge: Cambridge University Press.

Collins, R. (1986b) *Weber, a Skeleton Key*. Beverly Hills, CA: Sage.

Connor, O. (1996) 'Cultural sociology and cultural sciences', in B.S. Turner (ed.), *The Blackwell Companion to Social Theory*. Oxford: Blackwell. pp. 340–68.

Eden, R. (1983) *Political Leadership and Nihilism. The study of Weber and Nietzsche*. Tampa: University of South Florida Press.

Elias, N. (1978) *The Civilising Process. The history of manners*. Oxford: Basil Blackwell.

Gerth, H.H. and Mills, C. (1961) *From Max Weber: Essays in sociology*. London: Routledge & Kegan Paul.

Giddens, A. (1990) *The Consequences of Modernity*. Cambridge: Polity Press.

Giddens, A. (1991) *Modernity and Self Identity. Self and society in the later modern age*. Cambridge: Polity Press.

Giddens, A. (1992) *The Transformation of Intimacy. Sexuality, love and eroticism in modern society*. Cambridge: Polity Press.

Giddens, A. (1994) 'Living in a post-traditional society', in U. Beck, A. Giddens and S. Lash (eds), *Reflexive Modernization: Politics, tradition and aesthetics in the modern social order*. Cambridge: Polity Press.

Gneuss, C. and Kocka, J. (1988) *Max Weber. Ein Symposion*. München: Deutscher Taschenbuch Verlag.

Goldman, H. (1992) *Politics, Death and the Devil. Self and power in Max Weber and Thomas Mann*. Berkeley: University of California Press.

Gouldner, A.W. (1970) *The Coming Crisis of Western Sociology*. New York: Basic Books.

Green, M. (1974) *The von Richthofen Sisters. The triumph and tragic modes of love*. New York: Basic Books.

Heidegger, M. (1962) *Being and Time*. Oxford: Basil Blackwell.

Heidegger, M. (1977) *The Question Concerning Technology and other Essays*. New York: Harper and Row.

Hennis, W. (1988) *Max Weber: Essays in reconstruction*. London: Allen & Unwin.

Holton, R.J. and Turner, B.S. (1986) *Talcott Parsons on Economy and Society*. London: Routledge & Kegan Paul.

Kadarkay, A. (1991) *Georg Lukács. Life, thought and politics*. Oxford: Basil Blackwell.

Kalberg, S. (1994) *Max Weber's Comparative Historical Sociology*. Cambridge: Polity Press.

Käsler, D. (1988) *Max Weber. An introduction to his life and work*. Cambridge: Polity Press.

Lassman, P. and Velody, I. (1989) *Max Weber's 'Science as a Vocation'*. London: Unwin Hyman.

Lehmann, H. and Roth, G. (eds) (1993) *Weber's Protestant Ethic. Origins, evidence and contexts*. Cambridge: Cambridge University Press.

Liebersohn, H. (1988) *Fate and Utopia in German Sociology 1870–1923*. Cambridge, Mass.: The MIT Press.

Löwith, K. (1966) *Nature, History and Existentialism and other Essays.* Evanstone, Ill.: Northwestern University Press.

Löwith, K. (1970) *Meaning in History.* Chicago and London: University of Chicago Press.

Löwith, K. (1993) *Max Weber and Karl Marx.* London: Routledge.

Lyotard, J.-F. (1984) *The Postmodern Condition. A report on knowledge.* Manchester: University of Manchester Press.

Lyotard, J.-F. (1988) *Peregrinations: Law, form, event.* New York: Columbia University Press.

Lyotard, J.-F. (1989) 'The sublime and the avant-garde', in A. Benjamin (ed.), *The Lyotard Reader.* Oxford: Basil Blackwell.

McKinney, J.C. (1966) *Constructive Typology and Social Theory.* New York: Appleton-Century-Crofts.

Marcus, J. (1987) *George Lukács and Thomas Mann. A study in the sociology of literature.* Amherst: University of Massachusetts Press.

Marshall, G. (1982) *In Search of the Spirit of Capitalism, an essay on Max Weber's Protestant Ethic Thesis.* London: Hutchinson.

Mayer, J.P. (1944) *Max Weber and German Politics. A study in political sociology.* London: Faber & Faber.

Mills, C.W. (1959) *The Sociological Imagination.* New York: Oxford University Press.

Mommsen, W.J. (1984) *Max Weber and German Politics 1890–1920.* Chicago: University of Chicago Press.

Mommsen, W.J. (1989) *The Political and Social Theory of Max Weber.* Cambridge: Polity Press.

Moretti, F. (1987) *The Way of the World: The Bildungsroman in European culture.* London: Verso.

Nelson, B. (1981) *On the Roads to Modernity. Conscience, Science and Civilizations.* Totowa, MJ: Rowman and Littlefield.

Niethammer, L. (1992) *Posthistoire: Has history come to an end?* London: Verso.

Parkin, F. (1979) *Marxism and Class Theory. A bourgeois critique.* London: Tavistock.

Parsons, T. (1937) *The Structure of Social Action.* New York: McGraw-Hill.

Poulantzas, N. (1973) *Political Power and Social Classes.* London: New Left Books.

Rex, J. (1961) *Key Problems of Sociological Theory.* London: Routledge & Kegan Paul.

Ringer, F.K. (1969) *The Decline of the German Mandarins. The German academic community of 1890–1933.* Cambridge, Mass.: Harvard University Press.

Rojek, C. and Turner, B.S. (1993) *Forget Baudrillard?* London: Routledge.

Rorty, R. (1989) *Contingency, Irony and Solidarity.* Cambridge: Cambridge University Press.

Roth, G. (1987) *Politische herrschaft und Persönliche Freiheit.* Frankfurt: Suhrkamp.

Runciman, W.G. (1972) *A Critique of Max Weber's Philosophy of Social Science.* Cambridge: Cambridge University Press.

Sahay, A. (ed.) (1971) *Max Weber and Modern Sociology.* London: Routledge & Kegan Paul.

Salomon, A. (1935) 'Max Weber's sociology', *Social Research,* 2: 60–73.

Satterwhite, J.H. (1992) *Varieties of Marxist Humanism. Philosophical revision in Eastern Europe.* Pittsburgh and London: University of Pittsburgh Press.

Sayer, D. (1991) *Capitalism and Modernity. An excursus on Marx and Weber.* London: Routledge.

Scaff, L.A. (1989) *Fleeing the Iron Cage. Culture politics and modernity in the thought of Max Weber.* Berkeley: University of California Press.

Schroeder, R. (1992) *Max Weber and the Sociology of Culture.* London: Sage.

Sica, A. (1988) *Weber, Irrationality and Social Order.* Berkeley: University of California Press.

Stauth, G. and Turner, B.S. (1986) 'Nietzsche in Weber oder die Geburt des modernen Genius im professionellen Menschen', *Zeitschrift für soziologie,* 15: 81–94.

Stauth, G. and Turner, B.S. (1988) *Nietzsche's Dance: Resentment, reciprocity and resistance in social life.* Oxford: Basil Blackwell.

Stauth, G. and Turner, B.S. (1992) 'Ludwig Klages (1872–1956) and the origins of critical theory', *Theory, Culture and Society,* 9: 45–63.

Tenbruck, F. (1975) 'Das Werk. Max Webers', *Kölner Zeitschrift für Soziologie und Sozialpsychologie,* 27: 663–702.

Tenbruck, F. (1980) 'The problem of thematic unity in the works of Max Weber', *British Journal of Sociology*, 31 (3): 316–51.

Tribe, K. (ed.) (1989) *Reading Weber*. London and New York: Routledge.

Turner, B.S. (1981) *For Weber*. London: Routledge.

Turner, B.S. (ed.) (1990) *Theories of Modernity and Postmodernity*. London: Sage.

Turner, B.S. (1992a) 'The concept of the "world" in sociology: A commentary on Roland Robertson's theory of globalization', *Journal for the Scientific Study of Religion*, 31(3): 296–323.

Turner, B.S. (1992b) *Max Weber. From history to modernity*. London and New York: Routledge.

Turner, B.S. (1994) 'Max Weber on individualism, bureaucracy and despotism: Political authoritarianism and contemporary politics', in L.J. Ray and M. Reed (eds), *Organizing Modernity: New Weberian perspectives on work, organization and society*. London: Routledge. pp. 122–40.

Weber, M. (1930) *The Protestant Ethic and the Spirit of Capitalism*. London: Allen & Unwin.

Weber, M. (1966) *The Sociology of Religion*. London: Methuen.

Weber, M. (1975) *Roscher and Knies: The logical problems of historical economics*. New York: Free Press.

Weber, M. (1976) *The Agrarian Sociology of Ancient Civilizations*. London: NLB.

Weber, M. (1977) *Critique of Stammler*. New York: Free Press.

Weber, M. (1978) *Economy and Society*. 2 volumes. Berkeley and Los Angeles: University of California Press.

Weber, M. (1981) *General Economic History*. New York: Transaction Books.

Weber, M. (1995) *The Russian Revolutions*. Cambridge: Polity Press.

Weiss, J. (1986) *Weber and the Marxist World*. London and New York: Routledge & Kegan Paul.

Whimster, S. and Lash, S. (eds) (1987) *Max Weber, Rationality and Modernity*. London: Allen & Unwin.

White, S.K. (1991) *Political Theory and Postmodernism*. Cambridge: Cambridge University Press.

Winch, P. (1958) *The Idea of a Social Science*. London: Routledge & Kegan Paul.

CHAPTER 2

MAX WEBER'S RECEPTION INTO CLASSICAL SOCIOLOGY

The principal argument of this chapter is that Max Weber (1864–1920), despite his towering reputation in the second half of this century, was strangely neglected, especially in the English-speaking academic world, until the 1950s. Although Weber is now recognized as a founder of modern sociology, he did not, unlike Emile Durkheim (1858–1917), have a clear self-conception of himself as a 'sociologist' and he had no intention certainly of founding a school (Löwith, 1939; Wilbrandt, 1928). Trained as a jurist with an early interest in the historical development of the legal framework of economics, Weber's wide academic and political interests did not sit neatly within a narrow academic discipline. Despite these reservations, the uneven and late reception of Weber's sociology is a topic which is worthy of comment and discussion.

Within Germany itself, the discussion of Weber's work was limited to various commentaries on his methodological notions (especially the ideal type and the method of *verstehen*) and the negative ethical implications of his (alleged) relativism (Lassman and Velody, 1989). There was at the time considerable concern about Weber's political views and his criticism of the Kaiser, which gave rise to a critical debate around Weber as a public figure. Weber's criticisms of Wilhem II led some leading figures in Germany such as General Ludendorff to condemn Weber as a traitor. Weber's political sociology, as distinct from his political views with respect to the conduct of the war, came to have some significance for later discussions, but it did not figure very large in his early reception. There was some discussion of Weber's sociology of religion, but this commentary was largely confined to an evaluation of his essays on the Protestant Ethic (Lehmann and Roth, 1993). It was not until later that a robust interpretation of his comparative sociology of religion emerged. This chapter attempts to document that slow and partial evolution of an understanding of the stature and significance of Weber's sociological *oeuvre*. The final controversial feature of this appreciation is that, while Talcott Parsons (1902–1979) has been heavily criticized for his interpretation of Weber, it was primarily as a result of Parsons's efforts that Weber's sociology was eventually embraced by the sociological establishment in the United States. These observations on the historical development of the appreciation of Weber's sociology – its slow development, its uneven reception, its one-sided evaluation, its interpretation through Parsons's voluntaristic theory of action, and its eventual dominance – will themselves remain controversial.

The place and status of Weber in the canon of western sociology is also an issue of much dispute. Early interpretations of Weber saw Weberian sociology as a critical response and an alternative to Marx and Marxist sociology (Wiley, 1987; Antonio and Glassman, 1985). It was Albert Salomon (1945: 596) who declared that Max Weber had 'become a sociologist in a long and tense dialogue with the ghost of Karl Marx' and that the title *Economy and Society* was proof of this critical intention to undermine historical materialism. In particular, Weber's studies of the Protestant Ethic were received by many scholars in Germany as an idealist attack on Marxist materialism. The resulting critical debate with Felix Rachfahl, Werner Sombart, Hans Delbruck, H. Karl Fischer laid the foundations for what was to become the Protestant Ethic controversy which has lasted most of this century (Mommsen and Osterhammel, 1987). This view of Weber has declined in recent years to be replaced by the notion that Weber was following the footsteps of Friedrich Nietzsche (1844–1900) and writing not about industrial capitalism but about the more general notion of cultural modernism. Weber's contrast between erotic desire and asceticism, his emphasis on the will to power, his critical views on the moral basis of intellectualism, and his negative views of bureaucracy have been traced back to Nietzsche (Fleischmann, 1964; Stauth and Turner, 1988; Turner, 1996). Other interpretations have argued that Weber is not a sociologist but a political theorist whose emphasis on power has more to do with Nietzsche than with Marx (Hennis, 1988; Scaff, 1989; Tribe, 1989; Turner, 1992). These authors see Weber's work as a reflection on personality and life orders from within the perspective of Nietzsche's critique of modern culture and its discipline. Other writers, such as Karl Löwith (1897–1973) drew attention in the 1930s to the parallel between Heidegger and Weber as critics of rationalism and technology; instrumental reason had produced a technical civilization which would eventually undermine the cultured life (Löwith, 1993). These studies of Weber and cultural criticism helped to shift the perspective on Weber away from the economic sociology of capitalism to the cultural sociology of modernity (Sayer, 1991; Scaff, 1989). Given this emphasis on power and violence, it is hardly surprising that Weber is often criticized by feminist theory for his lack of understanding of the emotional life of human beings (Bologh, 1990). These different and unresolved views of Weber have, of course, played an important part in the critical reception of and responses to Weber and Weberian sociology.

The critical response to Weber's sociology has concentrated on his political theory (with respect to questions of power and authority), his methodological views (with respect to the problems of the social sciences), and his sociology of religion (with respect to the economic teachings of the world religions). Thus, Weber's political views, which emphasized the importance of power and leadership in society, have consistently given rise to controversy (Mommsen, 1984). He has been accused of laying some of the intellectual foundations for fascism and he has been criticized for promoting relativism. His methodological ideas, especially the use of the ideal type, continue to play an important role in the development of modern sociology. Finally, a variety of sociologists have argued that his comparative sociology, especially his comparative study of   religion and religious teaching on economics, is Weber's most important and lasting contribution to twentieth-century sociology (Tenbruck, 1975; 1980).

The Life and Works of Max Weber

Weber is commonly referred to as a founder of modern sociology. He offered a systematic and coherent framework for the sociological perspective, he developed a distinctive and profound philosophy of the social sciences, and he established a variety of substantive areas. Early evaluations of Weber noted his contribution to a variety of substantive fields such as his sociology of stratification (Cox, 1950), his analysis of power and status (Goldhammer and Shils, 1939), the study of bureaucracy (Bendix, 1945), the sociology of race (Manasse, 1947), rural sociology (Honigsheim, 1946) and even the status of women (Hacker, 1953). The general contribution of Weber to the sociology of institutions has been well documented in Julien Freund's classic *Sociologie de Max Weber* (1966). Weber grasped the fundamental characteristics of modern industrial civilization and his views about politics, leadership and science are, to say the least, challenging (Parsons, 1942). In the substantive fields of law, politics, economics and religion, he identified many of the key issues which became the basis of intellectual growth and specialization in the discipline. Finally, in his own life and writing on the concept of the calling in science and politics, he provided a robust role model of the sociologist as public intellectual. Despite these formidable accomplishments, Weber had a small student following in his own lifetime and remained relatively obscure outside Germany until the 1950s, if not the 1960s.

The historical details of Weber's life have been sympathetically documented by his wife Marianne Weber (1870–1954) in her famous biography (1975) and there are useful discussions of Weber's life in Arthur Mitzman's *The Iron Cage* (1971), Reinhard Bendix's *Max Weber. An intellectual portrait* (1960) and Paul Honigsheim's *On Max Weber* (1968). There are also important literature reviews of Weber's work by Constans Seyfarth and Gert Schmidt (1977), Vatro Murvar (1983) and Dirk Käsler (1988). A critical biography and bibliography of Weber which traces the rise of his sociological ideas on sociology as a whole has yet to be written. During his life, Weber had enjoyed the material and cultural benefits of his membership of the educated bourgeoisie (Honigsheim, 1926). He was in many respects the epitome of the so-called *Bildung* tradition of German culture and training. In nineteenth-century German society, it was the educated middle class (the *Bildungsbürgertum*) rather than the economic bourgeoisie (the *Wirtschaftsbürgertum*) which occupied a dominant place in the system of power, especially the bureaucracy and the state. Weber's political and cultural values reflect the history of this close association between the state bureaucracy and the cultured bourgeois class, which evolved during the course of the nineteenth century. In order to understand his place in German social sciences and the reception of his work, we must remember that Weber was a member of the German academic mandarins (Ringer, 1969).

Weber died of pneumonia on 14 June 1920 at the age of fifty-six years (Diehl, 1924). He was born in Erfurt on 21 April 1864 and studied jurisprudence at the universities of Heidelberg, Strasburg, Berlin and Göttingen, taking his doctoral degree in Berlin in 1888. He married Marianne Schnitger in 1893. He was appointed Professor of commercial and German law at the University of Berlin in 1893, in 1894 he became Professor of economics at the University of Freiburg and in 1897 became Professor of economics at Heidelberg. Weber experienced a profound psychological crisis in the summer of 1897 shortly after his father's death and, as a result of this crisis, illness prevented him from teaching and undertaking systematic research. This breakdown has been the topic of much psychoanalytic speculation, but it appears to have been connected with the conflict with his father and his complex attitude towards his own sexuality (Collins, 1986a). In 1903 there was evidence of his slow psychological recovery in that he began working on the essays on the Protestant Ethic (Weber, 1930). He became increasingly interested in the progress of the Russian revolutions of 1905 and 1917. Between 1911 and 1917, he undertook a prodigious investigation of the economic ethics of the world religions, which forms the backbone of his comparative and historical sociology (Collins, 1986b). During the First World War, Weber served as an administrator of military hospitals and became politically active towards the end of the war, participating eventually in the Versailles peace conference. He began teaching again at the universities of Vienna and Munich, and towards the end of his life delivered two powerful speeches on politics as a vocation and science as a vocation (Curtius, 1919).

From this brief sketch, we can deduce some obvious reasons for Weber's modest academic and political impact in his lifetime and the absence of a Weber school of sociology (Honigsheim, 1926). Obviously his psychological problems and illness prevented him undertaking a continuous academic career. The war also disrupted his academic research and in the aftermath of the hostilities Weber was involved for a short period in intensive political debate and activity. He died prematurely before either his political or scientific career could come to maturity. Furthermore, his works were generally published posthumously by his wife and many volumes were not translated into English until the 1950s. *General Economic History* was published in 1927, *The Religion of China* appeared in 1951, *Ancient Judaism* in 1952, *Max Weber on Law in Economy and Society* in 1954, *The Rational and Social Foundations of Music*, *The Religion of India* and *The*

City in 1958. Shortly afterwards *The Sociology of Religion* appeared in 1963. The controversial volumes of *Economy and Society* were published in 1968, which many regard as the core theoretical framework for Weber's general sociology. In the 1970s, *Roscher and Knies* (1975), *The Agrarian Sociology of Ancient Civilizations* (1976) and *Critique of Stammler* (1977) appeared. Finally, Weber's analysis of the history and sociological significance of the Russian revolutions appeared in 1995 as *The Russian Revolutions*. Thus it took almost seventy years from his death for his complete sociological works to appear in English.

The Early Reception of Weber's Sociology

Unlike Karl Marx (1818–1883), Weber left no great political following or intellectual discipleship and indeed outside Germany his work was relatively unknown (Scaff, 1989). Unlike Nietzsche, he has no cult following in the contemporary debate about modernity and postmodernity. Rheinhard Bendix (1960) towards the conclusion of his intellectual portrait observed that there was a key idea in Marx (the organization of production), in Durkheim (group membership) and Freud (the subconscious drives). In Weber, there was no single key idea and thus his sociology often appears as a fragmented *oeuvre*.

Following his death in 1920, there was in Germany some public discussion of the importance of Weber's sociology, his political ideas, his methodology and the significance of his work on ethics and power (Turner and Factor, 1984). This debate as I shall demonstrate later was organized around the central problem of relativism. Weber's views caused alarm because, in embracing value neutrality, he appeared to reject an ethical appreciation of political action. This apparently brutal view of power politics and the need for what he called 'elbow room' with respect to the eastern provinces appeared to confirm the view that Weber's political sociology indirectly supports the survival of the fittest. In his Inaugural Lecture at Freiburg in May 1895 (Tribe, 1989) Weber self-consciously employed concepts and expressions which were taken from Nietzsche's will to power. Weber's ethical relativism was clearly taken from Nietzsche's perspectivism, which recognized that truth exists only from a particular viewpoint or perspective. These notions were not simply part of Weber's political sociology; they also provided the agenda for his philosophy of the social sciences and his methodology (Jordan, 1937). These radical views on politics, ethics and methods caused great consternation and controversy in his generation, if within a rather narrow academic and professional environment.

Outside Germany, things were different. Apart from Theodore Abel's *Systematic Sociology in Germany* (1929), R.H. Tawney's work (1926) on *Religion and the Rise of Capitalism* and the study of religion and economic individualism by H.M. Robertson (1933), there was little discussion of

Weber's sociology in the English-speaking world before the Second World War and as J.P. Mayer (1944: 9) correctly noted in the foreword to *Max Weber and German Politics*, 'the political writings of Max Weber are almost unknown in this country'. The conflict between Germany and Britain in the war period and after also disrupted intellectual exchange and further contained the growth of interest in Weber's sociology.

In France, there was little interest in German sociology after Durkheim's death, apart from occasional contributions such as Maurice Halbwachs's article on puritans and capitalism (1925) and his general assessment of Weber in *Annales d'histoire economique et sociale* (1929). Julien Freund (1966) published his influential *Sociologie de Max Weber* and Raymond Aron's lectures at the Faculty of Letters and Human Sciences at the University of Paris were eventually translated into English as *Main Currents in Sociological Thought* (1968). Aron's principal interest was in Weber's analysis of power and he published a number of valuable contributions to this dimension of Weberian sociology. Aron was the only major French contributor to the 15th German Sociological Congress at Heidelberg to commemorate the centenary of Max Weber's birth in 1864. His paper 'Max Weber und die Machtpolitik' (1964) emphasized the importance of Darwin (struggle of the fittest) and Nietzsche (the will to power) in Weber's political sociology, which concentrated on the power struggles between nation states.

In Italy, Benedetto Croce, who first encountered Weber at the 1908 International Philosophy Congress in Heidelberg, was highly critical of the growth of positivism in sociology (Croce, 1905). Weber was critical of Croce's treatment of intuition and empathy in *Roscher and Knies* (Weber, 1975: 167–9). However, they were both critical of the methodological assumptions of historical materialism. Croce's views were influential in the development of Carlo Antoni's analysis of the development of the social sciences. *Dallo Storicismo alla Sociologia* was published in 1940 and translated in 1959. In Antoni's account of the problem of historicism and the growth of sociology, Weber played a crucial role (Antoni, 1962). For Antoni, Weber's work was a clear illustration of how the relativistic crisis in the historical sciences in the nineteenth century had prepared the way for the rise of sociology. The other figure in Weber's reception in Italy was his friend and colleague Robert Michels (1876–1936), whose work on the iron law of oligarchy was closely related to Weber's critique of the negative impact of bureaucracy on national leadership. Michels played an important role as an intellectual conduit between Germany and Italy, changing his first name to 'Roberto' as an indication of his involvement in Italian life. In 1911, Michels dedicated his principal academic work on *Political Parties* (Michels, 1962) to Weber. His obituary (Michels, 1920) clearly identified Weber as a master of modern social science, who had made a profound contribution to the study of political life. Michels in his obituary lamented the fact that, given Weber's huge intellectual talent, he had not enjoyed a major political career, and argued that, in part, Weber's failure to become a political leader was a function of the German system of social stratification, which did not permit intellectuals and academics to enter politics. Weber's relationship to both Michels and Gaetano Mosca (1858–1941) has been a component of the debate about Weber's relationship to fascism and *Fuhrerdemokratie* (Mayer, 1940; Mommsen, 1963; Nolte, 1963; Winckelmann, 1956).

Weber's reception into the United States has been much discussed (Roth and Bendix, 1959). Weber's sociology was discussed in a number of contexts in the United States. Theodore Abel (1929) gave an extensive overview of the nature of *verstehende Soziologie* in his *Systematic Sociology in Germany* and a series of articles in *Social Research* by Albert Salomon explored Weber's methodological notions (1934) and his political ideas (1935), but it was Parsons who explored Weber's sociology most systematically in a variety of publications and translations (Parsons, 1963). Parsons's commentary on Weber spanned Parsons's entire academic career. After his successful application to a German–American exchange fellowship programme, Parsons had arrived in Heidelberg in June 1925 and, after a language course in Vienna, spent the 1925/6 academic year at Heidelberg, working on a thesis on the concept of capitalism in German economic theory. Several aspects of this thesis were published in article form (Parsons, 1928; 1929). Prior to his arrival in Heidelberg, Parsons had been ignorant of Weber's work, but he became quickly captivated by the Protestant ethic thesis and Parsons's translation appeared in 1930 and a critical discussion of H.M. Robertson's treatment (1933) of Weber's sociology of religion and economic individualism followed later (Parsons, 1935). In 1936, Parsons published a substantial review of Alexander von Schelting's *Max Webers Wissenschaftslehre* (Schelting, 1934).

Parsons was fully engaged in a critical debate with utilitarianism as a philosophy and its manifestation in economic theory. In particular, Parsons argued that utilitarian notions of rationality could not explain social order, because rational actors would always resort to force and fraud to achieve their ends. Parsons found that Durkheim's attempt to come to terms with positivism and Weber's attempt to wrestle with economic rationality through the categories of *verstehende Soziologie* perfectly illustrated the utilitarian dilemma. As a result, this discussion of Weber played a prominent role in *The Structure of Social Action* (Parsons, 1937). Parsons continued to be interested in Weber's economic sociology and in 1947, he edited (with A.M. Henderson) and introduced part one of Weber's *Wirtschaft und Gesellschaft: Grundriss der verstehenden Soziologie* as *The Theory of Social and Economic Organization* (Parsons, 1947). The volume had been planned before the war, but war-time difficulties had severely delayed its publication.

In the same period, Frank Knight (1927) had translated the *Wirtschaftsgeschichte* and Hans Gerth and C. Wright Mills published their excellent selection *From Max Weber* (Weber, 1948) and thus provided an alternative view of Weber's sociology in terms of the importance of power, conflict and violence in social life. The posthumous *Wirtschaft und Gesellschaft* was not published in translation as *Economy and Society* until 1968. Parsons clashed subsequently with Mills over the analysis of American capitalism, and Mills attacked Parsons over the alleged abstraction of Parsons's system theory (Robertson and Turner, 1991). This disagreement over the analytical value of functionalism and conflict sociology was the beginning of a critical rejection of Parsons's interpretation of Weber's philosophy of science, Parsons's so-called convergence thesis in *The Structure of Social Action* and Parsons's account of Weber's sociology of religion (Alexander, 1983). These criticisms gave rise to an important debate over the interpretation of Weber, especially Weber's notions of power and authority. Parsons was attacked over his interpretation of *Herrschaft* or 'domination' as 'leadership' (Albrow, 1990). The main point of this attack was to suggest that Parsons's introduction of Weber into American sociology had domesticated Weber's vision to make it compatible with the bland and uncritical assumptions of structural functionalism (Cohen et al., 1975; Parsons, 1975; 1976).

It is clear that, as Parsons's sociology evolved, Durkheim, rather than Weber, became the dominant figure in Parsons's view of general sociology. Parsons found Durkheim's approach to religion and value systems especially compatible with his approach to social order and the social system. Hence Parsons was less interested in Weber's approach to power and conflict, as he came to develop a general theory of social system integration (Holmwood, 1996). In general, therefore, Parsons is accused of distorting Weber's tentative approach to conceptual construction in the social sciences in the interests of a general theory. The assessment of Lassman and Velody (1989: xiii) is typical in this regard:

> The immense contribution of Talcott Parsons in bringing the work of Weber to American and British audiences cannot be overestimated, a contribution which was furthered by his colleagues and students in a variety of directions. Yet the consequences of their efforts has been to offer a very particular account of the history of sociology and the place of Weber within this narrative.

Parsons's emphasis on system integration in his general theory of social systems was not only incompatible with Weber's approach to theory construction, but also incommensurable with Weber's radical approach to political domination as a condition of national economic growth. Weber and Parsons differed fundamentally over questions of political liberalism (Holton and Turner, 1986; 1989).

Despite these critical remarks on Parsons's treatment of Weber, he continued to publish directly and indirectly on Weber's sociology. For example, although Weber scholars have suggested that the comparative studies of religion should be regarded as the core of Weber and that *Economy and Society* has been overestimated, Parsons (1963) wrote one of the best evaluations we have of Weber's contribution to the scientific study of religion in his introduction to Weber's *The Sociology of Religion*. Other evaluations of Weber followed in the 1960s, including the 1965 paper on Weber's principles of value freedom and objectivity in *Max Weber und die Soziologie heute* (Parsons, 1971a) and the appreciation of Weber over the century 1864–1964 (Parsons, 1964). Behind these overt commentaries on Weber, Weberian sociology continued to influence Parsons's approach to modernity and modernization such as *The System of Modern Societies* (Parsons, 1971b).

Max Weber and the Crisis of Historicism

As Weber's stature and influence in sociology slowly increased outside Germany after 1945, he was often treated inappropriately in isolation from his time and context. Weber's analysis of the division between the natural and the social sciences was in fact part of a wider debate in German philosophy over the characteristics of science. The problematic nature of truth and reliability in Weber's formulation of sociology as a 'science' of social action was expressed in his ambiguous treatment of such topics as the ideal type, the fact-value distinction, and the concept of neutrality. His preoccupation with the methodological problems of sociology was bound up with his appreciation of the crisis of truth and meaning in Christianity, namely an appreciation of the problems of relativism and cultural specificity. Weber can be interpreted as a sociologist who was responding to Nietzsche's criticism of absolutist notions of truth. Nietzsche's slogan that 'God is dead' can be read as meaning that there are no 'final vocabularies' (Rorty, 1989) and that truth is always grasped from a certain perspective, truth is therefore always conditional. In short, while Weber was originally seen in the context of debates about Marxism and with the methodological problems of interpretative sociology, he is now more likely to be seen in relation to Nietzsche as a sociologist, whose main contribution was to the analysis of the crisis of values and meaning following the rationalization of European culture.

Weber's preoccupation with the problem of meaning and authority has to be set within the broader context of a crisis about Christianity. Biblical criticism had shown that the Christian Church and Christian values were historical truths, and that claims about religious universalism were essentially problematic. Hence, this religious crisis was then reflected in intellectual problems around the status of historical research. Weber was one figure in an intellectual movement (in sociology, philosophy, history and theology) which attempted to come to terms with this relativization of values and the secularization of European thought. The emergence of sociology in the late nineteenth century can therefore be seen as part of a larger reorientation of European social thought, which was brought about by the secularization of consciousness, the erosion of traditional values, the growing dominance of instrumental rationalism and the diversification of cultures through global trade and imperialism. Weber's general explanation for these developments was the process of rationalization – a theme which lies behind and constantly informs the critical responses to Weberian sociology.

This crisis of cultures was in the scientific world reflected in the debate about the nature of and relations between the natural sciences and the human sciences. Of course, the concept of 'science' had a broad meaning and significance in German, but it was recognized that there was a deep division between those sciences which generally addressed the life of the mind, consciousness or spirit (Geist) and those which concentrated on the natural world. While the natural sciences (Naturwissenschaften) explained phenomena in terms of causal arguments, the human sciences (Geisteswissenschaften) were concerned with understanding and evaluating the significance and importance of cultural phenomena. Thus in Germany while, for example, both physics and anthropology are 'sciences', they require vastly different methodologies and techniques, because anthropology has to address the symbolic significance and meaning of ritual acts and customs, which cannot be conceptualized within the framework of laws and causes. Rituals are rule-governed actions, not law-like events in the natural world. These problems, as we will see, dominated the philosophy of the social sciences in the sociological writings of Weber.

This division gave rise to a variety of approaches in which it was argued that the natural sciences were concerned with causes, while the human sciences dealt with reasons. In the natural sciences, the emphasis is on explanation, but in the humanities it is with hermeneutics and the problem of understanding and interpretation. While natural science examines behaviour, the social and human sciences concentrate on actions which are purposeful. Finally, the natural sciences frame their explanations in terms of laws and the social sciences, in terms of probabilities. Weber in Economy and Society defined sociology as a science which attempts to provide an interpretative understanding of the meaning and consequences of social action, that is actions which are meaningful. He characteristically referred to the science of society as 'interpretative sociology' (verstehende Soziologie).

Although these arguments about the differences between natural science and human science appear to be relatively clear, there is a deep problem about relativism, which is raised by the notion of interpretation. From a sociological point of view, the meaning of any action or cultural phenomenon (such as a symbol) is deeply embedded in its social and cultural context. The meaning of actions are quite simply particular to a given context. How is any general knowledge of society as such possible? If for example the meaning of the pilgrimage in Islam has to be interpreted within the context of Islamic values, can there be a universally relevant sociology of religion, or does relativism suggest that there has to be an Islamic sociology of religion for Islam and a Jewish sociology for Judaism?

This problem of the historical specificity of cultures and thus of cultural relativism is broadly the problem of historicism, namely the view that the meaning and importance of culture can only be understood historically within its specific temporal and spatial setting, that is contextually. This historical problem, as he points out for example in the chapter on Ernst Troeltsch, was particularly acute in the case of western Christianity. If the faith which has been inherited by the Christian churches in the west is a specific historical phenomenon which is peculiar to its time and place, how can Christian theology claim any universal authority and relevance for the prophetic message of Jesus Christ? The prophecy of Christ is simply one message, alongside many other claims about the nature of human existence and divinity. Similar problems about authenticity and authority are faced in the analysis of art and culture, where claims about aesthetics may simply appear as opinions rather than truths about cultural objects. For Antoni, these specific debates in theology (in the writings of Ernst Troeltsch), history (in the historical studies of Wilhelm Dilthey and Johan Huizinga), politics (in the political analysis of Friedrich Meinecke) and sociology (in the philosophy of the social sciences of Max Weber) in fact constituted a general and profound crisis of authority and certainty, not only in Germany, but in Europe as a whole – a crisis which spanned the entire nineteenth and early twentieth centuries.

Antoni (1962) identified a number of solutions – or attempted solutions – to this intellectual crisis, which formed a moral and spiritual crisis of confidence in European culture. Within his account of historical relativism, one can detect three forms of historicism: naturalistic, metaphysical and aesthetic. One solution to relativism attempted to develop the positivistic methods of the natural sciences as a basis for certainty in social inquiry. This solution tended to resolve history into (positivistic) sociology. By contrast, metaphysical historicism developed into idealism, which attempted to find some certainty outside time in the realm of pure thought (post-Kantian idealism) or pure faith (German theology). Aesthetic historicism concentrated on the experience of the historian as a point of common agreement, namely the aesthetic experience of reality could produce a form of certainty in the context of chaotic values.

Dilthey recognized clearly that the crisis of the authority of values and morality in German culture had been first experienced in debates about the character of the authority of the texts of Christianity, which had occurred through the evolution of biblical criticism. Biblical scholarship had raised profound problems in confidence in the authority and authenticity of the biblical foundations of authority. In western Christianity, as Troeltsch's typology of church-sect recognized, there had been two forms of authority. One type of authority, for example in the Roman Catholic Church, was based on tradition and the ecclesiastical authority of the Pope and the bishops. The so-called 'keys of grace' were in the hands of the clergy, who released grace through ritualistic acts, such as confession. By contrast, another form of authority was developed by the Protestant sects which sought a more direct and individualistic approach to the charismatic powers of Christ through a direct reading of the Bible and through personal experience of God, for example in conversion.

The problem for Protestant theology was that biblical criticism through the eighteenth and nineteenth centuries had made the biblical text into a historical document. In short, Protestantism through its rational inquiry into the Bible had exposed theological truth to historicism. As a result, the most obvious alternative source of authority was the conversion experience itself and as a result certain forms of Protestantism promoted feeling and experience as guarantees of the authority of faith. Throughout Europe various forms of pietism emphasized the feeling and the experience of the divine presence (through conversion, fellowship and contemplation) as the principal criterion of certainty. In Britain, the Methodist movement followed the teaching of John Wesley and the hymns of Charles Wesley, and conversion through emotional experiences of divinity became the main basis of faith. In Germany, this new emphasis on feeling and experience was given cogent intellectual expression by Friedrich Schleiermacher, whose early involvement with the Brethren convinced him that in a period of religious uncertainty the experience of grace was the fundamental phenomenon of religious activity. The anxieties of salvation and damnation were resolved in the quiet experience of fellowship and the warmth of grace. As Dilthey recognized, this attitude to religion spelt the end of traditional Protestantism with its stark emphasis on the truth of the Bible and the ever-present danger of evil and spiritual damnation.

Through the work of theologians like Schleiermacher, a solution to historicism emerged in which theology was converted into a psychology of feeling. Pietism offered the believer an experience of certainty by cultivating emotions and sentiment through the aesthetic stimulation of the emotions. It was for this reason that hymns and fellowship played such an important role in the development of Methodism in England. For Marx, this form of religiosity represented an opium of the people, because suffering could be borne through the comforts of sentimental religious songs and the dramatic effects of conversion.

Reflecting on Dilthey and Schleiermacher, Antoni recognized the importance of the concept of *Erlebnis* in the aesthetic solutions of historicism. As the translator's preface indicates, the concept of *Erlebnis* has no adequate English translation. The verb *erleben* means to experience and *Erlebnis* is an experience, but the term carries a much deeper significance in the historicist debate. It signifies the lived experience of everyday reality; it is the enjoyment of the experiences of the life-world. The collective experiences of *Erlebnis* represent the life-world of a community in its response to existence, and for Dilthey these collective representations of everyday life have a spiritual authority. In this world of collective or folk experience, there is a reality which can transcend the relativism of the historicist problem.

It is only a short step to the argument that industrial capitalism through the application of rational science technology has transformed the relationship between human beings and their environment; it has undermined the authenticity of the life-world through the commodification of culture. For Weber, rational capitalism has demystified the everyday world and incorporated the sphere of *Erlebnis* into the system of rational economic exchange. In Weber's pessimistic view of 'the iron cage', there is no escape from the process of rationalization which, through the application of science, has embraced all spheres of life including the spiritual domain (Bendix, 1960). It is the 'fate' of the modern world to suffer the routinization of life through bureaucracy, science and discipline in which the magical and charismatic aura of social existence is slowly but surely effaced.

While the overt thesis of Antoni's extraordinary study is the problem of historicism, the covert and more important argument is the general crisis of European culture, which, as we have seen, was a crisis of relativism in the intellectual class resulting in a profound sense of instability and uncertainty at the end of the century. Industrial capitalism and urbanization had totally transformed European social structure. There was a sense of the exhaustion of ideas, the collapse of Christian certainty and the inauthentication of the everyday world. This erosion of confidence was expressed in debates about anomie, alienation and *ennui*. One response was to seek out security in a re-evaluation of the importance of the irrational in theories of the unconscious realm in Freud, intuition in Bergson, revolutionary violence in Sorel or moral passion in Durkheim.

The covert theme of Antoni's exploration of the crisis of historicism is the quest for a political solution to the complexity and diversity which flowed from cultural relativism. This crisis in Germany was a question of the failure of liberalism as a political movement and the growth of Prussian authoritarianism. In one sense, Bismarck's unification of Germany and the autocratic policies towards working-class politics, the early trade union movement and the religious divisions in Germany between Catholics, Protestants and Jews were also a 'solution' to historicism – Bismarck's authoritarianism represented a political route out of the crisis of moral uncertainty. With the decline of organized religion, Troeltsch and Weber came to the pessimistic conclusion that moral solutions to the problem of civilization in Germany were no longer viable, and a strong and decisive political leadership for Germany, following the decline of Bismarckian Germany and the disaster of World War One, was essential if the state was to remain, alongside America and Britain, a powerful nation in the competition for world power. Troeltsch and Weber both felt that power politics would inevitably be Machiavellian insofar as politics is in its essence morally neutral (Mommsen, 1984). Power and values were the two central issues of Weber's sociology as a response to nineteenth-century historicism. In this regard, Weber was significantly influenced by the 'perspectivism' of the philosopher Nietzsche as expressed in the slogan 'God is dead'.

The covert theme of Antoni is the crisis of bourgeois liberalism and the rise of authoritarian fascism as the answer to European historicism. One of the most profound critics of Weber's philosophy of social science and his ethical relativism was Leo Strauss (1899–1973). Strauss, a Jewish refugee from Hitler's Germany, was a professor at the University of Chicago, and became a profound critic of liberalism, which he believed had undermined political leadership in Weimar Germany, thereby paving the way for fascism, and it was liberalism that threatened the United States with a similar catastrophe. For Strauss, Weber was paradoxically an important component in the crisis. His value neutrality obscured the importance of political philosophy. His relativism undermined values. His belief in the polytheistic nature of value conflicts was symptomatic of the religious crisis of the West.

Conclusion: Max Weber and Contemporary Sociology

The contemporary interest in Weber is a consequence of (1) the general and comprehensive nature of Weber's sociology as a paradigm for society as a whole, (2) the richness and complexity of his methodological approach (*verstehende Soziologie*), which provides us with a sophisticated understanding of the problem of values and meaning in historical and sociological analysis, (3) the contemporary relevance of his political and moral notions to a social order which is dominated by the rationalization process, (4) the depth and richness of his comparative sociology of religion as a perspective on the processes of secularization in modern societies, and finally (5) the relevance of his ambiguities about modernity and modernization in relation to the current concern with postmodernity and *posthistoire*.

Many students of Weber have argued that the core of his work was a study of the economic ethics of the world religions and their impact on the process of modernization (Turner, 1974). Weber's ambiguity about modernization can be related to the current debate about postmodernity. *Posthistoire* means that history has no pattern – at least no beginning, middle and end (Niethammer, 1992). This secularization of time follows from the erosion of Christianity as a dominant paradigm in a world where we are sceptical about grand narratives (Lyotard, 1979). This theme of postmodernity is anticipated by Antoni in the earlier debate about historicism, which was a debate about the sources of moral certainty and cultural authenticity in a world of rapid social transformation. While Rheinhard Bendix has argued that there is no single key to Weber's sociology, this presentation of the work of Weber is based on the assumption that the problem of the relevance of values does provide an interpretative key with which to unlock Weber's work.

It was thus forty years after Weber's death before he was fully recognized alongside Durkheim as a founder of modern sociology and it was not until the 1970s that the modern 'revival' of Weber was well under way. In the second half of the century, Weber's sociology became canonical and his analysis of capitalism was no longer treated as a simple rejection of Marxism (Weiss, 1986). Weber is a towering figure in twentieth-century social science, but his legacy remains an ambiguity and he has no clear intellectual following, despite the depth and breadth of his influence in both the social sciences and humanities. Of course, the very idea of a canon of sociology has been much disputed in recent years and many would argue that academic influence in the sense of becoming a founding father is undesirable.

References

Abel, T. (1929) *Systematic Sociology in Germany. A critical analysis of some attempts to establish sociology as an independent science.* New York: Columbia University.

Albrow, M. (1990) *Max Weber's Construction of Social Theory.* London: Macmillan.

Alexander, J.C. (1983) *Theoretical Logic in Sociology. Volume three. The classical attempt at theoretical synthesis: Max Weber.* London: Routledge & Kegan Paul.

Antoni, C. (1962) *From History to Sociology. The transition in German historical thinking.* London: Merlin Press.

Antonio, R.J. and Glassman, R.M. (1985) *A Weber–Marx Dialogue.* Lawrence, Kansas: University Press of Kansas.

Aron, R. (1964) 'Max Weber und die Machtpolitik', *Zeitschrift für Politik,* 5: 100–13.

Aron, R. (1968) *Main Currents in Sociological Thought.* London: Weidenfeld & Nicolson.

Bendix, R. (1945) 'Bureaucracy and the problem of power', *Public Administration Review,* 5: 194–209.

Bendix, R. (1960) *Max Weber. An intellectual portrait.* Berkeley: University of California Press.

Bologh, R.W. (1990) *Love or Greatness. Max Weber and masculine thinking – a feminist inquiry.* London: Hyman.

Collins, R. (1986a) *Max Weber. A skeleton key.* Beverly Hills, CA: Sage.

Colins, R. (1986b) *Weberian Sociological Theory.* Cambridge: Cambridge University Press.

Cox, O.C. (1950) 'Max Weber on social stratification: a critique', *American Sociological Review,* 15: 223–7.

Croce, B. (1905) 'A proposito di une discussione sulla sociologia', *La Critica,* 3: 533–5.

Curtius, E.R. (1919) 'Max Weber uber Wissenschaft als Beruf', *Die Arbeitsgemeinschaft Monatschrift fur das Gesamte Volkshochschulwesen,* 1: 197–203.

Diehl, K. (1924) 'The life and work of Max Weber', *The Quarterly Journal of Economics,* 38: 87–107.

Fleischmann, E. (1964) 'De Weber a Nietzsche', *Archives europeennes de sociologie,* 5: 190–238.

Freund, J. (1966) *Sociologie de Max Weber.* Paris: Presses Universitaires de France.

Goldhammer, H. and Shils, E.A. (1939) 'Types of power and status', *American Journal of Sociology,* 45 (2): 171–82.

Hacker, H.M. (1953) 'Marx, Weber and Pareto on the changing status of women', *American Journal of Sociology,* 12: 149–62.

Halbwachs, M. (1925) 'Les origines puritaines du capitalisme', *Revue d'histoire et de philosophie religieuses,* 5: 132–54.

Halbwachs, M. (1929) 'Max Weber: un homme, une oeuvre', *Annales d'histoire economique et sociale,* 1: 81–8.

Hennis, W. (1988) *Max Weber. Essays in reconstruction.* London: Allen & Unwin.

Holmwood, J. (1996) *Founding Sociology? Talcott Parsons and the idea of general theory.* London and New York: Longman.

Holton, R.J. and Turner, B.S. (1986) *Talcott Parsons on Economy and Society.* London and New York: Routledge.

Holton, R.J. and Turner, B.S. (1989) *Max Weber on Economy and Society.* London and New York: Routledge.

Honigsheim, P. (1926) 'Der Max-Weber-Kreis in Heidelberg', *Kölner Vierteljahrshefte fur Soziologie,* 5 (3): 270–87.

Honigsheim, P. (1946) 'Max Weber as rural sociologist', *Rural Sociology,* 1: 208–18.

Honigsheim, P. (1968) *On Max Weber.* New York: The Free Press.

Jordan, H.P. (1937) 'Some philosophical implications of Max Weber's methodology', *Ethics,* 48: 221–31.

Käsler, D. (1988) *Max Weber. An introduction to his life and work.* Cambridge: Polity Press.

Lassman, P. and Velody, I. (eds) (1989) *Max Weber's 'Science as a Vocation'.* London: Unwin Hyman.

Lehmann, H. and Roth, G. (eds) (1993) *Weber's Protestant Ethic. Origins, evidence, contexts.* Cambridge: Cambridge University Press.

Löwith, K. (1939) 'Max Weber und seine Nachfolger', *Mass und Wert,* 3: 166–76.

Löwith, K. (1993) *Max Weber and Karl Marx.* London: Routledge.

Lyotard, J.F. (1979) *The Postmodern Condition. A Report on Knowledge.* Manchester: Manchester University Press.

Manasse, E.M. (1947) 'Max Weber on race', *Social Research,* 14: 191–221.

Mayer, J.P. (1940) 'Sociology of Politics: an interpretation of Max Weber's political philosophy', *The Dublin Review,* 207: 188–96.

Mayer, J.P. (1944) *Max Weber and German Politics. A Study in political sociology.* London: Faber & Faber.

Michels, R. (1920) 'Max Weber', *Nuova Antologia,* ccix: 355–61.

Michels, R. (1962) *Political Parties. A Sociological Study of the Oligarchic Tendencies of Modern Democracy.* New York: Free Press.

Mitzman, A. (1971) *The Iron Cage. An Historical Interpretation of Max Weber.* New York: The University Library, Grosset & Dunlap.

Mommsen, W.J. (1963) 'Zum Begriff der "Plebiszitaren Fuhrerdemokratie" bei Max Weber', *Koner Zeitschrift fur Soziologie und Sozialpsychologie,* 15: 295–322.

Mommsen, W.J. (1984) *Max Weber and German Politics 1890–1920.* Chicago: University of Chicago Press.

Mommsen, W.J. (1989) *The Political and Social Theory of Max Weber.* Cambridge: Polity Press.

Mommsen, W.J. and Osterhammel, J. (eds) (1987) *Max Weber and His Contemporaries.* London: Allen & Unwin.

Murvar, V. (1983) *Max Weber Today – an Introduction to a Living Legacy, Selected Bibliography.* Brookfield, Wisconsin: University of Wisconsin-Milwaukee Symposium.

Niethammer, L. (1992) *Posthistoire. Has history come to an end?* London and New York: Verso.

Nolte, E. (1963) 'Max Weber vor dem Faschismus', *Der Staat,* 2: 1–24.

Parsons, T. (1928) '"Capitalism" in recent German literature: Sombart and Weber. I', *Journal of Political Economy,* 37: 641–61.

Parsons, T. (1929) '"Capitalism" in recent German literature: Sombart and Weber. II', *Journal of Political Economy,* 37: 31–51.

Parsons, T. (1935) 'H.M. Robertson on Max Weber and his school', *Journal of Political Economy,* 43: 688–96.

Parsons, T. (1936) '*Max Webers Wissenschaftslehre* by Alexander von Schelting', *American Sociological Review,* 1: 675–81.

Parsons, T. (1937) *The Structure of Social Action.* New York: McGraw-Hill.

Parsons, T. (1942) 'Max Weber and the contemporary political crisis', *Review of Politics,* 4: 61–76, 155–72.

Parsons, T. (1947) 'Introduction' to Max Weber. *The Theory of Social and Economic Organization.* New York: Free Press. pp. 3–86.

Parsons, T. (1963) 'Introduction' to *The Sociology of Religion.* Boston: Beacon Press. pp. xix–lxvii.

Parsons, T. (1964) 'Max Weber 1864–1964', *American Sociological Review,* 30 (2): 171–5.

Parsons, T. (1971a) 'Value-freedom and objectivity', in O. Stammer (ed.), *Max Weber and Sociology Today.* Oxford: Blackwell. pp. 27–50.

Parsons, T. (1971b) *The System of Modern Societies.* Englewood Cliffs: Prentice-Hall.

Parsons, T. (1975) 'Commentary on "De-Parsonizing Weber: A critique of Parsons' interpretation of Weber's sociology"', *American Sociological Review,* 40 (5): 666–9.

Parsons, T. (1976) 'Reply to Cohen, Hazeligg, and Pope, with special reference to their statement "On the divergence of Weber and Durkheim: A critique of Parsons"', *American Sociological Review,* 41 (2): 361–4.

Ringer, F.K. (1969) *The Decline of the German Mandarins. The German Academic Community 1890–1933.* Cambridge, Mass.: Harvard University Press.

Robertson, H.M. (1933) *Aspects of the Rise of Economic Individualism. A Criticism of Max Weber and his School.* Cambridge: Cambridge University Press.

Robertson, R. and Turner, B.S. (1991) *Talcott Parsons. Theorist of Modernity.* London: Sage.

Rorty, R. (1989) *Contingency, Irony and Solidarity.* Cambridge: Cambridge University Press.

Roth, G. and Bendix, R. (1959) 'Max Webers Einfluss auf die amerikanische Soziologie', *Kolner Zeitschrift fur Soziologie und Sozialpsychologie,* 11 (1): 38–53.

Salomon, A. (1934) 'Max Weber's methodology', *Social Research,* 1: 147–68.

Salomon, A. (1935) 'Max Weber's political ideas', *Social Research,* 2: 368–84.

Salomon, A. (1945) 'German sociology', in G. Gurvitch and W.E. Moore (eds), *Twentieth Century Sociology.* New York: The Philosophical Library. pp. 586–614.

Sayer, D. (1991) *Capitalism & Modernity. An Excursus on Marx and Weber.* London and New York: Routledge.

Scaff, L.A. (1989) *Fleeing the Iron Cage. Culture, Politics and Modernity in the Thought of Max Weber.* Berkeley: University of California Press.

Schelting, A. von (1934) *Max Webers Wissenschaftslehre.* Tubingen: Mohr.

Seyfarth, C. and Schmidt, G. (eds) (1977) *Max Weber Bibliographie: Eine Dokumentation der Sekundaerliteratur.* Stuttgart: Enke.

Stauth, G. and Turner, B.S. (1988) *Nietzsche's Dance. Resentment, Reciprocity and Resistance in Social Life.* Oxford: Basil Blackwell.

Tawney, R.H. (1926) *Religion and the Rise of Capitalism.* London and New York (Harmondsworth: Penguin, 1972).

Tenbruck, F. (1975) 'Das Werk Max Webers', *Kolner Zeitschrift fur Soziologie und Sozialpsychologie,* 27: 663–702.

Tenbruck, F. (1980) 'The problem of thematic unity in the works of Max Weber', *British Journal of Sociology,* 31: 316–51.

Tribe, K. (ed.) (1989) *Reading Weber.* London and New York: Routledge.

Turner, B.S. (1974) *Weber and Islam. A Critical Study.* London: Routledge & Kegan Paul.

Turner, B.S. (1992) *Max Weber. From History to Modernity.* London: Routledge.

Turner, B.S. (1996) *For Weber. Essays on the Sociology of Fate.* London: Sage. pp. ix–xl (second edition).

Turner, S.P. and Factor, R.A. (1984) *Max Weber and the Dispute over Reason and Value.* London: Routledge & Kegan Paul.

Weber, M. (1927) *General Economic History.* London and New York: Allen & Unwin.

Weber, M. (1930) *The Protestant Ethic and the Spirit of Capitalism.* London: George Allen & Unwin.

Weber, M. (1948) *From Max Weber. Essays in Sociology.* New York: Oxford University Press.

Weber, M. (1951) *The Religion of China.* New York: Free Press.

Weber, M. (1952) *Ancient Judaism.* New York: Free Press.

Weber, M. (1954) *Max Weber on Law in Economy and Society.* Cambridge: Harvard University Press.

Weber, M. (1958a) *The Rational and Social Foundations of Music.* Carbondale: Southern Illinois University Press.

Weber, M. (1958b) *The City.* New York: Free Press.

Weber, M. (1958c) *The Religion of India.* New York: Free Press.

Weber, M. (1963) *The Sociology of Religion.* Boston: Beacon.

Weber, M. (1968) *Economy and Society. An Outline of Interpretive Sociology.* New York: Bedminster Press, two volumes.

Weber, M. (1975) *Roscher and Knies. The Logical Problems of Historical Economics.* New York: Free Press.

Weber, M. (1976) *The Agrarian Sociology of Ancient Civilizations.* London: New Left Books.

Weber, M. (1977) *Critique of Stammler.* New York: Free Press.

Weber, M. (1995) *The Russian Revolutions.* Cambridge: Polity Press.

Weiss, J. (1986) *Weber and the Marxist World.* London: Routledge & Kegan Paul.

Wilbrandt, R. (1928) 'Max Weber. Ein deutsches Vermachtnis', *Die neie Rundschau,* 39: 449–64.

Wiley, N. (ed.) (1987) *The Marx–Weber Debate.* London: Sage.

Winckelmann, J. (1956) 'Die Herrschaftskategorien der politischen soziologie und die Legitimat der Demokratie', *Archiv fur Rechts und Sozialphilosophie,* 42: 383–401.

CHAPTER 3

MAX WEBER AND KARL MARX

Modern man has forgotten to listen to this silence. Our world becomes increasingly loud, noisy – deafening with noise. We can no longer hear and our words have become false.

Karl Löwith

Introduction

Sociology has, since its institutional foundation in the late nineteenth century, been subject to profound changes in paradigms and perspectives. Many of these conceptual revolutions have challenged the fundamental assumptions of their discipline by, for example, bringing into question the whole idea of 'the social' (Baudrillard, 1983). While the history of all academic disciplines can be written in terms of violent paradigmatic shifts (Kuhn, 1970), sociology appears more prone than most subjects to bewildering shifts in intellectual terrain. One can either regard this analytical instability in a negative fashion as indicating the lack of maturity of sociology as a social science, or one can see sociology as a disciplinary field which is acutely in tune with the broad sweep of cultural movements within modern societies. The swings and changes in analytical paradigms are thus a response to broader societal currents.

However, within this context of intellectual uncertainty, one relatively persistent dimension of sociology has been its unresolved and critical relationship to the legacy of Karl Marx. More precisely, the debate over the relationship between Marx's political economy and Max Weber's interpretative sociology, which has raged with varying degrees of intensity since the publication of *The Protestant Ethic and the Spirit of Capitalism* (Weber, 1932) in 1904, has determined many of the major issues for research in the social sciences in the twentieth century.

These controversies have been driven by many forces, both scientific and ideological. For example, the sociological curriculum has been transformed in the post-war period by feminism, to a lesser extent by ethnic politics, the black movement and more recently by ecological debates. Over a longer period, it has been coloured by the changing political fortunes of both Marxism as a social movement and by Marxist sociology as an academic discipline. Part of the hostility between Marxists and academic sociologists is a function of their family resemblance; they both subscribe to grand theories of the historical development of society and both claim to offer a scientific analysis of those conditions which will bring about revolutionary changes in social structure. They are pre-eminently explanations of the nature of modern societies, of which the capitalist economy is a central feature. Marxism and sociology have, however, typically adhered to profoundly different epistemologies, philosophies and presuppositions.

Although they can be distinguished in these terms, the fortunes of Marxism, socialism and sociology, especially in western Europe, have often been closely interrelated. Classical sociology at various points in its development was forced to confront socialism as a social fact and socialism as a competing theory of society. For example, Saint-Simon was simultaneously the founder of French socialism and sociology. Both Durkheim and Weber wrote extensively on the nature of socialism and Marxism. Durkheim in particular adopted a sympathetic approach to socialism as a moral regulation of the economy which would restrain the anomic effects of utilitarian ideology and market conflicts (Durkheim, 1958). Weber was highly critical of the rationalization of economic life which a centralized socialist economic plan would entail, but he was also significantly influenced in his view of the economic structure of the ancient civilizations by Marx's theory of slavery and feudalism (Weber, 1976). Weber also once claimed that the intellectual seriousness of scholars was to be judged by their attitude towards Nietzsche and Marx; Weber's own inaugural address at Freiburg University in 1895 was peppered with references and asides to Nietzsche's views on the will to power and to Marx's economic analyses (Tribe, 1989). Joseph Schumpeter, who was professionally an economist, contributed to the creation of economic sociology, but regarded the socialization of economic functions as a corrosion of entrepreneurial creativity (Schumpeter, 1934). Alternatively, sociological theorists have often been criticized precisely for their failure to take Marxism as a theory of society seriously. Thus, Talcott Parsons has been challenged because he treated Marxism as simply a version of utilitarian economic theory and therefore as an analysis of society that is consequently flawed by its narrow positivist assumptions (Gould, 1991). In fact, in Europe, sociology has often been inadequately represented in the academy as a consequence of its association with radical social movements.

While this intellectual and political relationship has been variable between different authors and sociological traditions, as a general rule, one can argue that Marxism and sociology have been typically opposed to each other, because they have in part been competing for a similar intellectual audience. Marxists have been critical of academic sociology since at least the 1930s when they objected to writers such as Karl Mannheim who had developed a relativizing sociology of knowledge that challenged Marxist approaches to ideology (Mannheim, 1991). By contrast, Marxist authors like Georg Lukács saw sociology as the manifestation of bourgeois irrationalism (Lukács, 1971). According to the 'official' view of Marxism and sociology, the whole orientation of Marxism has been towards a committed critique of capitalism as a system of unjust exploitation, whereas Weberian sociology, with its individualistic approach to

methodology and its separation of facts and values, has been either
overtly neutral in political terms or covertly an aspect of liberal social
philosophy.

This intellectual struggle between academic sociology and Marxist
political economy to dominate the character of sociology was probably at
its height from the 1960s to the late 1970s, when various manifestations of
French social theory, such as structuralism, were at the foreground of intellectual development. Louis Althusser (Althusser and Balibar, 1968)
adopted the idea of an 'epistemological rupture' from philosophers of science such as Gaston Bachelard to argue that Marxism was a science of the
transformation of modes of production, which avoided the common-sense
or subjective notions of sociology. This Althusserian structuralism was
adopted by writers like Nicos Poulantzas (1973) to claim that sociology, by
concentrating on the attitudes and experiences of individuals, could not
provide a scientific analysis of the determining structures of economics
and politics. This analytical contrast between the structuralism of scientific
Marxism and the methodological individualism of 'bourgeois sociology'
dominated much of the theoretical development of the social sciences in
the 1970s. In sociology, the theoretical contrast was often presented in
terms of Weber's methodological individualism and commitment to sociology as an interpretative perspective on social action, on the one hand,
and Marx's realist epistemology, structuralism and commitment to historical materialism as a science of modes of production on the other (Hindess
and Hirst, 1975). These debates, which were also reflections of broader
political struggles in western societies, largely ignored Weber's historical
analyses of the role of 'objective interests' in politics and economics, and
his preoccupations with the negative unintended consequences of action
(Turner, 1981). At the same time, Althusser was forced to argue that the
'early Marx' of the Paris Manuscripts was trapped in a humanistic paradigm which was eventually abandoned in favour of the scientific approach
of *Capital*, volume one (Althusser, 1966). The consequence was a largely
sterile debate about the character of orthodox Marxism: was the early
Marx's humanism compatible with the deterministic understanding of
Marxist Leninism by the Party?

One must also add that this intellectual contest was far more important
in Europe than in North America, partly because socialism as a political
force has never had much significance in American politics (Lipsett, 1960).
American sociology produced a number of radical sociologists such as
C. Wright Mills and Alvin Gouldner, but they were somewhat marginal to
the mainstream of American sociology in the 1950s and 1960s, which
remained liberal and reformist in politics, and empirical and applied in its
scientific orientation. Many of the American sociologists who fell outside
the applied tradition of main-stream American sociology were in fact either
European exiles (such as Hans Gerth and Leo Lowenthal) or Canadians
(such as Dennis Wrong).

The relationship between sociology and Marxism has in the last two decades gone through many phases, but basically the whole issue of sociology versus Marxism has in recent times been transformed by three inter-related changes: the dramatic political collapse of organized communism in 1989–90, which has inevitably brought into question the intellectual credibility of Marxism as a critical theory of society and history; the rapid re-establishment of sociology in the academies of the re-constituted east European universities in the 1990s, especially in Germany, Hungary and Poland; and the widespread interest in postmodernism as an alternative to the 'grand narratives' of humanism, the Enlightenment and Marxism (Turner, 1990). These socio-political changes have been significant for both sociology and Marxism, but it is obviously the case that there is a more general crisis of intellectual authority and direction in Marxism as a theory of society than in sociology.

Of course, Marxist intellectuals have often taken the view that organized communism either had no necessary relationship to Marxism as a theory of society, or that the Marxism of Karl Marx is still the most effective general criticism of the exploitation of workers in capitalism and of the authoritarian regimes of Soviet-style state socialism. In reality, the authority of Marxist theory has been severely challenged, not least for the failure of Marxism to anticipate the total collapse of east European communism and the Soviet Union. To argue that the collapse of organized communism as a political force and the destruction of state socialism as a form of society have no bearing on the intellectual credibility of Marxism would be rather like arguing that the discovery of the bones of Christ in an Israeli graveyard, the abdication of the Pope, and the closure of Christendom would have no relevance to the intellectual coherence of Christian theology. Radical thinkers like Ernesto Laclau are surely correct in arguing that socialist thought cannot simply turn its back on the history of 'actually existing Marxism'. Marxist theory has to be reconstituted from the foundations upwards and this reconstitution will necessarily involve a fundamental reappraisal of the scientific and political relationship between Marxism and sociology, that is between Marx and Weber.

Löwith's Heideggerian Existentialism

This convoluted and protracted debate explains the continuing interest in and importance of Karl Löwith's study of Weber and Marx which was published in Germany in 1932 in the *Archiv für Sozialwissenschaft und Sozialpolitik,* and was subsequently translated into English in 1982. Löwith wrote and worked in an academic and political context in Germany where Marxism and sociology were polarized. Weber's sociology of religion was welcomed by many German social scientists as the definitive answer to Marxist theories of ideology. With the rise of fascism in Germany in the

1930s, Marxism was of course very much under attack, but sociology was also regarded with some suspicion because it was itself associated with the Jewish intellectual community, which included such figures as Georg Simmel, Karl Mannheim and Norbert Elias. However, recent research on the history of German sociology under National Socialism has demonstrated that sociology was not an oppositional force and largely acquiesced in the reactionary university culture of the Nazi period (Turner and Käsler, 1992). By contrast, the members of the Institute of Social Research (the so-called Frankfurt School), which was initially inspired by Marxism, fled to the United States, where they lived as reluctant exiles (Jay, 1973). Löwith's study of Weber and Marx was thus published in a context of political instability, where scholarship was increasingly politicized. As we will see, Löwith's own work and life were bound up intellectually with the theory of history, the legacy of Hegelian idealism and Marxism, and bound up politically with the impact of fascism on Jewish intellectuals in Germany.

Löwith's study of Weber and Marx is now over sixty years old, but it is crucially important for three basic reasons. First, Löwith was able to show that, despite the very important differences between Marx and Weber, their sociological perspectives were held together by a convergent philosophical anthropology. Thus, while the political attitudes of Marx and Weber were diametrically opposed, they shared a fundamental interest in the problem of 'man'[1] in bourgeois capitalism. There was therefore an important convergence in their attitudes towards the negative features of bourgeois civilization, which Marx elaborated through the idea of 'alienation' and Weber through the idea of 'rationalization'. For both authors, capitalist society was, from their relatively similar views on ontology, inescapably problematic, but also revolutionary by comparison with the traditional civilizations of both the western world and Asia. Capitalism, which brought about a profound 'detraditionalization' of society (Beck, 1992) created enormous risks for humans, but also opened up new transformative opportunities. For Marx, the opportunity for social transformation was to be seized ultimately by the revolutionary struggles of the working class. For Weber, the transformative potential was an essential feature of capitalist modernization, but he was ambiguous about any ultimate escape from 'the iron cage'. In this sense, Weber's sociology was fatalistic, because it concentrated on the negative and unintended aspects of social action (Turner, 1981). Weber's sociology was driven by a concern for 'human dignity' (Löwith, 1982: 22), but Weber remained pessimistic about the opportunities for human freedom within a society which had been so thoroughly subjected to the processes of rationalization. This difference in their attitudes was neatly expressed by Löwith, namely 'Marx proposes a therapy while Weber has only a "diagnosis" to offer' (Löwith, 1982: 25).

Thus the first important feature of Löwith's general interpretation of Marx and Weber was that, by concentrating attention on 'this underlying anthropological concern' (Löwith, 1982: 20), Löwith was able to show that the differences between Marx and Weber in terms of their epistemological, scientific and political views were actually grounded in a similar philosophical anthropology. It is important to keep in mind that Löwith's thesis that there was a similar and crucial underlying philosophical anthropology in Marxism and Weberian sociology was published in 1932, many decades before recent interpretations which have presented similar arguments, for example about the impact of Nietzsche on Weber (Hennis, 1987). Löwith's work was highly original and anticipated many contemporary studies which have also focused on the underlying ontological assumptions of the social theories of Marx and Weber. Although a number of writers in the Marxist tradition have analysed the philosophical anthropology in Marx's early work such as *The Economic and Philosophical Manuscripts* of 1844 (Marx, 1964), the implicit understanding of 'man' in Weber continues to be neglected, with the possible exception of Wilhelm Hennis. Löwith's perspective on Weber provides an essential starting point for uncovering this hidden ontology in Weber's post-Christian analysis of human beings and their striving to achieve 'personality'.

Löwith's thesis continues to be important, secondly, because it was developed out of his philosophical indebtedness to Martin Heidegger. I shall show shortly that Heidegger was primarily concerned to understand the nature of Being, but Heidegger wanted to avoid the abstraction of traditional metaphysics which started with universal observations about Being. In *Being and Time* (Heidegger, 1962) which appeared in German in 1927, Heidegger rejected metaphysics by concentrating on the contingent facticity of Being in the everyday world. Being or *Da-sein* was always 'being-there' in time and space. However, human beings were constantly in danger of forgetting their place in this everyday world of Being. Human beings are to some extent always homeless beings; being without a place in the world, they are alienated from their reality. They are ontologically nostalgic (Turner, 1987) in this condition of existential homelessness (*Heimatlosigkeit*). Heidegger went on to develop a critique of technology in capitalist society (Heidegger, 1977) because it created conditions in which human beings are increasingly alienated from their own bodies. Heidegger, who was particularly interested in the importance of the human hand, refused apparently to use a typewriter, because it was a further alienation of mind and body (Derrida, 1989). Löwith as a student of Heidegger was of course profoundly influenced by this analysis of existence (Löwith, 1948) and the Heideggerian contribution to existentialism.[2] For Löwith, the Heideggerian analysis of the classical problem of essence and existence was the starting point of modern philosophy and hence the starting point for an adequate philosophical understanding of Marx and Weber. It was this Heideggerian dimension to Löwith's approach which made Löwith's analysis highly original and enduring. Heidegger's analysis of Being has been crucial to many developments in twentieth-century philosophy, such as phenomenology and existentialism, but it has also been increasingly important in post-structuralism and postmodernism. For example, Heidegger's hostility to traditional metaphysics, his close concentration on the etymology of basic concepts in philosophical analysis and the textuality of his philosophical method have been important in the development of so-called deconstructive techniques in modern philosophy, especially in the contributions of Jacques Derrida. Löwith's study of Weber and Marx from the perspective of Heideggerian existentialism has retained a freshness and relevance to modern philosophical discussion which should not be ignored.[3]

Thirdly, Heidegger's approach to the critique of metaphysics was in its turn shaped by Nietzsche's critique of conventional metaphysics, his hostility to traditional religious values and his commitment to the creation of a 're-valuation of values' which would overcome the mediocrity of the moral life of 'the herd' in modern society. Nietzsche's prophetic slogan that 'God is dead' was the starting point of modern philosophy which has been structured by the question which was central to Nietzsche's philosophy: what are the moral and social consequences of the death of God, that is the termination of a view of reality in which a personal god still made sense? The collapse of the certainties of the traditional view of reality had left an enormous chasm and Löwith interprets the development of modern philosophy as, in large measure, a response to this absence of certainty. Of course, Löwith has been primarily concerned with the modern development of existentialism as a response to the post-Christian world. In particular, Nietzsche, Kierkegaard and Heidegger have been philosophers who concentrated on the contingent character of life and the pathos of the human condition. While Pascal could still draw some comfort from the regularities of the physical world, modern existentialists (from Kierkegaard to Sartre) have viewed nature 'only as the hidden background of man's forlorn existence' (Löwith, 1952: 91). We might add that Weber's persistently bleak and negative view of the world (perhaps best summarized in his 'I want to see how much I can stand' announcement) was also part of this critical legacy. While Weber described himself as, in religious terms, 'unmusical', he was also deeply moved by the pathos of a post-Christian reality which had yet to produce an alternative world-view.

While Nietzsche was crucially important for the development of modern philosophy, it is only relatively recently that sociologists have recognized the importance of Nietzsche for sociology as a consequence of his impact on, for example, Weber, Simmel and Scheler (Stauth and Turner, 1988). It is for example impossible to understand Simmel's ideas about the tragedy of culture and the nature of social forms without understanding Simmel's dependence on Schopenhauer and Nietzsche (Simmel, 1991). Nietzsche is important for sociological theory because he formulated an analysis of cultural change which presents the problem of social cohesion in terms of an erosion of normative authority and politics. In short, Nietzsche developed an important understanding of the nature of ideology and the state. For Nietzsche the primitive form of ideology is idolatry. Having claimed that in modern civilization God is dead, Nietzsche was aware that new idols would fill the space which was left by this dead God; in particular, 'the herd' was increasingly subject to the state, which was the new idol that would rob people of their freedom. We can see Weber's anxieties about the slavery of modern people within the bureaucratic machine of the modern state and about the possibilities of personal autonomy in a world which had been transformed by the processes of rationalization. Weber went out of his way to use Nietzschean language in his Freiburg address of 1895 to comment on the importance of political struggle in economic life in which the quest for 'elbow room' was central to all political life. Löwith's Heideggerian interpretation of Weber and Marx was thus also important because it began the important task of uncovering the Nietzschean roots of Weber's pessimistic analysis of modern, rational society.

Löwith's Life and Works

Löwith was born in 1897 and died in 1973. His life was eventful. He was a student in Freiburg where he came under the influence of Husserl and Heidegger. Löwith described his student years in Freiburg as 'incomparably rich and fruitful' in his brief account of his 'curriculum vitae' (Löwith, 1959). It was Heidegger who directed Löwith's *Habilitationsschrift* on *Das Individuum in der Rolle des Mitmenschen* (Löwith, 1928). He had the status of *Dozent* lecturer at Marburg University prior to Hitler's climb to power in 1933. During these crisis years, he travelled to Italy, Japan and finally America in 1941, taking up positions at the Hartford Theological Seminary and the New School for Social Research in New York (1949–51). It was at Hartford Theological Seminary that Löwith wrote a number of influential articles on the philosophy of history, Marxism and existentialism for *Social Research*. He returned to Germany to take up a professorship of philosophy at Heidelberg University.

Löwith was thus starting his academic career in the context of significant developments in German philosophical thought. At the beginning of this century, 'the south-west school' of German philosophy at Heidelberg and Freiburg was the intellectual cradle of phenomenology and existentialism (in the work of Husserl and Heidegger), interpretative sociology (in the writing of Weber) and a rebirth of dialectical materialism (in the Marxism of Lukács). The writers who were influenced by E. Lask and Husserl included Karl Jaspers, Georg Lukács and Ernst Bloch. It was within this fountain of academic development in philosophy, history and sociology that Löwith's intellectual interests were formed.

Löwith's academic publications are extensive, but they are primarily journal articles. Some of his philosophical essays have been collected in his *Nature, History and Existentialism and Other Essays* (Löwith, 1966). His collected bibliography was edited by Klaus Stichweh in *Von Hegel zu Nietzsche* (Löwith, 1986) and a further version is to be found in Löwith's *Samtliche Schriften* (Löwith, 1981) which was edited by Klaus Stichweh and Marc B. de Launay. Löwith's reputation, especially outside German academic life, is based on three major texts, namely *Max Weber and Karl Marx* (Löwith, 1982) in 1932, *From Hegel to Nietzsche* (Löwith, 1964) in 1941, and *Meaning in History* (Löwith, 1970).

He published a number of short autobiographical essays of which the most interesting is *Mein Leben in Deutschland vor und nach 1933* (Löwith, 1986) which was written in Japan in 1939. This text is important because it contains an account of his meeting with Heidegger in 1936, and his reflections on Heidegger's philosophy in the context of German fascism. Löwith met Heidegger for the last time in 1936, when Heidegger was giving some lectures at the German–Italian Culture Institute. Löwith, Heidegger's student and now an exile from Germany, was particularly distressed by the fact that Heidegger wore the Party insignia on his lapel during a family excursion to Frascati and Tusculum. Löwith remarked that Heidegger 'wore it during his entire stay in Rome, and it had obviously not occurred to him that the swastika was out of place while spending the day with me' (Löwith, 1988: 115). Löwith's *Heidegger: Denker in Dürftiger Zeit* (Löwith, 1953) has yet to be translated.

Löwith's social theory was closely bound up with his intellectual engagement with Heidegger and hence with the problems of theological thought in the modern world. His constant concern with the problems of faith and scepticism (Löwith, 1951) was a product of the sense of crisis in post-war Germany and intellectually a product of his study of Kierkegaard and Heidegger. The presuppositions behind *Max Weber and Karl Marx* were primarily theological, but they are derived from a theology which was in large measure post-Christian. Of course, Löwith's intellectual and personal relationship with Heidegger cannot be easily separated from Heidegger's problematic and controversial relationship with fascism. Heidegger's personal commitment to National Socialism cannot be seriously doubted (Farias, 1987). What is at issue is whether there was some necessary or 'natural' relationship between Heidegger's philosophy of Being and his views on fascism (Wolin, 1988).

In this respect, Löwith's perspective on this issue is intrinsically interesting, because he recognized an analytical relationship between Heidegger's existentialist analysis of *Da-sein* as involving an authentic capacity-for-Being which is specific to each individual and which is an expression of their particular historical circumstances. Each individual is faced with the possibility of choice and personal responsibility. In fact within the context of the unfolding of German history, there is a duty (*Mussen*) to take a personal responsibility for one's Being. Löwith recognized some affinity between Carl Schmitt's 'decisionism' in political philosophy and Heidegger's existential notion of the 'throwness' of Being.

One might also suggest a parallel between this Heideggerian notion of existential responsibility and Weber's famous and influential notion of the ethic of responsibility, which Weber connected to the ideas of calling and personality. For Weber, the ethic of responsibility finds its most elevated expression in the callings or vocations of science and politics. It is an interesting coincidence that Weber's inaugural address for the chair of economics was also delivered at the University of Freiburg in 1895 in which Weber also alluded, in language which self-consciously borrowed from Nietzsche, to the need for strong political decision making if Germany was to survive in a competitive international context.

However, there is also a relationship between Hitler's idea of destiny, the fate of the German nation and his own charismatic calling to leadership. The facticity of our being propels us to a choice in which we may experience an authentication of life. Hitler's choice is one illustration of these ideas, but Heidegger's own rectorship of the University of Freiburg is another. Heidegger expressed these ideas about the authenticity of being and history in his 'The Self-Affirmation of the German University', the famous *Rekoratsrede* of 1933. In his momentous decision to act as rector and to support the National Socialist cause within the University, Heidegger's philosophy was transformed into contemporary German reality, 'and thus for the first time the master's will to action finds suitable terrain and the formal outline of the existential categories receives decisive content' (Löwith, 1988: 125).

Löwith and the Meaning of History

It is important to emphasize Löwith's academic relationship to Heidegger in order to understand Löwith's intellectual development, but more importantly to grasp his approach to Marx and Weber. Löwith's social philosophy is based on the view that the decisive feature of western culture is to be located in the break between the classical world-view in which there is no history but the harmonious repetition of the same and the Christian *Weltanschauung* in which the advent of Christ creates a teleological framework for reality. History now has a meaning, which is primarily the revelation of grace through the creation and fall of man, the advent, death and resurrection of Christ, the lives of the saints and the Church, and ultimately the creation of a Second Kingdom. Whereas the classical world recognized the existence of a perfectly organized cosmos that was rational, Christian theology saw reality in terms of a divine telos, but also recognized that the ways of God to humanity were often obscure. Indeed the Beatitudes, which for example appear to celebrate the frailty and humility of Christians, express irrational values from the perspective of Greek rationalism. Christian theology has thus typically seen the Christian gospel as an offence to a rational mind, because Christianity rests ultimately on faith and not upon reason.

This fundamental historical contrast, perhaps the original quarrel between the ancients and the moderns, shaped Löwith's entire approach to modern social theory, in particular his approach to Marx and Weber. It was for example the basic theme of *Meaning in History* and it shaped his approach to Hegel and Nietzsche in his famous account of the 'revolutionary bridge in nineteenth-century German thought' (Löwith, 1964). To take one illustration of his approach, Löwith thought that Nietzsche's problematic commitment to the doctrine of Eternal Recurrence was not an aberration but the core of Nietzsche's philosophy (Löwith, 1945). It was Nietzsche's views on the problem of history and the doctrine of the Eternal Recurrence which were constitutive of his ultimately ambiguous approach to religion, the problems of values and classical Greece. Nietzsche rejected Christianity as a form of decadence – as a form of neurosis – but he also recognized the radical implications of Christian eschatology. He was also aware that the modern doctrine of progress (and possibly the Darwinistic version of the idea of progress) were secularized versions of the Christian view of history as a progression of the faithful to the Kingdom of God. For Nietzsche, the Eternal Recurrence and its prophet Dionysus is an important component in his attempt to bring about a transvaluation of values. The Eternal Recurrence is seen by Nietzsche as a 'yes-saying philosophy' of self-affirmation against the Christian doctrine of a unique creation. Yet, as Löwith points out, Nietzsche is a modern man, who found an unconditional acceptance of the classical world-view problematic. Thus Nietzsche's 'great effort to remarry man's destiny to cosmic fate or to "translate man back into nature" as the original text could not but be frustrated' (Löwith, 1945: 283). Nietzsche's argument is, as a consequence, inconsistent. Nietzsche wanted to assert that the Eternal Recurrence was an objective fact which could be proved by modern physics and mathematics, but frequently presented the doctrine as a moral perspective or subjective viewpoint. Nietzsche was committed to a version of individuality in which human beings have to triumph over the limitations of society and history. This individuality was expressed in the idea that the principal task of every human being is to become who they are. This Nietzschean version of individuality, which is essentially a modern view, could not be reconciled with the classical idea that the world is simply an eternal cycle of impersonal repetition. In a world which threatens human beings by its aimlessness and lack of purpose, it is the nature of human beings to will to power. For Nietzsche, human beings will always prefer to will nothingness than not to will at all. The failure of Nietzsche's doctrine of the Eternal Recurrence 'was not that he revived the classical vision of the *kosmos* as an eternal recurrence of the same, but that he attempted to establish its truth by his own creative will, under the title of a "will to power"' (Löwith, 1952: 92).

This general view of the philosophy of history provides the context for Löwith's view of Marx. For Löwith, Marx's historical materialism is a secularized version of the Christian teleology. Despite the scientific vocabulary of the Marxist vision of history, Löwith treats Marx's philosophy of history as a global vision which depends fundamentally on the Christian scheme of eschatology, the doctrine of the Last Days and the Restoration of man to Grace. In Marxism, 'history' is located in the long interval between the loss of communal innocence in primitive communism and its restoration in the final transition to communism. The vale of tears in the Marxist historical framework is occupied by the creation of private property, the division of labour, the organization of a market by exchange values, and the brutalization of the working class by capitalists. In short, history is to do with human alienation. This interpretation of Marxism has often been challenged by Marxists who want to reject any association between Christianity and Marxism, but it is an association which is difficult to dispel. For example, the young Lukács's view of history as a series of revolutions, which has the effect of bringing about moral purification and redemption, had a definitely apocalyptic quality. Lukács is also highly relevant in this context, since it was Lukács's theory of alienation that combined Weber's theme of rationalization with a Marxist analysis of reification.[4]

Löwith identified the theme of alienation in Marx's social theory as constitutive of Marx's entire project. For Löwith, the theme of 'man's self-alienation in the early writings of Marx' (Löwith, 1954) was not merely an optional extra or a youthful aberration relating to Marx's humanism, but in fact a perspective which integrates the early writings on the anthropological condition of 'man' and the later writings on economic processes. Löwith takes a strong stand, therefore, on the integration and integrity of Marx's work as a whole. Marx's starting point is a critique of bourgeois social reality which is defined principally in terms of the alienation of human beings from themselves. Thus, *Capital* 'is not simply a critique of political economy but a critique of the man of bourgeois society in terms of that society's economy' (Löwith, 1954: 215). The 'man of bourgeois society' is characterized by the separation of the private world of individualized private property and morality and the public realm of dignity and reason. Marx explored this problem of self-alienation and externalization through religion, the economy and the polity. In religious alienation, the natural powers of 'man' are transferred to the divine powers of God (Feuerbach, 1957); economic alienation takes the form of commodification and, ideologically, as the fetishization of commodities; political self-estrangement is constituted by the separation of state and society; its social expression in capitalism is the historical creation of an alienated proletariat. Löwith never departed from this perspective on Marxism in which Marx's political economy is founded on the existential problem of the human condition.

Max Weber and Karl Marx

I have already indicated why Löwith's account of Marx and Weber has remained an original and powerful contribution to the development of social theory: it was thoroughly grounded in a philosophical understanding of the central issue of modern philosophy, namely the relationship between essence and existence. Löwith approaches Marx's materialist theory as a radicalization of Hegel's idealism: Marx's solution was to argue that in communism at the 'end' of history the individual essence of each human being is overcome and resolved (*Aufhebung*) in communal existence. This Heideggerian question concerning existence which Löwith poses in relation to Marx's materialism, provides the link between Marx's philosophical anthropology, Weber's post-Christian existentialism and the postmodern, deconstructive writings of Derrida and Vattimo.

It is not necessary to attempt to summarize the specific arguments of Löwith's *Max Weber and Karl Marx*. My aim is to pick out certain aspects of Löwith's account which relate to this 'anthropological concern'. This selective commentary provides the framework within which one can then ask the question: what is enduring in Löwith's social theology?

To start with an apparently trivial observation, it is interesting to note that this is a study of Weber and Marx, not Marx and Weber. In other words, we can read this as an interpretation of Marx through a prior and more fundamental study of Weber. One can imagine that Weber was politically not congenial to Löwith, given Weber's nationalism and authoritarian view of German politics (Mommsen, 1989). Löwith appears to be uncomfortable with the harsh words of Weber's Freiburg lecture in which Weber, in reviewing the political failure of both the Prussian *Junkers* and the bourgeoisie, 'presented some unpalatable truths to his own class'. However, Weber was part of a circle of German intellectuals which was greatly exercised by the historical role of Protestantism in western culture and by the general problem of Christianity in relation to the development of secular, bourgeois capitalism. Indeed, Weber's celebrated 'Protestant Ethic thesis' can be understood as a specific contribution to this theological debate in which some of the most important contributions came from elsewhere, such as from the theology of Ernst Troeltsch (1931). It is also clear that Löwith sympathizes with Weber's epistemological critique of Marxism as a 'science', a critique which was to some extent compatible with Heidegger's own deconstructive techniques. Löwith's study has, therefore, to be read from the perspective of Weber's criticisms of Marxism as a 'science' which had not faced up to the problems of Nietzsche's perspectivism.

One can thus argue that the most important feature of Löwith's interpretation of Weber is that he analyses Weber's philosophy of social science as the foundation of his sociology. This strategic reading of Weber is somewhat unusual because, as Friedrich Tenbruck (1980) has constantly complained, Weber's *Wissenschaftslehre* has been neglected by sociologists. While many students are familiar with the essay on '"Objectivity" in social science and social policy' (Weber, 1949) in the collection edited by Edward Shils and Henry Finch, the importance of Weber's methodological essays for understanding Weber's sociology as a whole has been undervalued. The brilliance of Löwith's approach is that he shows, at least implicitly, that both Weber's analysis of the 'bourgeois capitalist world' and his philosophy of the social sciences flow from a single source, namely the human problems of a world in which God is dead.

Weber accepted Nietzsche's argument that knowledge ('truth') is always knowledge from a particular perspective, that is from the standpoint of a system of values. Because God is dead, there is no grounding by which one perspective could have legitimacy over other perspectives. 'Truth' is therefore provisional and it is practical in the sense that it is relevant to specific aims and purposes. In contemporary terminology because there are no 'grand narratives' (Lyotard, 1979), we are confronted with many different, local, conflicting 'truths'. Weber's entire sociology, but especially his commentaries on the problem of understanding (*Verstehend*) the meaning of social actions, was an attempt to come to terms with this problem.

An examination of Weber's substantive historical research, his writing on sociological theory and his essays on the philosophy of social science leaves one with the conclusion that Weber was never able to resolve the epistemological problems of sociology. For example, Weber was unable to provide a satisfactory definition of the ideal type of rational action (Sica, 1988) – an ideal type which is fundamental to the whole structure of Weber's sociological work. The ambiguities of Weber's sociology reside in the fact that, while he recognized the problem of Nietzsche's perspectivism, he was reluctant to accept its logical implications that all social science propositions about 'social reality' were purely provisional approximations and that they were products of the particular presuppositions of the scientist. Thus,

> A chaos of 'existential judgments' about countless individual events would be the only result of a serious attempt to analyze reality 'without presuppositions'... Order is brought into this chaos only on the condition that in every case only a *part* of concrete reality is interesting and *significant* to us, because only it is related to the *cultural values* with which we approach reality.
>
> (Weber, 1949: 78)

In order to try to make this construction of presuppositions scientifically systematic, Weber developed the ideal type as a selection from reality, and tried to establish a coherent approach to concepts such as ethical neutrality, value judgement and value relevance, but it is very doubtful that this attempt at clarification was genuinely successful. However, what emerges from his deliberations is the conviction that social science cannot be presuppositionless, that value judgement is inevitable, and that the 'laws' of history were merely heuristic devices. The result was a devastating critique of the claims made by Marxists that political economy was an exact science which could predict the collapse of capitalism with precision. The 'economic interpretation' of history was merely a one-sided perspective which could be challenged by an equally one-sided spiritual interpretation.

The significance of Weber's extreme form of nominalism and constructivism is not what it tells us about his methodological agnosticism, but what it tells us about Weber's 'ontological insecurity' (Giddens, 1990: 92). As Löwith points out, Weber's methodological scepticism emerges out of his bleak view of 'man' in bourgeois society:

> The ideal typical 'construct' is based upon a human being who is specifically 'free of illusions', thrown back upon itself by a world which has become objectively meaningless and sober and to this extent emphatically 'realistic'.
>
> (Löwith, 1982: 38)

Weber's methodological individualism meant that social science concepts such as the economy and the state could not be interpreted as referring to objective, substantive phenomena. However, Weber's criticisms were not simply suggesting that collectivist, reified concepts were unscientific. He objected to the reification of concepts 'because such a view would be enmeshed in transcendent prejudices and ideals, while the world in which we are situated no longer justifies prejudices of that particular sort' (Löwith, 1982: 39).

Now the meaningless of this world has, according to Weber, been brought about paradoxically as a consequence of rationalization. As the world has become more routinized and rationalized, so it has become more disenchanted. Rationalization has destroyed the magic garden of faith and certainty, but it has not produced an alternative set of values which are credible. Science itself is not a value system, because it is primarily concerned with means rather than with ends. As the reflexive rationalism of the process of modernization has cut away the roots of the old monotheistic faiths, we are left in a world of competing, incommensurable values. Weber thus saw modern societies as cultural arenas within which there was a struggle between polytheistic values for social dominance.

Given deeply seated ontological insecurity, what responses might be possible on the part of a human being? In Weber's sociology, we find many clues and answers which were never presented in a single place. However, the two essays on 'Science as a vocation' and 'Politics as a vocation' (Gerth and Mills, 1991) provide us with a reasonably systematic summary. Weber was highly critical of those social groups or movements which sought to escape from the reality of this existential dilemma by for example retreating into the arms of the Church. Weber also rejected the possibility of embracing the Party. Marxism for Weber involved a further rationalization of life by regulating the market, controlling investment and centralizing authority. Marxism would intensify the negative impact of instrumental rationality on the life-world. He was equally critical of the emerging Freudian solution which sought a 'hygienic' answer to ethical dilemmas. He had more sympathy with the eudamonian and erotic response of the followers of Otto Gross who created small affective communities in search of sexual authenticity. Weber was also impressed by the prophetic writings of Stefan George and the circle of influential philosophers and artists that gathered around George at Heidelberg, but Weber could not believe that prophetic poetry was an adequate response to the rationalized world of bourgeois capitalism (Stauth and Turner, 1992).

Weber's own response to the crisis of perspectivism can be found in his discussion of 'personality' and in 'the ethic of responsibility', both of which are discussed by Löwith. As we will notice, Weber's response has a close affinity to Heidegger's view that responsibility and calling are necessary features of an adequate orientation to the daunting contingency of our being-in-the-world. Although human beings can never fully escape from the iron cage of the rationalized world of bourgeois capitalism, we have a duty to face up to this reality and in the process we become committed to the development of personality.

Now by 'personality', Weber does not have in mind a psychological construct. Rather 'personality' refers to a life-plan or a structure within which the chaotic events of the life-cycle can be located. A 'personality' is an organization of life-events which permits an individual to mature and develop. In this respect, Weber's 'personality' may have much in common with the ideal of the educated and civilized person of the educated middle classes of Germany (*Bildungsbürgertum*) and can also be seen as the socio-logical legacy of Goethe's *Bildungsroman*. Weber's view is that authenticity consists in 'facing up to reality' and in making a conscious choice about a life-style which can be rationally defended. Authentic personality involves a certain degree of isolation and separation in order to bring up a reflexive ordering of one's own personal and social reality. Weber's model of charis-matic authority and authenticity has a close relationship to this heroic image of personality, but it was also captured in his contrast between the 'ethic of ultimate values' and the 'ethic of responsibility'. A rational per-sonality is faced in principle by two competing but viable life-strategies. One can either stand by one's own values, regarding them as having an absolute authority, and make decisions by reference to these transcendental standards, without regard for consequences and implications. Alternatively, it is possible to organize one's life by reference to responsibility for more limited objectives and tasks, paying close attention to consequences and implications. Weber felt that the ethic of absolute ends had been rendered impossible and archane by secular social changes. A modern person could really only choose an ethic of responsibility, knowing that our values are not absolute but provisional, not universal but local.

Weber's difficult and hesitant attempts to formulate a response to the modern fragmentation of values and pluralization of life-worlds were finally expressed in the idea of *Beruf*, namely a calling or vocation. The term clearly has a religious connotation as a calling to service in the work of God. The idea of a 'vocation' is still associated with the idea of a spiritual vocation. Weber, accepting that secularization was a necessary feature of rationalization, rejected the possibility of a religious vocation as a personal solution to the meaninglessness of a rationalized social order, and accepted instead that an ethic of responsibility was perhaps best expressed through either a vocation in politics or a vocation in science. These concepts were fully articulated in two public lectures which Weber gave towards the end of his life in which he challenged the youth of a defeated Germany to face up to the tasks of their time and their generation: either search for truth and personal authenticity in the contemplative life of the world of science, a world we might add which was presupposition-less, or grasp the harsh and difficult post-war social and economic issues of Germany through a life of political action. One aspect of the tragedy of Weber's own life was that he was unable to fulfil his political ambitions in a life of practical politics and that, while he was a formidable scholar, he had relatively little impact in his own lifetime on the development of German social science. As Löwith tersely notes: 'it is characteristic of Weber that he did not in any way found a "school"' (Löwith, 1982: 21).

Weber's existential solution to the crisis of late nineteenth-century German culture was in terms of an ethic of responsibility and in terms of the notion of 'character' or personality. This solution as we have seen is full of complexity and uncertainty. For example, if rationality itself has been questioned by the very process of rationalization, is it possible to sustain the idea of a rational personality with a life-project and a set of norms about responsibility? In addition to the ambiguities of Weber's ideas about personality, it is also important to keep in mind that Weber's own answers were the cultural product of the *Bildungsbürgertum* tradition. This tradition assumed that a cultivated person should attempt to adhere to a number of civilized criteria of personal existence which included inner loneliness, personal cultivation, responsibility and loyalty. These values were the values of the old German educational elite, but these values were under attack from new social forces and conditions which were broadly associated with urban capitalism (Ringer, 1969). In particular, Weber was only too conscious that the processes of specialization with the rationalization of society made the achievement of personal integrity and wholeness extremely difficult to achieve. This anxiety was the basis of Weber's pessimistic comments in the conclusion of *The Protestant Ethic and the Spirit of Capitalism* about hedonists without a heart and vocational men without a soul. Specialization negated the whole tradition of the cultivated personality with broad interests and a general education, namely the enlightenment values of the age of Goethe. The tragic vision which characterizes Weber's despair was an effect of social changes in Germany which threatened these honorific standards.

To summarize Löwith's account of Weber and Marx in terms of 'this underlying anthropological concern', there was a fundamental convergence in basic values, but in terms of their response to the alienating features of bourgeois society, there was also a basic divergence. From Weber's philosophy of social science, Löwith showed how the underlying problems of a presuppositionless sociology were connected with Weber's attempt to come to terms with Nietzsche, in particular with the diagnosis of value pluralism and debasement as 'the death of God'. Weber's 'substantive sociology' was consequently shaped and organized around a theme of rationalization. This historical motif involves the complex of ideas that the world has become secular or disenchanted, that scientific ideas (instrumental rationalization) pervade everyday life, that there has been a specialization of social activities and authority, and that finally the world has been rendered increasingly meaningless by the erosion of charisma, religion or enchantment. For Weber, the world is predictable, but without an authoritative purpose, that is without grand narratives.

Within this broad scenario, we might distinguish between a specific and a general issue. Weber responded to the specific crisis of post-war Germany in terms of a nationalistic politics which was designed to minimize the magnitude of Germany's defeat. Weber's political sociology with its emphasis on the strong state, charismatic leadership and plebiscitary democracy was directed to the problem of Germany's position in world politics. When Löwith argued that Weber offered a diagnosis but not a therapy, this observation cannot apply to Weber's orientation to the specific crisis of Germany. Weber's answer may not be entirely palatable, but it was not based on acquiescence, quietism and retreatism. It was not merely a diagnosis. Weber's answer was quite specific: Germany must be a strong state. It was in terms of the macro-cultural characteristics of modern society where Weber adhered to a more pessimistic and negative world-view. For Weber, there was ultimately no clear escape from the iron cage of specialization and rationalization. Here the only plausible answer was one of stoical resolve.

The differences between Weber and Marx over these political issues were clear. While Marx also saw the bourgeois capitalist world in terms of self-alienation, Marx's teleology, which was the legacy of Hegel's secularized Christian theology, presented the historical role of the proletariat in terms of a resolution of the contradictions of bourgeois society. The proletarian victory would bring to an end the exploitation of human labour, the divisions of the private and the public realm, and the alienation of human beings. Marx's utopian vision of the end of history is, as Löwith argues, a powerful illustration of the chiliastic imagination which down the centuries has challenged ideologies which have celebrated and legitimized the permanency of existing social relations.[5] Whereas Weber's existential solution was individualistic, inward and despairing, Marx's solution was collectivist, external and hopeful. However, we have to keep in mind that Marx's own views on 'man's self-alienation' were eventually transformed into 'vulgar Marxism' in which the economic base mechanically determines the superstructure, and as Löwith points out, 'This is how Weber also regarded Marxism and combated it as a dogmatically economistic historical materialism' (Löwith, 1982: 68).

Löwith's legacy

Löwith's work will survive as a sensitive and informed study of Heideggerian existentialism, and also as a study which is located in the European sociological tradition of Weber and Marx. In its own way, Löwith's commentary is simultaneously an analysis of the human condition in bourgeois capitalism, namely an analysis of the paradoxical contingency and rationality, autonomy and alienation of modern times. What Löwith's approach does, in fact, is to question the simplistic dichotomies of spirituality/materiality and idealism/materialism. While 'vulgar Marxism' had constructed Marxism as a deterministic science of the mode of production, Löwith's probing of the anthropological concern of Marx's social theory presented a very different perspective on Marx as a philosopher who sought to comprehend the dilemmas of human beings within the ancient debate about essence and existence. In fact, Marx attempted in the 'Theses on Feuerbach' to throw off the old materialism which was deterministic and mechanical by taking on board the voluntaristic view of action in the old idealism. In this respect, both Weber and Marx emerge as critics of simplistic empiricism. Thus, one aspect of the legacy of Löwith is this sensitive appreciation for the complexity of the idea of 'materiality' in relation to any understanding of existence.

In retrospect we may see one of the great changes in western philosophy in the twentieth century in terms of the critique of Cartesian dualism, which provided the foundation of western philosophy since Descartes's publications on method. Descartes's famous foundation for modern science (*cogito ergo sum*) presented the idea of reality as a passive object, which the active, rational mind could comprehend directly without metaphysical presuppositions. Cartesianism was thus the origin of the subject/object division and also the dualism of mind and body. Western thought has wrestled with these ideas for decades, but in the twentieth century there has been, from many starting points, a concerted critique of the principal assumptions of mind/body dualism and the subject/object dichotomy. Husserl's Cartesian meditations have thus been critical for the philosophical development of Heidegger, Ricouer, Merleau-Ponty and Derrida. To simplify the issues, twentieth-century philosophy has broadly argued that reality cannot be separated from the knowing subject, because 'reality' is in some sense 'produced' by the paradigms which seek to understand it, and secondly mind and body are not separate; rather, according to writers like Merleau-Ponty, we are 'embodied'. In a more technical parlance, much of modern philosophy from Nietzsche onwards has been concerned to undermine the philosophical credibility and importance of the transcendental subject. The importance of these developments, especially in the work of Husserl, Lukács and Heidegger, has been captured by Goldmann:

> Man is not *opposite* the world which he tries to understand and upon which he acts, but *within* this world which he is a part of, and there is no radical break between the meaning he is trying to find or introduce into his own existence. This meaning, common to both individual and collective life, common as much to humanity as, ultimately, to the universe, is called *history*.
>
> (Goldmann, 1977: 6)

These philosophical arguments have, as it were, restored the human body to agency and cognition, and they have asserted the importance of factual, everyday reality to our practical embodiment. This attempt to understand everyday life is captured in the terminology of *Lebenswelt* (life-world), habitus and the immediate daily life. These ideas which have been crucial to mainstream philosophy have also found their way into the sociological work of Agnes Heller, Pierre Bourdieu and Jürgen Habermas, but they also played a part in the development of symbolic interactionism and ethnomethodology. The idea of everyday life is important in understanding the temporality of embodiment in a specific place; this idea of the intimate relationship between practice, body and place is fundamental, for example, to Bourdieu's attempt to provide a sociological critique of Kant's individualistic and neutral or disinterested notion of taste (Bourdieu, 1984).

In fact the body is crucial as both metaphor and concept in the 'materialism' of Marx and Heidegger, and this common theme further helps us to grasp the original nature of Löwith's approach to Weber and Marx. In this respect, it is absurd to suggest that while Marx and Lukács share a set of ideas about existence in common with Heidegger, there is one critical difference, namely that 'the latter conceived human being metaphysically' (Feenberg, 1981: 7). Heidegger's whole philosophy was constructed to bring a final end to metaphysics and his view of existence is specifically materialistic.

In the rather special terminology which Heidegger developed in order to articulate his critical views on abstract notions of Being, he constantly employs the idea of hand and place. Thus, as we have seen already, existence for Heidegger is captured by *Da-sein* ('Being-there'). But *Da-sein* also functions in Heidegger's philosophy as a substitute for 'man' or 'subject'. Similarly, the all-important contrast between *Zuhandenheit and Vorhandenheit* perfectly indicates the centrality of the hand in Heidegger's philosophy (Turner, 1992). *Zuhandenheit* is the equivalent in some respects of Marx's notion of praxis. *Zuhandenheit* or 'manipulability' literally means 'readiness-to-hand', but it signifies something very special about human beings: their great capacity for manipulating and transforming their material world, namely the practical character of human beings. *Vorhandenheit* (literally 'before the hand' or 'presence-at-hand'), by contrast, is that which is there but also that which presents itself to us as objective reality.

Vorhandenheit is everything which exists objectively outside or other than *Da-sein*. Presence-to-hand refers to the obstinacy and obduracy of the world of things. For Heidegger, the authenticity of existence or Being (*Da-sein*) is an aspect of the dialectic of readiness-to-hand and presence-to-hand in everyday life. Authenticity appears to be present in the very intimacy of the here-and-now world to the human hand. It is for this reason that Heidegger saw the development of technology such as the typewriter as a reification or alienation of the human capacities for immediacy in the direct manipulability of the readiness-to-hand. Thus, the Heideggerian concern for the authenticity of Being in a world of reified objects is parallel to Lukács's development of the concept of reification from Marx's notion of the fetishism of commodities.

Goldmann argues persuasively that this Heideggerian formula of *Zuhandenheit/Vorhandenheit* functions in Heideggerian philosophy as the counter-part to the Marxist idea of the 'identity of the subject and the object':

> By replacing 'totality' with '*Sein*' ('Being'), and 'subject' with *Da-sein* ('Being-there'), Heidegger creates a terminology which undoubtedly has the advantage of expressing, in the very structure of the formula, both the identity and the relative difference of the two concepts. He is then able to criticise ... any philosophy which still uses the terms 'subject'-'object' as continuing in the wake of traditional ontology in relation to which his own thought would constitute a radical break.
>
> (Goldmann, 1977: 13–14)

Heidegger's analysis of Being cannot be properly described, therefore, as metaphysical. But Heidegger attempted to develop an analysis of authenticity/inauthenticity at the level of ontology rather than of sociology. If there is a difference between Heidegger and Lukács, then it is in terms of Lukács's efforts to understand reification/inauthentication in the historical context of the development of the capitalist mode of production. Here again Weber and Marx could be said to converge, as Löwith suggests, in their critical understanding of capitalism in relation to Being via the concepts of rationalization and alienation. While both Marx and Weber have an ontological theory about the practical nature of human existence, they attempted to understand the problems of existence in bourgeois capitalism through a profound historical analysis of the development of the western world through slavery, feudalism and capitalism.

Notes

1 Throughout this discussion of philosophical anthropology in Marx and Weber, I shall use the term 'man' rather than its more appropriate alternatives such as 'humanity' or 'human beings'. Neither Marx nor Weber worked in a context where feminist criticism of sexist language was available. It is not entirely appropriate to correct their language. There is, however, an issue as to whether the underlying assumptions of late

nineteenth-century philosophical anthropology gave a privileged perspective to men in its analysis of the human condition.

2 There are reasons to be uncertain about referring to Heidegger as an existentialist. In this chapter, I shall follow Löwith (1948) in taking existentialism to be a philosophical perspective which treats the position of human beings as precarious creatures who inhabit a reality which is contingent, which argues therefore that existence precedes essence and which consequently regards the world as meaningless. Existentialism in its modern form is secular in denying that the world is shaped by a divine plan. As a result, one can argue that some aspects of Weberian sociology, with its emphasis on the ethic of responsibility, personality and choice, are compatible with existentialism (Löwith, 1982: 47).

3 Heidegger has been fundamental to the development of contemporary post-modernism. It is, for example, interesting to recall that Gianni Vattimo the author of *The End of Modernity* (1988) was a student of Löwith's at Heidelberg in the 1960s. Vattimo's understanding of postmodernism starts with the problem of history in Nietzsche and Heidegger, a problem which was also crucial to Löwith's understanding of Christian eschatology (Löwith, 1946).

4 Lucien Goldmann's neglected but important study of Lukács and Heidegger (1977) should be read in conjunction with Löwith's study of Weber and Marx. I have drawn extensively on this study to understand the complex meanings of reality, existence and materialism in Heidegger and Lukács. Goldmann has also been, perhaps indirectly, concerned with the origins of existentialism in his brilliant commentaries on Pascal in his study of the Jansenist movement in France in *The Hidden God* (Goldmann, 1964). Although Goldmann attempts to show how the transformation of the French class structure was a condition of the rise of the deterministic ideology of Jansenist soteriology, the hidden God of seventeenth-century France has a similar function to the dead God of Nietzsche's philosophy of the will. Both doctrines address the forlorn status of 'man' in the universe.

5 Mannheim's analysis of the history of utopian thought, which involved, amongst other cases, a study of the Anabaptists and socialist sects has provided the classical reference point for this debate (Mannheim, 1991). In twentieth-century Marxism, Ernst Bloch's monumental *The Principle of Hope* is an outstanding attempt to defend the idea that human beings *qua* human beings can only survive on the basis of some utopian commitment to the future as the Yet-To-Be (Bloch, 1969).

References

Althusser, L. (1966) *For Marx*. London: Allen Lane.

Althusser, L. and Balibar, E. (1968) *Reading Capital*. London: New Left Books.

Baudrillard, J. (1983) *In the Shadow of the Silent Majorities*. New York: Semiotext(e).

Beck, U. (1992) *Risk Society: Towards a new modernity*. London: Sage.

Bloch, E. (1969) *Das Princip Hoffnung*. Frankfurt am Main: Suhrkamp.

Bourdieu, P. (1984) *Distinction: A social critique of the judgement of taste*. London: Routledge & Kegan Paul.

Derrida, J. (1989) *Of Spirit: Heidegger and the question*. Chicago: University of Chicago Press.

Durkheim, E. (1958) *Socialism and Saint Simon*. London: Routledge & Kegan Paul.

Farias, V. (1987) *Heidegger et le Nazisme*. Paris: Editions Verdier.

Feenberg, A. (1981) *Lukács, Marx and the Sources of Critical Theory*. Totowa, N.J.: Rowman & Littlefield.

Feuerbach, L. (1957) *The Essence of Christianity*. New York: Harper & Row.

Gerth, H.H. and Mills, C. Wright (eds) (1991) *From Max Weber: Essays in sociology*. London: Routledge.

Giddens, A. (1990) *The Consequences of Modernity*. Cambridge: Polity Press.

Goldmann, L. (1964) *The Hidden God*. London: Routledge & Kegan Paul.

Goldmann, L. (1977) *Lukács and Heidegger: Towards a new philosophy.* London: Routledge & Kegan Paul.
Gould, M. (1991) 'The Structure of Social Action: at least sixty years ahead of its time', in R. Robertson and B.S. Turner (eds), *Talcott Parsons, Theorist of Modernity.* London: Sage. pp. 85–107.
Heidegger, M. (1962) *Being and Time.* Oxford: Basil Blackwell.
Heidegger, M. (1977) *The Question Concerning Technology and Other Essays.* New York: Harper & Row.
Hennis, W. (1987) *Max Weber's Fragstellung.* Tübingen: J.C.B. Mohr.
Hindess, B. and Hirst, P.Q. (1975) *Pre-Capitalist Modes of Production.* London: Routledge & Kegan Paul.
Jay, M. (1973) *The Dialectical Imagination. A History of the Frankfurt School and the Institute of Social Research 1923–1950.* Boston: Little, Brown.
Kuhn, T.S. (1970) *The Structure of Scientific Revolutions.* Chicago: University of Chicago Press.
Lipsett, M. (1960) *Political Man: The social bases of politics.* New York: Doubleday & Company.
Löwith, K. (1928) *Das Individuum in der Rolle des Mitmenschen.* Tübingen: Mohr.
Löwith, K. (1945) 'Nietzsche's doctrine of Eternal Recurrence', *Journal of the History of Ideas,* 6: 273–84.
Löwith, K. (1946) 'The theological background of the philosophy of history', *Social Research,* 13: 51–80.
Löwith, K. (1948) 'Heidegger: problem and background of existentialism', *Social Research,* 15(3): 345–69.
Löwith, K. (1951) 'Skepticism and faith', *Social Research,* 18: 219–36.
Löwith, K. (1952) 'Nature, history and existentialism', *Social Research,* 19: 79–94.
Löwith, K. (1953) *Heidegger: Denker in Dürftiger Zeit.* Frankfurt: Klostermann.
Löwith, K. (1954) 'Man's self-alienation in the early writings of Marx', *Social Research,* 21: 204–30.
Löwith, K. (1959) 'Curriculum vitae', *Archives de Philosophie,* 37: 181–92.
Löwith, K. (1964) *From Hegel to Nietzsche: The revolution in nineteenth-century thought.* New York: Holt, Rinehart & Winston. *Von Hegel zu Nietzsche. Der Revolutionäre Bruch im Denken des neunzehnten Jahrhunderts.* Hamburg: Felix Meiner Verlag, 1941.
Löwith, K. (1966) *Nature, History and Existentialism and Other Essays.* Evanston, Ill.: Northwestern University Press.
Löwith, K. (1970) *Meaning in History.* Chicago and London: University of Chicago Press.
Löwith, K. (1981) *Samtliche Schriften.* Hamburg: J.B. Metzlersche Verlagsbuchhandlung, 9 volumes.
Löwith, K. (1982) *Max Weber and Karl Marx.* London: George Allen & Unwin. 'Max Weber und Karl Marx', *Archiv für Sozialwissenschaft und Sozialpolitik,* vol. 66, 1932: 53–99 and 175–214.
Löwith, K. (1986) *Mein Leben in Deutschland vor und nach 1933.* Stuttgart: Metzler Verlag.
Löwith, K. (1988) 'My last meeting with Heidegger in Rome, 1936', excerpted from K. Löwith (1986) *Mein Leben in Deutschland vor und nach 1933.* Stuttgart: Metzler Verlag. Reprinted in R. Wolin (1988) 'Martin Heidegger and politics: a dossier', *New German Critique,* (45): 91–134.
Lukács, G. (1971) *History and Class Consciousness.* London: The Merlin Press.
Lyotard, J.-F. (1979) *La Condition Postmoderne: Rapport sur le Savoir.* Paris: Minuit.
Mannheim, K. (1991) *Ideology and Utopia.* London: Routledge.
Marx, K. (1964) *The Economic and Philosophical Manuscripts.* London: Lawrence & Wishart.
Mommsen, W. (1989) *The Political and Social Theory of Max Weber.* Cambridge: Polity Press.
Poulantzas, N. (1973) *Political Power and Social Classes.* London: New Left Books.
Ringer, F.K. (1969) *The Decline of the German Mandarins: The German academic community 1890–1933.* Cambridge. Mass.: Harvard University Press.
Schumpeter, J.A. (1934) *The Theory of Economic Development.* Cambridge, Mass.: Harvard University Press.
Sica, A. (1988) *Weber, Irrationality and Social Order.* Berkeley: University of California Press.
Simmel, G. (1991) *Schopenhauer and Nietzsche.* Urbana and Chicago: University of Illinois Press.
Stauth, G. and Turner, B.S. (1988) *Nietzsche's Dance: Resentment, reciprocity and resistance in social life.* Oxford: Basil Blackwell.
Stauth, G. and Turner, B.S. (1992) 'Ludwig Klages (1872–1956) and the origins of critical theory', *Theory, Culture & Society,* 9(3): 45–63.
Tenbruck, F. (1980) 'The problem of the thematic unity in the works of Max Weber', *British Journal of Sociology,* 81(3): 316–51.

Tribe, K. (ed.) (1989) *Reading Weber*. London: Routledge.

Troeltsch, E. (1931) *The Social Teaching of the Christian Churches*. New York: Macmillan.

Turner, B.S. (1981) *For Weber, Essays in the Sociology of Fate*. London: Routledge & Kegan Paul.

Turner, B.S. (1987) 'A note on nostalgia', *Theory, Culture & Society*, 4(1): 147–56.

Turner, B.S. (ed.) (1990) *Theories of Modernity and Postmodernity*. London: Sage.

Turner, B.S. (1992) *Regulating Bodies: Essays in medical sociology*. London: Routledge.

Turner, S. and Käsler, D. (eds) (1992) *Sociology Responds to Fascism*. London: Routledge.

Vattimo, G. (1988) *The End of Modernity: Nihilism and hermeneutics in post-modern culture*. Cambridge: Polity Press.

Weber, M. (1932) *The Protestant Ethic and the Spirit of Capitalism*. London: Allen & Unwin.

Weber, M. (1949) *The Methodology of the Social Sciences*. New York: Free Press.

Weber, M. (1976) *The Agrarian Sociology of the Ancient Civilizations*. London: New Left Books.

Wolin, R. (1988) 'Martin Heidegger and Politics: a dossier', *New German Critique*, no. 45 (Fall): 91–134.

CHAPTER 4

MAX WEBER ON ECONOMY AND SOCIETY

Introduction: Approaching Max Weber

It is common to refer to concepts which are the subject of endless dispute as 'essentially contested' (Gallie, 1955–6). We might usefully extend the idea to talk about 'essentially contested authors', that is authors the interpretation of whom gives rise inevitably and endlessly to controversy. Max Weber (1864–1920) is pre-eminently such an author. In recent years there has been a great revival of interest in Weber and Weberian sociology, but we do not appear to be anywhere near a scholarly consensus about the importance or meaning of his work. Weber has been attacked as a reactionary prophet of despair, as a bourgeois sociologist whose views on domination were part of the background of fascism, as one of the greatest minds of the twentieth century, or as a philosopher of modernity whose views on rationalization prepared the way towards the current dispute between modernists and postmodernists. These disputes over the meaning of Weber's work are ironic, since Weber regarded the interpretation of meanings which actors attach to social action as an essential aspect of sociology as a science. For Weber, sociology was interpretative sociology (*verstehende soziologie*). In interpreting Weber, there is the problem of whether Weber's work contradicts itself, namely whether Weber's own methodological writings are undermined by his substantive research (Scaff, 1984; Turner, 1974). There is the deeper question of whether Weber the person contradicts his work.

The aim of this chapter is to consider these changing interpretations of Weber's sociology as an appreciation of the enduring merits of Hans Gerth and C. Wright Mills's introduction to Weber (Gerth and Mills, 1948). Their selections and translations from Weber remain one of the most balanced introductions to Weber, in English, which we possess. Furthermore, given the notorious difficulties of Weber's German, they have offered us a lucid, but accurate translation. At the time of the publication of their selections little of Weber's sociology had appeared in English translation, apart from Parsons's translation of *The Protestant Ethic and the Spirit of Capitalism* (Weber, 1930). In 1944, J.P. Mayer published a valuable study of Weber's political sociology in his *Max Weber and German Politics* (Mayer, 1944). Of course, almost half a century after *From Max Weber* appeared, we have access to a far greater range of Weber's sociological publications, including the monumental *Economy and Society* (Weber, 1978a). There have also been re-translations of major parts of Weber's opus, such as the 'science as a vocation' lecture (Lassman and Velody, 1989) and various *Selections in Translation* (Runciman, 1978). In Germany, the publisher J.C.B. Mohr (Paul Siebeck) of Tübingen is currently publishing the entire collection of Weber's known works. Although there have been great advances in Weber scholarship, Gerth and Mills's approach to Weber has retained an originality and freshness which continues to command respect. Anticipating later commentary, it is valuable to mention two aspects of their approach to Weber, namely their awareness of the importance of the German philosopher Friedrich Nietzsche on Weber's world-view and the significance of Weber's interest in military and political questions for his general sociology of historical change.

Weber's Life

Weber's life has been the subject of a number of major inquiries. It is important to stress the fact that the biography by Weber's wife is both an essential text for any scholarly understanding of Weber, and a work of considerable literary and historical merit in its own right (Marianne Weber, 1926). There are also a number of major general discussions of Weber's life in relation to his intellectual development. In this context it is necessary to refer to Rheinhard Bendix's *Max Weber, An Intellectual Portrait* (1960), Paul Honigsheim's *On Max Weber* (1968) and, more recently, Dirk Käsler's *Max Weber* (1988). In addition, there are a number of interpretations of Weber's sociology which give prominence to certain (alleged) psychological problems in Weber's development which are held to explain, or at least throw light on, aspects of his intellectual development. For example, Weber's attitudes towards religion and sexuality are often seen in terms of the tensions between his mother's spirituality and father's secularity. Weber's early letters, especially to his mother, give us a wonderful insight into his development. Unfortunately, the *Jugendbriefe* have yet to be translated into English (Weber, 1936). Arthur Mitzman's *The Iron Cage* (1971) has been influential in identifying the intellectual consequences of Weber's rift with his father, the death of his father and his separation from Emmy Baumgarten in 1887. What emerges from these commentaries is a general understanding of Weber's tender but problematic relationship with women (his mother, Emmy Baumgarten, Marianne Weber and the von Richthofen sisters), and how these emotional issues form a part of his analysis of asceticism and the religious calling in his sociology of religion. Although the history of Max Weber and Marianne Weber in the rise of German feminism has yet to be written adequately, a valuable insight into the ambiguities of Weber's attitudes is offered in Green's study of the von Richthofen sisters (Green, 1974).

Subsequent interpretations of Weberian sociology have drawn attention to the contradictions between the discipline of intellectual life, the practical commitments which are necessary for a life in politics, and the ecstatic intensity of sexual and religious experience (Lepenies, 1985; Mommsen and Osterhammel, 1987; Turner, 1987). In this perspective, many of the oppositions and dichotomies in Weberian social theory can be seen as reflections upon the difference between the Apollonian principles (of order, form and rationality) and the Dionysian principles (of ecstasy, energy and creativity) which were explored by Nietzsche in the will-to-power problematic, and which were subsequently analysed in the literary masterpieces of Thomas Mann (Stauth and Turner, 1988). The degree to which these questions in Weber's academic work can be understood as a direct consequence of these psychoanalytic constellations is, of course, a matter of intense dispute.

There is little to be gained from merely repeating the personal and academic details of Weber's life, many of which are in any case discussed in the short but excellent 'biographical view' which is presented by Gerth and Mills (1948). However, while Weber's biographical details are relatively well known, it is still the case that many commentaries on Weber's sociology manage to divorce his sociology from its specific historical context. In my own approach to Weber's sociology, I take a strong position in the sociology of knowledge that Weber's conceptual apparatus is actually meaningless once divorced from the political issues which he sought to address in, for example, his political sociology. To take one crucial issue, Weber's views on leadership, bureaucracy and class structure were developed as part of a debate about the future of Germany and the legacy of Bismarck's chancellorship. Weber's apparently formal discussion of ideal types of leadership and bureaucracy are to be understood as contributions to a (initially) German political problem: clearly this claim does not in principle preclude the usefulness of Weber's conceptual apparatus in other contexts.

It is another feature of the merits of *From Max Weber* that Gerth and Mills took this historical and social location of Weber's sociology very seriously. They noted for example that 'Max Weber's life and thought are expressions of political events and concerns' (Gerth and Mills, 1948: 32). One of Weber's major political anxieties was for the future of a strong Germany in view of the political vacuum following Bismarck's resignation in 1890 (Gall, 1986). Thus, Weber's arguments in favour of the value neutrality and value freedom of sociology should not mislead us into assuming that either Weber or Weber's sociology were somehow politically disengaged. On the contrary, even Weber's discussion of the value neutrality of sociology has to be understood in the context of specific problems in the development of the German university system (Shils, 1976). Thus, in order to understand Weber's sociology, we have to understand his aspirations in the context of the changing national and international situation of Germany.

Max Weber was born in Erfurt, Thuringia in 1864 into an influential and affluent family, whose background and development exhibit many of the virtues which Weber came to explore in his famous 'Protestant Ethic' thesis (Weber, 1930), and which Thomas Mann developed in his novel *Buddenbrooks*. Weber's father, himself a member of a linen merchant family from Bielefeld, Westphalia, was a Councillor of Berlin, deputy of the Prussian Diet, and National-Liberal member of the Reichstag. Weber grew up in the Charlottenberg suburb of Berlin in an atmosphere of practical politics, and throughout his life was torn between a career in politics and the world of science – a conflict which he came to summarize brilliantly in his two lectures in 1919 on science as a vocation and politics as a vocation (Roth and Schluchter, 1979; Turner and Factor, 1984).

Weber's mother Helene Fallenstein Weber came from south Germany with a Huguenot background, and it was her austere Puritanism which came ultimately to shape Weber's ethical view of discipline, rectitude and personal ethics. Although he claimed to be 'religiously unmusical', it would be difficult to understate the continuous influence of religious ideas on his sociology. Weber's deep interest in the impact of religion on America, and in the Christian separation of politics and church was associated with his personal sympathy for the religious doctrines of W.E. Channing; his sociological analysis of religious institutionalization was a product of the influence of church historians like Ernst Troeltsch (1912); his conceptualization of charisma and his detailed knowledge of Old Testament prophecy (Weber, 1966) testify, not only to his profound understanding of the Abrahamic faiths, but to the moral influence of Israelite prophecy on his own view of history; and finally, Weber's view of the tragic character of the times in which he was living was shaped, above all else, by Nietszche's own prophetic proclamation that God was dead in *Thus Spake Zarathustra* in 1883–5 (Hollingdale, 1973).

Although Weber's health was always poor, he undertook his compulsory military service in Strasburg, becoming an *Unteroffizier* in 1884, but he was clearly relieved to return to his academic studies at the universities of Berlin and Göttingen, where he continued with his studies of law and history. Under Professor Goldschmidt, he began to prepare for his doctoral thesis on the history of commercial societies in the Middle Ages (*Zur Geschichte der Handelgesellschaften im Mittelalter*) and he eventually completed his *habilitationschrift* on the meaning of the history of Roman agrarian institutions for private and public law (*Die römische Agrargeschichte in ihrer Bedeutung für das Staatsrecht und Privatrecht*).

Very few commentaries on Weber's intellectual orientations have taken sufficient notice of his abiding focus on legal issues. It is not enough, for example, merely to take note of the fact that Weber undertook many important historical studies in law, which are reflected in the collection *Max Weber on Law in Economy and Society* (Rheinstein, 1954), or that Weber treated legal rationalization as an important foundation of modern capitalist activity. Among recent evaluations of Weber as a legal theorist, only Anthony T. Kronman (1983), after Talcott Parsons (1971), has fully understood that

Weber's notions of personality and rationality were deeply dependent on legal ideas of personality and responsibility (Holton and Turner, 1989).

Weber's legal training should also alert us to the fact that throughout his academic career he was hesitant about employing the word 'sociology' to describe his intellectual endeavours. Nevertheless, an involvement with social theory and social questions always shaped his approach to religion, law, politics and history. Thus, Weber joined the Association for Social Policy (*Verein für Sozialpolitik*) which had been founded in 1873 primarily by a group of German economists (including Wagner, Schmoller and Brentano). On behalf of the Association, Weber plunged into a survey of the position of rural workers in the East-Elbian region of Germany (*Die Lage der Landarbeiter im ostelbischen Deutschland*). In eastern Germany, the agricultural economy depended heavily (partly because of the continuity of traditional social relations on the *Junker* estates) on the influx of Polish and Russian migrant labour. Weber was interested in and concerned by the political and social implications of this dependency on foreign labour.

This apparently factual study of conditions in agricultural production in fact reflected two aspects of Weber's political orientation, but also the underlying assumptions of his sociology. First, Weber was intensely rationalistic, and much of his sociology is based on an assumption about the cultural superiority of German values. Weber feared that the dependence on Polish and Russian labour would eventually weaken the dominance of German culture on its eastern border. In his later political commentaries Weber was much exercised by the issue of Germany's foreign policy in a period when Britain and America appeared to be on the verge of a global monopoly of power. Weber's writing on economics, international relations and sociology not only presupposes a strong German state, but actually requires it. Second, Weber assumes that one of the great threats to German (and finally western) civilization is a Russian (Cossack) invasion. Weber was acutely aware of the military history of the flatlands of northern Europe, extending from Holland through Germany and Poland to the steppes of Asia. Germany's eastern sector had to be defended against such a threat, otherwise all attempts to reform and strengthen Germany would be pointless. Weber was impressed by the proposition that social policy, however excellent, was useless if the danger of a Cossack invasion could not be contained. Fear of a Russian occupation of Europe later fuelled Weber's intense interest in the first Russian revolution, about which he published two articles in 1906 on bourgeois democracy and constitutionalism in Russia (Weber, 1988). Weber did not, however, regard the prospect of a socialist revolution as an event offering the prospect of major changes in European societies. For Weber, socialist planning of the economy would require bureaucratic administration, rational legal systems, social surveillance and bureaucratic political management of a mass party. In short, a socialist transformation of society, based on the idea of a planned redistribution of wealth, would be merely a continuation and intensification of the rationalistic requirements of capitalism (Runciman, 1978).

Weber's nationalistic sentiments were also evident in his Inaugural Address, with the title 'The National State and Economic Policy' (Weber, 1988), on his acceptance of a professorship of economics at Freiburg University in 1894. Weber took it for granted that, while economic science can be value-free as an analytical and explanatory discipline, it has to be a national economic science in the services of a strong state as soon as it touches on questions of value. Weber thus contrasted the 'cosmopolitanism' of Smithian economics (that is Adam Smith's theory of international exchange) with his own view of economics as a discipline which serves a national interest. Weber's professorial address has therefore to be seen against the context of British and growing American economic dominance of the world economy.

A central motif of Weberian sociology is the question of struggle in human relationships. His Inaugural Address focused unambiguously on struggle as the driving force of social history. Rejecting utilitarian ideas about the greatest happiness of the greatest number, he flatly proclaimed that 'only in a hard struggle between man and man can elbowroom be won in our earthly existence'. There is no place in this outlook for international economic co-operation, and through this centrality of struggle to his economic and sociological framework Weber embraced the idea of the state as a power-state (*Machstaat*). International relations like all social relations can only be a struggle between states.

In 1896 Weber accepted a chair at Heidelberg, but he fell ill shortly after the death of his father in 1897 and was forced to withdraw from teaching to seek rest and cure through various convalescent vacations in Italy and Switzerland. He returned eventually to Heidelberg to work in 1902. In 1904–5 he published two articles which became the famous *The Protestant Ethic and the Spirit of Capitalism* (Weber, 1930), and he was immediately plunged into controversy over its scientific validity and empirical plausibility (Weber, 1978b). The debate about Weber's views on religion and capitalism has generated an enormous literature; in fact, it has proved to be one of the most enduring controversies in modern social science (Marshall, 1982). I shall return to this debate shortly, when I come to discuss Weber's relationship to Marx. It is important to note at this stage that it is unfortunate that the 'Protestant Ethic thesis' is often discussed in isolation from Weber's equally important commentary on American religious sects. The Webers visited America in 1904 when Weber was invited to St Louis for a scientific gathering where he gave a paper on the rural community in Germany past and present. Weber was overwhelmed by New York skyscrapers, mechanized production in Chicago and the general character of mass society as indicators of the future of Western civilization (Roth, 1985). It is interesting to compare Weber's sense of horrified, reluctant admiration for American capitalism with de Tocqueville's somber view of the future of *Democracy in America* (de Tocqueville, 1946) of 1835 and with the prophetically postmodern vision of Baudrillard's *America* (1988). Against these versions of America, Weber's commentary on religious sectarianism and business practice was an accurate insight into the peculiar union of secularity and religiosity in American everyday culture.

Weber's essay on the American sects – 'The Protestant sects and the spirit of capitalism' – appeared as part two of volume one of his collected writings on religion (*Gesammelte Aufsätze zur Religions-soziologie*), but it was excluded from Parsons's translation of the Protestant Ethic thesis. Another important feature of *From Max Weber* is the central focus which is given in general to Weber's sociology of religion, but more specifically to his essay on 'The Protestant sects and the spirit of capitalism' and his 'The social psychology of the world religions'. These two essays are an essential part of Weber's more general interest in religious rationalization as a source of modern culture, specifically economic institutions and values (Freund, 1968).

In fact the analysis of the impact of religious life in shaping western modernity resulted in a number of major studies of comparative religion which have appeared in English as *The Religion of China* (Weber, 1951), *Ancient Judaism* (Weber, 1952), and *The Religion of India* (Weber, 1958). These studies were never fully completed; for example Weber's comments on Islam are frustratingly brief (Turner, 1974). Nevertheless, they are essential contributions to Weber's analysis of Western rationalization (Tenbruck, 1975).

This great outpouring of Weber's genius was eventually brought to an end with the outbreak of the First World War, which Weber welcomed as 'great and wonderful', despite its ugliness, partly because it presented Germany with political choices which might transform the nation. Although Weber was patriotic and regretted that he was too old to fight, he was against a policy of territorial annexation, German settlement and colonialism. He argued for an autonomous Polish state in the east to protect Germany by offering a buffer to Russian antagonism. In *Der verschärfte U-Boot Krieg* in 1916 (Weber, 1988), he argued against the current offensive, and warned against antagonizing America, whose entry into the war would be a disaster for Germany.

Throughout the war, Weber was especially exercised by the problems of the legacy of Bismarck, the weakness of the German middle classes, the underdevelopment of working-class leadership, the external threat of America, Britain and Russia, the stifling effect of German bureaucracy, and the inadequacies of leadership during the war (as contrasted with the bravery of the average German in the trenches). These concerns were expressed in a number of wartime publications such as in 1918 *Parlament und Regierung in neugeordneten Deutschland* (Weber, 1988). These pamphlets should dispel the common notion that Weber's sociology is somewhat remote from practical political concerns.

These themes continued to dominate Weber's sociology after the war when, as professor at Vienna University, following the Russian Revolution of 1917, he gave a famous lecture to Austrian military officers on socialism (Weber, 1924). He argued that unlike small-scale and traditional forms of democracy in Greece and Switzerland, modern democracy has to be an administered, and therefore a bureaucratic, democracy. The socialist mass party will in the long run become dominated by a trained administrative class, which will over time cease to be responsible and responsive to the electorate. The planned market would eventually be joined by the planned polity. Although Weber paid tribute to Karl Marx as a social thinker of the first rank, Weber saw that there would be no general collapse of capitalism and that, rather than the 'dictatorship of the proletariat', modern socialism would be the 'dictatorship of administration'.

Weber hoped that in the aftermath of the war the bourgeoisie would be forced into a position of political leadership and that it would become detached from the protective umbrella of the official culture of the administrative classes (the *Obrigkeitsstaat*). Having left Vienna to take up a position in Munich in 1919, Weber started writing about and campaigning for political changes in Germany, especially the creation of a constitutional plebiscitary presidency (Mommsen, 1974). Weber was a member of the peace delegation which the German government sent to Versaille to conduct the negotiations for a permanent peace. His attitude towards the peace situation was a reflection of his general political philosophy: Tsarist Russia was the main enemy; the peace conditions were economically unacceptable, because they would destroy Germany as a strong European state; Germany should not accept war-guilt, since the war was essentially a defensive struggle against Russian domination of the eastern regions; and the German defeat was a political betrayal and not a military collapse. Consequently, Weber thought that the peace settlement which was ratified on 16th July 1919 was a disaster. He withdrew finally from politics to lecture on economic sociology at the University of Munich in 1919–20; these lectures were published posthumously (partly from student notes) as *General Economic History* (Weber, 1927). Exhausted and despairing of Germany's future, Weber fell ill and died of pneumonia on 14th June 1920.

Interpreting Max Weber

The Bourgeois Marx

With the publication of Weber's essays on Protestantism and capitalism, and with their translation by Parsons into English in 1930, Weber entered the world of social science as a bourgeois answer to Marx. It was held wrongly that Weber had argued against Marx that the origins of capitalism lay in spiritual values not material causes. In fact, Weber recognized the existence of forms of capitalism in the Catholic cultures of Italy and Spain. He saw that the causes of capitalism were complex and variable: they included modern technology, rational administration, a money economy, market demand, a disciplined labour force and the free political environment which the occidental city had made possible (Holton, 1985). Weber was, however, more concerned with how the 'spirit of capitalism' had combined with the this-worldly ascetic ethics of Lutheran and Calvinistic Protestantism to give western capitalism a peculiar and unique characteristic, namely its rational emphasis on calculation and predictability.

As Gerth and Mills pointed out, however, in their introductory comments on Weber's 'intellectual orientations', there were important epistemological, philosophical and methodological differences between Marxism (as it was developing in Germany) as a science of the laws of motion of the capitalist mode of production and Weber's more subtle and complex version of neo-Kantian philosophy of science. In principle, Weber opposed any notion of general laws in social history, remained sceptical even about the value of general concepts, and employed ideal types as limited, heuristic devices for specific tasks. In addition to having a strong sense of the importance of historically contingent events in social change, Weber adopted a flexible approach to the complex interaction of many causes (both material and idealist). In the case of capitalism, Weber was acutely aware of the complex 'elective affinity' between economic arrangements and religious belief, which was a fateful combination (Turner, 1981). He criticized Marxists and Christians with an interest in social policy for assuming that law-like predictions about future developments were at all possible. He insisted (inconsistently in practice) on the separation of facts and values, objecting strongly to those professors who used their chairs to preach overtly or covertly specific values. To these important differences, there was an important disagreement between Marx and Weber in terms of their general approach to the question of social stratification, where Weber gave greater prominence to power relations (Holton and Turner, 1989; Turner, 1988). However, the relationship between Marx's primarily economic analysis of classes and Weber's political analysis of social closure is still contested by scholars (Parkin, 1979).

With the revival of 'scientific Marxism' in the form of structural Marxism around the philosophers Louis Althusser, Etienne Balibar and Nicos Poulantzas, there was in the 1960s and 1970s a tendency to see Weber's sociology as an idealist, subjective and ideological reflection on capitalist social relations. By contrast, Marx was seen to have broken with common sense by developing a science of the structures of the mode of production. However, this rigid separation between Marx and Weber is no longer accepted in contemporary scholarship. There is by contrast a tendency to see both Marx and Weber as critical analysts of capitalism as a version of the more general phenomenon of modernity, since both were impressed by the dynamic capacity of capitalism to liquidate all historical and traditional certainties.

The Rationalization Theme

Against this bifurcation of social science around Weber versus Marx, there are equally strong reasons for identifying important convergences between Marx and Weber. The argument of Gerth and Mills about the parallels between Marx and Weber was thus a useful corrective to the tendency in radical social theory to separate them in order to emphasize the notion that sociology was ideology when contrasted with scientific socialism. One important component in their presentation of Weber was the attention given to Weber's views on militarism. Modern sociology has often been criticized for its failure to develop an adequate military sociology – its neglect of the impact of warfare on social change (Giddens, 1984). This accusation could not include the historical sociology of Weber. For example, Weber was particularly concerned to understand the interaction between changes in military technology, military organization and political structures. He saw the rise of modern citizenship as in part a consequence of the democratic implications of a mass infantry. Similarly, he contrasted the social impact of cavalry on the plains of Europe with the dependence of Asiatic armies on the foot-soldier.

This aspect of Weber's sociology permits one to argue that, whereas Marx was concerned to understand the monopoly of economic power in society, Weber drew attention to alternative monopolies. First, he was concerned with how the means of military violence were socially organized and distributed. Second, he looked at the institutionalism of spiritual powers in his religious sociology (Prades, 1966). It was for these reasons that Weber defined the state as an institution which enjoyed a monopoly of legitimate force, and the Church as an institution which sought a monopoly of spiritual power.

By arguing that Weber wanted to understand the institution of social closure (that is, how monopolies over scarce resources of wealth, spirituality and violence were constituted), we can get a better understanding of Weber's analysis of western history as the development of rationalization. By this process, Weber wanted to indicate the growing importance of rational science (instrumental rationality) in everyday life, and hence the corresponding disenchantment of the world and the erosion of religious powers. This secularization also involved the increasing dominance of the expert and professional knowledge, and the corresponding decline of charismatic authorities. These changes also required the specialization of tasks, and the growth in the division of labour. These bureaucratic changes in the organization of society were also associated with the separation of the worker from the means of production, the separation of the office worker from the means of mental production, and the alienation of the intellectual from control over the university. I have deliberately employed a Marxist terminology of alienation of workers from the means of production (both material and mental) to illustrate a convergence of Marx and Weber around the twin notions of rationalization (as disenchantment, specialization and powerlessness in the face of bureaucratic management) and alienation (as division, specialization and separation).

Both Marx and Weber responded to capitalism in the same mixture of horror and admiration. Capitalism for Marx destroyed the stagnation of traditional society and undermined what he referred to as the 'idiocy' of village and peasant life. It pushed humanity along the road of modernization, but at an enormous cost in terms of individual and collective suffering. One aspect of this suffering was alienation and dehumanization. Capitalism for Weber destroyed the securities of belief (the garden of enchantment) and disrupted the 'natural' rhythms of pre-modern means of production and consumption in the traditional household. Rationalization destroyed the authority of magical powers, but it also brought into being the machine-like regulation of bureaucracy, which ultimately challenges all systems of belief. The paradoxical outcome of rationalization was a world in which systems of meaning could no longer find an authority. Rational norms of authority are incompatible with charismatic and traditional powers. This relationship between alienation in Marx's analysis of capitalism and Weber's theme of rationalization as modernization was brilliantly developed in Karl Löwith's *Karl Marx and Max Weber* (Löwith, 1982) which was originally published in 1932 and which remains one of the most provocative and sensitive studies of the relationship between Mark and Weber. I shall return to the question about rationality as Weber's central question (Hennis, 1988; Tenbruck, 1975).

Nietszche and Weber

It is reported that in a discussion with Oswald Spengler in February 1920 Weber said that the moral stature and honesty of a present-day scholar might be measured by their attitudes towards Nietzsche and Marx (Baumgarten, 1964: 554ff.). It appears that Weber was especially influenced by Nietzsche from around 1892 onwards, and that the language of his Inaugural Address at Freiburg is shot through with images from Nietzsche's *Untimely Meditations* (Hennis, 1988: 146–51). Again it is an indication of the sophistication of Gerth and Mills's approach to Weber that they clearly recognized Nietzsche's influence on Weber's sociology of religion and on his commentary on moral systems in terms of a theory of resentment. Although the influence of Nietzsche on Weber's sociology is now widely recognized (Baier, 1982; Eden, 1983; Fleischmann, 1964; Hennis, 1988; Stauth and Turner, 1988) this Nietzschean influence was for a long time either neglected or denied. While this Nietzschean dimension to Weberian sociology is now generally accepted, the nature of that intellectual and moral relationship is still a matter of dispute.

In the Inaugural Address Weber appears to be responding to the emphasis on struggle and conflict in Nietzsche's view of the human condition. In particular, Weber's reference to the struggle for elbow-room as a motor of human history indicates Nietzsche's uncompromising view of human relations as relations of power. Thus in very general terms, it may be possible to read Weber as a 'sociologizing' of Nietzsche's notion of the will to power. It has been suggested often enough that Weber's ideas on charismatic leadership appear to represent a sociological version of Nietzsche's ideas about the historical functions of the Overman, who stands out against the herd-morality of the people. Furthermore, it may be that Weber's view on state-power and the problems of political leadership in the revaluation of values reflects the influence of Nietzsche (Turner, 1982). It is also important to note that Nietzsche's account of the implications of the death of God significantly influenced Weber's view of the plurality of beliefs (which he described as polytheism) in his lecture on 'science as a vocation'.

These interpretations of Weber and Nietzsche are, however, ultimately unsatisfactory. The deeper impact of Nietszche is in the area of morality, and of the possibility of a 'Science of Man' (Hennis, 1988: 107ff.). Weber's understanding of asceticism as simultaneously the basis of our modern civilization and as the necessary denial of our ontology (which is the psychological and culture cost of the idea of vocation in both lectures on science and politics) is a theme which was central to Nietzsche's contrast between Apollo and Dionysus. The ontology of human beings ('human nature') is thus seen to be, in some sense, out of joint with the cultural and social requirements of a modern civilization; indeed our human nature has to be suppressed by the sociological requirements of an industrial civilization. This argument was an important component of Nietzsche's philosophy, and we can also detect this influence in Weber and Freud. Although Weber publicly chose 'discipline' as some sort of solution for the life of an academic or politician, this discipline is seen to be ultimately life-denying (to use Nietzsche's terminology). It now appears that Weber's central questions involved an anthropological inquiry into human nature and into how our ontology is the product of certain 'life-orders' (Hennis, 1988). Talcott Parsons's presentation of Weber as a value-free sociologist of social action is now increasingly challenged by the view that Weber's work in fact belongs to a long tradition of German philosophical anthropology. In the twentieth century, the sociology of Arnold Gehlen is one of the most significant contributions to this German tradition (Berger and Kellner, 1965).

To see Weber in this light, however, opens up a new area of inquiry. If Weber is to be viewed as a philosophical anthropologist of the life-orders which produce certain types of personality, what is Weber's relationship to the romantic wing of anti-capitalist German poets and artists who also drew upon an anthropological tradition which had its roots in Nietszche? In specific terms, what was Weber's relationship to the cultural critics who gathered around Stefan George at Heidelberg, namely Friedrich Gundolf and Ludwig Klages? These prophetic poets occasionally assembled at Weber's famous afternoon discussions. While the ideas of the symbolist poetry of the George Circle are typically seen to be in opposition to Weber's sociology (as for example in Karl Mannheim's 'letter from Heidelberg'), Weber's notion that the ascetic life-order is ontologically destructive may not be so far removed from Klages's notions about the cosmic forces of love, or the discord between consciousness and spirit in his monumental *Der Geist als Widersacher der Seele* (Klages, 1929–32). In short, while Weber is often characterized as a 'liberal in despair' (Mommsen, 1974), if we pursue Hennis's thesis to its logical conclusion, it also makes sense to ask, not whether Weber was a philosophical anthropologist of despair, but whether he was a conservative cultural critic of the life-orders of capitalism?

Conclusion: Weber as a Theorist of Modernity

Hennis's diagnosis of Weber's texts is correct in one essential feature. To continue with the question about Weber's explanations of 'the origins of capitalism' (Giddens, 1971) now appears to be a limited and outdated exercise. Weber's own view of his work (namely to understand the characteristic uniqueness of our times) can probably be best understood as a quest after the nature of modernity. Weber's interests in rational law, administration, military technology, religious ethics and so forth can be seen in a broader context as a set of investigations into the peculiarities of modernity and in particular its fateful or even demonic properties.

Weber's attitude towards modernity was, as we have noted already, ambiguous. Like Marx, Weber believed that in capitalistic modernity 'All that is solid melts into air' (Berman, 1982). Modernization disrupts the traditional order and the ideology by which traditional authorities made the world intelligible and legitimate. Modernity questions everything and measures everything against a unitary principle of rationality.

But Weber recognized that this questioning of reality by reason was ultimately self-defeating and self-destructive. Rationality began to question its own horizons, recognizing its self-limitation. How can reason be rationally justified? Are there many forms of reason? Is reason (in the shape of instrumental rationality) in fact life-denying? Is rationality supported by various strategies which are artefacts of the grammatical structure of language, which is ultimately arbitrary? These questions had their origins in Neitzsche's probing of language, knowledge and power. As we have seen, these questions increasingly haunted Weber's sociology, finding their most condensed expression in the science as a vocation lecture.

In the last two decades, there has been a major revival of interest in Nietzsche as a theorist of the dilemmas of modernity, especially in the work of Michel Foucault, Jacque Derrida, Jean Baudrillard and Jean-François Lyotard (Boyne, 1990; Megill, 1985). These postmodern or post-structuralist theorists have in a variety of different ways questioned traditional assumptions and certainties about the rational project of modernity. Lyotard in particular has challenged the underlying legitimation of the 'grand narratives' (such as freedom, truth and reason) of modernity. Postmodernists argue that the modern project of reason was made possible by the dominance of western capitalism through the construction of a world economy based on colonial exploitation. For some postmodernists, the modern world of global mass media has brought about a dominance of media signs in which reality is eventually imploded by the sheer 'weight' of media messages. Reality becomes a hyper-reality in which signs only refer to other signs (Baudrillard, 1983). The combined effect of these transformations of modernity (which was based on the dominance of industrial capitalism) into a post-Fordist social system (which is based on post-industrial information systems) is to challenge the grand narrative of rationality as the central motif of capitalist production.

We can now see that Weber's anthropological analysis of the life-orders that produced modern Man (in the generic sense) in the production of a rationalized social system in many respects anticipated the contemporary debate between modernists and postmodernists (Holton and Turner, 1989). In particular, Weber's anxieties and uncertainties about the moral (and indeed spiritual) significance of modernity have been reproduced in our uncertainties about what sort of 'reality' might lie beyond modernity. Weber of course was at least clear in his own mind about one thing, namely that the world beyond modernity promised to be especially terrible. He once despairingly said the future will be an icy night of polar darkness. Weber's profound probing of the edges of that dark world is one reason why Weber's sociology continues to fascinate each new generation of scholars, as it did Hans Gerth and C. Wright Mills.

References

Baier, H. (1982) 'Die Gesellschaft–ein langer Schatten destoten Gottes', *Nietzsche Studien*, 10–11: 1–22.

Baudrillard, J. (1983) *Simulacra and Simulations.* New York: Semiotext(e).

Baudrillard, J. (1988) *America.* London: Verso.

Baumgarten, E. (1964) *Max Weber, Werk und Person.* Tübingen: Mohr.

Bendix, R. (1960) *Max Weber, An Intellectual Portrait.* London: Heinemann.

Berger, P.L. and Kellner, H. (1965) 'Arnold Gehlen and the theory of institutions', *Social Research*, 32: 110–15.

Berman, M. (1982) *All That is Solid Melts into Air: The experience of modernity.* London: Verso.

Boyne, R. (1990) *Foucault and Derrida.* London: Unwin Hyman.

Eden. R. (1983) *Political Leadership and Nihilism: A study of Weber and Nietzsche.* Tampa: University Presses of Florida.

Fleischmann, E. (1964) 'De Weber à Nietzsche', *Archives Européennes de Sociologie*, 5: 190–238.

Freund, J. (1968) *The Sociology of Max Weber*. London: Faber.

Gall, L. (1986) *Bismarck, the White Revolutionary, Volume 2, 1871–1898*. London: Allen & Unwin.

Gallie, W.B. (1955–6) 'Essentially contested concepts', *Proceedings of the Aristotelian Society*, 56: 167–98.

Gerth, H. and Mills, C. Wright (1948) *From Max Weber: Essays in sociology*. London: Routledge & Kegan Paul.

Giddens, A. (1971) *Capitalism and Modern Social Theory*. Cambridge: Cambridge University Press.

Giddens, A. (1984) *The Constitution of Society*. Cambridge: Polity Press.

Green, M. (1974) *The von Richthofen Sisters*. New York: Basic Books.

Hennis, W. (1988) *Max Weber: Essays in reconstruction*. London: Allen & Unwin.

Hollingdale, R.J. (1973) *Nietzsche*. London: Routledge & Kegan Paul.

Holton, R.J. (1985) *The Transition from Feudalism to Capitalism*. London: Macmillan.

Holton, R.J. and Turner, B.S. (1989) *Max Weber on Economy and Society*. London: Routledge.

Honigsheim, P. (1968) *On Max Weber*. New York: Free Press.

Käsler, D. (1988) *Max Weber, an introduction to his life and work*. Cambridge: Polity Press.

Klages, L. (1929–32) *Der Geist als Widersacher der Seele*. Bonn: Bouvier.

Kronman, A.T. (1983) *Max Weber*. London: Edward Arnold.

Lassman, P. and Velody, I. (eds) (1989) *Max Weber's 'Science as a vocation'*. London: Unwin Hyman.

Lepenies, W. (1985) *Die Drei Kulturen, Soziologie zwischen Literatur und Wissenschaft*. München: Carl Hanser.

Löwith, K. (1982) *Karl Marx and Max Weber*. London: Allen & Unwin.

Marshall, G. (1982) *In Search of the Spirit of Capitalism*. London: Hutchinson.

Mayer, J.P. (1944) *Max Weber and German Politics: A study in political sociology*. London: Faber.

Megill, A. (1985) *Prophets of Extremity: Nietzsche, Heidegger, Foucault, Derrida*. Berkeley: University of California Press.

Mitzman, A. (1971) *The Iron Cage: A historical interpretation of Max Weber*. New York: The University Library.

Mommsen, W.J. (1974) *The Age of Bureaucracy, Perspectives on the Political Sociology of Max Weber*. Oxford: Basil Blackwell.

Mommsen, W.J. and Osterhammel, J. (eds) (1987) *Max Weber and his Contemporaries*. London: Allen & Unwin.

Parkin, F. (1979) *Marxism and Class Theory, a Bourgeois Critique*. London: Tavistock.

Parsons, T. (1971) 'Value-freedom and objectivity', in O. Stammer (ed.), *Max Weber and Sociology Today*. Oxford: Basil Blackwell. pp. 27–50.

Prades, J.A. (1966) *La sociologie de la religion chez Max Weber, essai d'analyse et decritique de la methode*. Paris: Editions Nauwelaerts.

Rheinstein, M. (1954) *Max Weber on Law in Economy and Society*. Cambridge, Mass.: Harvard University Press.

Roth, G. (1985) 'Marx and Weber on the United States today', in R.J. Antonio and R.M. Glassman (eds), *A Weber–Marx Dialogue*. Lawrence, Kansas: University Press of Kansas. pp. 215–33.

Roth, G. and Schluchter, W. (1979) *Max Weber's Vision of History, Ethics and Method*. Berkeley: University of California Press.

Runciman, W.G. (1978) *Max Weber Selections in Translation*. Cambridge: Cambridge University Press.

Scaff, L. (1984) 'Weber before Weberian sociology', *British Journal of Sociology*, 35: 190–215.

Shils, E. (1976) *Max Weber on Universities. The Power of the State and the Dignity of the Academic Calling in Imperial Germany*. Chicago: University of Chicago Press.

Stauth, G. and Turner, B.S. (1988) *Nietzsche's Dance. Resentment, reciprocity and resistance in social life*. Oxford: Basil Blackwell.

Tenbruck, F.H. (1975) 'Das Werk Max Webers', *Kölner Zeitschrift für Soziologie und Sozialpsychology*, 27: 663–702; condensed and translated in 1980 as 'The problem of the thematic unity in the works of Max Weber', *British Journal of Sociology*, 31: 316–51.

Tocqueville, A. de (1946) *Democracy in America*. London: Oxford University Press.

Troeltsch, E. (1912) *The Social Teaching of the Christian Churches*. New York: Macmillan (1931).

Turner, B.S. (1974) *Weber and Islam, a Critical Study*, London: Routledge & Kegan Paul.

Turner, B.S. (1981) *For Max Weber: Essays on the sociology of fate*. London: Routledge & Kegan Paul.

Turner, B.S. (1982) 'Nietzsche, Weber and the devaluation of politics: the problem of state legitimacy', *The Sociological Review*, 30: 367–91.

Turner, B.S. (1987) 'The rationalization of the body: reflections on modernity and discipline', in S. Lash and S. Whimster (eds), *Max Weber, Rationality and Modernity*. London: Allen & Unwin.

Turner, B.S. (1988) 'Classical society and its legacy', *Sociological Review*, 36(1): 146–57.

Turner, S. and Factor, R.A. (1984) *Max Weber and the Dispute over Reason and Value*. London: Routledge & Kegan Paul.

Weber, Marianne (1926) *Max Weber. Ein Lebensbild*. Tübingen: Mohr; translated in 1975 as *Max Weber, a Biography*. New York: John Wiley.

Weber, M. (1924) 'Socialism', in *Gesammelte Aufsätze zur Soziologie und Sozialpolitik*, Tübingen: Mohr. pp. 492–518 and translated in W.G. Runciman (1978) *Max Weber, Selections in Translation*. Cambridge: Cambridge University Press.

Weber, M. (1927) *General Economic History*. New York: Collier, 1961.

Weber, M. (1930) *The Protestant Ethic and the Spirit of Capitalism*. London: Allen & Unwin.

Weber, M. (1936) *Jugendbriefe*. Tübingen: Mohr.

Weber, M. (1951) *The Religion of China*. New York: Macmillan.

Weber, M. (1952) *Ancient Judaism*. New York: Free Press.

Weber, M. (1958) *The Religion of India*. New York: Free Press.

Weber, M. (1966) *The City*. New York: Free Press.

Weber, M. (1978a) *Economy and Society*. Berkeley: University of California Press, 2 vols.

Weber, M. (1978b) 'Anticritical Last Word on *The Spirit of Capitalism*', *American Journal of Sociology*, 83(5): 1105–31.

Weber, M. (1988) *Gesammelte Politische Schriften*. Tübingen: Mohr.

CHAPTER 5

EMILE DURKHEIM ON CIVIL SOCIETY

Interpreting Emile Durkheim

Emile Durkheim (1858–1917) remains a major figure in social science as a whole and he is unambiguously a 'founding father' of sociology. Whereas other social theorists from the classical period of sociology (1890–1920) were often somewhat ambiguous about their status as 'sociologists', Durkheim appears to have had a clear vision of the importance of building sociology as a science of social facts. His sociology continues to play a profound role in shaping contemporary thought about the nature of modern life, and anybody who wants to understand modern French social thought must take Durkheim seriously. His work remains a rich and challenging resource for comprehending the complexity of the modern world, a complexity which Durkheim described, by adopting the moral philosophy of Jean Guyau (Orru, 1987) as 'anomic'. Unlike other dominant figures who have shaped modern social theory (such as Georg Simmel, Max Horkheimer, or Talcott Parsons) and who often wrote in a dense and often obscure prose, Durkheim's writing is direct, concise, and comprehensible. His books often start with a difficult analytical problem such as the meaning of 'religion' in the opening sections of *The Elementary Forms of the Religious Life* (Durkheim, 1961), but his arguments are invariably logical and clear. From the point of view of a student of sociology, Durkheim is in this sense an accessible author. Yet the clarity may be deceptive, because the underlying problems of Durkheimian sociology – can one have a *science* of morals? – are clearly immense.

The style and contents of *Professional Ethics and Civic Morals* (Durkheim, 1992) are, in this sense, typical. Durkheim's purpose was to explore the moral problems of an advanced, differentiated, and complex society, in which the economy had become somewhat detached from other social institutions. Much of the text is concerned to establish a clear analytical understanding of major concepts (sanction, property, morals, and contract), but this search for definitional clarity in order to remove the misconceptions of existing theories prepares the way for Durkheim's major concern, which was: how can we find a system of moral restraint which is relevant to modern conditions? The answer was, at least in part, in terms of the evolution of systems of professional codes and civic values, which would contribute to a regulation of the economy rather as the guilds had regulated medieval economic activity (Black, 1984). The state, which Durkheim saw as part of the moral apparatus of society, had an important part to play in regulating social life, but also, as we will see, in protecting the rights of the individual. This answer also provided a sketch of his sociology as a whole, which was, for Durkheim, essentially a science of morals.

Although the style and the content of the argument appear at this level to be relatively simple, Durkheim's sociology has been surrounded by a forest of contradictory and often misleading interpretation. Before turning to the thesis which is embedded in *Professional Ethics and Civic Morals* (hereafter *Civic Morals*), we need to understand some of the principal exegetical frameworks within which Durkheim's work has been received, especially in the English-speaking world. This overview of the tradition of interpretation is important, because I wish to argue that *Civic Morals* is a challenge to these paradigms of interpretation and reception. In particular, it is important to question two conventional views of Durkheim's sociology. The first is that his work is, in some sense, conservative, because it was primarily concerned to understand social order rather than social change, and the second is the claim that there is a major break between his early and his later sociology. I shall address these issues in this order.

French Society (1789-1918)

Between 1789 and 1914, France was subject to profound revolutionary changes which not only transformed French society but, in a real sense, created 'modern society' as a global phenomenon. The French Revolution and the Napoleonic period experimented with and then exported the elementary principles of modern democracy, namely liberty, equality, and fraternity (or secular solidarity). The destruction of the *ancien regime* resulted, however, in The Terror, and produced throughout Europe a conservative reaction against the excesses of the liquidation of the aristocracy and the monarchy. Perhaps the most famous response in the English-speaking world was Edmund Burke's *Reflections on the Revolution in France* which became, possibly in contradistinction to Burke's own ideas, a manifesto against revolution. Jeremy Bentham in his *Anarchical Fallacies* called the idea of natural rights in the 'Declaration of the rights of man and the citizen', with his characteristic vigour, 'nonsense upon stilts' (Waldron, 1987: 53).

The period between the Second Restoration (1815), the death of Napoleon (1821), and the Revolution of 1848 was marked by various unsuccessful attempts to create a stable government under a constitutional monarchy (Cobban, 1961). Marx in *The 18th Brumaire of Louis Bonaparte* wrote rather contemptuously of these political struggles as a 'farce' (Feuer, 1969: 360). However, the 1848 Revolutions throughout Europe raised once more the hope of a liberal, bourgeois alternative to the reactionary regimes which ruled over European affairs after the fall of Napoleon. The failure of the 1848 Revolutions, especially in France and Germany, was the context in which conservative social forces were able to maintain their traditional political role, despite the industrialization of Europe which placed considerable economic power in the hands of the urban bourgeoisie, which embraced various combinations of reformism, nationalism, and liberalism.

French society was further brutally transformed by military defeat in the Franco–Prussian War of 1870, in which Alsace-Lorraine, the birthplace of Durkheim and the focal point of a strong Jewish community, was annexed by Prussia. Military failure contributed to growing social tensions between social classes, and between Catholic conservatism, nationalism, and anti-Semitism, on the one hand, and liberal, secular, bourgeois groups, on the other. In France, these conflicts resulted eventually in the bloody confrontation of the Paris Commune of 1871. Karl Marx and Friedrich Engels, observing these events from London, expected an immediate, devastating, and final revolutionary struggle by the working class against the oppression of the capitalist system. Their revolutionary aspirations were soon dashed by the bloody suppression of the Commune.

The constitutional laws of 1875, which consecrated the Third Republic, emerged out of this traumatic period, but it did not provide a solution to the political divisions in France between a traditional Catholic political bloc and radical secular socialism. In this sense, the politics of the nineteenth century in France was an attempt to come to terms with the legacy of the French Revolution, and to settle the struggles between monarchy, republicanism, and Bonapartism within an effective constitutional framework. Military defeat in 1870 produced a deep nationalistic response in which the French population, including the intelligentsia, desperately sought a regeneration of the nation (Lukes, 1973: 41). In fin-de-siècle France, there was a significant wave of anti-Semitism, which had its parallel in most of the major cultural centres of Europe, but especially in Vienna. Jews were thought to be unpatriotic, but they were also assumed to be secular rationalists and therefore anti-clerical. They were, according to anti-Semitic mythology, simultaneously a threat to the state and the Church. These tensions were the backcloth to the famous 'Dreyfus Affair' (1894) which divided the French nation for over a decade (Miquel, 1968). Captain Alfred Dreyfus, an Alsatian Jew from a wealthy family, was accused of selling official military secrets to the Germans; he was eventually charged and convicted of treason. Knowing himself to be innocent, Captain Dreyfus failed to obey the code of military gentlemen by refusing to commit suicide or to confess. He was sentenced to life imprisonment on Devil's Island (Fenton, 1984: 14), but the case remained stubbornly open and contested. After a retrial and a presidential pardon, the Dreyfus case was finally closed by the Appeal Court in 1906.

The Affair further divided French society into Catholic, conservative nationalists and secular liberals and radicals. Much of the emotional fervour of the anti-Dreyfusards was directed against 'intellectuals' who were held to be a corrupting force in French society. It was in the context of that attack that Durkheim wrote his 'Individualism and the intellectuals' (Durkheim, 1969) for La Revue Bleue in 1898. Durkheim, who came from an established rabbinical family, was, as a university professor, inevitably caught up in the Affair, especially after a local newspaper in Bordeaux had suggested that Durkheim had encouraged his students to become politically active. Emile Zola's letter 'J'accuse' which was addressed to the President of the Republic in January 1898, accused the officers and judges who directed the case against Dreyfus of incompetence and prejudice. Zola's letter intensified the polarization between intellectuals and conservatives. Durkheim's attitude towards the Affair is revealing. He wanted to avoid clouding the issue with conflicts over politics and personalities. For Durkheim, the Affair was a moral rather than political turning-point in the history of the nation. The case, which was in reality a legal farce, was in Durkheim's opinion an opportunity for national renewal.

France was further devastated in the catastrophe of the trenches of Normandy in 1914–18. This national tragedy was also a personal disaster for Durkheim, many of whose intellectual disciples were slaughtered in the war. Over 30 per cent of the students from the Ecole Normale Supérieure who went to the firing line were destroyed. Durkheim wrote two pamphlets in connection with the war: *Qui a voulu la guerre?* (Durkheim, 1915a) and *L'Allemagne au-dessus de tout* (Durkheim, 1915b). Unfortunately, even during the war Durkheim, a Jew with a German name, came under criticism. His son André was killed in the Serbian retreat of 1915–16 (Giddens, 1978: 20). André Durkheim was a member of the intellectual community which had gathered around the journal *Année sociologique* which Durkheim had founded in 1896 (Nandan, 1980). His death was simultaneously a personal and intellectual tragedy. As a result of exhaustion and grief, Durkheim eventually succumbed to a stroke and, after a brief recovery, died at the age of 59.

Conservatism and Sociology

The origins of not only French, but of classical European, sociology have to be understood in the context of these profound social and political crises. Robert Nisbet (1967) in *The Sociological Tradition* has argued that sociology was an aspect of diverse intellectual movements which were responses to the industrial and the French Revolutions. This sociological response was filtered through three doctrines: socialism, conservatism, and liberalism. However, the most significant force shaping early sociology was in fact conservatism. The key ideas or 'unit ideas' of sociology, such as the problem of authority, the sacred, community, the problem of the individual, status in relation to social change, and organic wholeness are primarily aspects of this conservative intellectual legacy. Thus, sociology was an intellectual response to the sense of a lost community, the disappearance of the sacred as a source of values, the isolation of the individual in the city, and the resulting crisis of meaning. In this sense, sociology was a nostalgic refection on the loss of authenticity, personal spontaneity, social wholeness, and community (Stauth and Turner, 1988). Ferdinand Tönnies's famous distinction between *gemeinschaft* (community) and *gesellschaft* (association) (Tönnies, 1957) was a crucial contribution to the subsequent idea that modern societies are fragile and superficial, because they are not grounded in lasting values.

How did Durkheim stand, according to Nisbet (1967), within this tradition? Although Durkheim's search for a rational and positivistic theory of morals was a legacy of the Enlightenment project, Durkheim adopted and developed five themes which were derived essentially from a conservative tradition. These conservative themes were: the primacy of society over the individual; the necessity for moral restraint over human passions; the importance of authority in the organization of communities; the dependence of society on religious values; and the organic character of social relations. It is important to consider each theme in order to grasp fully the argument that Durkheimian sociology was part of a conservative reaction to social change. In order to clarify this presentation, it is important to note that, while there is much to commend Nisbet's interpretation, I shall eventually depart decisively from his exegesis to offer an alternative view of Durkheim.

Durkheim criticized the liberal and utilitarian traditions by arguing that 'society' is ontologically prior to the 'individual'. For example, in *The Rules of Sociological Method* (Durkheim, 1964), Durkheim defined sociology as the scientific study of social facts which are to be treated as things, that is social phenomena which exist independently of the subjective appraisal of individuals. Social facts are *sui generis*. Although this approach to sociology has often been condemned as positivistic and inadequate, it is possible to provide a defence of Durkheim's account, if we realize that he was not trying to define the research methods which sociologists are to employ in routine sociological inquiry (Gane, 1988). Durkheim was also trying to offer a method of 'reading' social facts which would avoid ideological and personal bias. By 'a social fact', Durkheim meant social phenomena which are external to an individual and which exercise a social or moral constraint over behaviour. Social facts include such phenomena as legal institutions, religious belief systems, and financial systems; they also include 'social currents' (Durkheim, 1964: 4) or what we would now term 'social movements'. The data of *Civic Morals* (legal sanctions, moral codes, customs, and so forth) are social facts in Durkheim's terms. The 'rules' of sociology attempt to outline how true knowledge of these social facts might be produced. Now Nisbet takes this treatment of the relationship between the individual and society in sociological methods as an example of conservatism, because the 'ideas, language, morality, and relationships' of an individual 'are but reflections of the anterior reality of society' (Nisbet, 1965: 25).

Second, human nature is such that moral constraint is essential for the well-being of humans and for the stability and safety of society. As Nisbet points out, the Enlightenment tradition saw Man as a creature of almost infinite capacity, whose nature had been stunted by religious control, political tyranny, or social corruption. As Rousseau had argued in *The Social Contract*, Man is born free, but everywhere he is in chains. By contrast the conservative tradition, especially under the influence of the Christian doctrine of the sinfulness of Man, regards human beings as creatures who need discipline in order to regulate their desires. We can take one famous example of this form of reasoning in Durkheim in his study of suicide (Durkheim, 1951), where the idea of anomie plays a pivotal role.

Durkheim adopted a view of Man which is best described as 'homo duplex'. Rather like the famous story of Jekyll and Hyde, human beings have two opposed natures. One is violent and passionate; the other is rational and sociable. The requirements of social stability demand the subordination of the animality of human beings by reason, if society is to avoid anarchy. Theories of society which are based on the assumption of 'homo duplex' typically argue that, whatever the individual cost, human sexuality must be regulated in the interests of social order. Sigmund Freud's treatment of this issue can be found in *Civilization and its Discontents* (Freud, 1930). For Durkheim, the problem of modern society is that, with the decline of the principle of mechanical solidarity which is based on a shared system of beliefs and morals (that is on the *conscience collective*), human beings are exposed to their own unregulated desires and ambitions, and they are exposed to profound changes in the organization of society. In particular, utilitarian individualism, which he thought was promoted primarily in the social thought of the English sociologist Herbert Spencer, encouraged egoism, ambition, and unlimited aspiration. The consequence of egoistic individualism (Marske, 1987) is that the social malaise of a society without an adequate normative structure or 'anomie' is intensified, and in *Suicide* (Durkheim, 1951) which he published in 1897, Durkheim attempted to show that the suicide rate was highest among those social groups which were most exposed to these anomic currents in society. Without normative restraint, individuals would succumb to such 'suicidal currents'.

In fact, Durkheim's argument in *Suicide* was far more complex than I have suggested, and he identified four different types of suicide, which have a specific causality. Some forms of suicide, such as fatalistic and altruistic suicide, are the products of too much regulation and social integration. Egoistic and anomic suicide were the types of suicidal behaviour which are most characteristic of contemporary society. Durkheim's analysis of suicide has been much debated and criticized (Atkinson, 1978; Giddens, 1965; Giddens, 1966; Lukes, 1973: 31), but I cannot in this chapter enter into this argument. The importance of *Suicide* for understanding *Civic Morals* is in terms of the light which it throws on Durkheim's critique of egoistic individualism as a process which uncouples the individual from the social structure.

Nisbet's third theme is the importance of authority in the conservative theory of society. The notion of authority 'runs like a leitmotif through all of Durkheim's works' (Nisbet, 1965: 59). It is an essential feature of his view of morality, where authority, especially in the form of discipline, plays an important role in shaping 'personality' through moral education. Once more, Durkheim was particularly critical of the liberal utilitarian tradition of Bentham and James Mill, who, according to Durkheim, confused liberty with lawlessness. Without restraint and authority, human beings would be committed to a life of anarchy. The problem of modern society is indeed the slow erosion of moral authority, and the task of *Civic Morals* was to describe this crisis and to offer a set of solutions for the creation of authoritative moral guide-lines. The problem of modern society is to discover an effective principle which will give moral force and ethical authority to social norms and practices, without which discipline will be merely an external regulation. In *The Elementary Forms*, Durkheim wanted to show how obedience to religious practices produced self-restraint and altruistic actions produced personal asceticism as a necessary basis of social life as a whole. It is only on the basis of 'a certain disdain for suffering' (Durkheim, 1961: 356), that society is possible at all.

This discussion allows Nisbet to get at the heart of Durkheim's conservatism, namely the centrality of religion, or more specifically the sacred, to Durkheim's sociological project as a whole. Here again Durkheim's approach departs significantly from the sociology of religion of Marx, Weber, or Simmel (Seger, 1957; Turner, 1991). Nineteenth-century theories of religion were largely individualistic and rationalistic, that is they treated religion as primarily a cognitive activity which was false from a scientific point of view (Goode, 1951). Religion was the consequence of Man's misunderstanding of natural reality. For example, animism was an attempt to explain nature by reference to spirits. Since these theories are false from a positivistic perspective, religion will disappear with the advance of science. Durkheim departed radically from these cognitive orientations, by treating religion as social, collective, and practical. His theories of religion were heavily influenced by the arguments of William Robertson Smith whose *Lectures on the Religion of the Semites* (1889) showed how the sacrificial meal between men and the gods created a sacral community, and by Fustel de Coulanges's study of *The Ancient City* (1901) where the changing structure of classical society is examined in terms of theological changes.

In his religious studies, Durkheim attempted to show that Australian aboriginal totemism, as the simplest known religion, provided an insight into 'the elementary forms' of all religious life. His second task was to identify the genesis of the fundamental categories of human thought (such as time and space); this issue in the sociology of knowledge was also considered in *Primitive Classification* (Durkheim and Mauss, 1963). His third objective was through an analysis of totemism to identify a number of generalizations about the universal functions of the sacred in social institutions.

Durkheim's work, which is a classic in the sociology of religion, has received ample commentary (Goode, 1951; Pickering, 1975; Robertson, 1970; Scharf, 1970; Seger, 1957; Turner, 1991). The core of his argument proceeds along two lines. First, he attacked existing, typically individualistic, arguments about the nature of religion, in order to arrive at his own solution. For Durkheim, religion is a 'unified system of beliefs and practices relative to sacred things, that is to say, things set apart and forbidden – beliefs and practices which unite into one single moral community called a Church, all those who adhere to them' (Durkheim, 1961: 62). His second line of approach was to argue that the 'elementary forms' of religion, by which he meant the basic structural characteristics of religion, provide an insight into social structures and processes as such. Religious beliefs are to be interpreted as the 'collective representations' of society; the unintended consequence of religious practices is to create a social bond; the practice of religious rituals creates a social enthusiasm or 'effervescence' by which social commitments are renewed; the training of the faithful in sacrifice and asceticism creates important norms of altruism and social service; and religious mythologies, which are dramatically re-enacted in the ritual, store up the collective memory of the social group, without which the continuity of this historical narrative of generations would be impossible (Wach, 1944). Talcott Parsons was probably correct or at least insightful, when he argued that Durkheim, starting with the proposition that society is the basis of religion, concluded with the equally revolutionary equation that the basis of society is sacred. The problem of modern society is that we are in a transitional period; the old gods are dead, and new ones are yet to be born. Nationalism may prove to be such a god, inspiring devotion and sacrifice.

Finally, Nisbet argued that the underlying metaphor in Durkheim's sociology was that society is organic, and that its developmental laws can only be understood in terms of collective processes such as social differentiation which cannot be reduced to individual psychology, and especially to individual rationality. Against the utilitarian tradition, Durkheim rejected the idea that society was the result of a social contract drawn up between individuals, and that the development of society could be conceived in terms of an original contract (Abercrombie, Hill, and Turner, 1986). Society is organic rather than contractual in Durkheim's more holistic perspective. He argued that a contract between individuals would be meaningless and ineffective unless it was based on deeply held values and beliefs, and unless it was sanctified by custom, ritual, and morality. The rejection of this utilitarian tradition occupied Durkheim in *The Division of Labor in Society* (1960), where he provided a specific attack on Spencerian sociology, but *Civic Morals* constitutes the core of Durkheim's critical offensive against individualistic/utilitarian accounts of property and contract; I shall turn shortly to this argument in detail in providing a description of the contents of his lectures on professional ethics and public morality. In conceiving of society as an organic whole and not as an aggregate of individuals, Durkheim has often been identified as a founder of 'structural-functionalism' as a distinctive school of sociology. Certainly Durkheim's view of historical change was primarily in terms of the dichotomy between mechanical and organic solidarity which he explored fully in *The Division of Labor in Society*.

This interpretation of Durkheim as a social theorist who laid the foundations for the analysis of social integration in social systems was promoted by Parsons in a number of major publications such as *The Social System* (Parsons, 1991: 367ff.), and in so doing Parsons has also, somewhat less directly than Nisbet, promoted the idea that Durkheim has to be seen as a theorist of social stability and social integration. For example, Parsons (1974) argued that Durkheim's account of solidarity in *The Division of Labor in Society* in terms of the *conscience collective* in mechanical solidarity in primitive societies and of social reciprocity in organic solidarity in advanced societies was a major solution to the Hobbesian problem of social order in the utilitarian tradition. Durkheim's analysis of the integrative functions of religious practice in both making and sustaining social communities provided Parsons with a theoretical source in classical sociology for his own emphasis on the importance of common values in the social cohesion of modern societies. In Parsons's early academic career, Weber's analysis of capitalism had been the primary intellectual stimulus for Parsonian sociology (Wearne, 1989), but as Parsons moved more towards an analysis of the allocative and integrative requirements of a social system Durkheimian issues appear to have become increasingly important. Thus, Parsons's appreciation of the significance of the psychological internalization of values which he took from Cooley (Parsons, 1968) was now supplemented by Durkheim's analysis of the integrative function of common beliefs to produce the cornerstone of Parsons's 'middle period', namely the internalization and socialization of values in social integration (Alexander, 1984; Robertson and Turner, 1989).

In the conventional paradigm of introductory textbooks for undergraduate sociology courses, there developed a tripartite version of classical sociology: Marx was a theorist of conflict and social change; Weber was a social philosopher of action and meaning; and Durkheim was a sociologist of social order, moral systems, and political stability. It has taken many years for a more complete interpretation of Durkheim to emerge, but recent perspectives on Durkheim have tended to take more notice of his political sociology (Giddens, 1986; Lacroix, 1981), his educational commentaries (Pickering, 1979), the complexity of his methodological views (Gane, 1988), his dependence on German moral philosophy (Meštrović, 1991), his sociology of law and justice (Green, 1989; Sirianni, 1984), the richness of his views on cultural strains in advanced societies (Alexander, 1988), and his awareness of the contradictions of modern society. These new emphases do not mean that previous perspectives on Durkheim were inaccurate or invalid; rather they produce an interpretation of Durkheim which is richer, deeper, and more comprehensive.

An alternative view of Durkheim's sociology was established by Alvin Gouldner's introduction (Gouldner, 1962) to Durkheim's *Socialism*, which had been posthumously published in 1928. Generally speaking, Gouldner's aim was to show that Durkheim's sociology was the intellectual legacy of Henri Saint-Simon (1760–1825) rather than Auguste Comte (1798–1857). This interpretation was a subtle strategy to demonstrate Durkheim's link with socialism rather than conservatism. Gouldner shows that we can in fact read Durkheim's *The Division of Labor in Society* as a polemic against Comte. Durkheim's position was not that modern society cannot exist without consensus, but rather that the reciprocity of organic solidarity produces a basis of social order without a normative consensus. Second, Gouldner argued that anomie was not normlessness, but rather a disjuncture between existing norms and changing social structures. Third, the real dislocation of modern society was the absence of intervening social institutions between the individual and the state; occupational and professional associations were intended to fill this gap. Another dislocation of modern society was the division between local commitments to the nation-state and the growth of internationalism, cosmopolitanism, and globalism. It is true that Durkheim defines socialism as a moral regulation of the market place, but in *Socialism* he was concerned to understand how a moral regulation of the economy would be possible. Gouldner's work was thus important in reasserting the significance of Durkheim's interest in economic and political issues.

The trend in more recent interpretations, therefore, has been to assert that there was an important radical dimension to Durkheimian sociology which has been neglected as a consequence of the concentration on his arguments about social solidarity and his condemnation of economic individualism. Giddens has made the valuable point that Durkheim was not in fact strictly interested in '"order" in a generic sense, but of the form of authority appropriate to a modern industrial State' (Giddens, 1986: 12). Furthermore, Durkheim's contributions to the sociology of law and the state were rather neglected by earlier interpretations of Durkheim (Pearce, 1989); it is precisely in this context that we need to take his *Civic Morals* seriously, as Durkheim's most elaborate reflection on state power in relation to individual rights.

Durkheim's impact on France was in fact always regarded as dubious by the conservative wing of French politics, because Durkheimian sociology was identified with anti-clericalism and the Dreyfusard lobby (regardless of Durkheim's own views on these issues). Durkheim's Jewish background and his clear identification with 'the intellectuals' were sufficient to put him outside the conservative bloc in French society. We can identify one aspect of Durkheim's sociology which was especially critical of existing economic institutions, namely the inequality of wealth in France, which Durkheim regarded as particularly destabilizing. An important feature of his economic sociology was, thus, his bitter condemnation of the inheritance of property within a society which had an ideology of egalitarianism.

In terms of the actual interpretation of Durkheim's sociology, part of Nisbet's (1965) argument about the conservatism of Durkheimian thought was its dependence on the French tradition of conservatism which included de Maistre and de Bonald. More recent interpretations of Durkheim have identified his dependence on German philosophy, especially on Schopenhauer. The importance of this viewpoint is to place particular weight on Durkheim's sociology as a science of morality (Meštrović, 1991). In this framework, we can see Durkheim's sociology as a reply to Kant's theory of morality and theory of knowledge. Briefly, we can see Kant's account of the moral imperative as an attempt to provide a rationalist justification for the Christian idea of brotherly (altruistic) love. Kant harnessed reason to ethics to explain why we should feel an obligation towards others; the categorical imperative claimed that we should treat others as we expected them to treat us. Morality was thus about reasonable obligation. Kant's epistemology and aesthetics ran in the same direction. Our knowledge of the world is determined or given by general categories of thought (cause, effect, time, and space). Knowledge is not imprinted on the mind by empirical reality. In the world of aesthetics, Kant argued that aesthetic judgement was disinterested, neutral, and objective; Kant thereby attempted to separate sensibility and aesthetics, because he denied that aesthetic judgements were emotive.

We can see Durkheim's account of ethics and knowledge as a reply to this Kantian legacy. In terms of the sociology of knowledge, Durkheim claimed, in *Primitive Classification* (Durkheim and Mauss, 1963), that the fundamental categories of thought were located in the organization of society; social forms produced the forms of thought. For example, the analytical notion of 'space' is modelled on social space. In terms of religious belief, as we have seen, Durkheim derived the concept of 'god', or more exactly the dichotomy of sacred and profane, from social life; it is society which inspires in us the sense of the holy. In general, Durkheim wanted to deny that a rational appreciation of duty, or a utilitarian respect for sanctions, would ever be sufficient as a basis of moral commitment. Morality required compassion, fervour, and a sense of the sanctity of moral obligations to induce a sense of commitment and duty. In this respect, Durkheim followed Schopenhauer rather than Kant in formulating an empirical science of morals which would avoid the formal, a priori reasoning in Kantian moral philosophy.

Although Durkheim's sociology, such as his sociology of education (Durkheim, 1977; Pickering, 1979), was clearly a social and political response to the crisis of French society in the late nineteenth century, his intellectual concerns were not unidimensionally driven by the legacy of French conservatism. While the intellectual legacy of Saint-Simon and Comte on Durkheim cannot be denied, Durkheim was also trying to come to terms with the intellectual legacy of Kant and Schopenhauer, and also with the impact in his own day of the political ideas of Heinrich von Treitschke whose pan-Germanism and state theory were condemned by Durkheim (Giddens, 1986: 230) as dangerous doctrines.

One strong argument against the view that Durkheim was conservative can be taken from *Civic Morals* itself, namely in Durkheim's critique of the injustice which is associated with and an inevitable outcome of the institution of inheritance. Because wealth which results from inheritance has no necessary relationship to merit, Durkheim argued that it 'invalidates the whole contractual system at its very roots' (Durkheim, 1992: 213). He then offered an attack on the social consequences of inheritance which would be worthy of Marx's prose:

> Now inheritance as an institution results in men being born either rich or poor; that is to say, there are two main classes in society, linked by all sorts of intermediate classes: the one which in order to live has to make its services acceptable to the other at whatever cost; the other class which can do without these services because it can call on certain resources, which may, however, not be equal to the services rendered by those who have them to offer. Therefore as long as such sharp class differences exist in society, fairly effective palliatives may lessen the injustice of contracts; but in principle, the system operates in conditions which do not allow of justice.
>
> (Durkheim, 1992: 213)

Durkheim claimed that, with a growing sense of justice in a modern democracy, the institution of inheritance clashed with contemporary norms of equality. Unfortunately the English translation appears to be stale and cumbersome. The French 'la conscience morale', is rendered as 'men's conscience' and 'le sentiment' as 'attitude' with the result that Durkheim's text is psychologized and rendered sexist.

Durkheim proposed a moral principle of distribution which would overcome these existing inequalities, namely 'the distribution of things amongst individuals can be just only if it be made relative to the social deserts of each one' (Durkheim, 1992: 214). Now Durkheim's notion of justice is largely incompatible with a conservative theory of private property rights, in which the right of heads of households to dispose of their own property according to their own interests is a fundamental principle of 'possessive individualism' (Macpherson, 1962).

Durkheim, however, recognized two forms of inheritance: wealth and talents. While the abolition of the privilege of inheritance would undermine economic inequality resulting from birth, the inheritance of talents, or what today we might call 'cultural capital' (Bourdieu and Passeron, 1990), is equally significant and is not solely related to economic class. Thus *Civic Morals* concludes with the problem of the inheritance of talents:

> To us it does not seem equitable that a man should be better treated as a social being because he was born of parentage that is rich or of high rank. But is it any more equitable that he should be better treated because he was born of a father of higher intelligence or in a more favourable moral *milieu*?

(Durkheim, 1992: 220)

While Durkheim could see no ready social or political solution to this moral problem, he believed that only a special type of consciousness based on charity and human sympathy may overcome the tendency to judge the moral worth of a person in terms of their social background.

In a conclusion which goes back to Schopenhauer's idea that compassion is the root of moral action, Durkheim argued that charity 'ignores and denies any special merit in gifts or mental capacity acquired by heredity. This, then, is the very acme of justice' (Durkheim, 1992: 220). These attitudes towards justice are hardly compatible with the social outlook of conservatism (Green, 1989). In summary, an inspection of 'Durkheim's writings on the growth of moral individualism, on socialism, and on the State, in the context of the social and political issues which he saw as confronting the Third Republic, shows how mistaken it is to regard him as being primarily "conservative"' (Giddens, 1986: 23). The political arguments of *Civic Morals* are particularly powerful evidence of such an interpretive 'mistake'.

Intellectual Continuity

Civic Morals is also relevant to the debate about the thematic and intellectual continuity of Durkheim's sociology. Here again it was Parsons who, in *The Structure of Social Action* (1937), had claimed that there was a profound discontinuity in the sociology of Durkheim. In particular, Parsons argued that Durkheim, especially in *The Division of Labor* of 1893 and *The Rules* of 1895, had embraced a positivistic theory of moral facts, while his later work such as *The Elementary Forms* of 1912 was based on idealism. Parsons attempted to show that a positivistic theory of morals which treats social facts as exterior, objective, and autonomous cannot solve the problem of how individuals become normatively committed to these moral facts. It fails to produce an adequate theory of internalization of moral facts, which can then become subjectively authoritative. It was only when Durkheim came to his final study of religion that he began to provide a theory of the emotive character of morality in terms of subjective affectivity. It is ritual practice and social effervescence which bring about the internalization of norms, but in Durkheim's sociology of religion these arguments are based on the view that 'society = god' – an equation which Parsons treated as idealism. In short, the analytical inadequacy of a positivistic theory of morals breaks down into idealism, producing an intellectual rupture at the heart of Durkheim's social science of morals. This position is difficult to sustain when we look at the development contents of *Civic Morals*.

In many respects, Parsons's interpretation of Durkheim was a major intellectual advance at the time. His emphasis on Durkheim's critique of Spencer's individualism in Durkheim's development of the idea of the non-contractual element of contract in *The Division of Labor* was especially significant (Parsons, 1981). However, a further feature of Parsons's interpretation involved dividing Durkheim's work into substantive topics. The 'early empirical work' concerned the occupational division of labour and the suicide problem in France, whereas 'the final phase' concerned religious ideas and questions of epistemology. The idea that Durkheim moved from empirical questions of social structure to epistemological problems of knowledge gave further credibility to the idea of a fissure in Durkheimian sociology. Again this division in terms of substantive areas is not tenable in terms of Durkheim's lectures on contract, property, the state, and religion in *Civic Morals*.

Professional Ethics and Civic Morals is in fact a collection of Durkheim's lectures, which had the title 'The nature of morals and of rights' and which Durkheim delivered at Bordeaux between 1890 and 1900. These lectures existed in manuscript form with Marcel Mauss; three of the six lectures were published in the *Revue de Metaphysique et de Morale* in 1937, twenty years after Durkheim's death. It is unlikely that Parsons would have known of the existence of these lectures when he first published *The Structure of Social Action* in 1937. Parsons's bibliographical notes at the end of *The Structure of Social Action* contain some references to work from Durkheim's Bordeaux period, but there is no reference to the material which now constitutes *Civic Morals*. Durkheim's lectures appeared in French as *Leçons de Sociologie, physique des moeurs et du droit* (Durkheim, 1950).

These lectures on professional ethics, civic morals, property, and contract are thus from what Parsons regarded as Durkheim's 'positivist' phase; chronologically, they belong with *The Division of Labor* and *The Rules*. They were part of Durkheim's attempt to create an autonomous sociological discipline whose main subject matter was to be the study of moral facts. If we can show that the themes of *Civic Morals* in fact cover Durkheim's entire sociological interests, both 'late' and 'early', and if we can show that these interests were not bifurcated around the materialism/idealism dilemma, then we have shown that Durkheim's sociology was not ruptured by this dilemma. More importantly, we will establish an evolution of Durkheim's sociological ideas over a period of almost twenty years.

It is not necessary to provide a general summary of Durkheim's *Civic Morals*. To avoid repetition, I shall focus on the core of Durkheim's argument across the six lectures with two questions in mind. First, do these lectures map out Durkheim's sociology as a whole by anticipating or discussing themes which are more fully developed later? Second, how does *Civic Morals* address theoretical or political issues which remain at the core of contemporary sociological debate? By answering these two questions, I hope also to address the query: why read Durkheim's *Civic Morals*?

The central issues of *Civic Morals* were part of the legacy from Saint-Simon in a number of important respects. The question behind Saint-Simon's work was the problem of the erosion of Christianity, the problems of industrialization, and the possibility of a 'religion of humanity' which, directed by sociological knowledge, would provide some coherence for a complex and differentiated society. Saint-Simon was thus exercised by the problems of political integration in Europe and, in various pamphlets and addresses, he attempted to conceptualize the institutions which would be necessary for a European parliamentary system (Taylor, 1975).

A similar set of issues provided the structure of the argument in *Civic Morals*. Durkheim starts by providing an outline of the scientific study of morals, with which we are perfectly familiar from *The Rules* or *Suicide*, but much of the core argument of *Civic Morals* is focused on the problems of social integration and government authority in a post-Christian, if not secular, society in which there is a high degree of social differentiation. There is also concern for the problems of global social order and a form of government which might ultimately transcend the limitations of the nation-state.

The problem facing modern Europe is the separation of the economy from society and the absence of any effective regulation of the market place. The division of labour and the development of the modern economy have produced, or been accompanied by, the evolution of occupational groups and professional associations. For Durkheim, these groups offer some stability for modern society, but there has been no significant development of business professions; there is no code of conduct which can regulate economic activity. Professional associations are, in any case, rather local in their organization and social effects, but the crucial issue is the absence of a set of professional ethics. The crisis facing Europe is the anarchy of the market place and the underdevelopment of moral regulation. This 'moral vacuum' (Durkheim, 1992: 12) can only be filled by the development of a 'corporate system', a code of business ethics, and state intervention in the market place. As Durkheim argued in *The Division of Labor* and *Suicide*, this lack of moral regulation means that individuals are exposed to the negative or anomic consequences of the business cycle and to their own unlimited desires and expectations. Durkheim was critical of this structural problem in modern societies, but he also attacked classical economists for failing to see the social consequences of unrestrained economic activity; economic functions were studied as if they had no social effects.

The social problem of modern society can be understood more effectively by examining the historical decline of the guild system which in Roman and medieval times had provided some ethical regulation of economic activity, by controlling their members, prices, and the conditions of exchange. Durkheim, in this historical sketch, adopts an argument which is characteristic of his sociological style of argumentation as a whole. He wants to show how these formal rules of conduct had a real effect on the behaviour of individuals, and he does this by a digression into religious history. The origins of the guild are to be found in the religious *collegium*. The cults which formed around craft activities provided festivals, feasts, collective sacrifices, and patterns of exchange such as the gift. These collective and ritual activities provided the social and moral force behind the original regulations on economic behaviour which are associated with the guild. In other words, Durkheim was never content to discover a formal obligation or regulation without showing how some collective and moral force brought about an affective commitment to some social practice. Morality and moral force is always to be discovered in 'something that goes beyond the individual, and to the interests of the group he belongs to' (Durkheim, 1992: 24). This type of argument was put to special use in *The Elementary Forms*, but we can also see it in operation in *Civic Morals*.

The crisis in the European socio-economic system can be best resolved through the development of a corporative structure which would organize the various branches of industry, provide an administrative and electoral system by which interests could be articulated, and thereby come to develop a macro-system of moral authority and regulation. The 'cells', so to speak, of this structure would be the professional and occupational associations to which individuals would be attached. However, the whole system could only function if the state became 'the central organ' of the whole system (Durkheim, 1992: 39). These relations between the individual, the professional associations, and the state are the subject matter of civic morals. These civic morals thereby determine the normative relationships between the individual and the state.

Given the widely held opinion that Durkheim failed to develop an adequate political sociology, it is a striking feature of *Civic Morals* that Durkheim gives special prominence to the state in regulating society and directing moral activity. For Durkheim, the state has the responsibility to 'work out certain representations which hold good for the collectivity ... [because] the State is the very organ of social thought' (Durkheim, 1992: 50–1). We can only understand these arguments by realizing that here, as elsewhere in Durkheim's sociology for example in *The Division of Labor*, he is attempting to counteract the arguments of Herbert Spencer. For Durkheim, the contemporary development of the state is not incompatible with the growing importance of the individual and individualism. The state is an essential feature of the evolution of individual rights, because it is only the state which has sufficient authority and collective power to create and protect individual rights. There is nothing about the state which must produce a political tyranny, and indeed it is the modern state which has liberated the individual from the particularistic forms of domination, which were typical of feudalism.

Of course, while Durkheim overtly developed a political sociology in *Civic Morals*, his political ideas assumed a moral framework (Wallwork, 1972: 103). The role of the state 'is to persevere in calling the individual to a moral way of life' (Durkheim, 1992: 69) and this leads Durkheim to the assertion that the state is 'the organ of moral discipline' (Durkheim, 1992: 72). One of the few recent studies in historical sociology which has recognized the importance of Durkheim's political ideas in *Civic Morals* is *The Great Arch* (Corrigan and Sayer, 1985: 6), but Durkheim is criticized for not recognizing that the moral authority of the state results from a social struggle over morality, and that moral regulation has to be enforced. In general terms, one objection to Durkheim's account of the state as a moral agency is the optimistic belief that state terror is not a significant problem. In a valuable analysis of Durkheim's sociology, Edward Tiryakian has suggested that Durkheim's optimistic view of the state as an institution which protects the individual from particularistic patterns of oppression is a consequence of Durkheim's Jewish origins. The fact that the First Republic in France had emancipated the Jews from the restrictions of the *ancien regime* provided Durkheim with a concrete model of the state as the protector of individual freedoms (Tiryakian, 1978: 198).

There is, however, an important additional element to Durkheim's argument which we should not ignore. For Durkheim, the possibility of state tyranny is limited by the presence of intermediary institutions between the individual and the state. In this respect, Durkheim's argument followed closely on Alexis de Tocqueville's analysis in 1832 of the problems of democracy in America, where he had claimed that a democratic despotism could only be avoided if there was an effective system of voluntary associations acting as a social buffer against political domination. This question of intermediary groups was essential to Durkheim's treatment of democracy. For Durkheim, the 'political malaise' has the same origin as the 'social malaise', namely 'the lack of secondary cadres to interpose between the individual and the State ... these secondary groups are essential if the State is not to oppress the individual: they are also necessary if the State is to be free of the individual' (Durkheim, 1992: 96). These 'cadres secondaires intercales entre l'individu et l'Etat' (Durkheim, 1950: 116) are essential both to individual liberties and to the effectivity of the state. Here again Durkheim looked towards professional and occupational associations to form this necessary intermediate stratum of institutions between the individual and the state. Indeed, these professional associations would become, according to Durkheim, the very foundation of political life. These institutions were necessary to avoid what we might usefully call 'political anomie'.

With these institutions and associations, the danger of political despotism would recede, but this situation still leaves open the problem of political commitment. What is the root of loyalty to the state? In Durkheim's argument in *Civic Morals*, to which he returned during the First World War, it is patriotism which is the core of this political commitment. Once more we can identify a typical Durkheimian sociological argument in his treatment of political loyalties. Patriotism is a type of secular religion, and thus it is possible to talk about a 'cult of the state' in which citizens are, as it were, the worshippers. Patriotism is constituted by 'the ideas and feelings as a whole which bind the individual to a certain State' (Durkheim, 1992: 73). But Durkheim thought that in modern times, there were two forms of political loyalty which he called 'patriotism' and 'world patriotism'. For some reason, Cornelia Brookfield has translated 'le cosmopolitisme' as 'world patriotism' which does not adequately convey Durkheim's meaning (Durkheim, 1950: 87). In ancient times, this division did not exist, because only one cult was possible: 'this was the cult of the State, whose public religion was but the symbolic form of the State' (Durkheim, 1992: 72). The evolution of modern society has produced a wider horizon for human consciousness as human beings become conscious of their involvement in 'humanity' on a global basis. Consciousness becomes more universal under these new conditions. This universal consciousness is at a higher moral level than mere patriotism, and the importance of this emerging universal consciousness is that it becomes possible 'to imagine humanity in its entirety organized as a society' (Durkheim, 1992: 74). Thus, in an argument which was very close to Saint-Simon's vision, Durkheim anticipated the idea of political globalization on the basis of a universalistic notion of humanity (Turner, 1990). This idea of cosmopolitanism was part of Durkheim's later condemnation of pan-Germanism and a feature of his critique of war 'which reduces societies, even the most cultivated, to a moral condition that recalls that of the lower societies. The individual is obscured' (Durkheim, 1992: 117). The actual expression used by Durkheim was much stronger: 'L'individu disparaît' (Durkheim, 1950: 140).

This brief commentary on some of the key ideas of *Civic Morals* is intended to argue that Durkheim's sociology is not in any simple sense 'conservative' and to show that there was no significant fissure or rupture in the development of his ideas. The Bordeaux lectures contained the essential features of his sociology as a whole, both in its 'early' and 'late' topics of analysis. One final argument which can support this claim is to note the importance of Durkheim's criticisms of Kantian philosophy in the final chapters on property.

I have already noted that in general we can see Durkheim's sociology as a response to Kant. First, in his sociology of knowledge, for example in *Primitive Classification* (Durkheim and Mauss, 1963), Durkheim argued that our knowledge of the world was not grounded in a set of a priori categories which were the structure of (the individual) mind. The fundamental categories of thought (time, space, causation and number) were collective and social categories which were modelled on the structure of society itself. The fundamental categories of mind are in fact collective representations of social life. This theory has, of course, been challenged on philosophical grounds (Needham, 1963), but I am only concerned at this stage to show the Kantian origins of this debate in Durkheim. In a similar fashion, Meštrović (1991) has convincingly demonstrated that Durkheim's moral and aesthetic views were an attempt to criticize the individualism and rationalism of Kant's moral argument concerning the nature of the categorical imperative. This debate with Kant was equally important in *Civic Morals*.

In a complex argument about the collective and sacred origins of property, in which ownership is compared with the concept of the taboo, Durkheim attempted to present a sociological alternative to Kant's discussion of property. After a lengthy and difficult argument, which the reader must study in detail, Durkheim came to a striking conclusion. Respect for property is not related to the individual personality; this respect has an origin which is exterior to the individual; it is, once more for Durkheim, an issue concerning the sacred/profane dichotomy. Thus 'Property is property only if it is respected, that is to say, held sacred' (Durkheim, 1992: 159).

Where does the sense of the sacred come from? Because the arguments of *The Elementary Forms* are probably quite familiar to the sociologist, we can easily anticipate how Durkheim will answer this question. However, from the point of view of exegesis, it is interesting to see how fully *Civic Morals* rehearses the arguments of his 'final phase'. For Durkheim, we can best understand religion as the 'way in which societies become conscious of themselves and their history' (Durkheim, 1961: 160). In a thesis which reproduced Fustel de Coulanges's ideas about the ancient world, Durkheim argued that

> The gods are no other than collective forces personified and hypostasized in material form. Ultimately, it is the society that is worshipped by the believers; the superiority of the gods over men is that of the group over its members. The early gods were the substantive objects which served as symbols to the collectivity and for this reason became the representations of it.

> (Durkheim, 1992: 161)

Once more the French original is inevitably superior:

> Les dieux ne sont autre chose que des forces collectives incarnées, hypostasiées sous forme matérielle. Au fond, c'est la société que les fidèles adorent; la supériorité des dieux sur les hommes, c'est celle du groupe sur ses membres. Les premiers dieux ont été les objets matériels qui servaient d'emblèmes à la collectivité et qui, pour cette raison, en sont devenus les représentations.

> (Durkheim, 1950: 190–1)

This argument, although it was anticipated by Fustel de Coulanges and William Robertson Smith, was the decisive origin of a *sociological* theory of religion which attempted to locate the nature of religious belief and experience in collective life. The experience of the holy is, in Durkheim's argument, produced by an exterior and superior authority (the society) through collective rituals, which in turn create a social effervescence. It was on this basis that Durkheim challenged the individualistic rationalism, not only of Kant's moral philosophy, but also of Kant's Protestant version of faith.

Thus, in its account of the nature of moral facts, the importance of civic morals and professional associations in regulating the relationship between the individual and the state, in its critique of economic individualism in Spencerian sociology and English utilitarianism, in its analysis of the social and political malaise of modern society, in its analysis of the social origins of religious ideas, and in its general critique of Kantian philosophy, *Civic Morals* provides a summary of Durkheim's sociology as a whole. That this volume should accomplish such a synoptic task is not surprising. Although these lectures on morals and rights were given originally in Bordeaux in the 1890s, they were repeated in 1904 and 1912 in the Sorbonne. In Parsons's exegetical framework these lectures therefore cover both Durkheim's 'early empirical work' and the 'final phase'. In the light of Durkheim's concern in the period 1912 to 1917 with patriotism, war, and religion, the continuities between his work at Bordeaux in the 1890s and later at the Sorbonne are more impressive and obvious than the alleged discontinuities. The central element of this continuity is that what we commonsensically think of in individual terms (mind, feelings, commitment, and so forth) are collective and social. In more specific terms, the force of emotive commitment to moral rules has to be found in compassion, and compassion has its origin in the sacred/collective character of social life.

Conclusion

In a recent collection of essays on *Durkheimian Sociology* (Alexander, 1988), Randall Collins has noted that 'Of the great classic figures of sociology, at the present time Durkheim's reputation is at its lowest' (Collins, 1988: 107). This low ebb is partly explained by the ways in which Durkheim has been (mistakenly) interpreted and received. Durkheim's reception has been initially through the English functional anthropologists and later he was embraced as the founder of multivariate statistics on the basis of his arguments in *Suicide*. Durkheim was also appropriated by conservatism as a leading figure. For Collins, Durkheim's work should be seen as a valuable contribution to conflict analysis, because, on the basis of *The Elementary Forms*, he produced a powerful theory of social solidarity, and this concept is essential to the development of conflict sociology. The abiding problem of Durkheimian sociology, however, is that it 'tended to minimize the significance of social classes and their conflicts' (Collins, 1988: 109). On the basis of a close inspection of *Civic Morals*, we can see that Collins's judgement is erroneous.

Civic Morals is dominated by a political and social analysis of the malaise of modern society, which is the failure of intermediary institutions to provide a linkage between the state and the individual. Professional ethics and professional associations, along with the development of a system of civic morals, are seen to be an antidote to this problem. However, Durkheim also believed that the state would have to help create a corporative system, in which an organic bond would emerge between the individual and the state. Without these associational and legislative changes, the anarchy of the economy would continue and society would remain anomic. However, despite these changes, the fundamental inequality between social classes would remain, because the system of inheritance guaranteed the unequal distribution of property in society across generations. This property system would continue to destabilize and delegitimize society, regardless of changes in the state and the professions. Durkheim's sense of justice was outraged by this inequality, because economic inequality prevented the development of compassion which he thought was the foundation of morality.

In retrospect, Gouldner's introduction to Durkheim's *Socialism* still provides us with one of the most accurate insights into the real nature and purpose of Durkheimian sociology. Gouldner argued correctly that one of the central issues in *Civic Morals* concerned inheritance and its moral consequences. Thus, Durkheim 'holds that it is the existence of social classes, characterized by significant economic inequalities, that makes it in principle impossible for "just" contracts to be negotiated' (Gouldner, 1962: 30). *Civic Morals* can thus be read as a treatise on the problem of justice in modern societies, and how the sense of injustice in relationship to the property system is a feature of their political instability. Durkheim's attempted answer to this problem was socialist in arguing that a new economic order – a corporative system – would be required to function as a replacement for the archaic order of the guild.

Durkheim's sociology of morals was not, therefore, a conservative theory of social order. It was a political response to the malaise which he saw in France in the second half of the nineteenth century, but it was also a socialist response to the negative impact of an anarchic economy on moral life. The capitalist economy had become differentiated from political and social life. In the absence of a system of moral regulation, capitalist economic relations would be regarded as illegitimate, because capitalist forms of inheritance and property relationships failed to reward merit and effort adequately. Durkheim did not look back with nostalgia to the medieval guild system, because he realized that the guild was no longer adequate to the task. The reform of an anomic society required a radical approach to political change and economic organization. Durkheim's analysis of the instabilities of a society based upon contract, his defence of the state as the basis of individual rights, and his ethical critique of inequality and inherited wealth have a clear relevance to the social and political problems of the late twentieth century. This relevance is one important reason for reading *Professional Ethics and Civic Morals*.

References

Abercrombie, N., Hill, S. and Turner, B.S. (1986) *Sovereign Individuals of Capitalism*. London: Allen & Unwin.

Alexander, J.C. (1984) *Theoretical Logic in Sociology, The Modern Reconstruction of Classical Thought, Talcott Parsons*. London: Routledge & Kegan Paul.

Alexander, J.C. (ed.) (1988) *Durkheimian Sociology: Cultural studies*. Cambridge: Cambridge University Press.

Atkinson, M. (1978) *Discovering Suicide*. London: Macmillan.

Black, A. (1984) *Guilds and Civil Society in European Political Thought from the Twelfth Century to the Present*. London: Methuen.

Bourdieu, P. and Passeron, J.-C. (1990) *Reproduction in Education, Society and Culture*. London: Sage.

Cobban, A. (1961) *A History of Modern France*. Harmondsworth: Penguin Books, 2 vols.

Collins, R. (1988) 'The Durkheimian tradition in conflict sociology', in J.C. Alexander (ed.), *Durkheimian Sociology*. Cambridge: Cambridge University Press. pp. 107–28.

Corrigan, P. and Sayer, D. (1985) *The Great Arch*. Oxford: Basil Blackwell.

Coulanges, F. de (1901) *The Ancient City*. Paris.

Durkheim, E. (1915a) *Qui a voulu la guerre?* Paris: Colin.

Durkheim, E. (1915b) *L'Allemagne au-dessus de tout*. Paris: Colin.

Durkheim, E. (1950) *Leçons de Sociologie, physique des moeurs et du droit*. Paris: Presses Universitaires de France.

Durkheim, E. (1951) *Suicide, A Study in Sociology*. New York: Free Press.

Durkheim, E. (1960) *The Division of Labor in Society*. New York: Free Press.

Durkheim, E. (1961) *The Elementary Forms of the Religious Life*. New York: Collier Books.

Durkheim, E. (1962) *Socialism*. New York: Collier Books.

Durkheim, E. (1964) *The Rules of Sociological Method*. New York: Free Press.

Durkheim, E. (1969) 'Individualism and the intellectuals', *Political Studies*, 17: 19–30.

Durkheim, E. (1977) *The Evolution of Educational Thought*. London and Boston: Routledge & Kegan Paul.

Durkheim, E. (1992) *Professional Ethics and Civic Morals*. London: Routledge.

Durkheim, E. and Mauss, M. (1963) *Primitive Classification*. London: Cohen & West.

Fenton, S. (1984) *Durkheim and Modern Sociology*. Cambridge: Cambridge University Press.

Feuer, L.S. (ed.) (1969) *Marx and Engels, Basic Writings on Politics and Philosophy*. London: Fontana.

Freud, S. (1930) *Civilization and its Discontents*. London: Hogarth Press.

Gane, M. (1988) *On Durkheim's Rules of Sociological Method*. London and New York: Routledge.

Giddens, A. (1965) 'The suicide problem in French sociology', *British Journal of Sociology*, 16: 3–18.

Giddens, A. (1966) 'A typology of suicide', *European Journal of Sociology*, 7: 276–95.

Giddens, A. (1978) *Durkheim*. London: Fontana.

Giddens, A. (ed.) (1986) *Durkheim on Politics and the State*. Cambridge: Polity.

Goode, W.J. (1951) *Religion among the Primitives*. Glencoe, IL: Free Press.

Gouldner, A.W. (1962) 'Introduction' to Emile Durkheim, *Socialism*. New York: Collier Books.

Green, S.J.D. (1989) 'Emile Durkheim on human talents and two traditions of social justice', *British Journal of Sociology*, 40: 97–117.

Lacroix, B. (1981) *Durkheim et le politique*. Montreal: Presses de l'Université de Montreal.

Lukes, S. (1973) *Emile Durkheim, His Life and Work, A Historical and Critical Study*. London: Allen Lane.

Macpherson, C.B. (1962) *The Political Theory of Possessive Individualism*. Oxford: Clarendon.

Marske, C.E. (1987) 'Durkheim's "cult of the individual" and the moral reconstitution of society', *Sociological Theory*, 5: 1–14.

Meštrović, S.G. (1991) *The Coming Fin de Siecle, An Application of Durkheim's Sociology to Modernity and Postmodernity.* London and New York: Routledge.

Miquel, P. (1968) *L'Affaire Dreyfus.* Paris: Presses Universitaires de France.

Nandan, Y. (ed.) (1980) *Emile Durkheim: Contributions to L'Année Sociologique,* New York: Free Press.

Needham, R. (1963) 'Introduction' to E. Durkheim and M. Mauss, *Primitive Classification.* London: Cohen & West.

Nisbet, R. (ed.) (1965) *Emile Durkheim.* Englewood Cliffs, NJ: Prentice-Hall.

Nisbet, R. (1967) *The Sociological Tradition.* London: Heinemann Educational Books.

Orru, M. (1987) *Anomie: History and meanings.* London: Allen & Unwin.

Parsons, T. (1937) *The Structure of Social Action.* New York: McGraw-Hill.

Parsons, T. (1968) 'Cooley and the problem of internalization', in Albert J. Reiss Jr (ed.), *Cooley and Sociological Analysis.* Ann Arbor: University of Michigan Press.

Parsons, T. (1974) 'Introduction' to Emile Durkheim, *Sociology and Philosophy.* New York: Free Press.

Parsons, T. (1981) 'Revisiting the classics throughout a long career', in Buford Rhea (ed.), *The Future of the Sociological Classics.* London: Allen & Unwin. pp. 183–94.

Parsons, T. (1991) *The Social System.* London: Routledge.

Pearce, F. (1989) *The Radical Durkheim.* London: Unwin Hyman.

Pickering, W.S.F. (1975) *Durkheim on Religion: A selection of readings with bibliographies.* London: Routledge & Kegan Paul.

Pickering, W.S.F. (ed.) (1979) *Durkheim, Essays on Morals and Education.* London: Routledge.

Robertson, R. (1970) *The Sociological Interpretation of Religion.* Oxford: Basil Blackwell.

Robertson, R. and Turner, B.S. (1989) 'Talcott Parsons and modern social theory: an appreciation', *Theory, Culture & Society,* 6: 539–58.

Scharf, B.R. (1970) 'Durkheimian and Freudian theories of religion: the case for Judaism', *British Journal of Sociology,* 21: 151–63.

Seger, I. (1957) *Durkheim and his Critics on the Sociology of Religion.* Columbia University, Monograph Series, Bureau of Applied Social Research.

Sirianni, C.J. (1984) 'Justice and the division of labour: a reconsideration', *Sociological Review,* 32: 449–70.

Smith, W.R. (1889) *Lectures on the Religion of the Semites.* Edinburgh.

Stauth, G. and Turner, B.S. (1988) *Nietzsche's Dance, Resentment, Reciprocity and Resistance in Social Life.* Oxford: Basil Blackwell.

Taylor, K. (1975) *Henri Saint-Simon 1760–1825, Selected Writings on Science Industry and Social Organisation.* London: Croom Helm.

Tiryakian, E.A. (1978) 'Emile Durkheim', in Tom Bottomore and Robert Nisbet (eds), *A History of Sociological Analysis.* London: Heinemann. pp. 237–86.

Tönnies, F. (1957) *Community and Association.* Michigan: Michigan State University.

Turner, B.S. (1990) 'The two faces of sociology: global or national', *Theory, Culture & Society,* 7: 343–58.

Turner, B.S. (1991) *Religion and Social Theory.* London: Sage.

Wach, J. (1944) *Sociology of Religion.* Chicago and London: University of Chicago Press.

Waldron, J. (ed.) (1987) *Nonsense upon Stilts, Bentham, Burke and Marx on the Rights of Man.* London and New York: Methuen.

Wallwork, E. (1972) *Durkheim, Morality and Milieu.* Cambridge, MA: Harvard University Press.

Wearne, B.C. (1989) *The Theory and Scholarship of Talcott Parsons.* Cambridge: Cambridge University Press.

CHAPTER 6

KARL MANNHEIM ON IDEOLOGY AND UTOPIA

Introduction: Karl Mannheim (1893–1947)

Although Mannheim helped to create the sociology of knowledge as a special branch of sociology, wrote a recognized classic on conservatism (Mannheim, 1986) and forged the modern link between planning and sociology, he has never enjoyed a secure reputation as a classical sociologist. In addition to his major work on ideology (Mannheim, 1936), he also wrote a number of major articles on central issues in sociology such as generations (Mannheim, 1952). Mannheim also did much to establish the study of the 'free-floating intellectuals' as a topic of modern sociology (Mannheim, 1986), but he has not been accorded the same intellectual status as his contemporaries – for example Max Weber and Georg Simmel.

The explanation for this relative neglect cannot be found in the obscurity of his publications or in the inaccessible presentation of his ideas in a tortuous style. Mannheim's major publications have been translated into English and, unlike many Jewish intellectual refugees from national socialism, Mannheim was able to secure an academic position at a key institution. Unlike other European exiles such as Norbert Elias (Goudsblom, 1988), Mannheim commanded considerable institutional influence over British sociology. With the support of Morris Ginsberg, the Martin White Professor of Sociology, Mannheim became a lecturer at the London School of Economics from 1933 until 1941, when he transferred to the Institute of Education at the University of London, eventually becoming Professor of Education in 1946. Mannheim was also the founding editor of a prestigious series with Routledge & Kegan Paul, namely the International Library of Sociology and Social Reconstruction, which did much to disseminate sociological ideas in British institutions of higher education. His untimely death in 1947 cut short a flourishing academic career, but it does not fully explain Mannheim's marginality as a 'founding father' of sociology.

Various explanations might be offered for this ambiguity in the history of the reception of Mannheim into the classical pantheon of the founding figures. One feature of Mannheim's work, which is also relevant in understanding *Ideology and Utopia*, is his penchant for the essay form. Mannheim tended not to write monograph-length pieces, and most of the books, which are now available in English, are in fact collections of discrete essays. One consequence is that his work is often repetitious and underdeveloped in terms of systematic presentation. Another ironic issue is that many of the characteristics which Mannheim admired in British life – pragmatism and liberalism – do not favour the emergence of an intelligentsia; Mannheim's assimilation into British culture may paradoxically have precluded his reception globally as a major modern intellectual. Finally, Mannheim, like Weber, left no school of disciplines behind him, because his sociology did not point to any single set of remedies for social ills. As Ernst Manheim in an obituary in the *American Journal of Sociology* noted, the complexity and difficulties of his work meant that 'no recipe is at hand to guide his disciples in continuing his work' (Manheim, 1947: 473).

In this chapter on Mannheim's study of ideology, I want to present various interpretations of Mannheim's work in order to locate *Ideology and Utopia* within the sociological map. A number of substantive aspects of his sociology – ideology, conservatism, democracy and intellectuals – are examined. The principal aim of this commentary is to establish the enduring relevance of Mannheim's views on Utopia, particularly in the context of the political turmoil in eastern Europe, and especially in Mannheim's native Hungary, at the time of writing this essay. This observation also provides the pretext for returning to an issue which dominated Mannheim's own intellectual interests: what *is* the role of the intellectual in modern society?

Mannheim's Life and Work

Mannheim was born in Budapest into a Jewish family; his mother Rosa Eylenburg was German and his father Gustav Mannheim was Hungarian. On graduating from a Budapest high school, he undertook university studies in 1912 at the universities of Budapest and Berlin, where he met Georg Simmel. He then followed further courses at Freiburg, Heidelberg and Paris. On returning to Budapest, Mannheim formed an association in 1915 with a group of intellectuals around Georg Lukács, which created the Free School for the Humanities in 1917. Mannheim was awarded a degree of philosophy in 1918 for his work on epistemology.

In the post-war crisis, a republic was formed under Count Mihaly Karolyi in October 1918, but this government also fell in 1919 to be replaced by a Hungarian Soviet Republic under the leadership of Bela Kun. In this revolutionary climate, Lukács and many of his followers joined the Communist Party and the new government. Mannheim, along with many lecturers from the Free School for the Humanities, taught at the reorganized University of Budapest. However, Béla Kun's Republican government was under attack from the bourgeoisie and the old landed aristocracy, but it also failed to win adequate support among the peasants and workers. After unsuccessful military activities against the Rumanians and Czechs, Béla Kun and his supporters fled to Vienna, the Rumanians occupied Budapest and eventually a counter-revolutionary army, led by Admiral Miklos Horthy de Nagybanya, reoccupied the capital, unleashing the White Terror. Lukács, Mannheim and many other, typically Jewish, intellectuals became refugees.

Mannheim fled to Heidelberg in 1920. Germany was also in a state of post-war revolutionary turmoil. In Heidelberg, Mannheim enjoyed some support from Alfred Weber, the brother of Max Weber, who had died in Munich in June 1920. Mannheim survived as a private scholar and published his dissertation on *Die Strukturanalyse der Erkenntnistheorie* in 1922, which was translated as 'Structural analysis of epistemology' in *Essays on Sociology and Social Psychology* in 1953.

It was in Germany that Mannheim began to write on a variety of specifically sociological topics, which included 'Das Problem einer Soziologie des Wissens' in 1925, 'Das konservative Denken' in 1927, his lecture on competition ('Die Bedeuteung der Konkurrens im Gebiete des Geistigen') at the conference of German sociologists at Zurich in 1928, and *Ideologie und Utopie* in 1929. These innovative developments around debates on epistemology, knowledge and ideology, which also involved writers like Max Weber, Max Scheler, Georg Simmel and Georg Lukács, were eventually to establish Mannheim as a major founder of the sociology of knowledge.

In 1926 Mannheim completed his habilitation, which qualified him to teach in a university. Working in the philosophy faculty at Heidelberg, he was apparently a popular teacher with considerable support within the student body. It was Mannheim's custom to do his intellectual work in a café with his postgraduate students and assistants such as Hans Gerth and Norbert Elias. In 1929 he moved to Frankfurt as a professor of sociology and economics. His growing eminence in Germany was, however, over-shadowed by the growth of German nationalism, anti-Semitism, and fascist influences inside the universities in the late 1920s. Hitler's chancellorship in 1933 marked the final collapse of democratic politics in Germany. In 1933, while he was on a lecture tour of the Netherlands, Mannheim received an offer to join the London School of Economics and he entered his second migration as a political refugee. This intellectual migration influenced his own views on the role of the 'free-floating intellectual', and one of his last published pieces was a reflection on 'the function of the refugee'.

In Britain, Mannheim's interests in epistemology and knowledge were eventually overtaken by the problems of post-war reconstruction, planning and democracy which are reflected in a range of articles, many of which were published subsequently as *Man and Society in an Age of Reconstruction* (1940), *Diagnosis of Our Time* (1943), *Freedom, Power and Democratic Planning* (1951) and (with W.A.C. Steward) *An Introduction to the Sociology of Education* (1962). These publications indicate Mannheim's increasing involvement in the problems of citizenship in post-war reconstruction and reformism, and his institutional location in the University of London. Indeed, Mannheim's sociology has been seen as 'the search for a democratic solution to the problem of achieving consensus in a mass society' (Wirth, 1947: 357). After his death, many of his articles were translated and edited as *Essays on the Sociology of Knowledge* (1952), *Essays on Sociology and Social*

Psychology (1953), *Essays on the Sociology of Culture* (1956) and *Structures of Thinking* (1982). Finally, a number of major interpretations of Mannheim have been published, which indicate a growing international appreciation of Mannheim's standing as a major twentieth-century social theorist. These publications include Gunter W. Remmling (1975) *The Sociology of Karl Mannheim*, A.P. Simonds (1978) *Karl Mannheim's Sociology of Knowledge*, David Kettler, Volker Meja and Nico Stehr (1984) *Karl Mannheim*, and Colin Loader (1985) *The Intellectual Development of Karl Mannheim*.

Interpreting Mannheim

Periodization

Various interpretations have been offered for the development and discontinuities of Mannheim's work. Several writers have suggested chronological frameworks which present a developmental view of Mannheim's *oeuvre*. For example, Remmling (1975: 9) divides Mannheim's development into four phases. In the first period (1918–32), he was primarily concerned with philosophical questions and with the sociology of knowledge. His major publication in that period was the German edition of *Ideology and Utopia* in 1929. In the second phase (1933–8), Mannheim turned to questions of planning, partly as a consequence of his migration to England and as a response to the problems of change in industrial societies. His major work in that period was *Man and Society in an Age of Reconstruction*, which was first published in German in 1935. In his third phase (1939–44), Mannheim was involved increasingly in questions concerning values, religion and education during his association with the Moot, an influential group of clergy and academics, who were concerned with social reform from a Christian perspective. The group included Alec Vidler, J. Middleton Murry and T.S. Eliot. His major work in this phase of his life was *Diagnosis of Our Time* in 1943. Finally, between 1945 and 1947, he turned towards the problem of power and politics, publishing *Freedom, Power and Democratic Planning*, which appeared posthumously in 1951.

Colin Loader adopted a similar interpretive strategy, describing Mannheim's work as a 'dynamic totality' (Loader, 1985: 3). Loader divided Mannheim's development into three major sections and two transitional periods. Loader recognized the eclectic character of Mannheim's interests and his dependence on the essay form, but he suggested that Mannheim did achieve a synthesis in terms of his cultural–philosophical interests (1910–24). This focus was followed by a political synthesis in 1929. Finally, there was a synthesis around democratic planning between 1938 and 1947. These three major periods broadly correspond to the three political contexts within which Mannheim worked in Hungary, Germany and England.

A number of commentators have remained dissatisfied with these attempts to periodize Mannheim's work. Thus, N. Abercrombie and

B. Longhurst (1983) attempted to identify thematic and epistemological features in Mannheim's development. They note that there are generally speaking three existing orientations to Mannheim's work, especially his studies of knowledge and ideology. First, there are a group of writers who see Mannheim as an exponent of Marxist sociology. Thus, M. Mulkay (1979) argued that Mannheim had extended Marx's idea that the economic base determines the superstructure of beliefs to incorporate the notion that the 'existential base' included generations, sects and occupational groups. Mannheim had also developed the idea of 'utopia' alongside the Marxist emphasis on ideology.

By contrast, a second group of writers (Adorno, 1967; Jay, 1970; Kettler, 1971; Lukács, 1980) argued that Mannheim had departed from Marxism. Their objections could be summarized by the argument that Mannheim's sociology of knowledge undermined the critical force of the Marxist analysis of ideology, which aimed to unmask the bourgeois ideology of capitalism. By contrast, in Mannheim's sociology of knowledge Marxism was itself simply another collection of beliefs, which could be analysed by a sociologist rather like Mannheim had analysed *Conservatism* (Mannheim, 1986).

Finally, other writers have seen Mannheim as part of the hermeneutic tradition. Thus, A.P. Simonds (1978) and Zygmunt Bauman (1978) believed that Mannheim's approach to conservative thought, Utopias, romanticism and consciousness represented hermeneutic attempts to understand their meaning and significance as cultural objects.

By contrast, Abercrombie and Longhurst argued that it was in fact difficult to claim that a single issue characterized or dominated Mannheim's work, because his interests and approaches had changed over time. They noted three major changes. First, Mannheim was concerned with the legacy of idealism in cultural analysis. This problem was dominant for example in his doctoral dissertation. Second, there was a hermeneutic stage, which was illustrated by his essay 'On the Interpretation of Weltanschauung' in 1921–2. The third and major stage was, however, dominated by the sociology of knowledge. In his sociology of knowledge, Mannheim rejected Marx, developed a view of social class as simply one dimension of domination, and embraced an essentialist view of struggle and competition as a necessary feature of the human condition as such.

This interpretation of Abercrombie and Longhurst has itself been challenged by Susan Hekman (1986). While she found their emphasis on the inconsistencies in Mannheim useful, Hekman claimed that these inconsistencies were produced by a single issue which influenced all of Mannheim's work, namely the question of an appropriate epistemological basis for the social sciences. Thus, she claimed that 'these inconsistencies are a result of his attempt to make a radical break with Enlightenment and positivist epistemology' (Hekman, 1986: 14). She concludes by arguing that this unsuccessful and incomplete quest for an alternative epistemology to positivism brought Mannheim, in his lifelong concern to understand the relationship between thought and existence, increasingly towards a hermeneutic and antifoundationalist position. To understand this claim, we need to examine another interpretive dispute in approaches to Mannheim which surrounds the issue of relativism.

Relativism and Relationism

Strong versions of the sociology of knowledge, especially those which have been influenced by a Marxist theory of ideology, are often thought to face a number of classic dilemmas. If it is argued that beliefs are socially determined, then the theory of social determinism is equally determined. There appears to be no escape from the trap of relativism. However, perhaps it is possible to argue that some beliefs are less determined than others. Furthermore, perhaps some formal, logical or mathematical propositions (such as $2 \times 2 = 4$) are not determined at all. The problem here would be to find a satisfactory division between scientific and other beliefs in order to argue that scientific beliefs are not socially determined. There are further problems with this argument. It does appear to be possible that the development and acceptance of scientific propositions are indeed socially determined. One classic example is to be found in the research of Ludwig Fleck (1979) on the production and acceptance of ideas in the scientific community. There does not appear to be grounds for giving natural science such a privileged position.

In any case, it appears to be logically important to distinguish between three separate issues: (1) are beliefs socially determined? (2) are beliefs true or false? and (3) are beliefs rationally held? If, as sociologists, we want to argue that all beliefs (including scientific beliefs) are socially determined, this may have logically little bearing on whether a belief is true and whether it is consistently and rationally held (Abercrombie, 1980; MacIntyre, 1971). Furthermore, symbols may be neither rational nor irrational. However, the problem is that unless we can distinguish between true and false beliefs, between ideological and neutral beliefs, between reason and unreason, then there are no grounds for critical evaluation. How can we choose between good and evil?

It has always been important to Marxism as a political movement to distinguish between ideology and science. Marx and Engels, however, held a number of rather different positions on the nature of ideology. They discussed a range of concepts relating to this question: the fetishism of commodities, false consciousness, the determination of consciousness by social being, ideology as a camera obscura, the base and superstructure metaphor, and the dominant ideology thesis. One position, which became common in traditional Marxism, claimed that it is the particular way in which beliefs are held in relation to interests, which permits us to decide on the ideological character of beliefs. Ideological or false beliefs are socially determined by class interests. Thus, one can in principle uncover the ideological beliefs of certain social classes by showing that they have an interest in obscuring the nature of reality in such a way as to gain some political or social advantage. For example, it has sometimes been suggested that individualism (Macpherson, 1962) functions as an ideology because it obscures the objective structure of class inequality; poverty appears as the fault of recalcitrant and lazy individuals. The major division is in fact around the beliefs of the capitalist class and the proletariat. Because the capitalist has an interest in the status quo, and thus an interest in legitimizing inequality, bourgeois beliefs are ideological. Because the proletariat has no objective interest in maintaining the current situation, working-class beliefs are not determined by class interest.

There are a number of notorious problems with this position. It is not clear that social class is the only framework within which one can understand interests and ideology. As Mannheim suggested, why not include generations, occupational groups or religious organizations? Then there is a major political problem, which is how to explain the apparent lack of enthusiasm for Marxism on the part of the working class in the advanced capitalist societies. Most of the solutions (false consciousness, dual consciousness, or hegemony) have proved to be inadequate (Abercrombie, Hill and Turner, 1980; Mann, 1973). However, it does not necessarily follow that, because the working class of the industrial capitalist societies have neither overthrown capitalism by revolutionary struggle nor voted for political parties which are willing to transform capitalism in some radical direction, the working class are successfully incorporated by consumerism, by a dominant ideology or by their false consciousness. The explanation of the stability of the western capitalist democracies in fact requires a far more complex explanation, which would include, among other issues, an analysis of the role of citizenship in the stabilization of the political system via the creation of social solidarity. Finally, the analysis of specific belief systems through a Marxist sociology of ideology has not always proved to be especially convincing. For example, although individualism is often thought to contribute to the legitimacy of capitalism, it can also be shown that certain varieties of individualism were anti-capitalist (Abercrombie, Hill and Turner, 1980).

These problems, which are broadly the problems of a relativist sociology of knowledge, haunted Mannheim's attempt to develop a sociology of the relationship between thought and social existence, which would avoid both reductionism and relativism. Mannheim developed a hermeneutic approach to culture as an alternative to the economic reductionism of certain forms of crude Marxism and, at least in his early Hungarian period, he was influenced by forms of idealism. Mannheim sought to distinguish a reductionist from an imminent critique of ideas. He drew on the work of Wilhelm Dilthey to develop an internal understanding of belief, which would supplement the external interpretations of Marxist sociology.

However, when his *Ideology and Utopia* first appeared in its German edition, Mannheim was criticized by members of the Frankfurt School (the *Institut für Sozialforschung*) because he had watered down Marx's critical use of ideology to understand the political requirements of the class struggle. But Mannheim was also charged by more conservative critics with relativism and it was further claimed that his sociology of knowledge would actually undermine commitment to liberal values, which were a necessary alternative to fascism. Mannheim felt the need to defend himself against some of these charges. He used various intellectual strategies to resolve these problems, but it is generally agreed that his solutions were both inconsistent and ultimately inadequate.

These solutions included: the hermeneutic tradition of interpretation as an alternative to reductionism; the differentiation of relativism and relationalism; and the idea of the free-floating intelligentsia. Hermeneutic interpretations are based on a tradition of critical reading which attempts to argue that the cultural sciences require techniques and methods which are quite separate from those of the natural sciences. While this argument is perfectly plausible, Mannheim in *Ideology and Utopia* often appears to explain ideological and Utopian beliefs in class terms, namely in terms of a theory of interest which is compatible with a Marxist sociology of beliefs. Mannheim does not appear to have adopted hermeneutic approaches consistently.

The distinction between relativism and relationism was also unsatisfactory, partly because it was used inconsistently. Relativism challenges belief by suggesting (often implicitly) that once a belief has been explained in terms of its context, then it has been explained away. Relationalism, in recognizing that beliefs have a context, challenges the idea of an absolute truth, but accepts the importance of a variety of truths which are related to a social context. The relational thinker can never be certain that his or her convictions are valid; it is for future generations to make such judgements. The relational thinker could have convictions, especially convictions about change, but they could not have a Utopian conviction about future conditions, however, through sociological knowledge, they might avoid the existential limitations of ideology. This distinction is similar to Weber's views on the ethic of responsibility and the ethic of absolute ends in his lecture on science as a vocation. In a world of pluralistic values, it is often difficult to be committed to an absolute goal in a consistent fashion. A person of some integrity should nevertheless embrace a moral life which is based on responsibility for actions. Such a person might choose a calling in science or in politics (Lassman and Velody, 1989). We can never be fully sure that this calling has validity, but our options are limited in a world without the guidance of God. However, for Mannheim, it was the free-floating intellectuals who might most successfully institutionalize a relational as opposed to a reductionist consciousness.

The Intellectuals

In *Ideology and Utopia*, Mannheim adopts, as part of his major argument, a typically Marxist position. The dominant class embraces ideology which blinds it to the possibility of social change, especially social change of a revolutionary character. The subordinate class, by contrast, is motivated by a desire for change; its Utopian vision blinds it to the possibility of perpetual stability. One could crudely argue that Mannheim adopts a Marxist theoretical strategy. Dominant classes seek to incorporate subordinate classes by supporting ideologies which justify the status quo as a natural order of events, especially an immutable order of arrangements. Their interests push them towards ideology. By contrast, because subordinate groups have nothing to lose but their chains, they have a Utopian orientation towards a future dispensation. The beliefs of both classes are situationally determined and interest-driven. Their beliefs are consequently relative, not relational.

Mannheim's concern for the role of intellectuals is a 'natural' development of this line of thought. Intellectuals are not an integrated social class, and they are not associated with a single political party. They are not in this sense directly determined by their class position or by a single class interest. However, one could also argue that Mannheim's intellectual concern for the role of an intelligentsia reflected his own biographical situation as a refugee from Hungarian counter-revolutionary forces and later from German national socialism. Furthermore, one might also note that much of classical sociology and radical Marxism were produced by a floating Jewish intelligentsia – Marx, Simmel, Durkheim, the whole of the Frankfurt School and of course Mannheim himself. These Jewish intellectuals were, so to speak, doubly alienated from European society as migrant refugees and as Jews alienated from a Christian social order. Finally, we can read Mannheim's views on the free-floating intellectuals in the late 1920s as a plea for the continuation of open and free debate about social issues in the context of the penetration of fascism into the German university system (Bensman, Vidich and Gerth, 1982: 18).

However, in *Ideology and Utopia* the discussion of the 'free-floating intellectuals' appears as a rather neutral discussion of the class position of intellectuals in modern societies. Adopting Alfred Weber's expression 'the socially unattached intelligentsia' (*freischwebende Intelligenz*), Mannheim argued that the intellectuals were not a class in Marx's sense and furthermore they were not attached to or identified with a specific social class. In contemporary societies, 'intellectual activity is not carried on exclusively by a socially rigidly defined social class, such as a priesthood, but rather by a social stratum which is to a large degree unattached to any social class and which is recruited from an increasingly inclusive area of social life' (Mannheim, 1936: 139). This structural independence from the class system opens up the possibility that intellectuals will be socially free from the determination of class interests and will therefore have an insight into social processes which are denied to other classes.

Mannheim in this brief passage on intellectuals opened up a debate which has continued with much vigour. However, there are both analytical and empirical problems with his argument – in addition to the fact that Mannheim did not continue or persist with this argument in his subsequent work. One issue is that intellectuals were often not free floating with respect to contemporary political movements such as fascism. While many intellectuals left Germany, an equally large group of influential intellectuals co-operated with national socialism. Today there is still a debate about the relationship or connection between Martin Heidegger, to take but one major German thinker, and national socialism. At a more general level, the precise way in which intellectuals might be free or independent is problematic. For example, in many European universities the intellectual as an academic has been regarded as a civil servant, and thus the exact character of their free-floating status is questionable. Because intellectuals like artists and musicians typically require some form of patronage if they are to work outside the state sector, their independence from social processes and from social interests is relative. The existence of an intelligentsia, their social class composition and their autonomy from social constraint are historical and sociological questions. Only in rather exceptional circumstances would an intelligentsia be 'unattached' in Alfred Weber's terms. It is consequently difficult from within a British tradition to understand Mannheim's views on the specific problems of German intellectuals. To understand the German context, we have to keep in mind the gradual erosion of the traditional educated strata of the middle class (the *Bildungsbürgertum*) and the transformation of the German professorate with the modernization of the German university system towards the end of the century (Ringer, 1969). Some aspects of this issue were analysed in Mannheim's *Conservatism*.

Although Mannheim's various attempts to resolve the difficulties which were raised by Marxist reductionism were ultimately inadequate or unsatisfactory, he did ask a range of questions which continue to dominate the sociology of knowledge generally and the sociology of intellectual life in particular (Abercrombie, Hill and Turner, 1986). While Mannheim sought to understand the social conditions which would make intellectuals autonomous in terms of their relationship to social class and political parties, the real issue is more specifically the organizational conditions under which intellectual life is conducted. Because intellectuals have typically existed as academics, the question of their independence is a more particular one, namely how will universities be funded and how will the tenure of academics be secured. In the modern period, the threat to intellectual life comes partly from threats to the ongoing funding of higher education and the conditions under which students have access to education. For example, the threat to the financial independence of universities in Britain during the global economic recession of the 1980s has given a new urgency to the problems of securing the independence and autonomy of intellectual life. This debate about the possible end of the intellectual as a recognized public figure (Bauman, 1987) has taken place in the context of new allegations about the involvement of major intellectual figures like Martin Heidegger and Paul de Man in fascist politics.

In short, Mannheim's concerns about intellectual integrity, the defence of values and the nihilist implications of relativism have retained their relevance and urgency. While some form of relativism appears to be an inescapable consequence of the sociology of knowledge, it is necessary to find alternatives to relativism if moral debate is to be possible. If intellectual life as critical culture is to survive, there must be some conditions for intellectual freedom; specifically intellectuals must enjoy a certain detachment from class and party. To understand these concerns more fully, we need now to turn to a discussion of the nature of Mannheim's analysis of ideology and Utopia.

Ideology and Utopia

Ideology and Utopia is the work on which Mannheim's reputation to date has largely rested. The German edition of 1929 consisted of two more or less independent essays and an introduction, which now form the three middle sections of the English version of 1936. The German edition thus contained part two ('Ideology and Utopia'), part three ('The Prospects of Scientific Politics'), and part four ('The Utopian Mentality'). In the English edition, part one ('Preliminary Approach to the Problem') was written for an English audience, whom Mannheim assumed would be unfamiliar with many issues which German academics would take for granted. Part five ('The Sociology of Knowledge') was originally an article ('Wissensoziologie') in Alfred Vierkandt's handbook of sociology (*Handwörterbuch der Soziologie* 1931).

These details are not trivial, because the English version 'has a character quite different from the original' (Wolf, 1971: lxi). In terms of style, whereas the German text is vigorous, passionate and committed, the English edition reads as a scholarly and measured commentary on the issues facing the sociology of knowledge. Reading the English version, it would be difficult to understand the political and moral dispute which arose from the German publication. Whereas the English version has been received as a treatise on the sociology of knowledge, the German version is a tract on the politics of certain types of mentality. While Mannheim became known for his theory of ideology, the German edition was equally a study of Utopian thought. Thus, the German study 'was a call to action, an attempt to involve intellectuals in the political process' (Loader, 1985: 95).

Partly as a consequence of these problems of translation and partly as a consequence of seeing *Ideology and Utopia* as a sociological answer to Georg Lukács's *History and Class Consciousness* (1971) which had appeared in German in 1923, commentaries on Mannheim have failed to give sufficient attention to the concept of Utopia in Mannheim's thought. For Mannheim, Utopia is the will for change; as such, Utopian thought is the major force of historical change. Utopian aspirations are associated with the quest for ecstacy, that is to transcend, and if necessary to transgress, existing social roles. The Utopian desire is to stand outside ourselves. In this light, Mannheim's discussion is parallel to Weber's contrast in his sociology of religion between the charismatic challenge to existing authorities and the traditional legitimation of social life as it is (Weber, 1965). Like Weber, Mannheim argues that modern history starts with the orgiastic chiliasm of the Anabaptists and modern politics starts when a Utopian mentality associated with a lower strata brings about the participation of a whole society in the quest for total change. The Utopian mentality of the Protestant revolution has subsequently influenced the whole of western history.

This definition of Utopia provides one method of defining ideology in negative terms, as the absence of a positive Utopia. Ideology thus belongs to the routinization of the social world, against which the Utopian movement is always an 'irrational' threat. In opposition to spiritual chiliasm, there developed an alternative Utopia which Mannheim described as the conservative Utopian mentality. However, while the ecstatic-chiliastic element tends to accompany all forms of revolutionary struggle, Mannheim noted a variety of modern, secular Utopian dreams for progress which have assumed a more rational and intellectual direction, for example the liberal-humanism of the bourgeois class in its struggle against the remnants of feudalism. The proletarian consciousness of industrial capitalism is also a descendant of the chiliastic experience of opposition, and has its location in the industrial working class. Just as the liberal Utopia was an attack on conservative and religious Utopias, so the socialist Utopia radicalized the liberal version of liberty and equality, and then attacked the bourgeois Utopia of personal freedom as an ideology, masking particularistic and cynical interests.

Again following Weber, Mannheim saw the emergence of a disciplined political party and an organized leadership as a 'routinization of charisma', that is organized socialism has to turn against its ecstatic-orgiastic origins in order to impose discipline. Within the sociology of religion, Ernst Troeltsch, at one time a close friend of Weber, had described this routinization in terms of a transition from a sect to a church in his *The Social Teaching of the Christian Churches* (1960), which was published in Germany in 1911. The oscillation between ideology and Utopia is a movement between charismatic leadership and administration, between the ecstatic experiences of the sect and the ordered ritual of the Church, and between the divine and the secular.

To see *Ideology and Utopia* in this framework (as a study of revolutionary politics rather than an academic treatise on epistemological problems in the sociology of knowledge) permits us to understand certain continuities in Mannheim's problematic. If Utopia is the driving force of history, where do intellectuals stand in relation to ecstacy? Mannheim outlined a number of options for intellectuals in terms of the choice between its social and its intellectual interests. For the radical socialist intellectual, there is no such tension or conflict, because intellectual and existential concerns are merged. Happily, their Utopian aspirations find an obvious and easy outlet. Alternatively, intellectuals might simply drop their ecstatic Utopian drives and settle into mediocrity. A third group might embrace nostalgia, thereby avoiding any engagement with the problems of modernity (Stauth and Turner, 1988). Another group will adopt a form of mystical withdrawal into a subjectivist or contemplative orientation. These orientations to the world in terms of Utopia closely resemble Weber's analysis of the tension within a Christian rejection of worldly values through the major alternatives of inner-directed and other-directed asceticism and mysticism. It was in terms of these tensions between the sacred and the profane that Weber (1965) conceptualized the direction of western modernity via religious orientations.

While these options all have their negative aspects, Mannheim was primarily concerned to assert the historical and existential importance of Utopia for the 'health' of society and the individual. He can contemplate the disappearance of ideology without difficulty, but the disappearance of Utopia 'would mean that human nature and human development would take on a totally new character. The disappearance of utopia brings about a static state of affairs in which man himself becomes no more than a thing' (Mannheim, 1936: 236). Without Utopian hope, human beings become alienated from human nature; they become thing-like. Without ideals, human beings are then subordinated to their animal impulses.

Thus, the concept of Utopia in Mannheim's German period was more than merely a component of a sociology of ideological and Utopian thought. Without Utopia, humanity would lose its will to create history, sinking into either self-pity or complacency. The conclusion of the German edition of *Ideology and Utopia* therefore contained an important moral message: without ideology and Utopia, human beings would abandon their 'reality transcending principle'. They would, to employ the words of Nietzsche's equally powerful view of Man as an historical animal, once more sink back into the herd. In this respect, the capacity for Utopian aspirations is a spiritual capacity. This moral challenge in Mannheim's analysis of Utopia, furthermore, carries with it a clear instruction to intellectuals: they have a responsibility to defend ideals against two corrupting forces: relativism and complacency engendered by the matter-of-factness of everyday relations.

Conclusion: The Civilizing Process

The implication of this chapter is that Max Weber and Alfred Weber played a major part in Mannheim's sociological development. Max Weber contributed significantly to Mannheim's views on sociological method and social structure. Weber's notion of the ethic of responsibility (embrace the tasks of politics and science within the limited horizon of values available!) had an importance for Mannheim's views on the seriousness of the sociological calling. We have seen that Alfred Weber's idea of the socially 'unattached intelligentsia' was equally significant. However, in the various secondary works written about Mannheim, perhaps insufficient weight has been given to Alfred Weber's cultural sociology in shaping Mannheim's analysis of Utopia and ideology. Furthermore, if we approach Utopia as a moral principle of a civilized society, then we should take more notice of Alfred Weber's contrast between social processes, civilizational process and cultural movements (A. Weber, 1920–1) as a framework for grasping the importance of Utopian movements.

As Germany moved rapidly towards an industrial and urban capitalist system, the cultural values which lay at the basis of the German notion of a 'cultured person' appeared to be fundamentally challenged. As we have seen, German values were organized around the idea of a *Bildungskultur* (a learned culture in which the personality is shaped by ideals); this concept was also linked to notions of restraint, individuality and sensibility. It was this culture which was challenged by industrialization. It was also challenged by new ideas of democracy and secularity. Mannheim's *Ideology and Utopia* appeared to conservative writers like Ernst Robert Curtius (1929) as a relativizing attack on established values .

In response to these social changes, German sociology developed a range of concepts and methods by which to understand these processes. Ferdinand Tönnies's conceptual distinction between *gemeinschaft* and *gesellschaft* was one of the most influential dichotomies in early sociology (Tönnies, 1955). The other contrast was between 'culture' and 'civilization', which Alfred Weber treated as processes or movements (*Kulturbewegung* and *Zivilisationsprozess*). In English, both 'culture' and 'civilization' indicate positive evaluations of persons or institutions; both are worth defending. However, in Germany in the late nineteenth century, these concepts represented opposite and contrasted processes. While 'Kultur' was positive and moral, 'Zivilisation' was the negative consequence of industrial modernization, secularization and the dominance of life-styles which resulted from capitalist relations of production. Civilization in this German context was thus negative modernization, or the corruption of traditional standards of excellence. The idea of a civilizational process (in the English sense of 'to civilize') was subsequently developed into a major theory of social change by Mannheim's Frankfurt assistant Norbert Elias (Mennel, 1989) in his two volume *The Civilizing Process* (Elias, 1978–82).

It is against this debate that we have to understand Weber and Mannheim's concern for the social role of the free-floating or unattached intelligentsia, because it was this group which might best respond to these civilizational changes without either persisting with merely conservative elitism or embracing a partisan socialism. The free-floating intelligentsia would require a vision of Utopia in order to guide the social forces which had been released by capitalist civilization. The traditional concept of *Bildung* (cultured education or learning) was typically elitist. The appropriation of *Bildung* required extensive training, self-regulation and restraint; it is difficult to imagine a democratization of this type of education. Mannheim eventually broke with Alfred Weber over the issue of culture, partly because Mannheim was moving towards a political interest in social change via planning and democracy. Mannheim, in rejecting both conservative and socialist responses to the *Zivilisationsprozess*, moved towards a version of the welfare state in which education would become available on an egalitarian basis. He also moved away from a German conception of personality within the *Bildungskultur* paradigm to embrace an American psychology of human development from the work of William James, W.I. Thomas and G.H. Mead in his *An Introduction to the Sociology of Education*.

In his later works on planning and reconstruction in a democracy, Mannheim was increasingly interested in how religious values might continue to be important and influential in the secular planning process, but the view of Utopia as both a challenge to established ways and as an aspect of the regulation of impulses disappeared from his English publications on social reform. In *Diagnosis of Our Time*, he saw the plural values of democracy (as the legacy of antiquity, Christianity and classical liberalism) as an important antidote to the fanatical values of the Nazi movement, but he did not specifically appeal to a spiritual or apocalyptic utopia to mobilize citizens against the Nazi terror. In *Man and Society*, he talked about the regulation of animal impulses through self-rationalization, self-regulation and reflection (Mannheim, 1940: 55–7), but the strong moral language of the German version of *Ideology and Utopia* is subordinated to an academic discourse.

As Mannheim became increasingly committed to the idea of rational planning within a democratic polity as the most desirable pathway to social change, the vision of Utopia as a historical force was replaced by his commitment to modern education as a method of preparation for citizenship. A modern educational system could institutionalize and rationalize the Utopian impulse and contribute to the transformation of eschatology into instrumental rationality. In this process, which Weber had called the 'routinization of charisma', the intellectual was also gradually transformed from an interpreter of social change into a legislator (Bauman, 1987).

Mannheim's final position was in many respects unsatisfactory; he never fully grasped the impact of interest-bearing groups and classes on both the political and the planning process, or the economic constraints on planning in a democracy. In any case, his position was incomplete, given his untimely death. However, his religio-moral view of the intellectual as the carrier of social values was a compelling perspective on the tensions of the intellectual in a secular calling. Mannheim's commitment to this project is also morally impressive in the context of his life as a refugee. However, in order to understand Mannheim's challenge to intellectuals as an unattached stratum, we need to pay close attention to *Ideology and Utopia*, but not in its longer and more sober English version. It is through an examination of the sections which were the original German version that we can understand this text as a passionate study of the Utopian mentality as the lever of history and as a defence against the nihilism of an industrial civilization.

References

Abercrombie, N. (1980) *Class Structure and Knowledge.* Oxford: Basil Blackwell.
Abercrombie, N., Hill, S. and Turner, B.S. (1980) *The Dominant Ideology Thesis.* London: Allen & Unwin.
Abercrombie, N., Hill, S. and Turner, B.S. (1986) *Sovereign Individuals of Capitalism.* London: Allen & Unwin.
Abercrombie, N. and Longhurst, B. (1983) 'Interpreting Mannheim', *Theory, Culture & Society*, 2(1): 5–15.
Adorno, T.W. (1967) 'The sociology of knowledge and its consciousness', in *Prisms.* London: Spearman.
Bauman, Z. (1978) *Hermeneutics and Social Science.* London: Heinemann.
Bauman, Z. (1987) *Legislators and Interpreters: On modernity, postmodernity and intellectuals.* Cambridge: Polity Press.
Bensman, J., Vidich, A.J. and Gerth, N. (eds) (1982) *Politics, Character and Culture: Perspectives from Hans Gerth.* Westport, Connecticut: Greenwood Press.
Curtius, E.R. (1929) 'Soziologie — und ihre Grenzen', *Neue Schweizer Rundschau*, 22: 727–36.
Elias, N. (1978–82) *The Civilizing Process.* Oxford: Basil Blackwell, 2 vols.
Fleck, L. (1979) *Genesis and Development of a Scientific Fact.* Chicago: University of Chicago Press.
Goudsblom, J. (1988) 'The sociology of Norbert Elias: its resonance and significance', *Theory, Culture & Society*, 4(2–3): 323–37.
Hekman, S. (1986) 'Re-interpreting Mannheim', *Theory, Culture & Society*, 3(1): 137–42.
Jay, M. (1970) 'The Frankfurt School's critique of Karl Mannheim and the sociology of knowledge', *Telos*, 20: 72–89.
Kettler, D. (1971) 'Culture and revolutions: Lukács in the Hungarian revolution of 1918/19', *Telos*, 10: 35–92.
Kettler, D., Meja, V. and Stehr, N. (1984) *Karl Mannheim.* London and Chichester: Tavistock.
Lassman, P. and Velody, I. (eds) (1989) *Max Weber's 'Science as a Vocation'.* London: Unwin Hyman.
Loader, C. (1985) *The Intellectual Development of Karl Mannheim, Culture, Politics and Planning.* Cambridge: Cambridge University Press.
Lukács, G. (1971) *History and Class Consciousness.* London: Merlin.
Lukács, G. (1980) *The Destruction of Reason.* London: Merlin.
MacIntyre, A. (1971) *Against the Self-Images of the Age.* London: Duckworth.
Macpherson, C.B. (1962) *The Political Theory of Possessive Individualism.* Oxford: Oxford University Press.
Manheim, E. (1947) 'Karl Mannheim', *American Journal of Sociology*, 52: 471–4.
Mann, M. (1973) *Consciousness and Action among the Western Working Class.* London: Macmillan.
Mannheim, K. (1936) *Ideology and Utopia.* London: Routledge & Kegan Paul.

Mannheim, K. (1940) *Man and Society in an Age of Reconstruction: Studies in modern social structure*. London: Routledge & Kegan Paul.

Mannheim, K. (1943) *Diagnosis of Our Time: Wartime essays of a sociologist*. London: Kegan Paul Trench.

Mannheim, K. (1951) *Freedom, Power and Democratic Planning*. London: Routledge & Kegan Paul.

Mannheim, K. (1952) *Essays on the Sociology of Knowledge*. London: Routledge & Kegan Paul.

Mannheim, K. (1953) *Essays on Sociology and Social Psychology*. London: Routledge & Kegan Paul.

Mannheim, K. (1956) *Essays on the Sociology of Culture*. London: Routledge & Kegan Paul.

Mannheim, K. (1982) *Structures of Thinking*. London and New York: Routledge & Kegan Paul.

Mannheim, K. (1986) *Conservatism: A contribution to the sociology of knowledge*. London and New York: Routledge & Kegan Paul.

Mannheim, K. and Steward, W.A.C. (1962) *An Introduction to the Sociology of Education*. London and New York: Routledge & Kegan Paul.

Mennel, S. (1989) *Norbert Elias, Civilization and the Human Self-image*. Oxford: Basil Blackwell.

Mulkay, M. (1979) *Science and the Sociology of Knowledge*. London: Allen & Unwin.

Remmling, G.W. (1975) *The Sociology of Karl Mannheim*. London: Routledge & Kegan Paul.

Ringer, F. (1969) *The Decline of the German Mandarins*. Cambridge, Mass.: Harvard University Press.

Simonds, A.P. (1978) *Karl Mannheim's Sociology of Knowledge*. Oxford: Clarendon Press.

Stauth, G. and Turner, B.S. (1988) *Nietzsche's Dance, Resentment, Reciprocity and Resistance in Social Life*. Oxford: Basil Blackwell.

Tönnies, F. (1955) *Community and Association*. London: Routledge & Kegan Paul.

Troeltsch, E. (1960) *The Social Teaching of the Christian Churches*. New York: Harper & Row.

Vierkandt, S.A. (1931) *Handwörterbuch der Soziologie*. Stuttgart: F. Enke.

Weber, A. (1920-1) 'Prinzipielles zur Kultursoziologie: Gesellschaftsprozess, Zivilisationsprozess und Kulturbewegung', *Archiv für Sozialwissenschaft und Sozialpolitik*, 47: 1–49.

Weber, M. (1965) *The Sociology of Religion*. London: Methuen.

Wirth, L. (1947) 'Karl Mannheim', *American Sociological Review*, 12: 356–7.

Wolf, K.H. (1971) 'Introduction: a reading of Karl Mannheim', in K.H. Wolf (ed.), *From Karl Mannheim*. New York: Oxford University Press. pp. xi–cxxxiii.

CHAPTER 7

KARL MANNHEIM AND THE SOCIOLOGY OF CULTURE

Introduction

Karl Mannheim (1893–1947) is famous for his contribution to the development of the sociology of knowledge (Turner, 1991), but his contribution to the sociology of culture is unfortunately less well known or appreciated. These two aspects of Mannheim's sociology are clearly closely related. Consequently, these essays on culture can be suitably read alongside Mannheim's influential *Ideology and Utopia* (1991). The sociological study of culture can be considered as an extension of the sociology of knowledge, because it develops a sociological perspective on the symbolic field. Although Mannheim's essays on the sociology of culture were begun originally in Germany before his exile in 1933, they have retained their intellectual freshness and relevance to our times.

There are two reasons why it is still very profitable to study these essays. Firstly, Mannheim developed a method of studying systems of ideas which has continued to be revolutionary in challenging our assumptions about the relationship between knowledge and society. This revolutionary method was in fact the sociology of knowledge which, among other things, is concerned with the social determination of ideas. His approach raised, and continues to raise, fundamental problems about the truth and falsity of ideas which are, for example, produced by the social competition between groups (Abercrombie, 1980; Meja and Stehr, 1990; Merton, 1945).

Secondly, Mannheim's views remain compelling because he explored issues which have continued to dominate contemporary debates. Two such issues are central to *Essays on the Sociology of Culture* (1956). They can be expressed in the form of two questions: What is the relationship between the social organization of intellectuals and the ideas which they produce? Given the changing nature of equality in contemporary societies, can we expect a certain democratization of culture? In this chapter I shall address myself to these two profoundly significant questions. However, before considering the problems of the intelligentsia and democratization, we need to concern ourselves briefly with the concept of 'culture'.

Sociology of Culture

Although the concept of culture is central to both sociology and anthropology, there is little agreement about its meaning or significance. Although there have recently been a number of major contributions to the sociology of culture (Archer, 1988; Wuthnow, 1987), Raymond Williams's observation that 'culture is one of the two or three most complicated words in the English language' (Williams, 1976: 76) is still obviously accurate. As a broad definition, we can say that culture refers to the symbolic and learned components of human behaviour such as language, religion, custom and convention. As contrasted with instinct, culture is often thought to mark out the significant division between the human and the animal world. In sociology, much of the difficulty with culture is whether it is necessary to have a sociology of culture or cultural sociology; that is, does sociology attempt to study a special phenomenon called 'culture', or should we attempt to develop a special perspective on social relations which would be encapsulated by the notion of 'cultural sociology'?

While there are these general difficulties, there are quite specific problems in terms of how we are to approach Mannheim's 'sociology of culture' in order to understand it properly within its German sociology context. Mannheim's understanding of the issues is developed in Part One, where he attempts to outline a sociology of mind in response to the legacies of idealism and materialism in German philosophy. He defines the sociology of mind as 'the study of mental functions in the context of action' (Mannheim, 1956: 20). The sociology of the mind will provide 'the wider frame of reference for our earlier inquiries into the sociology of knowledge' (Mannheim, 1956: 24). There are a number of problems and difficulties with Mannheim's presentation of the sociology of mind.

To begin with a problem of translation, the German term *Geist*, which has been translated here as both 'mind' and 'culture', is in fact problematic because of its very richness. As the translator's footnote on page 171 acknowledges, *Geist* in Mannheim's essay *Demokratisierung des Geistes* has been translated as 'culture' rather than 'mind', because Mannheim was concerned to understand social and cultural processes rather than processes in thought. In the English translation of the *Essays*, 'mind' and 'culture' are therefore employed interchangeably (Mannheim, 1956: 81). The English reader of Mannheim should not be misled by thinking that Part One on the sociology of the mind is either a psychological treatise or a contribution to analytical philosophy. Mannheim explores the legacy of Hegel's phenomenology and philosophy of mind in order to develop his own distinctive approach to culture and knowledge from a sociological point of view.

Geist is thus a particularly important concept in the development of German philosophy and social science. In discussing the concept, Mannheim typically analyses *Geist* from the point of view of the sociology of knowledge. The concept was part of a religious tradition, and it was Martin Luther who contributed to its transmission into German idealism. The educated German middle classes (*Bildungsbürgertum*) embraced the concept in 'their accommodation to the bureaucratic state and spiritualized the idea of freedom to mean intellectual indeterminism' (Mannheim, 1956: 31). For Mannheim, the consequence was to set up a false polarity between ideas and matter, but it also placed a special emphasis on the idea of individual autonomy. In short, German idealism blocked the emergence of the sociology of knowledge which has attacked the basic assumptions of 'the immanence theory' (Mannheim, 1956: 32). The argument of Part One is thus an attempt to clear the ground of misconceptions in order for the sociology of knowledge and the sociology of culture to emerge as legitimate lines of enquiry without the burden of the false starts in immanence theory. Mannheim's intention was, for example, to avoid the reification and separation of the individual and society. He argues that 'it is misleading to speak of the social determination of the individual – as though the person and his society confronted one another as discrete entities' (Mannheim, 1956: 46). The problem of the relationship between the 'individual' and 'society' has continued to dominate the sociological imagination without any clear resolution (Elias, 1991), but Mannheim's approach remains influential because he attempted to avoid reification (treating individual and society as dichotomous, static, concrete phenomena) and he approached the issue from a resolutely historical perspective.

Mannheim's intention is relatively clear, but there are still problems about translation. In referring to the human mind, *Geist* is normally contrasted with *Körper*, the body, as in 'body and mind'; it can also be used in the sense of 'spirit', as in the spirit of the times (*der Geist der Zeit*), or *Phänomenologie des Geistes* (phenomenology of the spirit). In the famous study by Ludwig Klages, we see this contrast in the idea of 'the mind as the antagonist of the soul' (*der Geist als Widersacher der Seele*) (Klages, 1981). The intellectual or conscious life of people was seen to negate their spiritual or emotional life. It is also contrasted with *der Seele* or 'soul'. In German philosophy, it was common to structure thought around these three realities — mind, soul and body. By interpreting *Geist* as 'culture', we are implicitly accepting these divisions between culture, spirituality and nature.

These intellectual divisions which were inherited from theology and philosophy eventually came to shape the way in which sociology was thought of as a discipline existing within the *Geisteswissenschaften* or, broadly speaking, 'the cultural and humanistic sciences' (Weber, 1949: 145). Weber saw sociology as 'a science concerning itself with the interpretive understanding of social action' (Weber, 1978: 4). The cultural sciences were to have their own special methods of inquiry which are appropriate to the study of the meaning of social action. This formulation of the contrast between *Geisteswissenschaften* and *Naturwissenschaften*, between what we commonly refer to as the social sciences and the natural sciences, has remained problematic: are they opposed or merely different? Is causal explanation with which we are familiar in the experimental methodology of the natural sciences inappropriate in social science? Is social science interpretation a form of explanation? These issues were central to the

Wissenschaftslehre of Weber (Weber, 1949; 1975; 1977), who claimed that socio-cultural analysis of human conduct was, by comparison with causal analysis in the natural sciences, 'qualitatively quite different' (Weber, 1975: 125). If we accept natural science as the only legitimate model of scientific activity, then we ultimately reduce values and meaning to observable behaviour. For many German sociologists and philosophers, this intellectual 'surrender' was merely a further step in the colonization and subordination of the life of the mind to the impulses of matter. Much of German phenomenology was bitterly opposed to this travesty, as they regarded it (Scheler, 1980).

It is important to understand that Weber's theory of social science methodology was very influential in the development of Mannheim's sociology of culture. In formulating a sociology of mind (culture), Mannheim was trying to avoid what he regarded as the pitfalls of reductionism; he wanted to avoid the use of mechanistic metaphors of causal explanation (such as levers, switches, motors or tracks) when dealing sociologically with the symbolic life of social groups. These essays on culture were regarded by Mannheim, following an expression of Montaigne, as merely 'attempts' (Mannheim, 1956: 24) at a final solution of the very difficult and complex philosophical difficulties facing the sociology of the mind. Hence sociological theory is at an exploratory and tentative stage of development. The essay form was thus best suited to an attempt at a sociology of mind.

Mannheim did not believe that it was necessary or desirable to exclude causal and functional analysis in sociology by concentrating only on meaningful interpretation of events; despite their very obvious differences it is unnecessary to polarize natural science and social science. For Mannheim, 'We identify such things as clans, nations, castes or pressure groups not causally, but through their structural setting' (Mannheim, 1956: 77). Sociology requires causal, functional and interpretative approaches. In accepting Mannheim's approach, however, the English-speaking reader needs to keep in mind the fact that the concept of science in German (*Wissenschaft*) has a much broader range of meaning than in English, where in everyday parlance 'science' means the methods of the natural sciences, especially controlled experimentation. The gap between the German and English understanding of 'science' is perhaps best illustrated by Weber's essays on interpretation in the methodology of social science in *The Methodology of the Social Sciences* (Weber, 1949) and J.S. Mill's argument (Mill, 1952) in *A System of Logic* in 1843, where he asserted that the methods of physical science are the only proper scientific methods (Oakes, 1975: 22). Because *Wissenschaft* is derived from *Wissen* or 'knowledge', the German debate about the methodology of the social sciences (the famous *Methodenstreit*) has not been so hampered by a specifically narrow understanding of 'science' (Apel, 1984).

There is one further issue which we must take into account if we are to understand the context of Mannheim's sociology of culture, namely the contrast in German social science analysis between 'civilization' and 'culture'. While in English it would not be considered inappropriate to use these terms as equivalent descriptions, in both French and German they had a distinctive and often opposed meaning. In France, the verb 'to civilize' had been overshadowed by the noun 'civilization' as the civilized West came to take its global superiority over uncivilized societies for granted in the eighteenth and nineteenth centuries. Civilization was associated with progress. By contrast, in Germany, *Zivilisation* was regarded as useful, but superficial. Genuine values coincided with *Kultur*, not *Zivilisation*. It was only through inner development and refinement that a person (in fact an intellectual) could obtain genuine culture (Elias, 1978). Education and culture (*Bildung* and *Kultur*) are crucial for drawing a line between the educated/cultured classes or nations, and those lives which are dominated by utility, or civilization. This debate was an important context for Mannheim's development, since at Heidelberg, where Mannheim worked from 1920 to 1929, Alfred Weber, the brother of Max Weber, developed a sociology of the 'civilizing process' around the contrast between culture and civilization. Mannheim argues that a sociology of culture must go beyond an ethnography of customs, which he associated with the existing historical studies of *Sittengeschichte* (Mannheim, 1956: 52). As sociologists, we must understand civilization as a long process of constant struggle between social groups to assert their interpretations over cultural forces. Thus Mannheim was concerned to understand the process of civilization as the growth of new patterns of self-regulation — 'contemporary society has evolved a great variety of controls which take the place of coercive power as the main guarantee of super- and subordination' (Mannheim, 1956: 98). This process of self-regulation was part of the growth of the 'self-discovery of groups' in the context of the democratization of culture and the autonomy of intellectuals.

Mannheim and the Intelligentsia

At various points in his academic career, Mannheim made an attempt to develop a sociology of the intellectuals. In *Ideology and Utopia*, he discussed the idea of the 'free-floating intellectuals' (Mannheim, 1991: 137) who might be able to achieve an independent, autonomous view of society as a whole. In *Conservatism*, Mannheim (1986) considered how various forms of conservatism were related to different patterns of intellectual life and to different social circumstances. In *Essays on the Sociology of Culture*, Part Two is devoted to an elaborate analysis of the historical development of the intelligentsia. Again there are problems in English where an educated reader might shrink from the idea of an 'intelligentsia' as a meaningful concept. The concept refers originally to an organized social group of educated people, typically in a revolutionary context. The debate originated in the contexts of the French and Russian Revolutions. The empiricism of English culture, the absence of a revolutionary (socialist) tradition, and the dominance of Oxford and Cambridge as training grounds for gentlemen and theologians, have blocked the acceptance in English of the idea of an intelligentsia.

Why is there this preoccupation with the life of intellectuals in the sociology of Mannheim? There is a cynical answer. A self-interest in the life of the intellectual might be expected from that social group which is narcissistically concerned with its own historical evolution and autonomy, namely academic intellectuals (Bauman, 1987: 8). There are two more respectable answers. The first is that, because the sociology of knowledge is concerned with understanding the structure and history of *systems* of belief and knowledge rather than the particular forms of knowledge held by individuals, it will be concerned with understanding the social organization of that group in society (the intelligentsia) whose special social function is collectively to produce, analyse and explain systems of belief. They are crucial to our understanding of the production of knowledge. Secondly, because the problem of relativism is endemic to the sociology of knowledge, it is important to understand the social location of intellectuals.

The problem of relativism, relationalism and reductionism in Mannheim's thought has been widely discussed and debated (Abercrombie, 1980; Abercrombie and Longhurst, 1983; Kettler et al., 1984; Meja and Stehr, 1990). I cannot analyse these problems here in any detail. However, relativism tends to be self-defeating: if all thought is relative to certain existential conditions (such as social class), then this statement about relativism also suffers from relativism. Hence, Mannheim attempted to articulate various solutions to the problem, including the weaker notion of a relationship between society and thought. Part of the problem is a confusion between the social determination of ideas, their truth and falsity, and the rational or irrational ways in which ideas might be held. The emergence of a scientifically valid view of the planetary system was a socially determined process, but whether or not it is true that the earth moves around the sun has to be established by scientific processes, which are also obviously determined. There is no *necessary* relationship between determinism and falsity. Once we accept the idea that there are no systems of thought which are not socially determined, then some aspects of Mannheim's problem simply disappear. Mannheim appears to have assumed that a belief system which is socially determined cannot be valid; he was therefore concerned to understand how some groups of intellectuals might be free floating: that is, not entirely determined by social interests and social forces. This quest to discover a 'socially unattached intelligentsia' (*freischwebende Intelligenz*, in Alfred Weber's words) is a rather misguided search, on the grounds that all systems of belief and knowledge are socially determined. Of course, we must keep in mind the social context in which Mannheim's views about the relationship between knowledge, intellectuals and politics emerged, namely in the context of the rise of fascism. The activities of Nazi students in the University of Heidelberg are particularly important historically. In retrospect, it now appears that many major thinkers such as Martin Heidegger were seriously compromised by fascism (Wollin, 1991). Mannheim and his assistant Norbert Elias (Mennell, 1989: 16) were forced to flee Germany, both eventually seeking exile in Britain. We can therefore see that the political role and social autonomy of intellectuals was, for Mannheim, both an intellectual and a personal issue.

Mannheim treats the rise of the intelligentsia as a historical issue, as part of the growing self-awareness or self-discovery of social groups. Whereas in medieval times the individual could live relatively naïvely in the context of well-worn traditions, in the contemporary world, where social change is extremely rapid and all-pervasive, customs and traditions are constantly superseded. Mannheim wanted to understand both the historical evolution of this consciousness of change, and how this consciousness was itself shaped by the competition between groups; that is, how the 'history of the human mind expresses the consecutive tensions and reconciliations of groups' (Mannhein, 1956: 94). In particular, he was interested in the coming-to-consciousness of the proletariat in terms of class-consciousness. He briefly referred to the emergence of a feminist consciousness as women entered the labour force under competitive market circumstances, but his main preoccupation was of course with the rise of consciousness among the intellectuals.

There are certain peculiar features of the intellectuals as a social group which Mannheim thinks are particularly significant. Firstly, their non-manual labour typically requires some system of patronage, whereby intellectuals can avoid entering into the labour force in order to withdraw into a contemplative role. In western societies, the two major patrons of the intellectuals historically have been the Church and the State, but this very dependence on patronage does, of course, threaten that autonomy which is an essential feature of their intellectual independence. This paradox has continued to exercise the attention of sociologists (Bauman, 1987; Gouldner, 1982; Jacoby, 1987). Secondly, the intellectuals are an interstitial stratum existing between social classes and parties. Thirdly, because these interstitial intellectuals are also recruited from a broad range of social groups and classes, they are potentially able to see social reality in neutral terms or from many perspectives. They are in this specific sense a 'relatively uncommitted intelligentsia' (*relativ freischwebende Intelligenz*) (Mannheim, 1956: 106).

Having provided a general outline of the problem of the sociology of the intellectuals, Mannheim then developed a more detailed historical view of the rise of the intellectuals in Europe in terms of a division of labour between manual and non-manual activities, between trades and professions, the growth of the concept of the cultured gentleman, and the growth of certification. This history is concerned to trace the shifting contexts of intellectual life – the Court, the Church, the State and, in modern societies, the University – and the changing organization of intellectual activity. Mannheim identifies an issue which is crucial to our understanding of the contemporary intellectual. This is the erosion of the authority of the intelligentsia as a closed and privileged status group and their transformation into a social group which has, in some industrial societies, forced the intellectual into the market-place of credentialization in search of employment in universities or government agencies or the media. Mannheim argues that 'the group of the learned has lost its caste organization and its prerogative to formulate authoritative answers to the questions of the time' (Mannheim, 1956: 117). With secularization, intellectuals no longer have the normative authority to pronounce definitively on events. For some writers, the dominance of large, commercially funded, public universities has meant that intellectuals can find employment as academics, but at the cost of their intellectual independence (Jacoby, 1987).

The role of the modern intellectual presents a number of paradoxes. The loss of religious patronage has been partly replaced in the post-war period with the patronage of the modern university, the growth of which was, in part at least, an effect of the democratization of higher education, especially in societies such as the United States (Parsons and Platt, 1973). Critics of these developments have suggested that the intellectuals have now lost their 'free-floating' character because, as hired labour, they are forced to serve interests over which they have little control. Furthermore, the modern university is merely an educational factory producing low-grade certification of a middle-class sector of the labour force. This rationalization of higher education undermines genuine academic vocations in a context where the intellectual is simply alienated labour. The political role of the intellectual-as-academic has become increasingly problematic and uncertain, but the relationship of intellectuals to modern culture is equally difficult. Is the intellectual somebody who merely reproduces the 'cultural capital' of the dominant social groups, and is the role of the university to preserve the hierarchy of aesthetic standards? Is the structure of the intellectual field produced by the competition for academic dominance between social groups (Bourdieu, 1988)? The question of the possibility of a democratization of culture as a development which is necessarily related to the democratization of politics through the institution of modern citizenship is thus necessarily connected with issues in the social organization of intellectual life.

Culture and Democratization

In this section I want to explore a rather traditional question; namely, is it possible to anticipate some democratization of modern culture as a consequence of the enhancement of citizenship rights? Although this issue was much debated – as I want to show subsequently by writers not only such as Mannheim, but by Theodor Adorno and Talcott Parsons in classical sociology – in our period this conventional question has acquired a new dimension, namely the consequences of a (partial) postmodernization of culture. I shall not in this chapter attempt to explore all of the complexities of the idea of postmodernization (Turner, 1990). By the postmodernization of culture in this discussion, I shall simply mean an increasing fragmentation and differentiation of culture as a consequence of the pluralization of life-styles; the employment of irony, pastiche and montage as cultural styles; the erosion of traditional 'grand narratives' of legitimation; the celebration of the principles of difference and heterogeneity as normative guidelines in politics and morality; the globalization of postmodern culture with the emergence of global networks of communication through satellites; and the erosion of industrial society and its replacement by post-industrialism.

The cultural consequences of these changes are very profound. They bring into question the traditional division between high and low culture, because postmodernization mixes and conflates these two aspects of a national culture. As a result, the traditional authority of intellectuals and universities (as carriers and producers of high culture) is challenged (Baumann, 1987). Secondly, mass culture, which emerged after the Second World War with the mass availability of radio, television and motor cars, and with the creation of the means of mass consumption, has also been eroded by a growing diversification of patterns of consumption and life-style (Featherstone, 1991).

While these claims are clearly contentious, I believe they can be defended with both sociological argument and evidence, but in this presentation I shall have to take much of this debate for granted. However, I want to point out a number of important qualifications to this claim. Firstly, just as in the neo-Marxist language of development theory, sociologists noted the continuity of traditionalism and underdevelopment alongside development, so we may expect traditional and modernist culture to continue alongside postmodernism. These elements or dimensions will persist in an uneven balance. Furthermore, as a response to both postmodernization and globalization, we can anticipate a corresponding (and literally reactionary) fundamentalization of culture and society by social groups who want to oppose postmodern consumerism, irony and relativism. The second aspect of my argument is equally controversial. The great majority of theorists have taken the somewhat pessimistic position that a democratization of culture is not feasible, and furthermore that the commercialization of culture is in fact an inauthentication of culture. By contrast, I want to present an optimistic interpretation. Postmodernization is a process which may offer us both the dehierarchization of cultural systems (and hence a democratization of culture), while also permitting and indeed celebrating the differentiation of culture which is an inevitable outcome of the differentiation of social structure and life-style in postindustrial civilizations. As I have said elsewhere, we can summarize the ethic of postmodernism under the slogan 'Here's to heterogeneity!' (Turner, 1990: 12).

Citizenship

I want to link Mannheim's idea of cultural democratization with the sociology of citizenship which was developed by the English sociologist T.H. Marshall (1950). What are the implications of this for citizenship as the crucial element in the democratization of modern societies? Firstly, I do not believe that the nation-state is any longer the most appropriate or viable political context within which citizenship rights are 'housed'. If we think about the meaning and history of citizenship, then there have been, in Europe, a number of important evolutionary steps towards modern citizenship: the public space of the Greek polis as a debating chamber for rational citizens; the development of Christendom as a religio-political entity within which political membership came to depend on the sharing of a common faith; the rise of the autonomous European cities of the late medieval period; and the development of nationalism and the nation-state as the carrier of rights (Turner, 1986a).

At present, there are socio-political and cultural changes which are challenging the idea that the state is the instrument through which citizenship is expressed. For example, in Europe the growth of community-wide institutions such as the European parliament and the European court of justice means that the sovereignty of the state is increasingly limited. There is a growing cultural awareness of a 'European identity' which transforms nationalistic conceptions of political citizenship. More fundamentally, the processes of globalization undermine – especially in the most privileged social classes in society – the emotive and institutional commitment to citizenship within the nation-state. At the same time that the state is eroded in terms of its political sovereignty and cultural hegemony by globalization, localism as a response to such changes 'squeezes' the state from below. The state has to respond simultaneously to these global pressures which challenge its monopoly over emotive commitments, and to local, regional and ethnic challenges to its authority. In a more profound fashion, the traditional language of nation-state citizenship is confronted by the alternative discourse of human rights and humanity as the normatively superior paradigm of political loyalty. This idea is certainly not new. Emile Durkheim in *Professional Ethics and Civic Morals* (1957) argued that the moral system of the state would give way eventually to a cosmopolitan ethic of humanity.

By examining the postmodernization of culture and globalization of politics, I have been preparing the way for an argument which claims that much of the traditional literature on democracy and citizenship is now antiquated. Let us take the theory of Marshall (1950), who defined citizenship in terms of three levels of entitlement (legal, political and social) which were institutionalized in the law courts, parliament and welfare state. In Marshall's theory, citizenship counteracts the effects of the capitalist market by providing individuals with minimum guarantees to a civilized life. In a capitalist society, citizenship and class stand in a relationship of tension or contradiction. A number of critics have noted that Marshall did not extend his idea of citizenship to include economic citizenship; that is, economic democracy. I want to take a parallel position by suggesting that Marshall failed to consider the nature of cultural citizenship in modern societies. It is in this context of the absence of a notion of cultural citizenship that we can more adequately appreciate the importance of Mannheim's attempt to outline a theory of cultural democratization.

By 'citizenship', I mean that set of practices which constitute individuals as competent members of a community. I adopt this definition in order, as a sociologist, to avoid putting too much emphasis on juridical or political definitions of citizenship. It would be more conventional for example to define citizenship as a status within a polity which determines the nature of rights and obligations. I prefer a sociological definition which identifies (1) a bundle or ensemble of practices which are social, legal, political and cultural, (2) which constitutes rather than merely defines the citizenship, (3) which, over time, becomes institutionalized as normative social arrangements, and (4) which as a consequence determines membership of a community. I am thus trying to avoid the idea that citizenship is a narrow juridical status which defines the conditions of participation in a state. Within this perspective then, cultural citizenship is composed of those social practices which enable a citizen to participate fully and competently in the national culture. Educational institutions, especially universities, are thus crucial to cultural citizenship, because they are an essential aspect of the socialization of the child into this national system of values.

There are some obvious problems with the way in which I have attempted to reiterate Mannheim's notion of the 'democratization of culture'. In those societies which have a large aboriginal population, such as Australia, the expansion of national-cultural citizenship may in fact be a form of cultural colonialism; cultural citizenship involves the destruction or co-optation of indigenous or aboriginal cultures. In this case, there may be a contradiction between citizen rights and human rights. A similar argument may well apply to societies which are divided by class so that cultural citizenship involves the exclusion or marginalization of subordinate class cultures by the cultural élite which surrounds the state. Both objections in fact amount to throwing doubt on the idea of a 'national' culture because very few modern societies have a uniform, national culture. Multiculturalism is the fate of us all. Finally, there is the view that formal participation in the national culture may simply disguise major *de facto* forms of exclusion. In Britain, to take a possibly trivial example, regional and class differences in speech and vocabulary continue to function in everyday life as major markers of cultural inferiority and superiority, despite the efforts of the BBC to legitimize certain regional accents as acceptable forms of speech.

Talcott Parsons played an important role in developing this notion of cultural citizenship in his discussion of his 'educational revolution' of the twentieth century. Parsons, who was in any case influenced by Marshall in his study of the absence of citizenship for the black American, adopted the notion of citizenship as part of his general view of the process of modernization (Holton and Turner, 1986; Robertson and Turner, 1991). We can regard citizenship within a Parsonian paradigm as the institutionalization of the *Gesellschaft* side of the pattern variables. Citizenship is a secular principle of membership of society which emerges with social differentiation and the institutionalization of achievement-ascription as dominant values of modern capitalism. For Parsons, therefore, especially in *Societies: Evolutionary and comparative perspectives* (Parsons, 1966) and *The System of Modern Societies* (Parsons, 1971), the rise of a mass, comprehensive and national system of education, and especially the university, was a critical step in the evolution of modern societies. Indeed, Parsons wanted to talk about an 'educational revolution' which in his view was as significant historically as the industrial and French revolutions. A comprehensive education system was the necessary prerequisite for the education of citizens as active participants in society, and on those grounds Parsons compared the historical experience of the USA favourably against Europe, where educational opportunity had remained narrow as a consequence of its class basis.

Cultural Democratization

However, one of the strongest arguments in favour of the idea of cultural democratization is to be found in Part Three of Mannheim's *Essays*. Mannheim rather baldly starts his argument with the statement that 'a democratizing trend is our predestined fate, not only in politics, but also in intellectual and cultural life as a whole. Whether we like it or not, the trend is irreversible' (Mannheim, 1956: 171). Although Mannheim recognized the dangers of cultural democratization in terms of Nietzsche's critique of the levelling consequences of the political dominance of the 'herd' ('democracy levels everything, it ushers in the dominance of mediocrity and the mass'), he argues that this position is ultimately a superficial view of the sociological relationship between aristocratic and democratic cultures (Mannheim, 1956: 175).

Mannheim felt that the underlying principles of democracy (the ontological equality of human beings, the idea of individual autonomy and the principle of open recruitment to élite positions in society) had fundamentally shaped the nature of culture in the modern world. He claimed that cultural democratization had the following socio-cultural consequences: (1) it was associated with 'pedagogical optimism' in which the educational system assumes that all children are able to achieve the highest levels of cultural excellence; (2) it is sceptical of the monopolistic character of 'expert knowledge'; and (3) cultural democratization brings about what Mannheim called the 'de-distantiation' of culture: that is, the erosion of the distinction between high and low culture (Mannheim, 1956: 208).

These democratic ideals which assume the ontological plasticity of human beings conflict sharply with the aristocratic ideal of charismatic cultural authority whereby the cultured person is transformed by illumination or conversion rather than education. The aristocratic ideal requires distantiation and wants to create an 'élite culture'. It is assumed that their knowledge, cultural techniques, patterns of speech and leisure activities will be 'unshareable by the many' (Mannheim, 1956: 211). This élite is a genuine leisure class which cultivates 'finickiness and delicacy' to distinguish itself from the masses.

In terms of the historical evolution of the democratic ideal, Mannheim claimed that a strong democratic trend is discernible from 1370 in late medieval art which developed 'intimate realism', where everyday life activities were represented in a naturalistic style. The highly stylized and unrealistic attitude of early medievalism was no longer attractive to new urban groups. Later the Reformation challenged the hierarchical assumptions of Catholicism and produced another stage in the historical development of democratic cultural norms. Baroque culture in the age of absolutism was treated by Mannheim as a reversal of this trend; baroque culture was characterized by ecstasy 'in the form of an intensification of fervour beyond all measure, in a kind of overheated and sublimated eroticism' (Mannheim, 1956: 224). Baroque effervescence contrasts strongly with modern popular cultural forms. Interestingly, Mannheim treated photography as the most characteristic expression of modern democratization. Its principle is supremely that of de-distantiation. Photography 'marks the greatest closeness to all things without distinction. The snapshot is a form of pictorial representation that is most congenial to the modern mind with its interest in the unretouched and uncensored "moment"' (Mannheim, 1956: 226).

The democratic cultural ethic also has its impact on religion where the traditional conceptualization of an all-powerful patriarchal God is the epitome of distantiation. The democratic trend brings about an equalization of the relationship between men and gods. Thus Mannheim argued that

> The metaphysical aura which surrounds the things of the world in pantheism is dispersed in modern naturalism, positivism and pragmatism. As a result of this radical this-worldliness, the mind of man becomes perfectly congruent with 'reality'... We have to do here with a radically analytical and nominalistic outlook that leaves no room for the 'distantiation' and idealization of everything.

> (Mannheim, 1956: 229)

A Critique of Cultural Democratization

I have briefly identified in Marshall, Parsons and Mannheim a view of modernization which involves the idea, or is compatible with the idea, that cultural citizenship will require a democratization of culture, or, in

Mannheim's words, will involve the replacement of an aristocratic ethos by a democratic one. The two main arguments against the possibility of cultural democratization which I want to consider are firstly, the studies of modern society which show that cultural divisions between classes are illimitable and irreducible, and secondly, those traditions of social analysis which suggest that any democratization of culture in capitalism will in fact produce the inauthentication of culture by a process of trivialization. Thus, from a sociological perspective, these claims about democratization of culture in modern capitalism do not appear immediately persuasive. To take two widely contrasted positions, Veblen's notion of 'the leisure class' (Veblen, 1899) suggests that some form of the high culture/low culture division is likely to persist in a capitalist society where the lower class is characteristically referred to as a 'working class' or 'labouring class'. An upper class is likely to assume a leisure life-style as a mark of distinction from subordinate labouring classes; hence the typical division in the occupational hierarchy between the manual and non-manual sectors. It is through leisure that these social classes can gain an easy familiarity with a cultured way of life.

The second example would be that the sociology of education has shown that the competitive educational systems which were characteristic of the post-war period, far from bringing about a major equalization of social outcomes, tended merely to reproduce the existing class structure. Formal equality of opportunity in the educational field was an important feature of the extension of citizenship rights to the whole population. However, the continuity of cultural deprivation and cultural differences between social classes meant that actual social mobility through educational attainment was well below the level anticipated by post-war educational reforms. The result has been that the educational system has reproduced the culture of the dominant class (Bourdieu and Passeron, 1990).

Pierre Bourdieu has further elaborated this idea in his study of social distinction (Bourdieu, 1984), which we can interpret as a sociological critique of Kant's theory of aesthetics. Whereas Kant wanted to argue that the aesthetic judgement is individual, neutral, objective and disinterested, Bourdieu wants to demonstrate empirically that taste is social, structured and committed. Our taste for goods, both symbolic and material, is simultaneously a classification which classifies the classifier; as such, it cannot be neutral and disinterested because it is a consequence of class position. Lifestyle, cultural taste, and consumer preferences are related to particular divisions within the occupational structure of society, and especially in terms of educational attainment. With the decline of a rigid status order in society, there is constant competition between classes and class factions to secure dominance over the definition of cultural taste (Featherstone, 1991). These patterns of cultural distinction are so profound and pervasive that they also dictate how the body should be correctly developed and presented, because the body is also part of the symbolic capital of a class.

Because the flow of symbolic goods is so extensive in the modern market-place, there develops the possibility of endless interpretation and reinterpretation of new cultural products. To provide this service, a class of new cultural intermediaries emerges (especially in the media, advertising and fashion) to inform society on matters of distinction. These intermediaries transmit the distinctive life-style of the intellectuals and the leisure class to a wider social audience. These processes within the world of consumer goods therefore force upper, educated social classes to invest in new knowledge and new cultural goods. These dominant groups will turn to 'positional goods' (Leiss, 1983) which are prestigious because of an artificial scarcity of supply in order to reassert their distinctive cultural distinction.

What is the implication of these studies of class and culture for the Mannheimian argument that we have entered a period in which the democratization of culture is inevitable? It implies obviously that any process of cultural equalization or levelling will be met by a counter-process of distantiation and hierarchization. Within a competitive market of symbolic goods, some pattern of social distinction will be imposed upon the market by cultural intermediaries. Although governments may attempt to reform the educational system to provide equality of educational opportunity, there will always be inequality in social outcomes, because different social classes and social groups already possess different types and amounts of cultural capital which they inevitably transfer to their children. Furthermore, because, for Bourdieu, intellectuals play a very important role in defining standards of appropriate cultural production and consumption, intellectuals as a stratum of cultural intermediaries have a distinctive, if often contradictory, interest in maintaining a hierarchy of taste.

In this sense, Bourdieu's work has very pessimistic implications for cultural democratization, because it would rule out any possibility of the majority of the population participating freely and fully in the 'national' culture. According to Bourdieu's work, any national culture will always be overlaid and structured by a class system which requires cultural distantiation. There may be two criticisms of, or alternatives to, Bourdieu's analysis which we should consider. The first is taken from Zygmunt Bauman's book *Legislators and Interpreters* (1987) in which Bauman argues that one important feature of modern society is that the state no longer exercises direct hegemony and regulation over culture. A fissure has opened up between the polity and the national culture, with the result that the intellectuals no longer have effective authority over cultural symbols. They have lost a considerable amount of social and political power as a result. This separation of politics and culture, and the conversion of intellectuals from legislators into interpreters, is associated with the postmodernization of cultures, namely their fragmentation and pluralization. Perhaps, therefore, the cultural field is more fluid and uncertain than Bourdieu suggests, and as a consequence it may be much more difficult than he imagines for cultural élites to impose their authority over cultural capital.

A second modification of Bourdieu's argument which may be important is that his view of the working class and working-class culture is extremely passive. In my typology, his view of cultural citizenship for the working class is private and passive. They are merely the recipients of the cultural products of the market. In *Common Culture*, Paul Willis et al. (1990) present us with an alternative view of the working class as active users and creators of culture which is resistant to total cultural incorporation. Following the work of Michel de Certeau (1984), Willis shows how consumers or users of cultural objects constantly change and modify cultural products to their own local needs and requirements. In short, people are not merely passive recipients of cultural products, and 'reception theory' has suggested that consumers have varied and complex methods of cultural appropriation (Abercrombie, 1990; Morley, 1986). This argument may be an important corrective to the 'top-down' view of cultural capital which appears to dominate Bourdieu's view of the cultural market-place in capitalism.

I shall now turn to the rather different issue of the inauthentication of culture by commodification and the growth of mass cultures in the western liberal democracies. Mannheim's essays were in fact originally composed in the early 1930s shortly before the rise of National Socialism forced Mannheim to seek asylum in England. Mannheim's optimistic view of the potential for cultural democratization thus contrasts sharply with the view of the 'culture industry' which was advanced by Theodor Adorno, who has provided one of the most sustained and original critiques of consumer culture. We must remember of course that Adorno's aesthetic theory was set within the specific context of the employment of film by the national socialists to manipulate public opinion, and that his attack on the culture industry took place within a wider set of objections to the problems of instrumental rationality and rationalization (Adorno, 1991). Adorno rejected the false universalism of mass art and entertainment, which he regarded as merely a respite from labour. Mass culture imposes a uniformity of culture on society; cultural production follows the same logic as all forms of capitalist production; real pleasure is converted into an illusory promise.

Although Adorno's aim was to break down the division between high and low art in conservative aesthetics, and to provide a critique of the falsification of culture by commodification, Adorno's own position has been criticized as an élitist defence of high art, given, for example, Adorno's rejection of jazz music as part of the culture industry. Adorno's form of critical theory has also been attacked as a nostalgic defence of high modernity against the emergence of popular culture (Stauth and Turner, 1988). Critical theory's attack on mass culture often in practice appears to be a condemnation of the Americanization of western popular culture. Other critics have argued that Adorno and critical theory failed to identify the oppositional and critical elements of popular culture – a theme developed in the work of the Birmingham Centre for Contemporary Cultural Studies, for whom popular culture is pre-eminently low and oppositional

(Brantlinger, 1990). Another argument against Adorno is that we no longer live in a world of standardized mass fashion. Instead, the world of popular taste is highly fragmented and diverse, catering to specific and distinctive audiences. Although a number of writers have recently come to Adorno's defence – for example Fredric Jameson in *Signatures of the Visible* (1990) – it is interesting that Walter Benjamin's 'Art in an age of mechanical reproduction', which was one target of Adorno's critique, has had more influence on our understanding of mass and popular culture than Adorno's aesthetics.

Conclusion

I have identified a number of important critiques of the idea of a democratization of culture in modern societies; yet it appears to be necessary to defend Mannheim, because the alternative (namely, acceptance of a pessimistic view of inevitable hierarchization) would leave us with no normative programme for educational and cultural reform. Pessimism is not a particularly useful framework for social change. By contrast, Mannheim never entirely abandoned the idea of Utopian mentalities as a requirement for social reorganization. Mannheim's views on cultural democratization, which were originally developed in Germany in the late 1920s and early 1930s, may as a consequence be seen as foundations for his subsequent writing in England on the problems of rational reconstruction of a democratic society in the aftermath of war, and the importance of planning for progressive social change (Mannheim, 1950). It is partly for that reason that I believe it is appropriate to compare and contrast Mannheim (1893–1947) and Marshall (1873–1982) on the nature of citizenship in modern societies. Marshall, whose ideas on citizenship became important in the development of social policy in Britain, was Professor of Sociology and Head of the Social Science Department at the London School of Economics from 1946. Both sociologists had a commitment to the principles of citizenship as a basis for attempting to transform inequalities in a democratic context. The difference between them is, not only the greater scope of Mannheim's sociology, but Mannheim's commitment to a principle of Utopian imagination as a counterweight to pessimism.

Sociologists tend to write about inequality, not equality (Turner, 1986b: 15), and therefore a sociologist like Mannheim who has an interest in the democratization of culture is likely to find himself working against the grain. Elias's ideas about civilization in an epoch which appears predominantly uncivilized (in terms of total war) received an equally negative reception in mainstream sociology. On the specific issue of cultural democratization, one important conclusion must be that the processes of hierarchization and democratization occur simultaneously in the cultural sphere as social groups compete with each other for social dominance, but an emphasis on cultural inequality in mainstream sociology has often neglected important aspects of cultural democratization. Thus the democratizating implications of the motor car, tourism, the cinema and television, are often ignored in favour of pessimistic analyses of the culture industry, the inauthentication of cultural meaning and the endless simulations in media representation (Baudrillard, 1990). Unfortunately, this critique of the cultural industry often leads implicitly to both an élitist defence of high culture against democratization and a nostalgia for lost communalism and wholeness. Thus Mannheim's contrast between the aristocratic and the democratic ethic in cultural life provides an important sociological insight into many of the educational and political dilemmas of our age, which is an antidote to nostalgia and élitism.

References

Abercrombie, N. (1980) *Class Structure and Knowledge.* Oxford: Basil Blackwell.

Abercrombie, N. (1990) 'Popular culture and ideological effects', in N. Abercrombie, S. Hill and B.S. Turner (eds), *Dominant Ideologies.* London: Unwin Hyman, pp. 199–228.

Abercrombie, N. and Longhurst, B. (1983) 'Interpreting Mannheim', *Theory, Culture & Society,* 2(1): 5–15.

Adorno, T. (1991) *The Culture Industry. Selected Essays on Mass Culture.* London: Routledge.

Apel, K.-O. (1984) *Understanding and Explanation, a Transcendental-Pragmatic Perspective.* Cambridge, MA: MIT Press.

Archer, M. (1988) *Culture and Agency. The Place of Culture in Social Theory.* Cambridge: Cambridge University Press.

Baudrillard, J. (1990) *Revenge of the Crystal. Selected Writings on the Modern Object and its Destiny, 1968–1983.* London: Pluto Press.

Bauman, Z. (1987) *Legislators and Interpreters. On Modernity, Post-modernity and Intellectuals.* Oxford: Polity Press.

Bourdieu, P. (1984) *Distinction. A Social Critique of the Judgement of Taste.* London: Routledge & Kegan Paul.

Bourdieu, P. (1988) *Homo Academicus.* Stanford, CA: Stanford University Press.

Bourdieu, P. and Passeron, J.C. (1990) *Reproduction in Education, Society and Culture.* London: Sage.

Brantlinger, P. (1990) *Crusoe's Footprints, Cultural Studies in Britain and America.* New York and London: Routledge.

Certeau, M. de. (1984) *The Practice of Everyday Life.* Berkeley, CA: University of California Press.

Durkheim, E. (1957) *Professional Ethics and Civic Morals.* London: Routledge & Kegan Paul.

Elias, N. (1978) *The Civilizing Process.* Oxford: Basil Blackwell.

Elias, N. (1991) *The Society of Individuals.* Oxford: Basil Blackwell.

Featherstone, M. (1991) *Consumer Culture and Postmodernism.* London: Sage.

Gouldner, A.W. (1982) *The Future of Intellectuals and the Rise of the New Class.* New York: Oxford University Press.

Holton, R.J. and Turner, B.S. (1986) *Talcott Parsons on Economy and Society.* London: Routledge & Kegan Paul.

Jacoby, R. (1987) *The Last Intellectuals, American Culture in the Age of Academe.* New York: Farrar, Strauss and Giroux.

Jameson, F. (1990) *Signatures of the Visible.* London: Routledge.

Kettler, D., Meja, V. and Stehr, N. (1984) *Karl Mannheim.* Chichester: Ellis Horwood, and London and New York: Tavistock Publications.

Klages, L. (1981) *Der Geist als Widersacher der Seele.* Bonn: Bouvier.

Leiss, W. (1983) 'The icons of the marketplace', *Theory, Culture & Society,* 1(3): 10–21.

Mannheim, K. (1950) *Freedom, Power and Democratic Planning.* London: Routledge & Kegan Paul.

Mannheim, K. (1956) *Essays on the Sociology of Culture.* London: Routledge & Kegan Paul.

Mannheim, K. (1986) *Conservatism, a Contribution to the Sociology of Knowledge.* London: Routledge & Kegan Paul.

Mannheim, K. (1991). *Ideology and Utopia.* London: Routledge.

Marshall, T.H. (1950) *Citizenship and Social Class and Other Essays.* Cambridge: Cambridge University Press.

Meja, V. and Stehr, N. (eds) (1990) *Knowledge and Politics, the Sociology of Knowledge Dispute.* London: Routledge.

Mennell, S. (1989) *Norbert Elias, Civilization and the Human Self Image.* Oxford: Basil Blackwell.

Merton, R.K. (1945) 'Sociology of knowledge', in G. Gurvitch and W.E. Moore (eds), *Twentieth Century Sociology.* New York: The Philosophical Library. pp. 366–405.

Mill, J.S. (1952) *A System of Logic.* London: Longman and Green.

Morley, D. (1986) *Family Television: Cultural power and domestic leisure.* London: Comedia.

Oakes, G. (1975) 'Introductory essay' to Max Weber, *Roscher and Knies. The Logical Problems of Historical Economics.* New York: The Free Press. pp. 1–49.

Parsons, T. (1966) *Societies: Evolutionary and comparative perspectives.* Englewood Cliffs: Prentice-Hall.

Parsons, T. (1971) *The System of Modern Societies.* Englewood Cliffs: Prentice Hall.

Parsons, T. and Platt, G. (1973) *The American University.* Cambridge, MA: Harvard University Press.

Roberston, R. and Turner, B.S. (eds) (1991) *Talcott Parsons, Theorist of Modernity.* London: Sage.

Scheler, M. (1980) *Problems of a Sociology of Knowledge.* London: Routledge & Kegan Paul.

Stauth, G. and Turner, B.S. (1988) *Nietzsche's Dance. Resentment, Reciprocity and Resistance in Social Life.* Oxford: Basil Blackwell.

Turner, B.S. (1986a) *Citizenship and Capitalism, The Debate over Reformism.* London: Allen & Unwin.

Turner, B.S. (1986b) *Equality.* Chichester: Ellis Horwood, and London: Tavistock.

Turner, B.S. (ed.) (1990) *Theories of Modernity and Postmodernity.* London: Sage.

Turner, B.S. (1991) 'Preface to the new edition', in K. Mannheim, *Ideology and Utopia.* London: Routledge. pp. xxxiii–lviii.

Veblen, T. (1899) *The Theory of the Leisure Class.* New York: Macmillan.

Weber, M. (1949) *The Methodology of the Social Sciences.* New York: The Free Press.

Weber, M. (1975) *Roscher and Knies, the Logical Problems of Historical Economics.* New York: The Free Press.

Weber, M. (1977) *Critique of Stammler.* New York: The Free Press.

Weber, M. (1978) *Economy and Society.* Berkeley, Los Angeles and London: University of California Press.

Williams, R. (1976) *Keywords, a Vocabulary of Culture and Society.* London: Fontana.

Willis, P., with Jones, S., Canaan, J. and Hurd, G. (1990) *Common Culture. Symbolic Work at Play in the Everyday Cultures of the Young.* Milton Keynes: The Open University Press.

Wollin, R. (1991) *The Politics of Being. The Political Thought of Martin Heidegger.* New York: Columbia University Press.

Wuthnow, R. (1987) *Meaning and Moral Order. Explorations in Cultural Analysis.* Berkeley, Los Angeles and London: University of California Press.

CHAPTER 8

GEORG SIMMEL AND THE SOCIOLOGY OF MONEY

Introduction

Simmel was born in 1858. Raised in the centre of the Jewish business culture of Berlin, Simmel studied history and philosophy, becoming a *Privatdozent* in 1885. Although he published numerous books and articles, Simmel was excluded from influential university positions as a result of the pervasive anti-Semitism of the period and it was not until 1914 that Simmel was finally promoted to a full professorship at the University of Strasburg. Like Durkheim, Simmel was both the object of anti-Semitic prejudice and a fervent supporter of the nationalist cause in the First World War. Simmel died in 1918 of cancer of the liver.[1] This basic and naive factual biography of Simmel in many respects provides many of the themes in Simmel's sociology. First, his sociology is held to be the brilliant reflection of the glittering, cosmopolitan world of pre-war Berlin and that his commentary on that world took the form of impressionism; his sociological essays are 'snapshots *sub specie aeternitatis*'.[2] Simmel's perspective has been regarded as an example of the nature of modern society as contained in Robert Musil's *The Man Without Qualities*, that is a social existence without roots, commitments or purpose.[3] Secondly, Simmel was and remained a social outsider, despite his good connections with Berlin's cultural elite. His writing has been as a result characterized as perspectivism and an aestheticization of reality. As an indication of this, Simmel's influence has in the past often rested on such minor contributions as 'The Stranger'.[4] Thirdly, because Simmel failed to secure an influential location within the German university system, there was no development of a Simmelian school of sociology at all comparable to Durkheimian sociology. Decades of sociological interpretation of Simmel's work have still left Simmel as a theoretical enigma on the ambitus of the sociological tradition. His sociology has been categorized as interactionist, formal and conflict sociology.[5] In more recent years, there has been a renewal of interest in Simmel which has begun to show a greater appreciation of the unity and stature of his sociology. This renewal has been brought about by the commentaries of Levine, Frisby, Robertson, and Robertson and Holzner.[6] More importantly, the translation of Simmel's *The Philosophy of Money*[7] by Bottomore and Frisby provides a new opportunity for a systematic evaluation of Simmel's sociology of modern culture. The main burden of this chapter is that existing commentaries have failed to focus on the central theme of 'alienation' and 'rationalisation' in *The Philosophy of Money* which provided the major theoretical backing for, on the one hand, Weber's analysis of capitalism as 'the iron cage' and, on the other, Lukács' so-called rediscovery of the alienation theme in the young Marx.

Despite his structural isolation from the core of the university system, Simmel was, in his own lifetime, regarded as brilliant. Even Weber, who in many respects fundamentally disagreed with Simmel, wrote in an incomplete manuscript of 1908 that Simmel 'deserves his reputation as one of the foremost thinkers, a first-rate stimulator of academic youth and academic colleagues'.[8] Certainly his lectures at Berlin brought him enormous attention from both colleagues and undergraduates. In the late 1890s Simmel was lecturing on sociology in the largest lecture theatre in the university and his courses continued until 1908 when Simmel turned his attention more definitely towards problems in philosophy, especially Kant, Schopenhauer and Nietzsche. His principal publications in sociology in this early period included *Über sociale Differenzierung, Die Probleme der Geschichtsphilosophie* and *Soziologie*.[9] *The Philosophy of Money* was published in 1900, although its contents were anticipated by a series of articles which appeared between 1896 and 1899.

The importance of Simmel's involvement in sociology in the 1890s was that it preceded Weber's turn to sociology from law and history; furthermore, Simmel's lectures and intellectual salon provided a massive impact on a group of intellectuals which in many respects came to dominate German social thought for many decades. For example, Lukács attended Simmel's lecturers in 1909–10 and participated in his private seminars, becoming one of Simmel's favourite pupils.[10] Simmel's approach to sociology was also influential in the development of Ernst Bloch, Max Scheler, Martin Buber, Karl Mannheim, Bernard Gorethuysen and Leopold von Wiese. Simmel was also a member of Weber's informal discussion group which assembled regularly in the Weber household. The relationship between Simmel, Weber and Lukács was the most significant of this network of German scholars.

Simmel's Sociology

In order to understand the argument of *The Philosophy of Money* it is important to provide a general interpretation of Simmel's social theory. Three themes can be said to embrace the core of Simmel's sociological perspective, namely relationalism, sociation and social forms.[11] For Simmel, no item of society can be understood in isolation, but only in terms of its interrelatedness with the totality. Thus, money as a social institution cannot be understood separated from the total social framework within which it is embedded. Money provides us with an insight into the total workings of a society and the structure of a society provides the context within which we can grasp the importance and nature of money as a social phenomenon. The implication of this argument, which is actually borne out by Simmel's very diverse empirical interests, is that any item of culture can be the starting point for sociological research into the nature of the totality. Fashion, the rules of chess or the use of knives at table would be as appropriate as money for understanding this totality. Nothing is trivial, because everything is related.

The second crucial feature of Simmelian sociology is the emphasis on what Simmel called 'sociation'. Simmel wanted to avoid both methodological individualism which ontologically claims that only individuals exist and sociological holism in which collective entities like the 'state' or the 'church' are reified and treated as autonomous social personalities. By contrast, Simmel argued that we can neither understand the individual nor society without starting from social interactions and without grasping that social structures are forged out of the process of sociation. Thus, commenting on the nature of exchange relations, Simmel observed that

> The exchange of the products of labour, or of any other possessions, is obviously one of the purest and most primitive forms of human socialization; not in the sense that 'society' already existed and then brought about acts of exchange but, on the contrary, that exchange is one of the functions that creates an inner bond between men – a society, in place of a mere collection of individuals. Society is not an absolute entity which must first exist so that all the individual relations of its members ... can develop within its framework or be represented by it; it is only the synthesis or the general term of the totality of these interactions.[12]

The third basic aspect of Simmel's position is that the forms of social life – groups, families, networks, exchange relations and so forth – which emerge out of the endless sociation of individuals assume a logic of their own, which over time becomes separated from the content of human interaction. Culture becomes reified as structures which are congealed. The 'tragedy of culture' lies in the fact that humanly created forms of life assume an autonomy and independence from the human beings who initially created them in the process of sociation. Money is, for Simmel, the classic illustration of this congealing of content into reified form; money is

> the reification of the pure relationship between things as expressed in their economic motion ... The activity of exchange among individuals is represented by money in a concrete, independent, and, as it were, congealed form, in the same sense as government represents the reciprocal self-regulation of the members of a community, as the palladium or the ark of the covenant represents the cohesion of the group, or the military order represents its self-defence ... This feature then assumes a structure of its own and the process of abstraction is brought to a conclusion when it crystallizes in a concrete formation ... The dual nature of money, as a concrete and valued substance and, at the same time, as something that owes its significance to the complete dissolution of substance into motion and function, derives from the fact that money is the reification of exchange among people, the embodiment of a pure function.[13]

The Philosophy of Money is thus to be seen as the study of how the form of exchange is detached from its content, of how money becomes a determining, autonomous feature of social relationships. The reification of exchange in money thus becomes one illustration of reification in general in a modern society based upon the money market, given the interrelatedness of all social phenomena.

In many respects *The Philosophy of Money* is a curious book. Ostensibly a critique of Marx's political economy, one aim of the analysis of money is

> to construct a new storey beneath historical materialism such that the explanatory value of the incorporation of economic life into the causes of intellectual culture is preserved, while these economic forms themselves are recognized as the result of more profound valuations and currents of psychological or even metaphysical preconditions.[14]

Yet there is almost no reference to Marx's discussion of money in *Capital* and, of course, the chapter on money in the *Grundrisse* remained unknown to Simmel. One can only surmise as to the intellectual influences that went into the making of *The Philosophy of Money*. Certainly, Simmel refers frequently to Kant and the book as a whole can be taken as representative of neo-Kantian epistemology, which was so dominant in social science at the end of the nineteenth century. In economic theory, Simmel was probably influenced by Carl Menger's *Principles of Economics* (1871) and *Problems of Economics and Sociology* (1882). It has also been suggested that Simmel followed David Hume in his account of inflation.[15] While Simmel came in later life to embrace a variety of philosophical views which were predominantly antirationalist, the main force behind his study of money was Kant, especially insofar as Simmel attempted 'a geometry of social life, a purely formal sociology'[16] out of the flux of incoherent sociation.

While *The Philosophy of Money* is a complex book, full of digressions, asides and minor tributaries, the central argument of the book is relatively easy to state. This argument has three components: (1) the historical transition from simple barter to a complex monetary system corresponds to a transition in society from *gemeinschaft* to *gesellschaft*; (2) the dominance of money is a reflection or representation of the prominence of impersonal, abstract social relationships; abstract money is the symbol of abstract social relations; (3) money creates greater interpersonal freedom through impersonal exchange relations, but at the same time makes human life more subject to bureaucratic, quantitative regulation. Money is thus consistent both with individuality and individuation. In terms of Simmel's historical argument, a simple system of barter or exchange gradually gives way to a situation in which some third element of measurement enters into the exchange of commodities. The value of two commodities in exchange is measured in terms of some other commodity which is held to be precious, such as shells, cloth or metals. Money, as a measurement of value, develops from precious metals, to coins of silver or gold, to leather money and finally to paper money. In this development, money ceases to have a face value and also becomes increasingly detached from a bullion backing. That is, money increasingly assumes a pure function as the mere symbol of value rather than itself being of value. This development is made possible by the changing nature of society and in particular by the growth of trust. The essentials of the argument are contained in the following quotation:

> A certain comprehensiveness and intensity of social relations is required for money to become effective ... and a further intensification of social relations is needed in order to intellectualize its effects. These conspicuous phenomena illustrate clearly that the inner nature of money is only loosely tied to its material basis; since money is entirely a sociological phenomenon, a form of human interaction, its character stands out all the more clearly the more concentrated, dependable and agreeable social relations are. Indeed, the general stability and reliability of cultural interaction influences all the external aspects of money. Only in a stable and closely organized society that assures mutual protection and provides safeguards against a variety of elemental dangers, both external and psychological, is it possible for such a delicate and easily destroyed material as paper to become the representative of the highest money value.[17]

The expansion of the society, backed up by state, law and custom, in association with an expanded social division of labour are the necessary preconditions for money to lose its intrinsic value and to acquire a purely functional significance. Above all, money presupposes inter-social trust, which in turn requires social stability. Without these conditions, money could not become a depersonalized phenomenon detached from intrinsic value. For Simmel, the centralization of social power in the institution of the state and the individuation of citizens are symbolically represented by the growing abstraction and impersonality of paper money.

The existence of a stable monetary system means that exchange can take place between persons or groups which are not related or connected socially or physically. Money makes exchange at a distance possible. It also means that every minute detail of human endeavour can have a price fixed upon it. Because of the divisibility of money into small change, there is in principle no limit to the quantification of human activity. Money is, therefore, a fundamental aspect of what Weber regarded as the process of rationalization in modern societies. The existence of money is a necessary basis for intellectualization of existence. A society based upon the representation of value by money

> Presupposes a remarkable expansion of mental processes ... but also their intensification, a fundamental re-orientation of culture towards intellectuality. The idea that life is essentially based on intellect, and that intellect is accepted in practical life as the most valuable of our mental energies, goes hand in hand with the growth of a money economy ... The growth of intellectual abilities and of abstract thought characterizes the age in which money becomes more and more a mere symbol, neutral as regards its intrinsic value.[18]

The intellectualization of life and the quantification of human performance are thus also linked with a process of secularization; money as the symbol of value replaces natural law as the metaphysical basis of conduct.

By making interpersonal relations more abstract, money also undermines the traditional world in which power was manifest in terms of overt interpersonal dependency. Just as exchange becomes more abstract, so the dependency on personalities recedes. In an argument which closely resembled Durkheim's analysis of the reciprocity brought about by the increasing social division of labour, Simmel observed that

> the dependency of human beings upon each other has not yet become wholly objectified, and personal elements have not yet been completely excluded. The general tendency, however, undoubtedly moves in the direction of making the individual more and more dependent upon the achievement of people, but less and less dependent upon the personalities that lie behind them. Both phenomena have the same root and form the opposing sides of one and the same process: the modern division of labour permits the number of dependencies to increase just as it causes personalities to disappear behind their functions.[19]

While money increases the range of economic dependencies through its infinite divisibility, flexibility and exchangeability, social interaction on the basis of money exchanges removes the personal element in social relations as a result of the abstractness and indifference of money. Although money liberates people from personal dependencies, it also makes the quantitative regimentation of individuals more precise and reliable as an aspect of social control. In this account of the negative consequences of money, we begin to detect in Simmel's sociology a definite perspective on the three dimensions of estrangement: reification, alienation and objectification.[20] For example, money ceases to be a means and is transferred into an end itself:

> Never has an object that owes its value exclusively to its quality as a means, to its convertibility into more definite values, so thoroughly and unreservedly developed into a psychological absolute value, into a completely engrossing final purpose governing our practical consciousness.[21]

Furthermore, in passages which are reminiscent of Marx on fetishism, Simmel employs religious analogies to come to terms with the nature of money. For example, the separation of money from any intrinsic value and its conversion into pure function represents 'the growing spiritualisation of money'.[22] In general terms, we have seen that Simmel treated money as belonging to the 'category of reified social functions'[23] and it is possible to suggest, therefore, that just as Marx treated religion as the fantastic representation of human alienation so Simmel regarded money as the reified representation of impersonal capitalism.

Marx, Lukács, Weber

It is often suggested that the extraordinary achievement of Lukács's *History and Class Consciousness* was to have rediscovered the themes of alienation and reification in the early Marx prior to the publication of the Paris Manuscripts.[24] A close reading of *The Philosophy of Money* and a knowledge of Lukács's dependence on Simmel's perspective on 'the tragedy of culture' suggest that, not only was Lukács's analysis of reified consciousness in bourgeois society mediated by Simmel's analysis of money as a reified social relationship, but Lukács's perspective depended in large measure upon Simmelian sociology. Lukács's borrowings from Simmel include the following: (1) the emphasis on society as, to use Althusserian terminology, an expressive totality in which the existence and meaning of any one element rests upon its interrelatedness with the whole; (2) the analysis of forms of bourgeois thought which have been separated from their real content and which assume a life of their own; and (3) the recognition that, while capitalism elevates the individual to major ideological importance in the doctrine of individualism as the justificatory basis of economics, law and politics, capitalism also undermines the autonomous individual by various processes of standardization, regulation and quantification. As one example, we can consider Lukács's employment of the content/form distinction in his criticism of what he calls the 'economic theory of capitalism'. The failure of such a theory consists in its failure to penetrate the phenomenal forms of capitalism relations and to grasp 'the real life-process of capitalism':

> They [economic theorists] divorce these empty manifestations from their real capitalist foundation and make them independent and permanent by regarding them as the timeless model of human relations in general. (This can be seen most clearly in Simmel's book, *The Philosophy of Money*, a very interesting and perceptive book in matters of detail.)[25]

Lukács's acknowledgement of Simmel's book as 'interesting and perceptive' hardly gives adequate recognition to Simmel's achievement. In addition, it should be noted that elsewhere Lukács was far more generous in his appreciation of Simmel's contribution to the sociology of culture generally. For Lukács, it was Tönnies's analysis of *gemeinschaft* and *gesellschaft* and Simmel's philosophical investigation into the development of money which had, more than any other sociological studies, brought about a clarification of cultural analysis.

In approaching the relationship between these theorists, I wish to advance the stronger claim that Simmel, not Lukács, 'rediscovered' the alienation theme in Marx's treatment of money in the capitalist economy. A number of crucial features of Simmel's argument are explicitly prefigured in Marx's manuscripts of 1844. For Marx, money represents the abstract relationships of private property which have become detached from the underlying human relations of exchange:

The reflexive existence of this relationship, money, is thus the externalization of private property, an abstraction from its specific and personal nature.[26]

Like Simmel, Marx perceived an evolutionary development of money from simple barter through to promissory notes as an abstraction of social relations:

paper money and paper substitutes for money such as bills of exchange, checks, promissory notes, etc., constitute the more complete existence of money as money and a necessary phase in the progressive development of the monetary system.[27]

Marx argued that the growth of trust and economic credit came to replace morality, since a person's worth was judged entirely in terms of their capacity to pay. Like religion, money is an expression of a world turned upside down:

money transforms the real essential powers of man and nature into what are merely abstract conceits and therefore imperfections – into tormenting chimeras – just as it transforms real imperfections and chimeras – essential powers which are really impotent, which exist only in the imagination of the individual – into real powers and faculties.[28]

While Marx's analysis of money became progressively more sophisticated and complex, his later commentaries on money retained the basic notion that money reflects but also reifies exchange relationships. For example, in the *Grundrisse* of 1857–8, we find Marx arguing that money becomes increasingly detached from the underlying social relations which initially give rise to money:

The need for exchange and for the transformation of the product into a pure exchange value progresses in step with the division of labour, i.e., with the increasing social character of production. But as the latter grows, so grows the power of money, i.e. the exchange relation establishes itself as a power external to and independent of the producers ... Money does not create these antitheses and contradictions; it is, rather, the development of these contradictions and antitheses which creates the seemingly transcendental power of money.[29]

It is also interesting that Marx emphasized in the *Grundrisse* the contradictory and alienating nature of money which is a means that is converted into an end; the following passage anticipated much of what Simmel was to assert some four decades later:

it is an inherent property of money to fulfil its purposes by simultaneously negating them; to achieve independence for commodities; to be a means which becomes an end; to realize the exchange value of commodities by separating them from it; to facilitate exchange by splitting it ... to make exchange independent of the producers in the same measure as the producers become dependent on exchange.[30]

While Marx's analysis of money in *Capital* became more detailed and while much of the early Hegelian language is stripped from the text, there is also an important continuity of attitude and purpose. For example, Marx quotes in *Capital* the same passage from Shakespeare's *Timon of Athens* (act 4, scene 3) which originally appeared in the notes on 'the power of money in bourgeois society' in the 1844 Manuscripts.[31] In *Timon of Athens*, we find the argument that money is an unnatural power which converts the morally bad into the morally good, the anti-social into the social, and the ugly into the beautiful. Marx adopted this poetic theme and converted it into the thesis that money assumes an autonomy and power over social relations so that money becomes the incarnation of social power:

> Just as every qualitative difference between commodities is extinguished in money, so money, on its side, like the radical leveller that it is, does away with all distinctions. But money itself is a commodity, an external object, capable of becoming the private property of an individual. Thus social power becomes the private power of private persons. The ancients therefore denounced money as subversive of the economic and moral order of things. Modern society ... greets gold as its Holy Grail, as the glittering incarnation of the very principle of its own life?[32]

One feature of this passage, as with the sections on the fetishism of commodities, which links Marx to Simmel is the prevalence of religious metaphors. By way of digression, one problem with the fetishism argument is that, strictly speaking, a fetish is typically a concrete object which represents an abstraction. The point about money, however, is that it is an abstraction used to represent concrete relations, that is real social relations of exchange. In both Marx and Simmel, the metaphors become very mixed because both want to argue that money as an abstraction becomes reified (that is, turned into a thing), while also arguing that money as a thing (a fetishized commodity) is converted into the abstract representation of society as a whole.

The point of this exegetical exercise has been to suggest that it is not Lukács but Simmel who, so to speak, unwittingly reconstructed Marx's analysis of money as alienation from the 1844 manuscripts. Despite very different starting points in epistemology, Marx and Simmel produced analyses which overlapped in many important respects. It also follows from this dependency of Lukács on Simmel that much of the influence accredited to Lukács in, for example, the field of literature belongs covertly to Simmel. In the sociology of literature, Goldmann is typically seen to be the main exponent of Lukács's position.[33] Goldmann, following Lukács, took the notion of totality as his principal methodological starting-point, accepted the distinction between form and content as a useful device of literary criticism and finally regarded the problem of 'the tragic vision' as central to modern society. All three components are, of course, essentially Simmelian since Lukács's Marxism was parasitic upon neo-Kantian sociology. While much of Goldmann's analysis of the philosophy of the

Enlightenment[34] is focused on the consequences of exchange relationships – such as the autonomy of the individual and universalism in social relations – for bourgeois culture, Goldmann does not refer to Simmel's study of money; he does however refer to the historian Gorethuysen and to the philosopher Heidegger, both of whom were significantly influenced by Simmel. The point of these comments is not to detract from the intellectual stature of Goldmann; the point is to suggest that the contemporary enthusiasm for forcing a sharp separation between Marxism and sociology is historically naive and analytically invalid.

While Simmel was thus important for several developments in twentieth-century Marxism, his principal impact on modern social theory was via Weber's sociology. Weber, for example, depended on Simmel's account of the interpretative method as the principal means of understanding the meaning of actions, although Weber also wanted to criticize some of the confusion in Simmel's treatment of subjective and objective meaning.[35] It has also been suggested that Weber's discussion of 'economic ethics' in *The Protestant Ethic and the Spirit of Capitalism* relied partly on Simmel's discussion of 'money in the sequence of purposes' in chapter three of *The Philosophy of Money*: it has been suggested that in *The Philosophy of Money* Weber discovered a method of transcending the ahistorical construction of ideal types because Simmel's approach permitted the historical construction of meaning – complexes as dynamic forms of cultural development.[36] Of course, Weber sought to criticize Simmel on a number of issues. For example, Weber objected to Simmel's failure to make an adequate distinction between the notion of 'the money economy' and 'capitalism' as a socio-economic system.[37] These observations on the Simmel/Weber relationship do not really get to the essential point: Simmel's philosophical inquiry into the development of an abstract and universal system of money as the measure of all human activity provided a fundamental model of the cultural manifestations of an underlying process of rationalization in western societies. Weber's account of rationalization in modern societies, especially as that process is manifest in the growth of the money economy, economics as a science, intersocietal exchange relations, detailed calculations for the measurement of human effort and economic predictions by systematic means, is an elaboration and extension of Simmel's account of money.

The concept of 'rationalization' in Weber's sociology has a variety of meanings and this variety in itself is evidence of the centrality of the concept to Weber's total corpus. There are thus a number of dimensions to the rationalization process.[38] Rationalization involves the separation of mental and manual workers from the means of production. In *Economy and Society*, Weber was explicit in his argument that the expropriation of the workers made rational calculation of capitalist activities possible, increased managerial rationality and created 'the most favourable conditions for discipline'.[39] In short, rationalization included alienation as the basis of calculation and discipline. Rationalization also involves intellectualization. This process involves the subordination of all areas of life to systematic scientific inquiry and management, at least in principle. In turn, this means the dominance of the expert over traditional authorities in the sphere of morality, social in relations and interpersonal behaviour. Rationalization is manifest in the progressive dominance of bureaucratic models of social organization, the dominance of bureaucratic personnel and the surveillance of the individual by the state. Rationalization results in 'the iron cage' whereby individuality is swamped by individuation. These aspects of rationalization finally produce secularization. Absolute values, whether those of religion or natural law, collapse in front of the wave of relativism generated by modern society, in front of the ethic of calculation and as a result of the prevalence of instrumental rationality. For Weber, rationalism ends in irrationalism because values can no longer be secured or anchored in transcendentalism or in any notion of universal interests. The differentiation of society brought about by bureaucratically-administered reality means that any quest for purpose in universal human interests is Utopian whistling in the dark.

These four dimensions of rationalization presuppose the existence of a money economy. In fact we have to state this situation somewhat paradoxically: money as both the effect and a condition of existence of rationalization. Money makes exact calculation possible and is the basis of all systems of rational accountancy. Money is a necessary requirement for bureaucratization since it makes possible the existence of salaried, white-collar employees, who can be hired and fired in fulfilment of exact functions. More generally, the development of free wage-labour as the essential feature of the capitalist economy could not take place without a money economy. The importance of money in Weber's economic sociology is illustrated by the discussion of money, credit and exchange in *Economy and Society*.

Unlike Simmel, Weber was fairly explicit about the sources of his analysis of money. He followed, for example, the approach of Ludwig von Mises's *Theory of Money and Credit* and G.F. Knapp's *The State Theory of Money*.[40] At this distance, it is all too easy to forget that the division between the social sciences, especially economics and sociology, had not been transformed into a system of exclusive property rights. Economists were as much as sociologists caught up in the so-called *Methodenstreit*.[41] Weber was, of course, primarily interested in the social consequences of money. These consequences are widespread and varied: the expansion of exchange relationships through indirect exchange; the growth of delayed obligations in the form of debt relationships; the transformation of economic advantages into control over money; the individuation of consumption; but these consequences are all dependent on

the most important fact of all, the possibility of monetary calculation; that is the possibility of assigning money values to all goods and services which in any way might enter into transactions of purchase and sale.[42]

Because a money system is so important for the development of calculation, discipline and exchange, Weber characteristically argued that the absence of a rational money system inhibited the development of modern capitalism. It is interesting for example, that Weber started *The Religion of China*[43] with an account of China's failure to develop a stable currency. This theme also played a part in the 'Protestant Ethic' thesis where Weber argued that, at the level of culture, Protestantism made money clean or at least religiously neutral by freeing it from the traditional ethical system that had frowned upon usury:

> What the great religious epoch of the seventeenth century bequeathed to its utilitarian successor was, however, above all an amazingly good, we may even say a pharisaically good, conscience in the acquisition of money, so long as it took place legally.[44]

The conditions for capitalist development, therefore, include the growth of exchange based on a money system, the development of banking and a set of attitudes which treats money as neutral from a moral point of view. In addition, a money economy is crucial for the emergence of bureaucratic administration and this in turn provides capitalism with a reliable, stable administrative framework. Indeed, Weber claimed that the money economy was the precondition for 'the unchanged and continued existence, if not for the establishment, of pure bureaucratic administration'.[45] For Weber, then, the development of money, especially paper money, was deeply associated with the origins, the development and the character of modern capitalism. In particular, money was the basis of rational calculation in capitalism and thus intimately related to rationalization, which brought about impersonality in social relations.

Weber was interested in a sociological problem – the relationship between rationalization and capitalism – not in the morality of a monetary system. He did, however, share with Simmel a metaphysics of modernity which was in essence the submergence of individuality within the administered society. Like Marx and Simmel, Weber's sociology was focused on the metaphysical pathos of means over ends or, as Alan Dawe expressed this paradox, 'the transformation of human agency into human bondage'.[46] The penetration of abstract money relations into all sectors of society was a necessary precondition of human alienation, but it was also the principal illustration of the reification of social relationships in a capitalist system. The difference between Weber and Simmel on the one side and Marx on the other was that for Weber and Simmel socialism was not the termination of reification but the logical outcome of that process of bureaucratic rationalization, which was inextricably linked with abstract relationships.

Conclusion

In this discussion of Simmel's philosophy of money, the similarities between Simmel, Marx, Weber and Lukács have been stressed in order to underline the common theme of money as alienation and rationalization.[47] This emphasis on convergence and overlap may seem somewhat perverse in the current theoretical conjuncture where priority is typically given to difference and divergence. It is certainly clear that these 'sociologists' (insofar as they share that designation) started out from very different epistemological positions. Simmel's sociology is often seen as a social version of the Kantian a priori categorization and his sociology as a whole is interpreted within a neo-Kantian paradigm. In his analysis of value-problems, Simmel came close to the neo-Kantian Baden school which was associated with Windelband and Rickert.[48] However, we should also note the significant influence of Nietzsche on Simmel in the idea of cultural forms negating the will, where the will represents untrammelled energy or content in opposition to Apollonian form. The impact of Nietzsche's problem of the devaluation of values in a nihilistic culture had a significant set of common theoretical consequences for both Simmel and Weber which have yet to be systematically assessed.[49]

Marx's engagement with the analysis of money in the context of capitalist expansion was shaped by very different intellectual and social forces.[50] In Marx's economics, money had diverse social functions: a measure of value, a medium of circulation, a means of payment, a medium of universal exchange and a means of hoarding wealth. Behind these various social functions, Marx attempted to show that as a commodity money embodied abstract labour and that the value of money was determined by the conditions of production rather than by market conditions of demand and supply. Marx's treatment of money was meant to be a critique of bourgeois political economy which was content to analyse the phenomenal forms of money. Although Marx's treatment of value, money and prices has been subject to an extended criticism, we can readily appreciate the sociological merit of Marx's perspective which was to uncover the manner in which money was in fact a mediation of social relations.[51] Marx's analysis of the circuits of money-capital was never simply a formal exercise in economic sociology as an ideal typical conceptualization. One contrast between Marx and Simmel would be in terms of Simmel's neo-Kantian formalism as opposed to Marx's attempt to locate the character of money in real economic processes. In other aspects of their orientation to social analysis, it is equally difficult to equate Marx with Simmel. In their treatment of conflict, it is highly misleading to draw a parallel between Simmel's sociology of conflict and Marx's class analysis, since Simmel's approach to human conflict was inspired primarily by Nietzsche.[52] Whereas Marx's theory of money in terms of the labour theory of value was intended as a sustained critique of classical economics, Simmel was often content to appropriate existing economic assumptions about money and exchange. Similarly Lukács sought to transcend the 'antinomies of bourgeois thought', of which the essentialist distinction between form and content would be a leading example.

Weber's sociology has also on occasion been criticized for its formalism, abstraction and conservatism.[53] This interpretation of Weber fails, however, to examine the fatalistic theme of Weberian sociology where intentions are always subverted by consequences. In the case of Weber's treatment of money, we can again detect this fatalistic theme which he shares with Simmel, whereby means dominate ends. However, Weber was not content merely to trace out the unfolding logic of exchange through history as a teleological progression from concrete barter to abstract exchange through universalistic money. The development of money was closely tied to the extension of bureaucratic social relations which were in turn an expression of economic requirements for stability and predictability. Weber was not concerned with any human attributes (such as 'greed') in the explanation of the development of money: indeed he specifically denied that economic sociology required any such assumptions. Money develops either because it makes 'budgetary management' (*Haushalten*) more rational or because it facilitates the exact calculation of profit and consequently stimulates entrepreneurship. Weber's economic sociology was not grounded in notions of human 'need', but rather sought to understand the structural conditions that favoured the growth of a rational money system.[54] By contrast, Simmel's approach was primarily concerned to develop a phenomenology of money as a medium of human experience of social reality.

Although money is a major institution within modern societies and a necessary feature of the social expression and distribution of prestige, it is peculiar that we do not possess a fully developed sociology of money. In Marxism there are a number of classic texts on money which have built critically on the legacy of Marx; the principal illustration would be Rudolf Hilferding's *Finance Capital* which was published in 1910.[55] In sociology, it is important to realise that one of the few significant contributions to theory in economic sociology and specifically to an understanding of money came from Talcott Parsons and Neil Smelser.[56] Given the importance of the problem of economic rationality in Parsons's sociology, it is an odd feature of Parsons's intellectual development that Simmel was virtually ignored in *The Structure of Social Action* and *Economy and Society*. Similarly, the strong argument for an economic sociology in Neil Smelser's *The Sociology of Economic Life* recognizes Durkheim and Weber as precursors, but entirely neglects Simmel.[57] Finally, despite the influential view that Simmel provided a major basis for the development of symbolic interactionism, studies of the ritual role of money in symbolic exchanges in the everyday world by symbolic interactionists typically ignore *The Philosophy of Money*.[58]

The recent revival of interest in the sociology of Georg Simmel has yet to provide a fully developed evaluation of his contribution to economic sociology. This neglect is unfortunate since the great merit of Simmel's study was that it elaborated a genuinely social view of the role of money as an institution. The absence of a systematic sociology of money means that social-science approaches to money and exchange are commonly dominated by a narrow and inadequate economic framework. The originality of Simmel was to have perceived money as a central feature of the development of a culture which is dominated by the process of rationalization. Like the Protestant Ethic thesis, *The Philosophy of Money* is a classic study of the roots of modernity and modern consciousness. To dismiss Simmelian sociology as formalistic is to miss the importance of Simmel's contribution to a sociology of modernism and more specifically it is to ignore Simmel as a major founder of economic sociology.

References

1. For an outline of Simmel's life, L.A. Coser, *Masters of Sociological Thought, Ideas in Historical and Social Context*, Harcourt Brace Jovanovich, 1971.
2. D. Frisby, *Sociological Impressionism, A Reassessment of Georg Simmel's Social Theory*, London, Heinemann, 1981. For a critical review of Frisby, see Roland Robertson's book review in *Theory, Culture and Society*, vol. 1, no. 1, 1982, pp. 94–7.
3. On the importance of Musil, see D.S. Luft, *Robert Musil and the Crisis of European Culture 1880–1942*, Berkeley, University of California Press, 1980.
4. K.H. Wolff (ed.), *The Sociology of Georg Simmel*, New York, Free Press, 1950.
5. For example, F.H. Tenbruck, 'Formal sociology' in K.H. Wolff (ed.), *Essays on Sociology, Philosophy and Aesthetics by Georg Simmel*, Columbus, Ohio, 1959, pp. 61–99; N.J. Spykman, *The Social Theory of Georg Simmel*, New York and D. Levine, 'Sociology's quest for the classics' in B. Rhea (ed.), *The Future of the Sociological Classics*, London, George Allen & Unwin, 1981, pp. 60–80.
6. D. Levine, 'Introduction' to Georg Simmel, *On Individuality and Social Forms*, Chicago, University of Chicago Press, 1971; Frisby, D., *Georg Simmel*, London, Tavistock, 1984; R. Robertson, *Meaning and Change, Explorations in the Cultural Sociology of Modern Societies*, Oxford, Blackwell, 1978 and R. Robertson and B. Holzner (eds), *Identity and Authority, Exploration in the Theory of Society*, Oxford, Blackwell, 1980.
7. G. Simmel, *The Philosophy of Money*, trans. by T. Bottomore and D. Frisby, London, Routledge & Kegan Paul, 1978.
8. M. Weber, 'Georg Simmel as sociologist', *Social Research*, vol. 39, 1972, p. 158.
9. For additional discussion of Simmel and his work, J. Freund, 'German sociology in the time of Max Weber' in T. Bottomore and R. Nisbet (eds), *A History of Sociological Analysis*, London, Heinemann, 1978, pp. 149–86; R. Heberle, 'The sociology of Georg Simmel: the forms of social interaction' in H.E. Barnes (ed.), *An Introduction to the History of Sociology*, Chicago, University of Chicago Press, 1958, pp. 249–73 and H. Maus, *A Short History of Sociology*, London, Routledge & Kegan Paul, 1962.
10. For biographical notes on Simmel and Lukács, I. Mészáros, *Lukács Concept of the Dialectic*, London, Merlin Books, 1972.
11. For alternative interpretations of the structure of Simmel's thought, M.S. Davis, 'Georg Simmel and the aesthetics of social reality', *Social Forces*, vol. 51, 1973, pp. 320–9 and S. Hobner-Funk, 'Aestheticism in George Simmel's "Philosophy of Money"', Proceedings of the 10th World Congress of Sociology, Mexico City, 1982.
12. Simmel, 1978, *op. cit.*, p. 175. For a discussion of Simmel's analysis of money, S.P. Altmann, 'Simmel's philosophy of money', *American Journal of Sociology*, vol. 9, 1903–4, pp. 46–68.
13. Simmel, *op. cit.*, p. 176.
14. *Ibid.*, p. 56.
15. D. Laider and N. Rowe, 'Georg Simmel's *Philosophy of Money*: a review article for economists', *Journal of Economic Literature*, vol. 18, 1980, pp. 97–105.

16. Coser, 1971, *op. cit.*, p. 202.
17. Simmel, 1978, *op. cit.*, p. 172.
18. *Ibid.*, p. 152.
19. *Ibid.*, p. 296.
20. P. Berger and T. Luckmann, *The Social Construction of Reality*, London, Allen Lane, 1967.
21. Simmel, 1978, *op. cit.*, p. 198.
22. *Ibid.*, p. 198.
23. *Ibid.*, p. 175.
24. G. Lukács, *History and Class Consciousness*, London, Merlin Press, 1971. On Lukács's discovery of the young Marx, A. MacIntyre, *Against the Self-Image of the Age*, London, Duckworth, 1971. For a general evaluation, I. Mészáros (ed.), *Aspects of History and Class Consciousness*, London, Merlin Book Club, 1971.
25. Lukács, *op. cit.*, p. 95.
26. K. Marx, *Writings of the Young Marx of Philosophy and Society*, (trans. by. L.D. Easton and K.H. Guddat), New York, Anchor Books, 1967, p. 267.
27. *Ibid.*, pp. 268–9.
28. K. Marx, *Economic and Philosophical Manuscripts of 1844*, (ed by D.J. Struik), London, Lawrence & Wishart, 1970, pp. 168–9.
29. K. Marx, *Grundrisse, Foundations of the Critique of Political Economy*, London, Penguin Books, 1973, p. 146.
30. *Ibid.*, p. 151.
31. On alienation as 'universal saleability', I. Mészáros, *Marx's Theory of Alienation*, London, Merlin Press, 1970.
32. K. Marx, *Capital*, London, Lawrence & Wishart, 1974, vol. I, pp. 132–3.
33. M. Evans, *Lucien Goldmann, An Introduction*, London, Harvester Press, 1981.
34. L. Goldmann, *The Philosophy of the Enlightenment*, London, Routledge & Kegan Paul, 1973.
35. M. Weber, *Roscher and Knies, The Logical Problems of Economics*, New York, Free Press, 1975, p. 152.
36. D. Frisby, *Georg Simmel*, Chichester and London, Ellis Horwood and Tavistock, 1984, p. 143; Levine, 1971, *op. cit.*, p. xlv; G. Marshall, *In Search of the Spirit of Capitalism, An Essay on Max Weber's Protestant Ethic Thesis*, London, Hutchinson, 1982, p. 33.
37. M. Weber, *The Protestant Ethic and the Spirit of Capitalism*, London, Allen & Unwin, 1965, p. 185
38. For a discussion of the various dimensions of rationalization, R. Brubaker, *The Limits of Rationality, An Essay on the Social and Moral Thought of Max Weber*, London, Allen & Unwin, 1984. On the development of rationalization, W. Schluchter, *The Rise of Western Rationalism, Max Weber's Developmental History*, Berkeley, University of California Press, 1981.
39. M. Weber, *Economy and Society, An Outline of Interpretive Sociology*, Berkeley, University of California Press, 1978, vol. I, p. 138.
40. L. von Mises, *Theories des Geldes und der Umlaufsmittel*, Munich, 1912 (trans. as *The Theory of Money and Credit*, London, 1934) and G.F. Knapp, *Staatliche Theorie des Geldes (The State Theory of Money*, London, Royal Economic Society, 1924). For Weber's commentary, *Economy and Society, op. cit.*, vol. I, pp. 184–93.
41. L. von Mises, *Epistemological Problems of Economics*, New York, New York University Press, 1981.
42. Weber, 1978, *op. cit.*, p. 81.
43. M. Weber, *The Religion of China, Confucianism and Taoism*, New York, Macmillan, 1951.
44. Weber, 1965, *op. cit.*, p. 176.
45. H. Gerth and C. Wright Mills, *From Max Weber, Essays in Sociology*, London, Routledge & Kegan Paul, 1961, p. 205.
46. A. Dawe 'The relevance of values' in A. Sahay (ed.), *Max Weber and Modern Sociology*, London, Routledge & Kegan Paul, p. 47.

47. The definitive study of the relationship between Marx and Weber in this area is still K.Löwith, *Max Weber and Karl Marx*, London, George Allen & Unwin, 1982.

48. W. Outhwaite, *Understanding Social Life, The Method called Verstehen*, London, George Allen & Unwin, 1975.

49. Various aspects of the issue are considered in R.Robertson, *Meaning and Change, Explorations in the Cultural Sociology of Modern Societies*, Oxford, Basil Blackwell, 1978; E.Fleischmann, 'De Weber à Nietzsche', *Archives Eropéennes de sociologie*, vol. 5, 1964, pp. 190–238; B.S. Turner, *For Weber, Essays on the Sociology of Fate*, London, Routledge & Kegan Paul, 1981; B.S. Turner, 'Nietzsche, Weber and the devaluation of politics; the problem of state legitimacy', *Sociological Review*, vol. 30 9(3), 1982, pp. 367–91.

50. S. de Brunoff, *Marx on Money*, London, Pluto, 1976.

51. On abstract exchange, A.Sohn-Rethel, *Intellectual and Manual Labour, A Critique of Epistemology*, London, Macmillan, 1978; for the classical critique of Marx's theory of money, Eugen von Bohm-Bawerk in Paul M.Sweezy (ed.), *Karl Marx and the Close of his System*, London, Merlin, 1975; for a defence of Marx's transformation of value into prices, G. Carchedi, 'The logic of prices as values', *Economy and Society*, vol. 13(4), 1984, pp. 431–55.

52. For a misleading comparison, J.H. Turner, 'Marx and Simmel revisited: reassessing the foundations of conflict theory', *Social Forces*, vol. 53(4), 1975, pp. 618–27.

53. This interpretation is prominent in N.Poulantzas, *Political Power and Social Classes*, London, New Left Books, 1973. For a critique, B.S. Turner, 'The structuralist critique of Weber's sociology', *British Journal of Sociology*, vol. 28, 1977, pp. 1–16.

54. This perspective on Weber's economic sociology is outlined in T.Parsons's introduction to M. Weber, *The Theory of Social and Economic Organization*, Glencoe, Ill, The Free Press, 1947, pp. 3–86.

55. R. Hilferding, *Finance Capital, A Study of the Latest Phase of Capitalist Development*, London, Routledge & Kegan Paul, 1981.

56. T.Parsons and N.J. Smelser, *Economy and Society, A Study in the Integration of Economic and Social Theory*, London, Routledge & Kegan Paul, 1956.

57. N.J. Smelser, *The Sociology of Economic Life*, Englewood Cliffs, New Jersey, Prentice-Hall, 1963.

58. Two principal examples would be A. Birenbaum and E. Sagarin (eds), *People in Places, The Sociology of the Familiar*, London, Nelson, 1973 and M. Truzzi (ed.), *Sociology and Everyday Life*, Englewood Cliffs, New Jersey, Prentice-Hall, 1968.

CHAPTER 9

TALCOTT PARSONS ON THE SOCIAL SYSTEM

Introduction: Interpretative Difficulties

The general problem of *The Social System* is that it is both one of the most influential and systematic textbooks of modern sociology, and one of the most ferociously criticized books. Naturally its author has had a rather similar career. Parsons's first major publication – *The Structure of Social Action* (1937) – has proved in the long run to have been one of the most coherent and profound attacks on utilitarian theories of social action in the social sciences, thereby establishing Parsons as, among other intellectual roles, a leading contributor to the analytical problems of economic theory. His next major book *The Social System* (1951), along with *Toward a General Theory of Action* (Parsons and Shils, 1951), established Parsons as the central figure in so-called structural-functionalism, which, as a style of theoretical work, has been generally condemned as hyper-abstract, logically faulted, and conservative. One paradox in the life of Parsons is, therefore, that here we find an author of two major contributions to modern sociology which are held to be mutually exclusive positions. This contradiction also partly explains why, despite Parsons's very obvious stature as a modern thinker, 'the conventional attitude towards his theory is one of critical aloofness' (Munch, 1981: 710).

The purpose of this chapter on Parsons's *The Social System* is to see whether this contradiction or tension in fact exists and whether it can be resolved in any way. Because Parsons's prose (especially in his later work) is notoriously dense and cumbersome, my aim here is also to facilitate the reader's access to the text. One of Parsons's severest critics once wrote that Parsons's work is 'full of sham scientific slang devoid of clear meaning, precision and elementary elegance' (Sorokin, 1996: 56). While I do not share that view of Parsons's work, it would be misleading to pretend *The Social System* is an exciting piece of prose or an elementary introduction to sociology. Part of the task of this chapter is, therefore, to answer the question: why read Parsons?

Those who are already familiar with Parsons's work will note the irony of this question. Parsons's *The Structure of Social Action* starts with the notorious question, adopted from Crane Brinton's *English Political Thought in the Nineteenth Century*: 'who now reads Herbert Spencer?' The answer was of course, nobody, but, since Parsons's subsequent work had at least some resemblance to Spencer's functionalism (Peel, 1971), Parsons's own question was ironically prescient. Fortunately, the answer to the question 'who now reads Parsons?' is very definitely not nobody. As we will see shortly, there has been, since Parsons's death in Munich in 1979, a major revival of interest in Parsons's work, not only in his own culture (Alexander, 1984; 1987), but also in Germany (Habermas, 1987; Luhmann, 1982; Munch, 1987), in England (Hamilton, 1983; Savage, 1981), and in many other societies (Bourricaud, 1981; Buxton, 1985; Holton and Turner, 1986; Robertson and Turner, 1989). Indeed, for some commentators on the current sociological theory scene, the re-evaluation of Parsons is part of a broader revitalization of sociology, which has been dubbed either 'neofunctionalism' (Alexander, 1985) or 'the new theoretical movement' (Alexander, 1988).

However, my question is not whether Parsons is still the focus of attention, but 'why read Parsons?' Partly anticipating a fuller answer to this question in this chapter, there are broadly speaking three components to my defence of Parsons's work in general and *The Social System* in particular. First, it is literally impossible to understand the mainstream debates of modern sociology without some comprehension of Parsonian sociology, because Parsons's treatment of the notions of social action, social structure, function, culture, and social system shaped, directly or indirectly, many subsequent developments in sociology, both in America and Europe. Of course, it was often in *opposition* to Parsons that these developments took place. For example, Anthony Giddens's 'structuration theory' (Giddens, 1968; 1976) was typically developed against Parsons's views of power, system, and action. Second, Parsons's approach to theory provides us with a powerful model of systemic social theory, which is addressed to the fundamental problems of the social sciences as such. While many sociologists work in splendid isolation from other social sciences, Parsons's sociology is overtly intended to engage with analytical issues in 'adjacent' social sciences such as the cultural anthropology of Clyde Kluckhohn, the 'institutional economics' which was developed in opposition to much conventional economics, and the psychoanalytic tradition of Freud. Although Parsons was highly sympathetic towards interdisciplinarity (partly because of his involvement in the Harvard Department of Social Relations), *The Social System* also provides a powerful and interesting defence of sociology as an autonomous discipline. Third, sociology, like other social sciences, often occupies an unstable and uncertain location between small-scale descriptive and empirical research which has little general significance, and large-scale theoretical research, which has little obvious implications for applied investigations, but enjoys general relevance. Parsons's sociology, I want to argue, goes a long way to bridging this gap between theoretical and empirical sociology.

Talcott Parsons: His Life and Times

Parsons's life (1909–79), which was frankly uneventful in historically significant terms, has been sketched often enough, although we do not as yet possess a full intellectual biography, comparable to, for example, Reinhard

Bendix's intellectual biography of Weber (1969). I shall not attempt to present a biography of Parsons at this stage. The intention here is to comment on aspects of Parsons's intellectual development in order to throw some light on the issues that engaged Parsons in writing *The Social System,* which can only be understood in the context of Parsons's entire *oeuvre.* Three broad intellectual forces influenced Parsons's sociological approach from his early student days at Amherst College until his death in Munich over half a century later.

The first of these was the reformist Protestantism of the Parsons's household to which we can trace his abiding concern for the problem of human values in western society. This interest in values was not simply an historical interest, because Parsons wanted to argue that the problem of value-orientation was actually fundamental to the very structure of social action (hence the title of his masterpiece on the problems of utilitarian social thought). Parsons remained committed to the idea that human values were essential for *sociological* analysis. From Protestantism, Parsons took the basic idea that human action could not be understood scientifically without recourse to value analysis. In this respect, it is interesting to compare Parsons and Weber, since Weber was also fundamentally influenced in his world-view by Protestantism, especially the reformist philosophy of W.E. Channing (Mayer, 1944: 24ff.). Weber's idea of personality as a general plan for one's life was derived directly from his liberal Protestant background, and continued to shape his attitude towards human action as value-directed (Holton and Turner, 1989).

Locating Parsons within a broader tradition of classical sociology, we should note that Parsons, like Marx, Durkheim, and Weber, was particularly exercised by two questions. The first was 'what has been the contribution of Christianity, by comparison with Greek, Roman and, to a lesser extent, Islamic culture to the evolution of European civilization?' The second question was 'to what extent has the influence of Christian values diminished with the growing dominance of capitalist institutions since the end of the sixteenth century?' For Parsons, Christianity had fundamentally shaped western capitalist civilization through its emphasis on individual responsibility, asceticism, rationalism, and its separation of politics and spirituality. In that regard, Parsons definitely followed the lead provided by Weber's *The Protestant Ethic and the Spirit of Capitalism* which Parsons had translated. However, Parsons differed from Weber in arguing that Christianity and capitalism were not necessary incompatible. Parsons, for example, regarded many aspects of secular America (such as cultural pluralism) as the fulfilment of Christian values (such as tolerance) (Robertson, 1982). Weber's sociology was dominated by themes of fatalism and pessimism (Turner, 1981); Parsons's sociology, and for this he was severely criticized by left-wing opponents, was shot through with what we might call American triumphalism. By comparison, Weber's overt nationalism with regard to Germany has passed with little comment.

Second, Parsons's biography and his sociological views were strongly influenced by his admiration for professional medicine as a secular calling. Parsons's intention had been to study biology and philosophy, and to follow medicine as a career. Although Parsons became 'diverted' by sociology, the interest in medical issues remained an enduring aspect of his sociological ideas. For example, the medical profession and the so-called 'sick role' are key issues in *The Social System* where medical values represent a central illustration of social action which is not dominated by utilitarian values of self-interest. A professional person is expected to be altruistic, oriented towards community service and regulated by professional ethics, not short-term market considerations. Parsons also became increasingly influenced by psychoanalytic theory, especially by the theories and therapeutic techniques of Freud. Parsons used Freudian ideas about transference to explain the social relationships between doctor and patient; he also used Freud's ideas about the Oedipus complex to explain the social functions of the incest taboo in the organization of the modern family (Parsons, 1954).

However, while Parsons's conception of social action was influenced by the notion of regulation by professional ethics, he also adopted medical, and more specifically, biological ideas in developing his views on the social system. There is a tension here between his interest in medical practice as a model of how values shape social action, and his interest in the biology of organic systems as a model of how social system parts (institutions) function to improve the adaptive capacities of the social system in relation to its environment.

Here, then, is a critical issue in the interpretation of Talcott Parsons to which I have already alluded by counterposing the relationship between *The Structure of Social Action* and *The Social System*. Should we regard Parsons's sociology as primarily a contribution to the analysis of (what Parsons called) a voluntaristic theory of action, or a contribution to the deterministic theory of the structure of social systems? In the first type of theory, the agency of the social actor appears to assume a primary theoretical position, whereas in the second case it is the structure of social relations which has primacy. This dilemma is the (by now) classic set of dichotomies between idealism and determinism, idealism and materialism, and agency and structure. We can adopt two positions with regard to Parsons's version of these contradictions. In the first position, we can argue that Parsons was irredeemably trapped by these theoretical problems, and offered no final solution to these issues (Dawe, 1970; Giddens, 1984). If we adopt this argument, then we are claiming that ultimately Parsons's general theory as a whole (but not necessarily parts of it) is logically inconsistent and incoherent. Parsons's theory has therefore finally to be rejected. For example, Habermas argues that Parsons's theory cannot ultimately cope with the communicative nature of social interaction, and continued to treat culture as an objective system part. Parsons's early action theory was overwhelmed by his subsequent systems theory (Habermas, 1987: 203).

A second position would be to deny that in general terms Parsons's sociology is caught in a cleft stick between agency and structure, and that his theory goes a long way towards reconciling those ancient contradictions. In this respect, we would have to argue that Parsons's theory is strictly speaking neither a theory of action nor a theory of systems; it is in fact an action–systems theory. This second position would not argue in some absolute sense that Parsons had overcome these difficulties, but (1) that his theory is not hopelessly locked into or trapped by these dilemmas, and (2) that as a result it is possible to develop Parsons's work in ways which remain fruitful for the future development of sociology. Parsons's theory is capable of repair (Holton and Turner, 1986). This orientation to Parsons's sociology appears to be the position adopted by what has come to be known as 'neofunctionalism' (Alexander, 1985), which accepts many of the criticisms traditionally made against Parsons, but wants to defend the general aims of Parsonian sociology through repairing the Parsonian legacy. In this introduction to Parsons's *The Social System*, I shall in general terms adopt the theoretical spirit of neofunctionalism for one simple reason. In sociology, we have been so deeply involved in self-criticism that we are in danger of self-destruction. In order to see if the tree is still growing, we constantly take it up by the roots to see if all is well. To continue the analogy, this introduction to Parsons adopts a strategy of theoretical pruning rather than extensive cutting. Before turning to this exercise, we need to examine Parsons's involvement with the biological sciences more closely.

In social theory, employing analogies and metaphors from biological sciences has been a common strategy in the development of theoretical frameworks on social systems. This strategy was basic to the 'organic analogy' which was common to social Darwinism and to Spencer's evolutionary sociology. Parsons's views on the systemic qualities of social relations was influenced at Harvard by L.J. Henderson's study group on V. Pareto, by Walter B. Cannon's *The Wisdom of the Body*, and by Claude Bernard. It was from these influences that Parsons came to see social change in terms of an evolutionary adaptation of a social system to its environment, especially in terms of the structural differentiation of the parts of a system. The idea of homeostasis also came to assume an importance in Parsons's work, namely the tendency of 'disturbances' of the system to result in a new level of equilibrium. The major assumptions of this type of theory are therefore (1) all social systems are defined in terms of the relations between their 'internal' parts, and between the system and its environment; (2) the notion of functional contribution is essential in understanding the continuity of various parts of a system, and sociology is directed primarily to the analysis of the functional significance of institutions in the survival of social systems; and (3) it is the social system and not its social parts or institutions which is the referent of functional significance (Haines, 1987). In common-sense terms, the task of sociology is to discover how various institutions (such as the family, the school, or the church) function, that is how they contribute to the continuity and survival of society as a whole. In his later work, this concern for continuity and change in social systems was extended and developed by an interest in the new science of cybernetics, that is how social systems are directed and regulated by the storage and transmission of information.

So far we have seen that Parsons's early sociology was significantly influenced by two major issues: religious values, and biological sciences. Against Marxism, Parsons argued that capitalist society could not be understood in exclusively economic (or materialistic) terms. Like Weber and Durkheim, Parsons was acutely interested in the impact of religious values on political and economic issues. We can see this influence in the whole contents of *The Social System* which is a study of the value-orientations which are fundamental to social interaction, and which provide the normative structuring of social relationships. Second, Parsons's interest in biological sciences involved him in a lifelong concern for the scientific interrelationship between the natural and the social sciences. The third major influence on his early development was the nature of economics as a science.

The importance of economic theory for the development of Parsons's sociology has for a long time been seriously neglected (Holton and Turner, 1986). Partly because Parsons was criticized for his idealism – namely his persistent interest in the role of values – it has not occurred to his critics to look to economic analysis as a central theme of Parsonian sociology. Where did this interest in economic theory come from? First, Parsons had come under the influence of Walter Hamilton, who taught institutional economics at Amherst, but this intellectual concern was greatly reinforced when Parsons came, after a brief period at the London School of Economics, to spend a scholarship at Heidelberg (1925–6). In Germany, Parsons wrote a dissertation on the concept of capitalism in German social-science literature, from which Parsons published two short articles, but these studies laid the basis for many of his subsequent contributions to economic sociology, not only in his critique of utilitarian economic ideas in *The Structure of Social Action*, but also in his translations from Weber and in many occasional papers on economic ideas and theorists. However, it has to be borne in mind that this engagement with economic theory and economic history was not merely a passing phase in Parsons's intellectual development. Parsons continued to write on economic sociology with, for example, Neil Smelser (Parsons and Smelser, 1956), but he was also an economics tutor at Harvard in 1931 and was the Marshall lecturer in economics at Cambridge University, England in 1953.

However, even these details disguise the real importance of economics in Parsons's intellectual career. This influence took two forms. The first issue was that Parsons took economics to be the most developed of the action theories within the social sciences and thus a model of how sociology might evolve towards a more mature status with the university curriculum. Parsons came to develop a four sub-system model of the social system around four 'tasks' facing a social system in relation to its environment. These four sub-systems (the AGIL system) were adaptation (the economy), goal-attainment (the polity), integration (cultural system of general values which is concerned with law and social control), and latency (the normative problem of motivation to fulfil positions in the social system). There are, as we will see, definite problems with this model, but at this stage we can note that Parsons thought that economics was a science of economizing action with special reference to questions of adaptation between the environment and the social system; economics was particularly about the allocation of scarce resources. The first continuous influence of economics as a discipline was thus in terms of Parsons's general concern for sociology as a discipline, its relationship to other disciplines and the problem of curriculum reform within the university.

The second form in which economics influenced Parsons's thought was as a model of social exchange in general. Conventional demand-and-supply economics has been concerned to comprehend the nature of maximizing behaviour in the exchange of commodities between individuals in a market. These exchange relations are typically undertaken, not in terms of a material exchange of commodities, but symbolically in terms of money as a medium of exchange. The capitalist buys labour power, not by providing the worker directly with the means of existence (clothing and food), but in terms of a wage in the form of money. However, money is itself only a symbol of value, because in principle the worker could be paid in terms of precious shells, postage stamps, a cheque, or other tokens. Georg Simmel, whose work significantly influenced Parsons, despite the fact that Simmel did not appear in *The Structure of Social Action* (Levine, 1980), argued in *The Philosophy of Money* (Simmel, 1978) that money as a symbol of the value of exchange was a measure of trust, and hence a measure of the extent of trustworthy social interactions. Parsons took money to be a generalized medium of exchange and by analogy argued that there may be a number of such media in society. In particular, he looked at power, influence, and commitment as circulating media of exchange which permit social actors to achieve desirable objectives. These media of exchange relate back to Parsons's model of the four sub-systems (AGIL). Money is the medium of exchange between the adaptive sub-system and its boundaries; power is the generalized medium of the polity; influence of the integrative sub-system; and commitment of the latency sub-system. As we shall see, Parsons's predilection for argument by analogy, his view of power as a medium of exchange, and his particular approach to money have all been criticized (Ganssmann, 1988). At this stage, I am not directly concerned with this criticism; my purpose has been simply to establish the influence of economic theorizing on Parsons's intellectual development.

From Structure to System

Secondary commentary on the major texts of sociology should never be substituted for reading the texts themselves. However, in this introduction to Parsons's *The Social System*, there is a strong warrant for offering a sympathetic reading of Parsons's major works, in the context of the hostile reception of his systems theory in the 1960s and 1970s. Furthermore, since Parsons is often accused of inconsistency, perhaps there is also some justification for reading Parsons's work sequentially. It is certainly the case that it is difficult to understand *The Social System* without some grasp of *The Structure of Social Action*.

In *The Structure of Social Action*, Parsons developed three interconnected arguments. The first was that classical social theory was unable to provide an account of action, in terms of a rationalistic and positivistic epistemology, and an explanation of social order without contradicting its own premises. For example, classical economics assumes that economic actors are rational and egoistic. They satisfy their needs by egoistically attempting, through exchange, to maximize their competitive advantage. Parsons argued that such theories cannot then explain social order, because it is perfectly rational for economic actors to use force and fraud to achieve their individual goals. The society implied by economic theory is atomistic, unstable and possibly violent. Parsons argued, following Hobbes's famous description of such a society as 'nasty, brutish and short', that an atomistic society of this character would involve a war of all against all.

Classical economic theory in fact 'solved' this problem by importing certain residual assumptions about common sentiment, human cooperation and 'the hidden hand' of history to explain how society was possible at all, but these supporting assumptions are not compatible with or deducible from rational, utilitarian assumptions. Parsons invented the idea of the 'residual category' to criticize these illicit theoretical strategies. But, one might object, does not social contract theory in Hobbes, Locke and Spinoza solve the issue of order and preserve the notion of egoistic rationality? If actors form contractual agreements to keep the peace, then social order can be obtained by rational actors, who continue to behave competitively. Parsons's argument against these assumptions, following Durkheim's notion of the 'noncontractual element of contract', is that the enforcement of contracts depends upon shared agreements (values) about the importance of contracts which make these agreements morally enforceable. In short, most rationalistic accounts of action and order are either incoherent or they are compelled to introduce some notion of coercive force to achieve a stable social order.

The second feature of Parsons's argument was that, through an examination of four major social theorists (Marshall, Pareto, Weber, and Durkheim), we can detect a theoretical convergence towards what Parsons called a voluntaristic theory of action. This convergence took place precisely because their rationalistic and positivistic theories could not simultaneously explain social order and rational action without recourse to residual categories. One special difficulty with these theories is that, because they defined rational as that which is compatible with experimental natural science, they could not arrive at a satisfactory theory of values, culture and meaning. From a positivistic perspective, all religious beliefs and practices appear to be irrational. Against these reductionist views, Parsons argued that religious symbols, for example, were neither rational nor irrational; they were simply non-rational. Religious symbols stand for experiences of ultimate reality, about which natural science has little or nothing to say. Without an adequate theory of the non-rational aspects of action, sociology would never develop a satisfactory understanding of the meanings which actors attach to social action.

The third major theme of *The Structure of Social Action* was that the development of a sociology of values is an essential task of sociology as a social science, if we are to grasp how the meaning of social action for the individual and the integrative functions of common values for the social system are necessarily linked. Social order is possible if social actors share a culture of common values, which unites them together to share and perform co-operative activities. It is these general values which determined the ultimate goals of action and which structure the norms by which the means of action are selected. These general values, or what Parsons was to call the cultural system, store up, as it were, the collective meaning of action and society for the whole collectivity. Action is meaningful because rational actors have available to them common values which define action, and social order is possible because these general values bind social actors together into social systems in such a way as to permit (without guaranteeing) a peaceful resolution of social conflicts.

Thus, the idea of a realm of relatively autonomous social values which cannot be reduced to material interests or environment was an essential feature of *The Structure of Social Action*. In this respect, *The Social System* can also be seen as an attempt to develop a general sociology of values. The aim of Parsons's book is, therefore, to derive the principal components of a social system from the structure of social action. His argument as a result focuses principally on the idea of what he calls 'value-orientations' and cultural patterns of action, and their relationship to the motivational aspects of social processes.

In *The Social System*, Parsons adopted a mode of theoretical activity based on a quest for symmetry and pattern, which characteristically involved either three-fold or four-fold diagrams or boxes. Thus, a system of social action can be divided into three principal components: the cultural, social and personality systems.

The modes of motivational orientation of action are cognitive, cathetic, and evaluative; similarly there are cognitive, appreciative and moral value-orientations of a social actor towards the action situation; cultural patterns and institutions are also organized around belief systems (which give some emphasis to knowledge and cognition), expressive-symbolic systems (which correspond to the cathetic principal), and finally there are systems of value-orientation (which embody moral obligations, corresponding to evaluative activities).

For many critics of Parsons, this use of parallels, analogies and symmetrical relations, often in a rigid 2 × 2 box, become the most unattractive and implausible aspect of Parsons's version of social system theory. For example, it was argued that Parsons's model of cognitive, cathetic and evaluative orientations was no more than a common-sense claim that, when acting, human beings are either knowing, feeling or judging things. In defence of Parsons, it could be pointed out that many philosophical accounts of ethics, for example Aristotle and Kant, are based on such a tripartite system of action. Furthermore, Parsons came to use the idea of expressive symbols very creatively when he saw aspects of modern social movements as an 'expressive revolution'. These theoretical models should be treated as heuristic devices to develop sociological theory, rather than as rigid, permanent features of Parsonian sociology (Adriaansens, 1989).

Another feature of Parsons's development of sociological theory was the introduction of the pattern variables. These patterns refer to the structure of role-definitions which are claimed to confront action as a system of conflicting choices. To take one example which is central to Parsons, a doctor, while following a professional-ethical code in the examination of a child, treats the child in a universalistic, neutral, and specific fashion. The doctor is, in principle, indifferent to the child's particular social characteristics (lower class, white, Catholic), because the doctor is guided by a professional interest in the child's symptoms. The child's mother, by contrast, is characterized by her particularistic, emotional and diffuse relation to the child. Parsons wants therefore to indicate in terms of values and actions the very significant differences between the family and the professional situation. They exhibit very different pattern variables, which in fact are related to the famous distinction between *gemeinschaft* and *gesellschaft*, which were first systematically described by Tönnies (1912). The pattern variables are claimed to be universal and inescapable: they are affectivity v. affective neutrality; self v. collective orientation; universalism v. particularism; achievement v. ascription; specificity v. diffuseness.

These apparently formalistic accounts of value-orientations, cultural institutions and pattern variables are in fact directly related to Parsons's early analyses of voluntaristic action and social order in two ways. First, Parsons wanted to show that the interchange between personality and cultural systems had important implications for the stability of the social system. Where social actors have 'internalized' values through socialization in the family, then in terms of personality they receive gratification in conforming to the dominant pattern of values in the social system. There is a double contingency between actor and culture. The cultural system is reinforced by actions which conform to the dominant culture; the social actor receives gratifications to personality as a consequence of carrying out actions which are compatible with dominant values. Social order is maintained because social actors are rewarded for their support. It is for this reason that much of *The Social System* is given over to the discussion of deviance.

The second relation is that in his account of the pattern variables Parsons is once more addressing the question of the Hobbesian problem of order. Social relations work in the sense that they are not random but structured by fundamental value patterns which morally coerce action. Furthermore, in his description of the universalistic, affectively neutral, collective, specific and achievement-oriented action, Parsons was giving an account of social action which is contrasted strongly with market-oriented (capitalistic) actions. We can see Parsons's vision of society as thus a clear alternative to a society dominated by 'possessive individualism' (Macpherson, 1962). It is thus crucial to see that the pattern variables are at the heart, not only of Parsons's view of modern professional behaviour, but of sociology itself. In fact, Parsons, towards the conclusion of his study, actually argues that sociological theory is 'that aspect of the theory of social systems which is concerned with the phenomena of the institutionalization of patterns of value-orientation in the social system' (Parsons, 1951: 552).

This issue is particularly marked in Parsons's analysis of the professions, which is an issue closely associated in *The Social System* with the analysis of the sick role, but its influence is far more wide-spread in Parsons's work as a whole. In fact, this issue is sufficiently important for me to want to claim that the key to *The Social System* is to be found in the pages (428ff.) where Parsons discusses how the pattern variables shape the relationship between doctor and patient. For Parsons, being sick is a social condition, because it involves entry into a social role. There are important expectations surrounding being sick, namely being sick involves normative expectations on the part of doctor and patient whose social relationships constitute a social system. In particular, Parsons emphasized the importance of universalistic, neutral and collective orientations on the part of the professional doctor.

Parsons was, however, also concerned to set the sick role within the broader context of general social values. Given the achievement and activistic values of individualistic American culture, being sick was, in an important sense, being deviant. Sickness typically involves withdrawal from work and passivity. Sickness involving a temporary, passive withdrawal from work is potentially a threat to the values of the whole system. Hence, the doctor emerges in Parsonian sociology as very much the guardian of the established order, as the gate-keeper of deviance, and as the embodiment of the 'sacred' order of normality. The pattern variables in this context (especially affective-neutrality) permit the doctor to function as the disinterested guardian of the society as a whole.

The *Social System* is a diverse and complex text, but I hope I have already suggested certain ways of reading Parsons which show the relevance of his approach to contemporary concerns. For example, Parsons's views on the symbolic importance of medical power is particularly important in the context of social responses to AIDS, IVF programmes, to chronic illness and ageing, and to the human dangers of the medical-industrial complex. Although Parsons's medical sociology has often been criticized, it is one aspect of his work where the charge of empirical irrelevance cannot be sustained. Furthermore, Parsons's awareness of the cultural and symbolic significance of medical authority anticipated many contemporary, radical paradigms which take medical power and medical knowledge as their starting point (Turner, 1987).

Parsons and American Sociology

Critics of the influence of Parsons's structural-functionalism often overlook the fact that his personal influence in American professional sociology was both limited and short term. For example, J. Goudsblom's suggestion (1988) that, by comparison with the lack of institutional power on the part of Norbert Elias, the success of Parsonian sociology is partly explained by Parsons's dominance of organized sociology in America is wide of the mark. Parsons's early work on European theory was slow to gain recognition (Camic, 1989). In retrospect, we can now see how important Parsons was in introducing classical European sociology (especially Weber and Durkheim) to American academic life, but at the time Parsons was somewhat remote from mainstream American sociology, which continued to be dominated by American academics such as Robert Park, Charles Cooley, Franklin Giddings, Albion Small, William Sumner, William Thomas and Lester Ward. Parsons's theoretical interests appeared peripheral to the local, applied, and empirical orientation of the Chicago School.

It was not until the 1950s that Parsons's influence began to have some general impact, partly through his postgraduate students, who included Bernard Barber, Kingsley Davis, Robert Merton, Wilbert Moore and Robin Williams. Parsons had also been elected president of the American Sociological Association in 1949. Parsons was also literally pouring out an apparently endless and effortless number of volumes and articles on a wide diversity of topics. However, while Parsons's sociology was becoming influential, his approach to sociology was also coming under sustained and often antagonistic criticism.

There were, so to speak, three waves of critical opposition to Parsonian sociology, or more specifically what had become known as 'structural-functionalism' (Alexander, 1987). There was the ethnomethodological critique of the followers of Harold Garfinkel, who argued that social order was grounded in the taken-for-granted practical rules over everyday life which was sustained by the ongoing practices of knowledgeable members.

Second, symbolic interactionists, following the work of Erving Goffman, also argued against what they took to be Parsons's functionalist account of social order. For symbolic interactionists, order was an emergent property of micro-social interaction, which could only be sustained by co-operative negotiation between social actors. The point was that social stability was inherently precarious.

It was, however, the criticisms of what can be broadly called conflict theory which proved in the long term to be the most troublesome and thorough-going critique of Parsons. He was held to be a conservative thinker, whose social theory could not explain social change or social conflict, partly because he denied or neglected material interests, which in turn were linked to fundamental cleavages in the social structure (such as social class). These criticisms were presented in a wealth of critical volumes which were in direct opposition to Parsons's approach to the explanation of social order. These influential critical works included: R. Dahrendorf 'Out of Utopia' (1958); A. Giddens '"Power" in the recent writing of Talcott Parsons' (1968); Alvin Gouldner *The Coming Crisis of Western Sociology* (1971); D. Lockwood 'Some remarks on the social system' (1956); C. Wright Mills *The Sociological Imagination* (1959); J. Rex *Key Problems in Sociological Theory* (1961).

The Social System in particular came under sharp attack. The emphasis on values and norms was held to preclude any proper understanding of the role of material forces, technology and social class in shaping the social structure. Hence, Parsons had difficulty explaining violent social change (for example, revolutions), and could only conceptualize change in evolutionary terms as the internal differentiation of social systems as an adaptive adjustment to the environment. It was further held that, because of this difficulty, Parsons could only explain opposition in society in terms of deviation from a set of central norms. As such, Parsons's sociology depended on a version of the dominant ideology thesis (Abercrombie, Hill and Turner, 1980), because it could not conceptualize a situation where a social system might have several competing systems of values.

Conflict theorists also argued that there were also a number of technical problems in Parsons's analytical scheme which compounded these problems. We can mention three of these issues. First, there was the conventional problem that Parsons found it difficult to reconcile an action perspective (as in *The Structure of Social Action*) and a system perspective (as in *The Social System*) (Scott, 1963). Second, it is in fact difficult to identify a 'social system', and to define a 'social system' in relation to a 'society'. Parsons treated the social relations between two social actors (a doctor and a patient) as a social system, but clearly Great Britain is also a social system, which is composed of several societies (England, Scotland and Wales). Is the nation-state (France for instance) a society or several societies? Because the legitimate existence of the nation-state is typically contested, there can be no naïve equation of nation-state, society or social system. Third, Parsons's theory of the social system (and more generally structural-functionalism) has difficulty in identifying the sources of social change, and this objection is really to ask a question about the relationship between sociological and historical explanations. Parsons often referred to 'social strains' as explanations of social change (as in his well-known writings on McCarthyism), or in his essays on Fascism he saw the legacy of the German class system in relation to the military bureaucracy as an explanation for the rise of national socialism (Parsons, 1942). However, it is not clear how these events and circumstances can be reconciled with the very general nature of his sociology of the social system. In part, this problem was an aspect of Norbert Elias's critique (1978) of Parsons's lack of any sense of historical contingency.

These objections clearly represent a formidable critical reception of Parsons's sociology. I shall return to a modest defence of Parsons shortly. However, I want to suggest that behind these critical comments there are two more basic, but often unstated, attacks on Parsons. The first is that his work almost entirely neglected the contributions of Karl Marx to social science. The second is that his work represents, often overtly, a defence of American civilization as the cutting edge of modern progress. These two issues are clearly interrelated.

From the vantage point of having lived through the revolutions of 1989, it is now increasingly difficult to understand, or empathize with the dominance of structuralist Marxism in sociology in the 1960s and early 1970s. The events of 1968 were associated with a period of remarkable Marxist theoretical developments, especially in Germany around critical theory, and in France around structuralist Marxism. While these intellectual movements had little impact on American social theory, there were strong radical student movements in the USA, which were, at least for a time, influenced by critical theory through the work of Herbert Marcuse. Parsons had rather little sympathy for such student movements on campus. While Marx was enjoying a major revival in university lecture halls around the world, Parsons's general theory was almost entirely closed to the influence of Marxist theory. Marx was very briefly considered in *The Structure of Social Action*, where he was dismissed as merely a variant of utilitarian economic theory. Parsons sustained this view of Marx as a utilitarian for the remainder of his intellectual career (Gould, 1989). Parsons also wrote almost nothing specifically about Marx or Marxism. This neglect of Marxist social theory during the radical decades of the post-war period further reinforced the view that Parsons's sociology was ideologically conservative.

Parsons's refusal to engage with contemporary Marxist theory was related to Parsons's view of the role of America in post-war reconstruction. Parsons took the view that the defeat of German and Italian fascism was a triumph of liberal, pluralist politics and for capitalism as an economic system. America was the illustration of successful and 'progressive' social evolution which, despite the problems of racism, urban violence, organized crime and class inequalities, offered the most promising alternative to Stalinism and international communism. Parsons acknowledged many of the social achievements of Russian society, but remained sceptical about its adaptive capacities. Parsons did not therefore accept the radical criticisms of American society which were common in the 1960s (Lidz, 1989). Parsons felt that the critical positions adopted in *The Lonely Crowd* (Riesman, 1950), *The Power Elite* (Mills, 1956), *The Sane Society* (Fromm, 1956), *America as a Civilization* (Lerner, 1957) and *The Authoritarian Personality* (Adorno et al., 1950) were superficial and, behind the smoke screen of academic neutrality, merely vented old ideological slogans. Parsons's intention was to write a general study of American society as a reply to these critics, which was to be called *The American Societal Community*, but very little of this work was finally completed. What remains is a collection of (largely unpublished) manuscripts. The critical objection to Parsons was, therefore, not only that his sociology was flawed by a range of technical problems, but that, in addition to his critique of Marxism, his analysis of values was by intention a defence of American civilization against right-wing social movements (such as McCarthyism) and against power blocs in the world-system of politics (such as Russian communism), which threatened the future of cultural pluralism.

A Defence of Parsons

One problem with the criticism of Parsons in the 1960s was that it typically focused on a narrow range of Parsons's own work, specifically *The Social System*. The revival of interest in Parsons in the 1980s has been characterized by its focus on the work of Parsons as a whole. What emerges from this more complete overview is an appreciation of its theoretical comprehensiveness (Sciulli and Gerstein, 1985). In addition, there is a growing appreciation of the applied and empirical virtues of Parsons's framework (Holton and Turner, 1986). As a result of these contemporary evaluations of Parsons's complete contribution to sociology, many of the conventional objections to Parsons no longer appear so compelling or convincing. It is also important to point out (as a moral evaluation of Parsons as a person) that Parsons attempted to reply systematically to his critics.

A modest defence of Parsons would include the following observations. Against the conventional view of Parsons as a conservative, it is now more than ever clear that Parsons was in fact a New Deal liberal, who attempted to defend progressive political changes, such as full citizenship rights for American blacks. It is not valid, furthermore, to argue that Parsons's sociology neglected questions about broad historical changes; Parsons was specifically concerned, like Weber, with the general pattern of western development out of Christian and Greco-Roman civilizations. It is also possible to defend Parsons against the idea that his Grand Theory had little to do with the understanding of empirical problems. For example,

Parsons's essays on the German social structure, on intellectuals, or his various articles on the professions are clear illustrations of his ability to write about specific issues and empirical problems. Although Parsons correctly described himself in the dedication of *The Social System* as 'an incurable theorist', he also retained clear and specific political interests in contemporary issues such as university curriculum development, or race relations, or American foreign policy issues.

Although these comments are reasonable and appropriate, they are hardly original or compelling. Returning to my observations at the beginning of this chapter, there are three broad areas of defence which we should address in more detail. The first is that Parsons's sociology established many of the broad parameters of contemporary debate in sociology; these parameters include (1) how is social order to be explained, and how important are shared values in such an explanation? (2) what is the nature of social action, and how can we best defend the idea of voluntaristic action against various forms of utilitarianism? (3) what are the essential characteristics of a modern society in terms of its values and social structure, and how much of this 'modernity' is the product of capitalistic economic development? and, finally (4) how can sociology contribute to understanding and fostering progressive social relations, that is relations which exist without recourse to forms of authoritarian compulsion? These questions, which were central to Parsons's sociology, have remained crucial to mainstream sociology and are even central to the sociological alternatives presented by Parsons's critics.

Although Parsons was blind to many current issue – gender, feminist theory, the analysis of symbolic exchange at the micro level, the negative features of American foreign policy, the repression brought about by western imperialism, the devastation of aboriginal cultures by westernization, and the possibilities of 'underdevelopment' as a necessary consequence of so-called western development – two features of Parsonian sociology continue to dominate contemporary sociology.

The first is the growing recognition that classical sociology failed to develop an adequate perspective on culture, and that various forms of development of modern capitalism have made cultural issues more rather than less prominent in 'post-industrial' society. Given Parsons's preoccupation with cultural anthropology, his tripartite theoretical model of society, culture and personality, and his predilection for value analysis, Parsons's contribution to cultural sociology is a crucial feature of his general sociology. This aspect of work has yet to receive adequate attention (Robertson, 1988).

The second thematic issue in Parsons's sociology was its anti-nostalgic stance towards modernity (Holton and Turner, 1986). While mainstream sociology, which has followed Marx and Weber, has in practice been a sociology of capitalist society, Parsons has been unambiguously a theorist and protagonist of modernity. Classical sociology retained an often unspoken nostalgia for the conservative values of a stable rural community; the basic unit-ideas of sociology (such as the sacred, community, authority, and status) reflect this undercurrent of commitment to the world represented by pre-industrial agrarian communities (Nisbet, 1967). While writing about *gesellschaft*, sociologists have often embraced a set of values which are more relevant to *gemeinschaft* (Holton and Turner, 1989). Parsons, by contrast, was unambiguously modernist in his acceptance of secularization, differentiation, pluralism of values, bureaucratization of administration, urban cultures and modern forms of citizenship. There is nothing in Parsons's sociology to compare with the constant angst which Weber exhibited towards modernity and towards the problem of discovering a scientific or political calling in post-religious society (Lassman and Velody, 1989). Given the current debate about modernity and postmodernity, it is not a risky prediction to assume that Parsons may well be revived as the spokesperson of modernity, and that this revival may (with considerable irony) put Parsons in the same camp as Habermas in wishing to complete the project of rational modernity.

The second major defence of Parsons is that his theoretical endeavours over half a century represented a sustained and systematic attempt to develop a single coherent approach to sociology, replacing the legacy of rationalistic utilitarian social theory with a voluntaristic theory of action. Parsons's critics have recently paid tribute to this serious quest for analytic coherence. Thus Habermas (1987: 199) has written that Parsons has left a body of theory which is 'without equal in its level of abstraction and differentiation, its social-theoretical scope and systematic quality'. This action theory would (1) take into account the centrality of norms and values in the choice of the ends of action and the regulation of means to ends, and (2) would maintain a view of the social actor as a rational being who is also motivated by feelings and by evaluations. Parsons's sociology thus attempted to provide a coherent overview of the domain of sociological enquiry which would systematically integrate, following Weber's account of action, social action and social relationship, a voluntaristic theory of action with what we might call a culturalist theory of the social system.

Although many critics of Parsons have argued that there is a hiatus between his action theory and his social systems theory (and therefore that Parsons does not provide us with a systematic general theory of sociology), by calling Parsons's theory of social systems a culturalist theory, we can recognize the strong connection between the importance of values in his action theory and the pattern of cultural orientations in his systems theory. Some aspects of this relation were outlined in a neglected study of Parsonian theory (Chazel, 1974). As Chazel points out, there is a direct line of theoretical development from the idea of action orientation in the unit act in *The Structure of Social Action*, the emergence of the pattern variables in *The Social System*, and the final development of the four-system (GAIL) model of his later systems theory. This development, in fact, was an attempt to spell out the implications of classical sociology – especially Tönnies's distinction between *gemeinschaft* and *gesellschaft* – for the analysis of modern societies.

The pattern variables remained a constant theme in Parsons's sociology and they therefore indicate, against his critics, an important feature of the continuity of his work. While some commentators have suggested that they were abandoned in Parsons's later work, this is not the case. The pattern variables represented for Parsons, not simply a theoretical framework, but a moral code as well. We have seen this implicit moral theory in his treatment of the importance of professional ethics in guiding the doctor's relationship to the (subordinate and often helpless) patient. On a larger canvas, if we treat Parsons's work as a whole as the quest for a sociological and historical account of the origins of (what I shall call) 'progressive social systems', then the continuity of the pattern variables becomes obvious. Progressive social systems are characterized by their pluralism, their tolerance of value-diversity, their structural differentiation, their capacity to solve system problems without recourse to totalitarian violence, and thus their institutionalization of universalism, achievement-orientation and altruism. On these grounds, there would be scope for extensive criticism of the failure of America to achieve these universalistic norms. The race relations issue in American society would be one prominent illustration. Parsons was keenly aware of these criticisms, but he thought that the institutionalization of citizenship norms would eventually reduce such forms of discrimination, without necessarily eradicating racism, and that these changes would permit sufficient social solidarity for the American community to avoid civil war.

As I have noted, this vision of modern society was Parsons's translation of Weber's 'Protestant Ethic thesis' into contemporary sociological theory, which Parsons then combined with the idea that, at this particular point in history, American society most successfully embodied the Weberian 'Protestant Ethic' (Robertson, 1982). Therefore, America is at the cutting edge of the process of modernization. This thesis first emerges in *The Social System* and then is fully developed in *Societies* (1966) and *The System of Modern Societies* (1971); it also underpinned the whole incomplete project of *The American Societal Community*. These volumes argued that the historical origins of western liberalism lay in the institutionalization of democracy in the Greek polis and in the individualism which was an important feature of Christian doctrine. In these studies, Parsons adopted an optimistic and modernist view of historical change, not as an evolutionary development towards a social paradise, but as a process which allowed human beings some grounds for hope that (to use Weber's pessimistic metaphor) the iron cage was not the only possible outcome of collective endeavour.

The final defence of Parsons's sociology would centre around his vision of sociology itself. Throughout the post-war university boom, sociology was regularly the target of public criticism. From the left, it was regarded as a bourgeois defence of capitalism, masquerading as an objective science. From the right, it was regarded as a thinly disguised academic version of Marxism, dressed up in the language of an objective academic discipline. Both sides agreed the sociology had to go. Of course, this situation is not new. Simmel's lectures on sociology at Berlin were regarded as subversive. At other times, sociology has been dismissed by anti-semites as a 'Jewish Science'. For those sociologists who, following Weber's idea of a calling in science, are passionately committed to their discipline, Parsons's sociology provides an unrestrained and unrepentant defence of sociology as a vital science of social action, whose special area of focus is the integrative role of common values, especially the maintenance of the pattern variables. Although anthropology and sociology were for Parsons closely connected, anthropology was rapidly becoming a theory of culture. Sociology and anthropology were specifically regarded as an alternative to a utilitarian theory of rational action, because their province lay primarily with phenomena which were nonrational.

There are very good grounds for seeing the task of sociology in a wider context. Parsons's account of the nature of sociology is ambiguous. While allocating sociology to the study of the integrative sub-system, Parsons also tends to see sociology as a general theory of action, for which political, economic and psychological phenomena are significant. In short, it is not clear whether sociology is a special discipline concerned with the institutionalization of value-patterns or whether it is a general science of the social. In this discussion of sociology as a science, it is important to keep in mind that, at least in the German context, the use of the word 'science' (*Wissenschaft*) has a much wider terrain than in an Anglo-Saxon context, where 'science' is reserved for positivistic, experimental, natural sciences. Because Parsons was steeped in German scientific culture, he felt less anxious than most in employing 'science' in his description of those disciplines which study action.

Whether or not one agrees with Parsons's version of sociology, I believe we have to respect Parsons as a committed scientist, whose own life was also shaped by the pattern variables he sought to describe in *The Social System*. Weber is reputed to have said that 'much of what is sailing under the name of sociology is a swindle' (Mayer, 1944: 87). In the case of Parsons, as with Durkheim, we are confronted by a man for whom sociology is a calling. With Parsons's sociology we are offered not a swindle, but the genuine article.

References

Abercrombie, N., Hill, S. and Turner, B.S. (1980) *The Dominant Ideology Thesis*. London: Allen & Unwin.
Adorno, T.W., Frenkel-Brunswik, E., Levinson, D. J. and Sanford, R.N. (1950) *The Authoritarian Personality*. New York: Harper.
Adriaansens, H.P.M. (1989) 'Talcott Parsons and beyond: recollections of an outsider', *Theory, Culture & Society*, 6(4): 613–21.

Alexander, J.C. (1984) *Theoretical Logic in Sociology, Vol. 4: The modern reconstruction of classical thought: Talcott Parsons.* London: Routledge & Kegan Paul.

Alexander, J.C. (ed.) (1985) *Neofunctionalism.* Beverly Hills: Sage.

Alexander, J.C. (1987) *Twenty Lectures: Sociological theory since World War II.* New York: Columbia University Press.

Alexander, J.C. (1988) 'The new theoretical movement', in N.J. Smelser (ed.), *Handbook of Sociology.* Newbury Park: Sage. pp. 77–101.

Bendix, R. (1969) *Max Weber, an Intellectual Portrait.* London: Methuen.

Bourricaud, F. (1981) *The Sociology of Talcott parsons.* Chicago and London: University of Chicago Press.

Buxton, W. (1985) *Talcott Parsons and the Capitalist Nation-State.* Toronto: University of Toronto Press.

Camic, C. (1989) 'Structure after fifty years', *American Journal of sociology,* 95: 38–107.

Chazel, F. (1974) *La theorie analytique de la societe dans l'oeuvre de Talcott Parsons.* Paris: Mouton.

Dahrendorf, R. (1958) 'Out of Utopia: towards a reorientation of sociological analysis', *American Sociological Review,* 64: 115–27.

Dawe, A. (1970) 'The two sociologies', *British Journal of Sociology,* 21: 207–18.

Elias, N. (1978) *The Civilizing Process, Vol.1 The History of Manners.* Oxford: Basil Blackwell.

Fromm, E. (1956) *The Sane Society.* London: Routledge & Kegan Paul.

Ganssmann, H. (1988) 'Money – a symbolically generalised means of communication? On the concept of money in recent sociology', *Economy & Society,* 17(3): 285–316.

Giddens, A. (1968) '"Power" in the recent writing of Talcott Parsons', *Sociology,* 2: 257–72.

Giddens, A. (1976) *New Rules of Sociological Method, a Positive Critique of Interpretative Sociologies.* London: Hutchinson.

Giddens, A. (1984) *The Constitution of Society, Outline of the Theory of Structuration.* Cambridge: Polity Press.

Goudsblom, J. (1988) 'The sociology of Nobert Elias: its resonance and significance', *Theory, Culture & Society,* 4(2–3): 323–37.

Gould, M. (1989) 'Voluntarism versus utilitarianism: a critique of Camic's history of ideas', *Theory, Culture & Society,* 6(4): 637–54.

Gouldner, A.W. (1971) *The Coming Crisis of Western Sociology.* London: Heinemann.

Habermas, J.(1987) *The Theory of Communicative Action, volume two, The Critique of Functionalist Reason.* Cambridge: Polity Press.

Haines, V.A. (1987) 'Biology and social theory: Parsons's evolutionary theme', *Sociology,* 21(1): 19–39.

Hamilton, P. (1983) *Talcott Parsons.* London and New York: Tavistock.

Holton, R.J. and Turner, B.S. (1986) *Talcott Parsons on Economy and Society.* London: Routledge & Kegan Paul.

Holton, R.J. and Turner, B.S. (1989) *Max Weber on Economy and Society.* London: Routledge.

Lassman, P. and Velody, I. (eds) (1989) *Max Weber's 'Science as a Vocation'.* London: Routledge.

Lerner, M. (1957) *America as a Civilization.* New York: Simon and Schuster, 2 vols.

Levine, D.N. (1980) *Simmel and Parsons, Two Approaches to the Study of Society.* New York: Arno Press.

Lidz, D. (1989) 'The American value system: a commentary on Talcott Parsons's perspective and understanding', *Theory, Culture & Society,* 6(4): 559–76.

Lockwood, D. (1956) 'Some remarks on *The Social System*', *British Journal of Sociology,* 7: 134–45.

Luhmann, N. (1982) *The Differentiation of Society.* New York: Columbia University Press.

Macpherson, C.B. (1962) *The Political Theory of Possessive Individualism.* Oxford: Oxford University Press.

Mayer, J.P. (1944) *Max Weber and German Politics, a Study in Political Sociology.* London: Faber.

Mills, C. Wright (1956) *The Power Elite.* New York: Oxford University Press.

Mills, C. Wright (1959) *The Sociological Imagination.* Harmondsworth: Penguin Books.

Munch, R. (1981) 'Talcott Parsons and the theory of action I: the structure of the Kantian core', *American Journal of Sociology,* 86: 709–40.

Munch, R. (1987) *Theory of Action: Towards a synthesis going beyond Parsons.* London and New York: Routledge.

Nisbet, R. (1967) *The Sociological Tradition*. London: Faber.

Parsons, T. (1937) *The Structure of Social Action*. New York: McGraw-Hill.

Parson, T. (1942) 'Democracy and the social structure in pre-Nazi Germany', *Journal of Legal and Political Sociology*, 1: 96–114.

Parsons, T. (1951) *The Social System*. London: Routledge & Kegan Paul.

Parsons, T. (1954) *Essays in Sociological Theory*. New York: Free Press.

Parsons, T. (1966) *Societies Evolutionary and Comparative Perspectives*. Englewood cliffs, NJ: Prentice-Hall.

Parsons, T. (1971) *The System of Modern Societies*. Englewood cliffs, NJ: Prentice-Hall.

Parsons, T. and Shils, E.A. (eds) (1951) *Toward a General Theory of Action*. Cambridge, Mass: Harvard University Press.

Parsons, T. and Smelser, N. (1956) *Economy and Society*. London: Routledge & Kegan Paul.

Peel, J.D.Y. (1971) *Herbert Spencer: The evolution of a sociologist*. London: Heinemann.

Rex, J. (1961) *Key Problems in Sociological Theory*. London: Routledge & Kegan Paul.

Riesman, D. (1950) *The Lonely Crowd*. New Haven, CT: Yale University Press.

Robertson, R. (1982) 'Parsons on the evolutionary significance of American religion', *Sociological Analysis*, 43: 307–26.

Robertson, R. (1988) 'The sociological significance of culture: some general considerations', *Theory Culture & Society*, 5(1): 3–24.

Robertson, R. and Turner, B.S. (1989) 'Talcott Parsons and modern social theory: an appreciation', *Theory Culture & Society*, 6(4): 539–58.

Savage, P. (1981) *The Theories of Talcott Parsons: The social relations of action*. London: Macmillan.

Sciulli, D. and Gerstein, D. (1985) 'Social theory and Parsons in the 1980s', *Annual Review of Sociology*, 11: 369–87.

Scott, J.F. (1963) 'The changing foundations of the Parsonian action scheme', *American Sociological Review*, 29: 716–35.

Simmel, G. (1978) *The Philosophy of Money*. London: Routledge & Kegan Paul.

Sorokin, P.A. (1966) *Sociological Theories of Today*. New York: Harper.

Tönnies, F. (1912) *Gemeinschaft und Gesellschaft*. Berlin: Karl Curtius.

Turner, B.S. (1981) *For Weber, Essays in the Sociology of Fate*. London: Routledge & Kegan Paul.

Turner, B.S. (1987) *Medical Power and Social Knowledge*. London: Sage.

THE EARLY SOCIOLOGY
OF INSTITUTIONS

PART II

THE EARLY SOCIOLOGY
of INSTITUTIONS

CHAPTER 10

THE SOCIOLOGY AND ANTHROPOLOGY OF RELIGION

The study of religious phenomena, including magic and mythical systems, was an important general feature of the origins of contemporary social science. Indeed, speculation about religion represented a continuous theme in sociology and anthropology, running through the nineteenth century and into the classical period of the sociology of religion with writers like Emile Durkheim, Max Weber, Herbert Spencer and Georg Simmel. With the nineteenth-century growth of European colonialism, there developed a consistent preoccupation with so-called primitive tribes, 'lower races', primitive cultures and finally with primitive mentality. Increasing evidence drawn from reports by colonial administrators, missionaries and amateur anthropologists fired speculation about the contrasting nature of advanced civilizations and primitive communities, where magical beliefs were seen to be exotic illustrations of the underlying primitive mentality of these colonized societies. Religion was seen to be analogous to the relationship between childhood and adulthood in so far as primitive religions provided an insight into the historic origins of human communities as such. In addition, the strange customs of primitive peoples in far flung colonies provided, as it were, a living experience of Otherness for European observers. These nineteenth-century comparative inquiries laid much of the foundation for modern orientalism and lingering racist attitudes towards primitiveness. These studies were based on a powerful orientalist assumption about the uniqueness and superiority of the West in the evolutionary scale of human societies. However, out of this encounter with primitive cultures, a more mature and sophisticated sociology of belief systems began to emerge.

While this interest in primitive religion was overtly embedded within an emergent social science of comparative civilizations, the implicit theme in these studies of primitive religion was in fact the growing ambiguity and uncertainty of the role of Christian belief and practice within a social environment which was itself increasingly secular and where intellectual debate was dominated by the assumptions of natural science, rather than of theology and philosophy. While early contributions to sociology and anthropology probed the beliefs and practices of primitive cultures, they were equally, but more covertly, an investigation and interrogation of the role and nature of Christianity within a social environment where moral and social authority was passing from ministers of religion to natural scientists. Anthropology and sociology raised relativistic problems about the truth value of primitive religion and as a consequence they inevitably raised relativistic questions about the rationality and validity of Christian mythology and Christian practice. These tensions between science and religion in the West were beautifully illustrated in Mrs Humphry Ward's famous novel *Robert Elsmere* (1888) in which the religious beliefs of Elsmere were gradually compromised and then undermined by his exposure to the relativistic thrust of anthropology, leading eventually to his transition from Unitarian belief to a humanistic, sceptical adherence to the philosophy of T.H. Green.

We have to see the rise of the anthropology and sociology of religion against the background of the dominant mode of natural science thought in the second half of the nineteenth century, namely a mode of scientific theorizing shaped by the dominance of an evolutionary paradigm. Social Darwinism, with its emphasis on conflict and struggle as the motors of evolutionary adaptation, provided a general social theory of historical development and social differentiation. Karl Marx integrated political economy and social Darwinism to generate a powerful theory of history and social formations, in which the stages of the mode of production were linked together into an evolutionary chain from primitive communism, through feudalism, to capitalism and socialism. While Marx's view of history was a product of this combination of social Darwinism and moral economy, his analysis of religion was based upon a critique of Hegel's idealism and Ludwig Feuerbach's sensualism, adopting many of the leading components of German biblical criticism and secular theology of his generation. In Marx's view, religious beliefs were seen to be closely related to the particular economic conditions of given modes of production. Thus, Roman Catholicism was well suited to the political and economic structures of feudalism, whereas the individualistic beliefs of Protestant Christianity were seen to be highly consistent with the economic individualism of competitive capitalist economies. Marx, adopting an evolutionary view of religious beliefs, assumed along with Friedrich Engels that religion would evaporate in the face of the hot blast of scientific reason and materialism. Marx's secular critique of traditional Christian belief was widely shared by Victorian intellectuals. The contemporary philosopher Alasdair MacIntyre has cogently argued in his essay on 'The fate of theism' (MacIntyre and Ricoeur, 1969) that it was in the final decades of the nineteenth century that atheism ceased to be a viable option for intellectuals because theism itself could no longer be taken seriously.

Nineteenth-century theories of economic industrialization were also theories of secularization, because social scientists assumed that, with the growth of industrial capitalism, the transition from rural to urban society had destroyed the social and moral control of the Church. The social and historical development of Europe was divided chronologically into separate ages of faith and ages of secularity. For writers like Claude Saint-Simon, the 'feudal–theological system' was gradually being replaced by a new social order based upon the industrial classes and positivistic science. In the industrial–scientific system, the government of human beings would be transformed into the administration of things. He predicted the rise of a new religion based on humanism and science. For Auguste Comte in his positivistic philosophy, medieval society, which was characterized by the dominance of the Catholic Church and by militarism, was being rapidly replaced by a new social system in which scientists and industrialists would have dominant social roles. In the sociological writings of Herbert Spencer, the separation of military from industrial society had become a commonplace idea among dissenting liberals. The collapse of the old military–theological system created a general crisis in social organization and individual consciousness, at least a crisis for conservatism.

While the sociology and anthropology of religion were sharply divided into various contrasting and conflicting theories, there existed a core of general notions about the nature of religion and science which provided the underlying theme for the analysis of religion in the late nineteenth century. The first assumption was that rationality was an emerging principle of industrial society and that rationality was defined operationally by the methods of experimental science. Truth was ultimately produced by the evidence made available to the human senses by the intervention of experimental science which was an embodiment of human reason. Scientific reason became the unambiguous benchmark for the evolution of civilization, a benchmark which neatly constructed primitiveness as Otherness. As a result, the belief systems of primitive people were regarded as unscientific and therefore as irrational. Primitive belief systems were the effect of a primitive mentality which perceived reality in ways entirely different from those which orchestrated reasoning in the natural sciences. This view was defended at some length by Lucien Lévy-Bruhl in his *Primitive Mentality* (1923). The second assumption was that human history was characterized by an evolutionary scheme in which human societies passed through a series of definite and necessary stages from simple to more complex societies. Within this evolutionary scheme, humanity passed from primitive magic and fetishism through religion to contemporary science. Third, along with the assumptions of the dominant system, individualism was taken to be the primary moral and political characteristic of an advanced civilization. In thinking about primitive religion, social philosophers imagined primitive individuals in isolation attempting to make sense of their natural environment through a system of magical beliefs. The emphasis was thus upon the cognitive apprehension of reality by isolated individuals who were quaintly perceived as ancient philosophers.

With the later development of anthropology and sociology in the twentieth century, these assumptions were eventually jettisoned through internal criticism, as a consequence of improvements in the methodology of field research and through the accumulation of more reliable comparative ethnographic data. We can see in the development of anthropology and sociology of religion a growing awareness and appreciation of the non-rational, that is an appreciation of the role of symbol and metaphor in human thinking outside the framework and criteria of experimental natural science. Social scientists also turned increasingly to questions about the function and consequences of religion, rather than focusing on the truth or falsity of their belief systems. Finally, the social sciences have taken an increasingly critical view of individualism as a universal criterion of civilizational progress. The social philosophers who provided the framework within which a contemporary view of religion began to develop came to reject many of the evolutionary assumptions of nineteenth-century theological approaches to religion.

Within a traditional and philosophical approach, religion was thought to evolve through a series of stages from fetishism, through polytheism, to monotheism and eventually to a Protestant view of theology as a rational and reasonable framework within which to understand humanity and nature. Evolutionary views of religion had been upheld by David Hume in *The Natural History of Religion* in 1757. The notion that religion had its origins in fetishism was developed by Ch R. de Brosses, a contemporary and correspondent of Voltaire, in *Le Culte des dieux Fétiches ou parallèle de l'ancienne religion de l'Egypte avec la religion actuelle de la Nigritie* in 1760. De Brosses took the notion of fetishism from the Portuguese word for talisman and he argued that religion was the survival of earlier forms of fetishism involving the worship of stones and other physical objects. German scholars of the method called *Kulturkreislehre* attempted to establish as evolutionary scale which was based on the assumption that hunter–gatherer communities represent the lowest form of human existence. These societies developed along three lines: matrilineal and agricultural, patrilineal and totemic, and patriarchal and nomadic.

While the notion of fetishism was deployed by Marx as a criticism of obsessive attachment to consumerism as an ideology of social relations under capitalism, nineteenth-century theorists like Max Müller and Herbert Spencer came to reject fetishism as a general explanation of religion and Müller in particular treated fetishism as a corruption of earlier forms of religion. Totemism was also much debated by the nineteenth-century writers as an illustration of primitive religious practices. Early writers on the sociology of religion were much exercised therefore by questions of polytheism and monotheism. Wilhelm Schmidt's theories of the origin of the idea of God attempted to establish a notion of primitive monotheism, but generally speaking, early theories of religion adhered to an evolutionary scheme in which polytheism gave way eventually to monotheism. A monotheistic belief system was also thought to be more compatible with natural science, because God was not necessarily a personal deity but simply the First Cause.

On the basis of these assumptions about reason, evolutionary growth and individualism, we can develop a useful scheme in order to understand early approaches to the social scientific analysis of religious belief and practice. A variety of models are in fact available for this categorization. R.R. Marett saw the study of religion as essentially a comparative empirical science in his *The Threshold of Religion* (1909). Having made a distinction between individualistic and sociological approaches, he came to define comparative religion as 'a branch of empirical sciences which aims at describing in formulae of the highest generality attained, the historical tendencies of the human mind considered in its religious aspect' (Marett, 1909: 168). The assumption behind comparative religion was that it involved some departure from primarily philosophical and theological approaches. The emergence of comparative religion required a greater devotion to an appropriate methodology, an argument emphasized by Alexander Le Roy (1923) in his *The Religion of the Primitives*. In contemporary anthropology and sociology, more complex categorization has emerged. For example, E.E. Evans-Pritchard (1965) in his *Theories of Primitive Religion* distinguished early psychological approaches starting with R. de Brosses and theories which examined the importance of the idea of the soul in the work of E.B. Tyler, Max Müller and J.G. Frazer and the sociological theories of Emile Durkheim, Robert Hertz, Henri Hubert and Marcel Mauss. These approaches were contrasted with the work of Lucien Lévy-Bruhl who through his *La mentalité primitive* which was first published in 1922, attempted to provide an account of prelogical thought. He rejected individualistic psychology in favour of a social understanding of primitive representations. The most useful categorization of theories of religion was however developed by William J. Goode (1951) in his *Religion Among the Primitives*. Goode distinguished between animistic–manist theories which were particularly influential among the English anthropologists, naturalistic theories which were embraced by writers like Max Müller, psychoanalytic theories which were embraced by writers like Sigmund Freud in his *Totem and Taboo, The Future of an Illusion* and *Moses and Monotheism*. Goode also identified theological and cultural historical approaches and finally notes the emergence of sociological interpretations of religion through the work of William Robertson Smith, Emile Durkheim and his followers, such as Henri Hubert and Marcel Mauss.

In this chapter on the origins of anthropological and sociological theories of religion, I shall closely follow the classificatory scheme of Goode. However, we should note that the rationalistic, individualistic and cognitive assumptions of nineteenth-century social philosophy found their most profound critique in the work of Talcott Parsons, particularly in his *The Structure of Social Action* (1937), in his introduction to Max Weber's *The Sociology of Religion* (1966) and finally in his general theory of society in *The Social System* (1951). Parsons attempted to demonstrate that on the basis of a rationalist theory of economic action, it was impossible for social scientists to explain the nature of social order without some recourse to a notion that general values provide the foundation for society. Parsons criticized the rationalist theory of social action because it could not provide us with a theory of social solidarity. Indeed, force and fraud are perfectly consistent with rational choice theory. Hence Parsons looked towards religion as an illustration of the origins of social solidarity in common rituals and common values. Parsons analysed Durkheim's *The Elementary Forms of the Religious Life* as a paradigm for the development of a sociology of solidarity and he showed that the Durkheimian School had laid the foundations for modern sociology by understanding the ritualistic nature of social order, particularly in common collective rituals.

The attempt to distinguish between magic and religion had been one of the consistent themes of nineteenth-century theories of religion. Magic was often seen to be an early or primitive version of religious belief or practice. Magic came to be seen as primarily an individualistic response to the dilemmas and dangers of social arrangements and natural catastrophes. It is interesting, for example, that Durkheim argued that 'there is no Church of magic ... the magician has a clientele and not a Church' (Durkheim, 1961: 60). This notion of the social dimension of religion in opposition to magic was, as we will see, an important step in the development of a genuinely sociological view of religious belief and practice.

Turning then to nineteenth-century theories of religion, animism – which was widely adopted among English social philosophers including Tylor, Frazer and Spencer – exhibited all the essential hallmarks of rationalistic and individualistic approaches to religion. It was based upon the assumption that religion provided 'the ancient philosopher' with a general but false explanation of natural and human phenomena. The concept of the soul was treated by Tylor as a basic premise of religion understood as a type of philosophy. Thus, Tylor argued that 'the ancient savage philosophers probably made their first step by the obvious inference that every man has two things belonging to him, namely, a life and a phantom' (Tylor, 1891: volume 1, 429). By regarding religion as a philosophy, Tylor sought to explain the primitive understanding of the world in terms of a belief in the soul. For example, the soul provided the ancient philosopher with a useful way of distinguishing between being awake and being asleep. On the basis of this approach, Tylor came to give religion one of its most simple but influential definitions, namely religion is the belief in spiritual beings. If religion was a cognitive philosophy based upon the belief in the soul, magic was defined by Tylor as 'a sincere but fallacious system of philosophy' (1891: 135). Another version of this approach was adopted by Spencer in his *Principles of Sociology* (1880–96) where he emphasized the importance of the concept of mana. This concept was adopted by western observers from Melanesian theories of religious power and generalized to provide an understanding of primitive religion as such. Mana is the distinctive characteristic of sacred beings. It is defined by R.H. Codrington in his *The Melanesians* (Codrington, 1891: 118–119), where he defined mana in these terms 'as a force altogether distinct from physical power which acts in all kinds of ways for good and evil and which is of the greatest advantage to possess and control'. Codrington showed that the peoples of the Pacific have a belief in a sacred power which is not individualized and is not associated with spiritual beings. Mana is capable of residing in almost any object or place. Western philosophers use the concepts of animism and manism to provide an account of the false philosophy of primitive religion as an account of the mysteries of nature and of human existence.

An alternative approach was adopted by Müller and Schmidt which has been defined by Goode and others as naturism. In this tradition religion is seen to be a human response to the majesty and awful character of nature. Overwhelmed by the beauty and majesty of the natural environment, human beings sought an explanation for this wonder in terms of spiritual beings. Müller's theory therefore posits feelings and strong emotions in the face of natural phenomena which inspired a sense of terror or wonder in human beings. Müller combined this notion with a theory of language. He argued that belief in spirits and supernatural beings was the result of a linguistic mistake, that is, the confusion between the metaphorical use of terms and their denotative use. Primitive people came to personify nature through the misuse of language in relation to the beauty of nature. In particular, myth was, according to Müller, treated as a disease of thought.

Although these nineteenth-century theories of religion were influential, they came under extensive intellectual criticism. This criticism laid the foundation of modern approaches to religion in anthropology and sociology. Animism–manism and naturism, as I have indicated, shared a common set of assumptions – the centrality of the individual, positivism, natural science as an exclusive paradigm of rationality, evolutionism and orientalism. Sociological theories emerged out of a critical dialogue with these approaches. Durkheim, in *The Elementary Forms of the Religious Life*, provided the principal ingredients of the basic sociological approach. He criticized Tylor's 'minimum definition' and his idea that religion as a general philosophy was false. For Durkheim, 'there are no religions which are false. All are true in their own fashion, all answer, though in different ways, to the given conditions of human existence' (Durkheim, 1961: 15). Sociology attempted to discover 'the ever-present causes upon which the most essential forms of religious thought and practice depend' (1961: 20). Durkheim also attacked the individualistic definitions of religion in animism by arguing that belief in spiritual beings was not universal to religions. For example, Theravada Buddhism is non-theistic. Durkheim proposed to define religion as a 'unified system of beliefs and practices relative to sacred things, that is to say things set apart and forbidden – beliefs and practices which unite into one single moral community called a Church, all those who adhere to them' (1961: 62). Tylor and Frazer, by concentrating on the individual's rational apprehension of the world, failed to draw attention to the emotional character of religious practices and the obligatory nature of involvement in religious institutions. Belief in the sacred character of the totem was not a voluntary or private option. Durkheim also dismissed Müller's naturism as merely the vision of nature of modern city-dwellers; for traditional societies, nature was more likely to be seen as regular and monotonous. Totemic objects are often far from awe-inspiring and indeed Müller's view of nature approaches anthropomorphism.

If Durkheim laid the foundation for modern approaches to the sacred in the work of Robert Hertz, Henri Hubert, Marcel Mauss and Roger Callois, this sociological breakthrough was only possible on the foundations built by the methodological critique of Andrew Lang, by the theoretical insights of Fustel de Coulanges and W. Robertson Smith, by the ethnographic discoveries of anthropologists, missionaries and others, and by the comparative approach to primitive religion of Robert Lowie. The edifice of Durkheimian sociology of totemic religion was based on the ethnographic reports of Baldwin Spencer and F.J. Gillen (1904) on Australian Aboriginal belief and practice.

We can understand the evolution of the sociology and anthropology of religion, therefore, in terms of a growing critical awareness of the methodological limitations and weaknesses of traditional approaches in speculative comparative religion and philosophical approaches to mythology. For example, Andrew Lang showed that the philological approach to mythology by Müller and Schmidt was unreliable, being merely a form of armchair anthropology. Lang criticized the notion that myths could be easily compared through merely textual methods and recommended the use of comparative folklore. Although these criticisms were valid, as Evans-Pritchard (1965: 5) complained, the early study of religion 'has been the happy hunting ground of men of letters and has been speculative and philosophical in a rather old-fashioned way'. Major studies such as Frazer's *The Golden Bough* (1935) were constructed haphazardly on the basis of selective evidence taken from around the world. The result was a caricature of the mentality of 'primitive man'.

Against this speculative and selective background, two sociological contributions proved to be transformative. There was first the social–historical approach to classical society and religion by Numa Denis Fustel de Coulanges in 1864 in *The Ancient City* (1956) and the second breakthrough took place in William Robertson Smith's writing on sacrifice. Fustel de Coulanges traced the history of religions, especially in terms of the conception of god, in ancient society from the religion of the hearth-gods to the emergence of a unified notion of a supreme deity. His thesis was that beliefs about the gods were mythical reflections of the underlying political structure of Roman society. As society became more unified and integrated, a universalistic notion of monotheism evolved, resulting in the Christian conception of a high god. The polarity between polytheism and monotheism reflected not a psychological disposition among believers, but a structural transformation of society itself. The nature and role of myth were functions of the structure of society. This notion in some ways was compatible with the approach of W. Robertson Smith, whose perspective on religious practices combined German biblical criticism with evolutionary anthropology. Smith's articles in the *Encyclopaedia Britannica* in 1875 caused anxiety in the Scottish kirk and he was eventually dismissed from the chair of Hebrew at the University of Aberdeen for his alleged indifference to biblical authority and to the uniqueness of the gospel.

In Smith's approach, the meaning of religious beliefs and symbols was dependent on their social and cultural location; the 'truth' of religious claims was local and variable. In primitive societies, where there was no development of a professional theological stratum of priests and hence no systematic theology, practice embodied belief in rituals and rites. Smith was particularly interested in the rituals of sacrifice. One of the most fundamental religious acts involves an exchange of goods between human beings and their gods, and these exchanges often take the form of a ritual meal where food (which may include human sacrifice) is offered to the gods. In the totemic meal, the collective consumption of the sacred totem forged a bond between the individual and the sacred. These totemic meals illustrate the obligatory nature of religious rituals which serve to bind the group together. The word 'religio' itself also means to bind together and thus religion can be defined as a set of practices with respect to sacred powers, where the enactment of these rituals creates and recreates the group. Mythology can thus be read as the collective history of the group, especially in its dealings with the sacred.

Smith's analysis in his *Lectures on the Religion of the Semites* (1889) gave rise to the possibility, of course, that the central liturgical practice of Christianity, namely the Eucharistic meal, was itself the legacy of ancient cannibalistic and totemic festivals wherein 'primitives' ate their own god. Indeed in the Eucharistic injunction 'Take, eat. This is my Body which is given for you', it is difficult not to avoid the conclusion that the ritualistic core of the Christian cult is a totemic meal. Smith attempted to avoid this relativistic threat to Christian orthodoxy by arguing that Christianity was a spiritual religion in which the totemic meal had a symbolic function by indicating the altruistic nature of divine love. The Christian celebration was not based on a false equation between hygiene and holiness, because Holy Communion celebrated a spiritual, not a physical, bond between God and His flock. Smith's critics within the Church were not entirely convinced that he had safeguarded the integrity and uniqueness of the gospel from an inevitable comparison with primitive totemic systems.

Regardless of the theological squabble within the Church, Smith's treatment of religion laid the foundation for Durkheim's analysis of totemism which embraced the theoretical lessons of Fustel de Coulanges and Smith with the ethnological studies of Australian Aboriginal communities to produce a masterpiece of twentieth-century sociology in *The Elementary Forms of the Religious Life*, the subtitle of which was *The Totemic System in Australia*, in 1912. His study had three distinctive aims. The first was to study the simplest religious system, namely Australian totemism, in order to understand the elementary forms of religious life. The second was to study the elementary forms of thought such as the distinction between sacred and profane, and third to establish generalizations about social relations in all human societies. In this study, Durkheim demolished the individualistic, cognitive and evolutionary arguments of Frazer, Tylor, Müller and Spencer. He sought a universalistic definition of religion which recognized that the sacred/profane distinction was a fundamental form of all religious systems. His classical definition was, following Smith, that 'religion is a unified system of beliefs and practices relative to sacred things, that is to say, things set apart and forbidden – beliefs and practices which unite into one single moral community called a Church, all those who adhere to them' (Durkheim, 1961: 62).

While this definition laid the foundation for contemporary sociology, it still reflected some of the assumptions and limitations of traditional comparative religion. Durkheim argued that religion survived because it satisfied fundamental functions of social life, namely the need for social solidarity. The collective effervescence of ritual life reintegrated individuals into the group. Thus religion was a form of social glue (Turner, 1991: 38–62). In the ritual act, therefore, the worshippers gave homage, not to God, but to the social group. Durkheim's theory held to the traditional assumption, at least implicitly, that the belief statements of religious systems are false, because they refer, not to a divine person, but to society itself. His sociology was evolutionary in the sense that socialism was to replace traditional religious systems as the social glue of advanced, industrial society. His approach has also been criticized on the grounds that it is often difficult to generalize from simple totemic systems to more complex modern beliefs, but even this contrast suggests an evolutionary scale in which Australian Aboriginal totemism is held to be more simple than, for example, the collective rituals and beliefs which surround contemporary sport. In modern societies, the enthusiasm and collective emotions which arise through loyalty to football clubs are often compared to religious devotions. One final problem with Durkheim's functionalist account of the social consequences of religious practice is that it neglected the historical dimensions of religious institutions, especially the organizational structures and roles of ecclesiastical organizations. These aspects of religion were developed more in the German tradition of sociology by Ernst Troeltsch and Max Weber. Whereas British and French anthropologists had concentrated on the general nature of religious and magical symbols and customs, German sociology arose around a specific concern with the historical role of Christianity in western society, and with the organizational forms of Christian institutions. In his famous *The Protestant Ethic and the Spirit of Capitalism* (1930), which Weber published in German as two essays in 1904, he analysed the relationship between Protestant beliefs and the individualistic and secular culture of emerging capitalism. In *The Social*

Teaching of the Christian Churches (1931), Troeltsch developed a contrast between sect and church as a model of organizational development and change in Christianity, a model which used Weber's analysis of charismatic breakthrough (Weber, 1966). Weber's study of prophetic religions illustrated the perpetual struggle between traditional modes of authority and charismatic revolutions; in institutional terms, this contrast can be seen in terms of a distinction between the authority of priests and the radical claims of prophets. In this framework, the traditional Christian Church represented an institutionalization of charisma.

In conclusion, the intellectual environment of contemporary sociology and anthropology has obviously changed considerably from the late nineteenth century which provided the context for these early studies of 'primitive religions'. In general, there is much less confidence in the authority of science as a unitary, universal and rational perspective on society. Anthropological research itself has made us more sensitive to the relativity of human culture. Sensitivity to the meaningful nuances of other cultures is combined with a recognition that the methodology of traditional field work does not produce empirical facts from which obvious conclusions can be drawn. The evolutionary perspective of social Darwinism is no longer a secure basis for pronouncing on the development of human societies from primitive to advanced systems. We are more sensitive to the moral problems of racist paradigms which boldly talked about 'primitive mentalities' than the armchair anthropologists of Victorian Britain. In addition, contemporary sociologists are much less confident in our ability to announce that modern industrial societies are inevitably exposed to cultural processes of secularization. Nietzsche's declaration that 'God is dead' was an important call for a new philosophy in the last century, but contemporary sociologists are more impressed by the vitality of Islam under modernization and by the revival of religions in post-communist societies.

References

Codrington, R.H. (1891) *The Melanesians.* Oxford: The Clarendon Press.

Durkheim, E. (1961) *The Elementary Forms of the Religious Life.* New York: Collier Books.

Evans-Pritchard, E.E. (1965) *Theories of Primitive Religion.* Oxford: Clarendon Press.

Frazer, J.G. (1935) *The Golden Bough.* New York: Macmillan.

Freud, S. (1927) *The Future of an Illusion.* London: Hogarth Press.

Freud, S. (1939) *Moses and Monotheism.* New York: Knopf.

Freud, S. (1950) *Totem and Taboo.* London: Routledge & Kegan Paul.

Fustel de Coulanges, N.D. (1956) *The Ancient City. A Study of the Religion, Law and Institutions of Greece and Rome.* Garden City, N.Y.: Doubleday.

Goode, W.J. (1951) *Religion Among the Primitives.* New York: Free Press.

Le Roy, A. (1923) *The Religion of the Primitives.* London: Burns, Oates & Washbourne.

Lévy-Bruhl, L. (1923) *Primitive Mentality.* London: George Allen & Unwin.

Lévy-Bruhl, L. (1985) *Primitive Mythology.* St. Lucia: Queensland University Press.

MacIntyre, A. and Ricoeur, P. (1969) *The Religious Significance of Atheism.* New York and London: Columbia University Press.

Marett, R.R. (1909) *The Threshold of Religion*. London: Methuen.

Parsons, T. (1937) *The Structure of Social Action*. New York: McGraw Hill.

Parsons, T. (1951) *The Social System*. London: Routledge & Kegan Paul.

Smith, W.R. (1889) *Lectures on the Religion of the Semites*. Edinburgh: Adam and Charles Black.

Spencer, B. and Gillen, F.J. (1904) *The Northern Tribes of Central Australia*. London: Macmillan.

Spencer, H. (1880–96) *The Principles of Sociology*. 3 vols, New York: Appleton.

Troeltsch, E. (1931) *The Social Teaching of the Christian Churches*. New York: Macmillan.

Turner, B.S. (1991) *Religion and Social Theory*. London: Sage.

Tylor, E.B. (1891) *Primitive Culture. Researches into the Development of Mythology, Philosophy, Religion, Language, Art and Customs*. London: John Murray.

Weber, M. (1930) *The Protestant Ethic and the Spirit of Capitalism*. London: George Allen & Unwin.

Weber, M. (1966) *The Sociology of Religion*. London: Methuen.

CHAPTER II

THE SOCIOLOGY OF THE CITY

Introduction: Cities and Civilization

In the history of the human species, cities are a relatively recent development. The earliest cities appeared simultaneously between 3000 and 4000 BC in the Nile Valley and in Mesopotamia. Around 2000 BC cities also developed in Crete, in the Yellow River in China, Greece and the Indus Valley. Cities arose independently in the New World in Central Mexico around 300 BC. The Mayan and Aztec cities arose in the first millennium AD, but large cities are a product of the industrial revolution and the demographic transformation of the eighteenth and nineteenth centuries. The two principal conditions for the emergence of the city are an agricultural surplus and an administrative system which exists over and above the family and kinship. Generally, an agricultural surplus required new technologies and urban administration required writing systems (Gist and Fava, 1974: 1–25; Gledhill, Bender and Larsen, 1988). In AD 900 cities like Beijing, Agra and Constantinople had populations of half a million. We should not, however, imagine that the history of cities and urbanization is simply one of continuous, uninterrupted evolution. Before the modern period, there were significant periods of urban decay and renewal. The crisis of the Roman empire in the third century and the barbarian invasions of the fifth century were important in shaping medieval society which, unlike classical Rome, was based on a peasant economy and a warrior caste. Feudalism resulted in a reduction of inter-city trade and a decline of the urban economy (Le Goff, 1988).

Urbanization as a historical process was both uneven and complex. For example, although London, with a population of half a million by the end of the seventeenth century, was the largest city in Europe, England was not an urban society before the industrial revolution. Unlike France with its large provincial cities such as Rouen, Orleans, Amiens and Rheims, England had few significant regional centres, apart from Bristol, Norwich and York with populations around thirty thousand. Furthermore, England had no city-states and could not match the political and administrative development of Florence or Venice. In 1801 more than three-quarters of the British population lived in the country, but the industrial revolution and, somewhat later, the growth of railways provided the economic back-drop to a number of important Georgian experiments in both town planning and housing development such as New Town in Edinburgh, the Bath Circus, the Cheltenham Promenade and the Crescent at Buxton (Downes, 1979). Yet London remained 'a disorderly sprawl, as much of a haphazard muddle as any English rural village' (Laslett, 1965: 58–9).

Although the history of the city in the West is not a single, unified narrative of urban evolution, the idea of the city has had a common character and location in the European imagination. We can argue that cities, like nations, are 'imagined political communities' (Anderson, 1983: 15) in that, regardless of demographic size, spatial characteristics and socio-economic functions, the urban community is a product of shared experiences, cultural practices, urban rituals and political processes. Members of a city the size of Bangkok do not know each other intimately or interact with each other regularly, and yet the idea of Bangkok is central to their understanding of 'community'. The city is an important component of the ideology of the West.

The city has been a fundamental social institution in the history of western civilization; this intimate interaction between the city and western culture is probably fundamentally illustrated by the etymology of such terms as civilization, civility and citizenship. The cultivated and educated citizen (*cité-zein*) is the inhabitant of a city and for historical sociologists like Norbet Elias (1978) the civilizing process whereby the manners of individuals are cultivated and developed into a socially acceptable etiquette of everyday behaviour, requires the cosmopolitan context of an urban environment, namely a city-state. Elias argued in *The Civilizing Process* that the historical evolution of civilization moves from the violent lives of men on horseback to the refined manners of the court and later to the puritanical code of the bourgeois household, but this social transformation ultimately required the larger context of a city environment. In common-sense terms, the primary values of western society have been associated with the moral order produced by the city, namely the values of urbanity and the urbane personality. By contrast, the countryside was connected with the negative notion of the pagan (*paganus*) whose life, because it existed outside the city, was characterized by illiteracy and vulgarity. Life beyond the city walls was characterized by violence, pillage and uncertainty. Karl Marx, one of the most trenchant critics of nineteenth-century capitalism, condemned the countryside and its values as mere 'rural idiocy' in his writings on the political conservatism of the French peasantry. Marx looked towards the urban bourgeoisie as the primary vehicle for the destructive creativity of modernity and to the urban environment as the breeding ground of nihilism. Marx's writings on rural France and the industrial revolution in England have provided inspiration for contemporary interpretations of the radical nature of urban life and its impact on the modern mentality. Marshall Berman's *All that is Solid Melts into Air* (1982) is a potent example.

The city ramparts were also the ramparts of a civilized and Christian existence. Augustinian theology employed self-consciously the metaphor of the city as a description of the great struggle between pagan and Christian virtues in his narrative of *De civitate Dei*. The fall of the Eternal City to barbarian invaders in 410 was the background to the Augustinian theory of virtue. Augustine's stoic acceptance of the importance of human misfortune (including deprivation, war, treachery and loss of friends) as a critique of pagan notions of possible happiness can be seen as a philosophical reflection on the decay of the public arena of Roman culture. Classical Greek and Roman norms of civility and rationality were associated with the public space of the city-state. Within this classical tradition, the private was always associated with moral (de)privation; privacy was not a desirable condition, because it was associated with the world of slavery and female domestic labour.

From medieval times, there was forged, against a background of barbarian invasion and urban decay, an intimate but necessary relationship between the growth of university scholarship and city culture. The medieval university was based, at least in principle, on the idea that the university as an institution should be open to all classes. The Renaissance universities also embraced the cosmopolitan dimensions of cultural universalism and the reform of German universities in the nineteenth century was based on an assumption that science (*Wissenschaft*) required an environment which supported the public spirit (*Civismus*). In short, universities need 'civic humanism' (Bender, 1988).

Within the sociological literature on the city, nineteenth-century writers like Numa Denis Fustel de Coulanges (1956) associated the growth of a universalistic doctrine of brotherhood and co-operation with the spread of urban Christianity in the ancient world. His famous study of *La cité antique* in 1864 traced the historical evolution of classical society from a fragmented set of communities to an integrated civilization organized around the universalistic message of Christianity. Religious rituals were seen to be fundamental in shaping the history of the city from the ancestor cults of Greece and Rome to the universalistic eucharist of Christianity. Fustel de Coulanges is regarded by many as the first modern historian of the city-state and of the revolutions which produced modern society. He had a significant impact on Emile Durkheim's general sociology and on the early sociology of religion (Turner, 1991).

In the development of social theory, the theory of the city has occupied a fundamental position in the sociological imagination and in the historical narrative of western culture and its civilized institutions. The city has become part of the fundamental discourse about the Occident, embodying a system of dichotomous contrasts and evaluations between the Otherness of the Oriental world and the rational culture of the autonomous western city. The city was seen as an integral and essential component of western history, values and institutions. This fundamental distinction was associated with the early sociology of the city, which was developed by Max Weber in his elaboration of the peculiarities of the West and his systematic contrast between the autonomous associations and democratic institutions of western cities with the predatory, patrimonial Islamic cities of the Far East. For Weber, the city was the cradle of western capitalism with its autonomous guilds and its independent associations, whereas the Islamic city was merely a military fortress, the location of the patrimonial power of pillaging caliphs. According to Weber (1958: 80) 'Neither the "city" in the economic sense, nor the garrison, the inhabitants of which are accoutred with special political-administrative structures, necessarily constitute a "community". An urban "community", in the full meaning of the word, appears as a general phenomenon only in the Occident.'

Fernand Braudel (1974: 400) appears to follow Weber in claiming that 'Capitalism and towns were basically the same thing in the West'. Braudel identified three ideal types in the historical development of cities: towns which were undifferentiated from their rural hinterland, towns which were closed inwardly by ramparts and fortifications and finally towns which were part of the sovereignty exercised by princes and states. In Europe, the city dominates the countryside, economically and politically, and within the city, life is organized by the craft and merchant guilds. These guilds are the historical seed of 'associational democracy' as celebrated by early theorists of pluralism and democracy like Alexis de Tocqueville. Here again the Islamic city is seen to be different – 'Towns similar to those in medieval Europe – masters of their fate for a brief moment – only arose in Islam when the empires collapsed. They marked some fine moments for Islamic civilization. But they only lasted for a time (to the advantage of the marginal towns)' (Braudel, 1974: 409). Within the conventional framework of western Orientalism, the Islamic city has been defined somewhat generally as the product of a patrimonial polity and is the seed, not of citizenship, but of dictatorship (Turner, 1974: 9–106).

In order to understand the significance of the city in western sociological theory, we have to understand the importance of the city for debates about individual freedom and democracy, and we have to grasp the ideological importance of the city as a strategic concept in Orientalism which specified a radical difference between the oriental despotic city as a military camp and the democratic institutions of the western city (Said, 1978; Turner, 1974; 1978). The political uncertainty of the Islamic patrimonial cities undermined the sociological conditions which were necessary for free trade, for independent banking institutions and the evolution of a mercantile culture. This contrast was fundamental to the prevalent notion that 'the city air makes a man free' (*Stadtluft macht frei*), namely that within an urban western environment the possibilities of independent freedom and democracy were maximized.

Romanticism and the Village

The city as an intellectual and ideological notion was an important part of the long-standing debate between the 'ancients and moderns' (Schorske, 1963). While many scholars applauded the virtues of the ancient city, radical critics like Voltaire spoke approvingly of London as a centre of art, commerce and freedom. It was a significant aspect of social mobility in an industrial civilization as opposed to the hierarchical structures of feudalism. Adam Smith in *The Wealth of Nations* in 1776 agreed with Voltaire perceiving the city as the principal connection between the raw commodities of the countryside and the division of labour in urban industry. However, the growing prosperity of the city, in producing an unstable and unpredictable social environment, also created a psychologically volatile climate, which he contrasted romantically with the tranquillity of country pursuits. In the middle of the eighteenth century, the Scottish physician George Cheyne, who provided medical advice to David Hume and Alexander Pope, claimed in his *Essay on Health and Long Life* in 1724 that the coffee-house diet and life-style enjoyed by the London elite was resulting in chronic melancholy and obesity. William Blake encountered 'Marks of weakness, marks of woe' in his poem on London and Oliver Goldsmith championed rural virtues, deploring the slow but inevitable destruction of the peasantry and the rural community. The Lake District poets perfected a literary tradition which treated rural tranquillity as a necessary condition for stability of the mind and poverty and deprivation became a central topic of the realism of the nineteenth-century novel (Lukács, 1971). The realist novel saw the city through the eyes of writers like Charles Dickens, as a place of petty corruption, working-class crime and competitive individualism. In twentieth-century literature, this critique of the city as the context of secular modernity was continued in the work of T.S. Eliot in 'The Love Song of J. Alfred Prufrock' and in 'The Waste Land' where Eliot reflects bleakly on the 'Unreal City,/Under the brown fog of a winter dawn,/A crowd flowed over London Bridge, so many,/I had not thought death had undone so many.' Eliot's *The Waste Land*, drafted in the autumn of 1921, was inspired by the post-war ruin of Europe and by Joseph Conrad's *Heart of Darkness*, which opens with a scene of the red sails of barges drifting in the Thames Estuary. From the point of view of philosophy, this condemnation of the modern city and its underlying technology reached its apex in the philosophical critique of metaphysics in Martin Heidegger's 'The question concerning technology' of 1955 in which he laments, among other things, the damming of the Rhine for electronic power-stations and its use by the tourist industry (Heidegger, 1977: 16). As we will see, aspects of Heidegger's philosophical criticisms of modernity provided the foundation for postmodern criticism of the city, 1950s urban redevelopment and modernist architectural style in the work, for example, of Le Corbusier (Jenks, 1995; Lash, 1990). As a conclusion, we can note that a dichotomous view of the countryside as either the scene of idyllic, Arcadian virtues or a backwater of boorish manners has continued with remarkable persistence down the centuries, during which time the rural economy was transformed from peasant production to a capitalist agribusiness (Newby, 1979).

In fact the rise of social theories of the city has been profoundly marked by the influence of romanticism which idealized the rural communalism of the traditional village and regarded the city as a dangerous and alienating environment. This critique of the modern city was particularly important in the work of Lewis Mumford (1895–1990), whose *Technics and Civilization* (1934), *The Culture of Cities* (1938) and *The City in History* (1961) shaped the underlying values and assumptions of both urban sociology and town planning.

Mumford shared with Patrick Geddes the basic metaphorical notion that the city was ultimately a social organism whose evolution, at best, might be helped by 'conservative surgery', decentralized management and devolved planning. Mumford, influenced by Geddes's approach to the conservation of the architectural heritage of Edinburgh and by his synthetic philosophy of the natural and social sciences, deplored the scale of the growth mania of urban America, rejecting the notion that escalating sky-scrapers, increasing physical size, and soaring land prices were necessarily an index of urban progress. In 'The intolerable city' (Mumford, 1926) he argued that the burden of progress was borne by citizens who could no longer afford to live in New York and by cultural activities (museums, parks and art galleries) which could not compete with business for space and accommodation.

Mumford's principal focus was in fact historical; he sought to understand the erosion of a balanced, organic and decentralized civilization and its replacement by a centralized, militaristic (or at least belligerent), metropolitan system of power. In more particular terms, he studied the decline of the contained, compact and comfortable medieval city and the rise of the aggressive, anonymous, centralized megalopolis. For Mumford, the medieval town provided robust opportunities for communal and associational life, for private spaces and solitude. A city like London in the fourteenth century, with a population of 40,000, was still open to country living and rural life-style. By contrast, the industrial cities of the nineteenth century were characterized either by row after row of bourgeois shops and homes, or by the sordid squalor of Charles Dickens's 'Coketown'. The age of 'carboniferous capitalism' would be replaced eventually by Tyrannopolis in which gangster-dictators would have control or by Nekropolis, where the city would be converted into a tomb by war and disease. Mumford's solutions were modest, but practical; they involved experiments with green-belts, urban resettlement and the creation of inner-city communities and 'villages'. Many of these ideas were expressed in his report for a plan for the city of Honolulu in 1938 (Miller, 1989).

The Urban Revolution

As we have seen, the city played an important part in western romanticism where it has been a target of considerable conservative criticism. The city is simultaneously the product of social change (such as urbanization), the engine of social transformation and the geographical space within which modern change has occurred. As a result, the city plays an important part conceptually in theories of social change. We examine first the European context and the idea of the city as both the site and the motor of social history.

In order to understand the debate about the city and social change, it is important to start with an examination of the conceptual problems in defining the city. Beginning with the work of archeologists on pre-history, the classification of the city as an urban context has been an important feature of the literature on cities. If we take the work of Gordon Childe, we can start by establishing a number of important criteria for the early antiquity of the city and for its sociological definition. In his article on civilization, cities and towns in *Antiquity*, Childe (1957) identified a number of important criteria for the definition of a city. Childe was interested in the city as the location for the development of various juridical institutions and arrangements such that a city is a community 'that comprises a substantial proportion of professional rulers, officials, clergy, artisans and merchants who do not catch or grow their own food, but live on the surplus produced by farmers or fishermen who may dwell within the city or villages outside its walls' (Childe, 1957: 37). Thus a city involves a particular framework of government which comes into existence with the development of an agricultural civilization with a surplus to support such intellectual or mental workers. This transition in history permits us to speak of an 'urban revolution' analogous to the notion of an industrial revolution or a Neolithic revolution. Thus the origins of cities are closely associated with the growth of the institution of writing as a bureaucratic process of management and surveillance. The transition of the city from its ancient origins into a modern form is closely connected with the emergence of literate culture and the role of writing as a strategy of political regulation.

In Europe therefore, the origin of the city is linked to the growth of a bureaucratic status group whose principal cultural asset was the manipulation of a literary culture as part of a political regime of control. Alongside these bureaucratic developments, the growth of the city is associated with major population changes. For example, the work of Michel Foucault (1991) on governmentality and surveillance can be seen as a reflection upon the demographic transformation of Europe, namely the rise of the highly populated cities of the eighteenth and nineteenth centuries. The rise of governmentality as a political practice is connected with anxieties about the impact of population change on the European urban scene. If sociology had its origins classically in the period 1890–1920, then we can see the rise of sociology as in part an intellectual reflection upon urban density and population change. Throughout the nineteenth century, the cities of Europe experienced a profound population transformation which was the result of urban migration and a demographic transition involving a decline in the birth rate and an increase in the surviving populations through improvements in sanitation and medical intervention.

Cities are defined in these terms by reference to an agricultural surplus, the demographic transition, the institution of writing and bureaucratic institutions of government. From a sociological perspective, these criteria are not entirely satisfactory for understanding the city. Sociologists are interested in the city more as a system of social relations than as a geographical or demographic phenomenon. It was Aristotle who argued that the city-state was based upon a shared social reality of equal citizens within a public arena; the private world was one of unequal members. A common space in itself was not sufficient to define a city. Greek philosophers who feared difference espoused the notion of the ideal city in terms of its wholeness and unity rather than location in space (Saxonhouse, 1992). Urban sociology may have had its roots in urban geography, but it developed as an analysis of the city as a social form. Sociologists have been interested firstly in the city as an administrative and political agency, secondly in the city as a way of life, and thirdly with the mentalities (or cultures) which are associated with urbanism. The analysis of the city as a political system is the legacy of Weber's sociology of the city. The study of the city as a way of life was, as we will see, the contribution of the Chicago School of sociology, and finally the perspective on urban living in terms of mentality has to be understood by reference to Georg Simmel's contribution to the sociology of culture. I shall consider these dimensions in this sequence.

The City, Politics and Power

The city has played an important role in political and administrative control. In *The Preindustrial City*, Gideon Sjoberg (1960) argues that the traditional city had a number of common features. It was walled and played a part in the defence of an urban elite. This walled area contained religious and government buildings, and within this central space markets developed. Sjoberg's emphasis on defence functions is to some extent a criticism of Weber who claimed that a city is always a market. Cities exist as mechanisms for the consolidation of the power of a dominant class. While Anthony Giddens (1985) believes that Sjoberg's argument is an exaggeration, he supports the view that cities are vehicles for the expansion of administrative power over rural areas. Therefore, the rise of the city-state was closely associated with the development of writing. The development of writing is an essential basis for the development of surveillance.

There is some general agreement among historians that the city-state has its origin in the existence of an agricultural surplus, the rise of urban elites and writing systems which permitted more sophisticated forms of control and surveillance. But with the rise of commercialism and intercontinental trade, the city also provided the context for immunities from feudal lords, for the growth of craft guilds and for civic culture. The historical study of the city and democracy were given a specific scholarly focus by Henri Pirenne (1936) who, through the study of the cities of Belgium and the Netherlands, established the broadly-based thesis that the rising urban culture of the European city provided the context for not only merchant immunities but for a robust context for democratic practice and behaviour. Pirenne was sensitive to the changing fortunes of the trading communities of urban Europe after the expansion of Islam closed off international trade routes following the expansion of the Umayyad caliphate westward and consequently the Islamic occupation of North Africa and Spain.

One can find a similar preoccupation with the city and political development in German scholarship. In pre-Bismarckian Germany, academics like Johann Winckelmann and Johann Wolfgang Goethe looked backwards towards Greece and classical Rome for a model of civilized virtues. Prior to the unification of Germany, there was no single, dominant city among the many Germanic principalities. The political and cultural supremacy of Berlin only emerged towards the end of the nineteenth century. Following the impact of the French Revolution, nationalists like Johann Gottlieb Fichte extolled the virtues of the traditional German city and its burghers who were inspired by a communitarian morality which was productive of civic virtues. Fichte's voluntaristic theory of knowledge, his rejection of revelation in favour of secular reason, and his activist assumptions about rights were a reflection of his commitment to the tradition of independent cities. In Fichte's 'science of rights', the independent city was seen as the vehicle of liberty and progress. The themes of communalism were taken up by historians like Otto von Gierke (1990) who traced the legacy of community (*Genossenschaft*) through the evolution of German constitutionalism. Broadly speaking, Gierke treated the development of German political structures in terms of an ever shifting balance between communal forms of fellowship and self-regulation within the walls of the city and the rise of an authoritarian constitution (*Obrigkeitsverfassung*). By the end of the Middle Ages in Germany, the authority of the city craft guilds had declined, government by councils not citizens prevailed, and passive rights had replaced rule of the people. The defeat of the populist elements of the Reformation further strengthened the principle of authoritarian sovereignty (*Obrigkeit*).

A similar set of notions are expressed through a tradition of writing on the city and the metropolitan government in the work of writers like Frederic W. Maitland, whose history of English constitutionalism was the basis of his approach to political reform in the city. Gierke and Maitland were principal intellectual sources for Weber's historical and sociological analysis of the autonomy of the western city. For Maitland (1898), the Royal charter of medieval times did not constitute a corporation; rather it conferred recognition on an urban community which already enjoyed liberties and immunities. After the fifteenth century, there was a tendency for charters to recognize, not the traditional autonomy of cities, but the responsibility of the citizens to the state. The modern city emerged in the context of nineteenth-century legislation which treated the city as an important component of the representative and administrative system of the state. In North America, the ideal of active citizenship was the aim of municipal reforms and became a major theme of political theory in the work of William Bennet Munro (1912). The city was a context for active citizenship, municipal reform and progressive politics; it was the training ground for civic education and urban political participation. Social scientists came to regard the modern city as 'the laboratory of representative government' (Capes, 1922: 3).

Urbanism as a Way of Life

These studies were closely associated with the growth of the European urban environment, but from a social science point of view it was in North America that urban sociology found its most congenial context for research and theoretical development. For example, the so-called Chicago School provided a strong tradition of urban research on marginal groups, on social disorganization, on the ghetto, on marginal occupations and on urban poverty. The Chicago School was motivated by a doctrine of pragmatism, amelioration and empirical research. However, against this matter-of-fact approach to urban data there was also a strong sense of a loss of innocence, the dominance of moral decay and the erosion of civilized practice. Against a background of urban decay, the Chicago School and its followers embraced implicitly a positive image of the early colonial environment, the autonomous city and the free and authentic citizen. Out of this mixture of pragmatism and romanticism, there emerged a variety of theories of spatial order, zoning, ethnic segregation and social ecology. The Chicago School provided one of the most detailed and significant descriptions of the modern urban city which was genuinely sociological in its direction and dimensions.

Whereas the European urban sociologists were concerned with comparative and historical issues relating to the rise of capitalism, the American sociologists were initially preoccupied with the impact of ethnic migration and cultural diversity. They developed a particular interest in the origin of cities, their geographical location and their spatial development. Following a positivist epistemology, they saw their scientific role in terms of developing a detailed picture of the 'facts' of urban life. These questions about origin, location and spatial characteristics gave rise to a number of influential studies, but *The City* (Park, Burgess and McKenzie, 1925) was particularly important.

From this research tradition, there emerged the so-called 'ecological theory of the city'. For Robert E. Park the city was a natural environment of modern people, which followed specific laws of development. The city grew as a complex network of communities, which came to be associated over time with specific neighbourhoods and particular suburbs. These neighbourhood communities are populated by ethnic communities, organized around a definite division of labour. For Park, the city was an organization of social communities in space, an organization which follows its own laws of evolutionary development. The Chicago School's approach to the city was thus based on broad assumptions that the city provided a 'natural' laboratory or framework for sociological study, there was an important cultural division between city and country, which was conceptualized in terms of a rural–urban continuum, and in an urban society the city came to define the whole life of the society. The more specific theory of the city was the concentric-zone theory of urban development. This theory states that the growth of the city is determined by a social struggle over land values, which ensures that the dominant group controls the most significant urban land. The central business district is the key to this pattern of land distribution, while newcomers and less powerful communities are relegated to the urban periphery. The city grows as a result in terms of a series of circles or zones. As ethnic communities are integrated into the dominant culture, they experience social mobility which results in geographical mobility. Minority groups are transferred from the ghetto to more prestigious areas in the city. It is possible to map these social changes in order to produce a geographical history of the city in terms of population transfers between zones. This approach resulted in a number of influential studies of the city (Anderson, 1923; McKenzie, 1923 and 1933; Reckless, 1933; Schmid, 1937; Thrasher, 1927; Wirth, 1928; Zorbaugh, 1929).

Although the ecological theory was concerned initially with the spatial organization of cities, it did recognize the importance of cultural specialization within the city and encouraged the study of the city as a cultural phenomenon (Sennett, 1969). This trend towards a cultural analysis can be noted in Louis Wirth's famous essay on 'Urbanism as a way of life' in which Wirth (1938) attempted to specify the principal features of the large modern city. In addition to population density, he noted: heterogeneity of ethnic communities, life-styles and cultures; social relations which are transitory, anonymous, and effectively neutral; occupational specialization and the division of labour; separation of residence and work place; secularization of thought and values, which is facilitated by a money economy; standardization through the growth of mass markets; dependence on formal rules of conduct, which are indicated by the dominance of the clock and traffic signals; and the predominance of secondary and segmental contacts. Wirth's seminal essay has been both criticized and elaborated by subsequent research. Urban relationships are not necessarily or invariably impersonal. Empirical research suggests, for example, that consumers often adopt a personalized approach to shopping (Stone, 1954).

The Chicago School laid the foundations for contemporary urban sociology, but it was also influential in the sociological analysis of race relations, studies of social stratification and urban organization. It influenced the famous 'Yankee City studies' of W.L. Warner and P. Lunt (1941) who developed a six-class model of social hierarchy, and in contemporary sociology the housing-class theories of John Rex (1970) in his research on discrimination within the city. The Chicago School established a tradition of qualitative, urban ethnography with a special focus on minority groups, ethnic communities and social class. Concentric-zoning theory has been modified by the application of marginalist economic principles to take into account the interaction between transport costs and rent in shaping the city. The structure of the city changes in response to consumer preferences of the rich. If urban congestion has a sufficiently negative impact on transport, the rich will prefer to live in the central city, thereby pushing the poor outwards. The legacy of the Chicago School is therefore important for contemporary theories of social justice (Harvey, 1973).

The Urban Mentality

The city is a social system in which relations between strangers are dominant and thus the growth of the city is a measure of the erosion of traditional patterns of existence and a measure of the growth of modernity. In the nineteenth century, the stranger was an isolated traveller between the local community (*Gemeinschaft*) and the cosmopolitan society (*Gesellschaft*); in contemporary society globalization forces strangeness upon the whole of society. For Georg Simmel (1971a), the archetypal stranger was the Jewish trader. Because he is involved through exchange relations with the local community, he is both remote and proximate. He remains emotionally detached, while still involved through economic relations. Whereas the stranger was the exception in Simmel's world, the stranger has now become a way of life (Harman, 1988). Many social commentators came to the opinion that urbanization eventually created a new type of personality who was less committed to values and primarily influenced by the quest for status and influence. This personality type was described by David Riesman (1950) as 'the other-directed personality' in his influential book on *The Lonely Crowd*. Such personalities do not depend on their own commitment to a set of inner values ('the inner-directed personality') but follow instead the fluctuating judgements of their contemporaries. The other-directed personality is not situated within the family or the neighbourhood. Instead 'The other-directed person is a cosmopolitan' (Riesman, 1950: 25). Theories of urban anomie became popular in the 1950s and 1960s. Riesman's commentary on 'the lonely crowd' found an echo in Christopher Lasch's development of the critique of narcissism (1979) and the narcissistic personality.

These American anxieties about the moral superficiality of the cosmopolitan personality can be traced back to the origins of twentieth-century sociology in Europe. As a result of urbanization and related population changes, we can argue that sociology had its origin in a specific anxiety about the social control problems presented by population pressures within the urban environment. For example, a number of commentators have suggested that Durkheim's theory of the division of labour, the notion of anomie and the emphasis on the collective consciousness are sociological accounts of demographic pressures on social arrangements in France in the late nineteenth century. Other writers were impressed by the emergence of a new type of personality which was associated with the anonymous, anonymic and alienated populations of the large cities of Europe.

In his 'The metropolis and mental life', Simmel (1971b) argued that urban life, with its constantly shifting and changing environment, stimulated the intellectual aspects of human personality, while the rural community was based on emotional ties. It also encouraged a matter-of-fact approach to life which was expressed in what he called the blasé attitude. The money economy of the city required a calculating, impersonal attitude to life, which in turn depended on punctuality and exactness. The bustle of everyday life created an attitude of distance and withdrawal, even indifference and detachment from mundane commitments and involvements. The city, in short, was the institutionalization of modern, economic individualism.

On a more imaginative and literary plane, writers like Charles Baudelaire (Benjamin, 1976) also wrote about the urban mentality and the urban personality through the concept of the urban *flâneur*, a voyager floating without commitment through urban space. It has been a common theme of modern social theory that the urban culture of the city gave a new prominence to the visual and therefore to the eye as an organ of the human senses. The gaze is a fundamental feature of modern cultures. As such, visual culture is connected with the growth of shopping malls as places for viewing commodities, with the growth of gas lighting which made streets safe, with advertising boards which represented commodities within a new consumer aesthetic, and with the *flâneur* as a social role. This tradition of writing about the urban environment also found a poignant expression in the work of Walter Benjamin (1970) on his childhood experiences in Berlin, on the shopping revolution in Paris and Berlin, and on the emergence of a commercial culture in the new shopping malls of Europe (1982). Benjamin fully recognized the revolutionary nature of Baudelaire's vision of the city with his focus on the bohemian artist, the urban dandy, the street vendor, and the detective. The crowds strolling through the arcades, the passengers gazing from the trams, the prostitutes in the gas-lit streets and the petty urban criminal – these figures populated the imagination of writers and poets like Baudelaire whose art was closely associated with the new aesthetic of decadence. Baudelaire's poetry expressed the arrival of an artistic crisis, namely the death of the rural lyric. The detective story was the literary genre most suited to the new urban conditions involving anonymity, calculation, the individual contract, and the faceless masses. The railway journey became a favourite crime scene of the urban detective story. The Great Exhibition of 1851 and the building of the Crystal Palace celebrated and created a new era of commodification in a population for whom shopping and advertising were a new experience (Richards, 1991: 17).

We can see the origins of the postmodern debate in this urban experience of consumer diversity, simulation and fragmentation. If Benjamin recognized Baudelaire as the literary precursor of the modern urban imagination, Benjamin has been identified as an important figure in the emergence of postmodern theories of the city (Buci-Glucksmann, 1994). The postmodern urban aesthetic recognizes the playful, artful and transitory qualities of modern life, with its emphasis on a 'throw-away culture', the cycle of fashion, and its simulated environments. The emphasis on novelty and on the artificial is an essentially urban experience. There is as a result an important continuity between Marx's work on the revolutionary character of the nineteenth-century bourgeoisie, Baudelaire's celebration of the *flâneur*, Simmel's analysis of the urban mentality and Benjamin's analysis of the arcades. While the detective story gave expression to an urban sensibility, there were profound social changes which underpinned these cognitive and aesthetic developments, in particular demographic changes, the rural–urban exodus, the decline of rural communities and the growth of urban slums. Much of the early theory of the city thus emerged out of a geographical preoccupation with space, with migration and with city zones and it was expressed morally and theoretically within a vision which was focused on social control and population pressure.

Poverty, Social Class and the City

As we have seen, there was a profound ambiguity in early theories of the city, which was identified with anomie and alienation on the one hand, and with democratization and liberty on the other. In giving an account of these developments, I have given a certain prominence to an analysis of the cultural dimension of urbanization. It is now appropriate to give fuller recognition to changes in the material conditions of people experiencing urbanization (Briggs, 1968). There is considerable literature on the impact of the urban environment on physical and moral deprivation. For example, was the industrial city associated with improving standards of health or was it associated, through urban poverty, with increasing infant mortality and morbidity? There is now an important amount of social science literature on the demographic transformation of western societies which has analysed the consequences of urbanization on the health of urban populations, especially in the second half of the nineteenth century. Edward Shorter's studies of family life in the nineteenth century show that middle-class infant mortality increased with the practice of sending young children out to the country to be raised by peasant women (Shorter, 1977). The analyses of medical historians on the impact of rural wet nurses on the urban infant populations show a pattern of increasing morbidity and mortality. Rapid urbanization was also connected with an increase in mental illness; different types of mental illness were associated with both social class and city zones (Faris and Dunham, 1939).

In the historical study of the city, the urban environment has been seen paradoxically in both a positive and a negative light, on the one hand by contributing to the democratic evolution of European society and on the other, by contributing to the mental and physical deprivation of the working class. This dual image of the city continues into modern writing on the urban environment. One important theme within this genre therefore is the role of the city as a context for the historical growth and evolution of the so-called dangerous classes and for the making of the working class. Much of the early sociology of the city was concerned with the problem of poverty, the rise of an organized and politically active working class and the negative effects of urban poverty on health in terms of both morbidity and mortality. Friedrich Engels was one of the earliest continental theorists of poverty and it was Engels who saw Britain divided into two tribes which have relatively little contact with each other, namely the very rich and the very poor. *The Condition of the Working Classes in England* (Engels, 1958) which was published in 1845 became a classic study of urban poverty and deprivation. The analysis of urban poverty eventually produced a significant legacy of social science analysis which can be illustrated by Charles Booth's *Life and Labour of the People in London* (Booth, 1889–91) and by the path-breaking work of B. Seebohm Rowntree (1922) in his classic study of town life. It was Rowntree who, through an analysis of diet and household expenditure in the city of York, provided an early objective measurement of the poverty line which came to shape much of the social policy work of Britain in the first half of the twentieth century. His surveys provided one of the most detailed analyses of household expenditure in relation to the life-cycle of families and individuals. The work of Rowntree was complemented by similar research undertaken by writers like A.L. Bowley and A.R. Burnett-Hurst (1915) in their study of work and poverty. The debate about an objective poverty line continues to exercise the imagination and research of social scientists in the late twentieth century.

The analysis of urban poverty gave rise to a complementary literature on urban poverty alleviation and the positive programmes for restructuring and developing the urban environment. Planning was essential for a civilized existence (Howe, 1912). For example, in the work of sociologists like Karl Mannheim the importance of planning and urban development became a fundamental basis for the development of sociological writing about democratic planning in an advanced urban environment. He argued that in a mass society the individual becomes atomized and as a result an effective democracy requires planning to overcome individualism and egoism (Mannheim, 1951).

Within a similar genre one can see the sociological work of Geddes on urban planning as a response to the negative consequences of urban disorganization and anomie. Geddes had an optimistic vision of the positive role of rational planning on the urban environment. His work was based upon a conceptual scheme which had been developed by the French sociologist Frederic Le Play in which sociology is the study of the organic relationship between place, work and family. Armed with this paradigm, he insisted upon the importance of detailed empirical observation of city life. The creation of Outlook Tower in Edinburgh was to further the development of urban planning based on a comprehensive understanding of regional needs.

A major problem of issue for town planning is urban inequality and poverty. In more recent sociology, there have been various attempts to understand the city as a cause of social inequality. I have already referred to the work of John Rex who analysed the issue of housing classes as a feature of racial stratification in the city. In the 1960s Ray Pahl (1975) developed a theory of the city which emphasized the importance of 'urban managers' (estate agents, social workers and workers in local authority bureaucracies) in the distribution of resources and the creation of systematic social inequalities. These inequalities are in turn the focus of urban class struggles and social movements. These theories were criticized because urban managers often appear to be the intervening variable, not the independent variable, in the explanation of urban stratification. Other critics suggested that Rex's housing classes were in fact primarily phenomena of racial injustice (Saunders, 1981).

Conclusion

In conclusion, there are various ways in which we can conceptualize the history of the sociology of the city. Castells (1977) usefully distinguishes between the tradition which treats 'urbanization' as the geographical or spatial concentration of human populations in which the city is defined by its density and scale. By contrast, urbanization has been regarded as a crucial feature of modernization in disseminating values, norms and behaviour ('urban culture') which constitute secularization. Contemporary sociology has either attempted to transcend this dichotomy by developing a Marxist political economy of the formation of urban structures or to rewrite urban sociology as a more comprehensive sociology of space (Urry, 1996). Peter Saunders (1985) as a result distinguishes between the following intellectual traditions: (a) the city as an ecological community (Park et al.,); (b) the city as a cultural form (Simmel); (c) the city as a system of resource allocation (Rex and Pahl); and (d) the city as a unit of collective consumption (Castells). Although these transformations of perspective on the city represented important changes in intellectual direction in urban theory, there are important continuities with early debates about urban class inequality, deprivation and poverty.

Early sociological writings on the city were characterized by a number of important topics. First, there was the historical comparative research of writers like Durkheim, Weber and Pirenne who were interested in the contribution of the city to the evolution of rationalism, democracy and western civilization. Their research gave rise to two major historical questions on the role of the city in the creation of industrial capitalism and the relationship between the city and the growth of democratic associations. Second, there has been a tradition of geographical and demographic analysis of the impact of populations on systems of belief, patterns of control and bureaucratic processes. This debate was associated with an analysis of the place of writing in the development of the government of large, urban populations. Third, there has been a social-problems approach to the city emphasizing the importance of poverty, prostitution, family decay and deprivation. This focus on urban deprivation and city planning characterized a diversity of traditions such as civics education, Fabianism and, in America, the Chicago School.

The future direction of urban sociology lies within a broader sociology of space which is generically concerned with the spatial dimensions of social relations and social interaction in the context of an understanding of globalism. Finally, within contemporary literature there is a growing interest in the globalization of the city, the rise of the city as a powerbase of industrial societies and the impact of internet communication systems on the virtual reality of the urban environment. Although these changes are profound and significant, there are also continuities with previous research on urban mentalities, cosmopolitan life-styles and the heterogeneity of urban cultures.

There are profound anxieties about the city in contemporary sociology which are concerned with questions relating to globalization, the economic role of the megapolis and the impact of urban pollution on health and individual welfare. Urban deprivation is growing as a result of uncontrolled migration out of the country-side, rapid population growth, the failure of policies of urban renewal and the negative impact of International Monetary Fund programmes on cost containment in the Third World. As a result, it is estimated that currently there are a billion people without sanitation, two hundred and fifty million without access to safe water, and six hundred million who are homeless. It is argued by epidemiologists that 80 per cent of disease can be attributed to poor drinking water. This deprivation is one cause of growing urban crime, drug abuse and terrorism. Social scientists believe that, given the prospect of a collapse of urban civilization in the early part of the next century, the Green agenda for the natural environment should be complemented by the Brown agenda. These arguments are of course reminiscent of the debate at the end of the nineteenth century which also identified urban poverty and urban renewal as key political issues in the continuity and maintenance of democracy. This similarity is one further reason for an interest in the early history of urban sociology.

References

Anderson, B. (1983) *Imagined Communities. Reflections on the Origin and Spread of Nationalism.* London: Verso.
Anderson, N. (1923) *The Hobo: The sociology of the homeless man.* Chicago: University of Chicago Press.

Bender, T. (ed.) (1988) *The University and the City. From Medieval Origins to the Present.* Oxford: Oxford University Press.

Benjamin, W. (1970) *Berliner Chronik.* Frankfurt: Suhrkamp.

Benjamin, W. (1976) *Charles Baudelaire. A Lyric Poet in the era of High Capitalism.* London: Verso.

Benjamin, W. (1982) *Das Passagen-Werk.* Frankfurt: Suhrkamp, 2 vols.

Berman, M. (1982) *All that is Solid Melts into Air. The Experience of Modernity.* New York: Simon and Schuster.

Booth, C. (1889–91) *Life and Labour of the People in London.* London: Macmillan.

Bowley, A.L. and Burnett-Hurst, A.R. (1915) *Livelihood and Poverty.* New York and London: Garland Publishing.

Braudel, F. (1974) *Capitalism and Material Life 1400–1800.* London: Collins.

Briggs, A. (1968) *Victorian Cities.* Harmondsworth: Penguin Books.

Buci-Glucksmann, C. (1994) *The Baroque Reason.* London: Sage.

Capes, W.P. (1922) *The Modern City and its Government.* New York: E.P. Dutton & Co.

Castells, M. (1977) *The Urban Question. A Marxist Approach.* London: Edward Arnold.

Childe, G. (1957) 'Civilization, cities and towns', *Antiquity,* 13: 36–8.

Downes, K. (1979) *The Georgian Cities of Britain.* Oxford: Phaidon.

Elias, N. (1978) *The Civilizing Process. The History of Manners.* Oxford: Basil Blackwell.

Engels, F. (1958) *The Condition of the Working Classes in England.* Oxford: Blackwell.

Faris, R.E.L. and Dunham, H.W. (1939) *Mental Disorders in Urban Areas. An Ecological Study of Schizophrenia and Other Psychoses.* Chicago: University of Chicago Press.

Foucault, M. (1991) 'Governmentality', in G. Burchell, C. Gordon and P. Miller (eds), *The Foucault Effect. Studies in Governmentality.* Hemel Hempstead: Harvester Wheatsheaf. pp. 87–104.

Fustel de Coulanges, N.D. (1956) *The Ancient City. A Study of the Religion, Laws and Institutions of Greece and Rome.* New York: Doubleday.

Geddes, P. (1950) *Cities in Evolution.* New York: Oxford University Press.

Giddens, A. (1985) *The Nation-State and Violence.* Cambridge: Polity Press.

Gierke, O. von (1990) *Community in Historical Perspective.* Cambridge: Cambridge University Press.

Gist, N.P. and Fava, S.F. (eds) (1974) *Urban Society.* New York: Harper and Row.

Gledhill, J., Bender, B. and Larsen, M.T. (eds) (1988) *State and Society. The Emergence and Development of Social Hierarchy and Political Centralization.* London: Unwin Hyman.

Harman, L.D. (1988) *The Modern Stranger. On Language and Membership.* Berlin: Mouton de Gruyter.

Harvey, D. (1973) *Social Justice and the City.* London: Edward Arnold.

Heidegger, M. (1977) *The Question Concerning Technology and Other Essays.* New York: Harper & Row.

Howe, F.C. (1912) 'The city as a socializing agency', *American Journal of Sociology,* xvii: 590–601.

Jenks, C. (ed.) (1995) *Visual Culture.* London and New York: Routledge.

Lasch, C. (1979) *The Culture of Narcissism.* New York: Norton & Co.

Lash, S. (1990) *Sociology of Postmodernism.* London and New York: Routledge.

Laslett, P. (1965) *The World we have Lost.* London: Methuen.

Le Goff, J. (1988) *Medieval Civilization 400–1500.* Oxford: Basil Blackwell.

Lukács, G. (1971) *The Theory of the Novel. A Historico-Philosophical Essay on the Forms of Great Epic Literature.* London: Merlin Press.

Maitland, F.W. (1898) *Township and Borough.* Cambridge: Cambridge University Press.

Mannheim, K. (1951) *Freedom, Power and Democratic Planning.* London: Routledge & Kegan Paul.

McKenzie, R.D. (1923) *The Neighbourhood.* Chicago: University of Chicago Press.

McKenzie, R.D. (1933) *The Metropolitan Community.* New York and London: McGraw-Hill.

Miller, D.L. (1989) *Lewis Mumford. A Life.* Pittsburgh and London: University of Pittsburgh Press.

Mumford, L. (1926) 'The intolerable city: must it keep growing?', *Harper's Magazine,* February, pp. 286–7.

Mumford, L. (1934) *Technics and Civilization.* New York: Harcourt, Brace.

Mumford, L. (1938) *The Culture of Cities.* New York: Harcourt.

Mumford, L. (1961) *The City in History. Its Origins, its Transformations and its Prospects.* New York: Harcourt.

Munro, W.B. (1912) *The Government of American Cities.* New York: Macmillan.

Newby, H. (1979) *Green and Pleasant Land? Social Change in Rural England.* London: Hutchinson.

Pahl, R. (1975) *Whose City?* Harmondsworth: Penguin Books.

Park, R.E., Burgess, E.W. and McKenzie, R.D. (1925) *The City.* Chicago: University of Chicago Press.

Pirenne, H. (1936) *Economic and Social History of Medieval Europe.* London: Routledge & Kegan Paul.

Reckless, W.C. (1933) *Vice in Chicago.* Chicago: University of Chicago Press.

Rex, J. (1970) *Race Relations in Sociological Theory.* London: Weidenfeld and Nicolson.

Richards, T. (1991) *The Commodity Culture of Victorian England. Advertising and Spectacle 1851–1914.* London: Verso.

Riesman, D. (1950) *The Lonely Crowd.* New Haven and London: Yale University Press.

Rowntree, B.S. (1922) *Poverty. A Study of Town Life.* London: Longmans, Green & Co.

Said, E. (1978) *Orientalism.* London: Routledge & Kegan Paul.

Saunders, P. (1981) *Social Theory and the Urban Question.* London: Hutchinson.

Saunders, P. (1985) 'Space, the city and urban sociology', in D. Gregory and J. Urry (eds), *Social Relations and Spatial Structures.* London: Macmillan. pp. 67–89.

Saxonhouse, A.W. (1992) *The Fear of Diversity. The Birth of Political Science in Ancient Greek Thought.* Chicago and London: University of Chicago Press.

Schmid, C.F. (1937) *Social Saga of Two Cities. An Ecological and Statistical Study of Social Trends in Minneapolis and St. Paul.* Minneapolis Minnesota Bureau of Social Research. Minneapolis Council of Social Agencies.

Schorske, C.E. (1963) 'The idea of the city in European thought: Voltaire to Spengler', in O. Handlin and J. Burchard (eds), *The Historian and the City.* Massachusetts: The MIT Press and Harvard University Press. pp. 95–114.

Sennett, R. (ed.) (1969) *Classic Essays on the Culture of Cities.* Englewood Cliffs, New Jersey: Prentice-Hall.

Shorter, E. (1977) *The Making of the Modern Family.* London: Fontana.

Simmel, G. (1971a) 'The stranger', in D.N. Levine (ed.), *On Individuality and Social Forms.* Chicago: University of Chicago Press. pp. 143–9.

Simmel, G. (1971b) 'The metropolis and mental life', in D.N. Levine (ed.), *On Individuality and Social Forms.* Chicago: University of Chicago Press. pp. 324–39.

Sjoberg, G. (1960) *The Preindustrial City.* Glencoe Ill. Free Press.

Smith, A. (1976) *The Wealth of Nations.* Oxford: Oxford University Press.

Stone, G.P. (1954) 'City shoppers and urban identification: observations on the social psychology of city life', *American Journal of Sociology,* 60(2): 36–45.

Thrasher, F.M. (1927) *The Gang.* Chicago: University of Chicago Press.

Turner, B.S. (1974) *Weber and Islam. A Critical Study.* London: Routledge & Kegan Paul.

Turner, B.S. (1978) *Marx and the End of Orientalism.* London: Allen & Unwin.

Turner, B.S. (1991) *Religion and Social Theory.* London: Sage.

Urry, J. (1996) 'Sociology of time and space', in B.S. Turner (ed.), *The Blackwell Companion to Social Theory.* Oxford: Basil Blackwell. pp. 369–95.

Warner, W.L. and Lunt, P. (1941) *The Social Life of a Modern Community.* New Haven: Yale University Press.

Weber, M. (1958) *The City.* Glencoe, Ill.: Free Press.

Wirth, L. (1928) *The Ghetto.* Chicago: University of Chicago Press.

Wirth, L. (1938) 'Urbanism as a way of life', *American Journal of Sociology,* 44 (July): 1–24.

Zorbaugh, H.W. (1929) *The Gold Coast and the Slum. A Sociological Study of Chicago's Near North Side.* Chicago: University of Chicago.

CHAPTER 12

THE SOCIOLOGY OF SOCIAL STRATIFICATION

Introduction

In the twentieth century, the sociological analysis of social class, and more broadly the study of social stratification, became a basic and defining characteristic of the sociological curriculum and a major focus of empirical research. In the universities, sociology as a discipline developed in part as a contribution to the analysis of the negative functions and consequences of social inequality in industrial capitalism, where social inequality was seen to stem largely from economic inequality and ultimately therefore from the location of individuals and families within the class structure of industrial capitalism. Sociology attempted to provide answers to the question, how does economic class difference function in a welfare-capitalist system?

Although the study of social class came, as a consequence, to structure the sociological understanding of industrial society, there were traditional difficulties with the analysis of class. These analytical problems were simple, but enduring:

1 How can class be adequately defined so as to distinguish clearly class inequality from other forms of stratification?
2 How many classes are there?
3 What, if any, are the main patterns of mobility between classes?
4 Is class inequality an inevitable, necessary and permanent feature of human society, or merely a consequence of the growth of the capitalist mode of production?

Class analysis became, therefore, an essential feature of the study of a capitalist industrial system and the political search for alternatives, particularly in the debate about socialism as a revolutionary stage of social history beyond capitalism. With the collapse of organized communism towards the end of the 1980s, sociologists began to express serious doubts about the viability and prospects of class analysis, partly because 'class' no longer appeared to express adequately the patterns of social inequality in *late* industrialism (Lee and Turner, 1996). For example, it is felt that class analysis has not been particularly successful in explaining or expressing the nature of gender divisions and sexual inequality in industrial society (Crompton, 1996). The sociological analysis of class has gone through a number of major changes since the publication of Charles Booth's study of the *Life and Labour of the People in London* in the late 1880s. To understand the origins of the sociology of class is, therefore, to some extent to grasp the history of sociology as such.

The Political Economy of Capitalism

Social classes had, of course, been understood and analysed long before the origins of sociology as a formal university discipline towards the end of the nineteenth century and before writers like Auguste Comte used the term 'sociology' to describe the idea of *philosophie positive* in 1838. Classical Greek philosophers had attempted to describe the problems of Greek politics through an understanding of the differences between slaves and slave-owners, and Christian theologians in medieval times had sought to understand the applications of natural law to human society, which they knew was unjust and unfair. The theological debates about a 'just wage' can be seen as debates about class differences. However, from the point of view of the origins of social science, modern class analysis starts with the debates of the classical economists like Adam Smith (1723–1790), David Ricardo (1772–1823) and Jeremy Bentham (1748–1832), who adapted the traditional moral philosophical discourse of ethical behaviour to the new problems of the capitalist market-place.

It was clear by the eighteenth century that a new economic environment had arisen as a result of the transformation of agricultural production, the rise of the wool industry, the expansion of overseas trade and a variety of technological innovations and inventions which had reduced the costs of production. Smith published *Wealth of Nations* in 1776, which attempted to express in economic terms many of the social issues arising from the development of the capitalist mode of production. Smith, as the title of his treatise indicates, was primarily concerned with the production and distribution of wealth in a context of international trade and competition. He believed that the division of labour was a crucial feature of economic growth through a process of specialization. His famous illustration was the factory production of pins. One man, without specialized machinery, could make around twenty pins per day, but in a small factory with machinery employing ten men on specialized activities, it should be possible to produce 48,000 pins per day. The social cost of this specialized production is the decline in the mental abilities of labour. In the language of contemporary sociology, the consequence of mechanization is the alienation and de-skilling of the work force by technical change. There is an inevitable 'degradation' of labour through mechanization (Braverman, 1974).

Smith's theory of the division of labour was an important basis for his price theory. With the specialization of labour, it was important for the price of goods in a system of market exchange to reflect precisely the production costs of commodities. In this theory, Smith was responding to the classical discussion of the relationship between price and value. In a pre-capitalist market, Smith believed that the price of goods directly reflected the amount of labour which was necessary to produce a commodity, but in an advanced economy the cost of goods would also need to reflect the cost of wages, the rent of land and other factors of production, the demand for goods in an international market, and the need for profit for future investment. Smith also recognized another complexity, namely that price is expressed in money, but the value of money is also variable. In this analysis of the components of the price of commodities in the production process, we have the ingredients of a general theory of capitalism, namely that in the competition for wealth the labour force (the working class) will become 'alienated' from society and, in turn, society will be divided and fragmented in the social struggle over wages, profits and rent.

It was the so-called 'labour theory of value' (that the value of a commodity is determined by the amount of labour time invested in it) which provided the foundation of the controversy between Ricardo and Marx over the exploitation of labour in relation to the creation of profits for capitalist accumulation, and thereby laid the basis for the emergence of a genuine sociology of classes. In this way, classical economics evolved into the political economy of class conflict and then into the sociology of class relations. In economic theory as such, the primary concern of economists was with the constraints on wealth creation rather than on the nature of class structure

Classical economics assumed that economic growth depended on the amount of capital which was available for investment and hence the secret of economic growth was on how and who made decisions about capital investments. The limitations of industry, according to utilitarians like Jeremy Bentham, were determined by the limitations of capital. The principal cause of economic stagnation was government interference in the form of preferential taxation, artificial levies, government monopolies and bounties; economic stimulation would result from the state withdrawing from the market-place in order that naked self-interest could produce economic growth through the simple greed for profit. Government interference did not produce wealth because it could not produce investment capital; it merely transferred existing capital into stagnant areas. Diverting capital to help the working class in terms of 'relief' was also a mistaken fallacy of governments. Classical economics assumed that there was a fixed fund for wages, and thus class struggle could not increase the amount of wages available in a given year.

Classical economics was thus based on a set of assumptions about scarcity rather than abundance. There was, in addition to a scarcity of capital and profit, a scarcity of space, and so capitalist society was one in which social classes struggled for 'elbow-room', and 'the end product of crowdedness and shortage was not just social friction but class war. In confronting the problems issuing from an economy of scarcity, the liberals were driven to do what practically every political theory must; namely, to justify a system inherently unequal in its distributive principle' (Wolin,

1961: 323). In particular, liberals who believed in fundamental individual freedoms and embraced a theory of minimal government intervention (the so-called 'nightwatchman state') had to argue the case for the state as the basic institution for maintaining social security, and hence for defending an unequal and unfair principle of distribution. This contradiction in liberal political economy can be recognized as the starting point of Marxist class theory.

Marxism and Class Analysis

While Karl Marx (1818–1883) was a major critic of classical economics, his political economy of capitalism also contained a moral attack on what he saw as the hypocrisy of liberal political theory, and in this respect he continued the legacy of Smithian economic analysis. Marx attempted to prove that the defining characteristic of capitalism was the exploitation of the working class by the owners of productive capital, namely the bourgeoisie. In Marx's economic sociology, 'exploitation' had a technical and specific meaning. With the economic expansion of society through capitalist growth and colonial development, there was a surplus which was in fact the foundation of class society. In capitalism, class exploitation occurs when surplus value is extracted by industrial capitalists from the labour of the working class. Given the existence of private property, the working class sells its labour in order to live, but the capitalist uses the labour of the worker to create a surplus over the wage which is paid for the workers to reproduce themselves, that is to buy the necessities of life. While the wage covers the cost of labour, labour creates a surplus value which is the real source of profit. Thus, 'profit-making' is simply exploitation, where the working class is alienated from ownership of its own labour and from the products of its labour.

Marx developed a dynamic and historical view of this process, because he treated capitalism as a contradictory and ultimately self-destructive mode of production. Capitalists have to compete with each other in order to secure advantages in the market, to reduce production costs and to increase their profits. Two routes to these objectives are through increased specialization and the reduction of costs by the increased use of machinery, that is through technological innovation. However, replacement of labour by machinery (or by 'dead labour' as Marx called it) has the paradoxical outcome of reducing the rate of profit, because the real source of surplus value is labour itself. This assumption gave rise to the famous and controversial 'law' of the tendency of the rate of profit to fall.

We need not at this stage enter into the controversy surrounding the validity of this law. From the point of view of this introduction, it is enough to note that Marx identified a number of fundamental crisis tendencies in the economic processes of capitalism, all of which pointed towards various forms of class conflict. For example, the economic contradictions of the capitalist mode of production included:

1   The falling rate of profit resulted in regular economic restructuring of enterprises and the destruction of inefficient firms.
2   It drove capitalists to seek cheaper labour in colonial labour markets and cheaper natural resources from within a world market.
3   It required increasingly exploitative working conditions, including the use of child labour.

These processes, as Marx explained in *The Communist Manifesto* of 1848 (Marx and Engels, 1968), resulted in:

1   A radical polarization of the class system into two large contending classes, namely the bourgeoisie and the proletariat.
2   The immiseration and pauperization of the working class.
3   The radicalization of the working class which was transformed through political struggle from a class-in-itself to a class-for-itself.

As the working class became more politically organized through the violence of class conflict, the conditions for revolutionary struggle were established whereby, under the guidance of the communist party, capitalism would be overthrown and the early stages of socialism established. The final communist revolution would remove exploitation through the destruction of private property and the alienation of the working class. This social revolution would thus be the end of the history of class society.

Marxism involved a radical attack on the liberal ideology of capitalism, because Marx attempted to expose the ideological covering of capitalism, which obscured the real nature of exploitation in capitalist industrial relations. Notions of individual freedom, which were the ideological expression of private property, obscured the underlying relations of economic exploitation which were the real causes of capital accumulation. While Marx was obviously a radical critic of capitalism, his theory of capitalist history was also paradoxically a celebration of capitalism, which had destroyed the traditional stagnation of feudalism and which had been the midwife of socialism. In a similar fashion, capitalist forms of colonialism, however brutal and violent, had dragged Asia into modern history by destroying what Marx referred to as 'the Asiatic mode of production'. By creating private property in land, the British colonial administration in India had created social classes and thus set up the mechanisms by which profound change could take place in India for the first time. Indian history, before the British, had been merely a history of successive conquests and in fact 'Indian society had no history at all, at least no known history' (Marx and Engels, 1972: 81). We can see in Marx's analyis of colonialism, especially in his understanding of the 'social stationariness' of India and China (Turner, 1974), that Marxist class analysis was not merely a classificatory scheme for describing relations of inequality in capitalism; it was fundamentally a theory of historical change within which class conflict was the causal mechanism which brought about profound transformations of the mode of production.

Class analysis in Marxism was thus the fundamental basis of the so-called economic interpretation of history, and it represented a major departure from classical economics. Whereas the economists had recognized important differences in the role of workers and capitalists, they had treated class as simply a collection of individuals with similar economic functions; Marx had attempted to describe the structure of capitalist society in terms of objective class relationships. This difference was very clearly recognized by Joseph Schumpeter who also noted that 'the glamour' that surrounds the economic interpretation of history 'depends precisely on the strictness and simplicity of the one-way relation which it asserts' (Schumpeter, 1987: 13). The principal sociological criticism of the Marxist interpretation of history was that this 'strictness and simplicity' could not be sustained by the empirical evidence about actual capitalist societies. For example, in Germany by the end of the nineteenth century, it was clear that the social classes had not become polarized and the working class was not pauperized. There appeared to be an increase in the real standard of living of the working class which had shared in the economic expansion of a united Germany, and the working class generally embraced German nationalism in the period leading up to the First World War. In addition, the class structure was fragmented around a diversity of class fractions which were associated with both cultural and skill differences; in particular, the development of the capitalist economy created a new white-collar class which reflected the growth of a service sector. These differences suggested that it was important to distinguish status and class as variables of social stratification.

The failure of the strict and simple economic interpretation of history resulted in German Marxism in a political movement referred to as 'reformism', which advocated a peaceful route to socialism which did not necessarily involve open class conflict. It also laid the basis for the growth of the sociology of stratification, which attempted to resolve some of the analytical difficulties in Marxist theory. Sociologists responded to Marxism in terms of the following arguments:

1   There are important cultural dimensions to class differences, which often appear as 'life-style' differences in social class behaviour, for example in the notion of the 'leisure class' (Veblen, 1899).
2   They have shown that economic expansion in capitalism gave rise to a large and dynamic middle class (Abercrombie and Urry, 1983; Cole, 1950).
3   Sociologists have identified changes in the organization of capitalism whereby there is an important differentiation of management and ownership (Berle and Means, 1932).

4   Sociological research on occupational groups such as 'black-coated workers' indicates that there are important differences between class, status and work situations between individuals (Lockwood, 1958).
5   Scarcity of resources can be expressed in various ways, thereby giving rise to many types of class such as, for example, 'housing classes' (Rex and Moore, 1967).
6   Finally it has been argued that with the growth of liberal democracy there has been an expansion of welfare provision for the working class, and therefore citizenship functions to limit the negative impact of class in capitalist society (Marshall, 1950).

These sociological responses to Marxism have their intellectual origin in the sociology of Max Weber (1864–1920), and hence the history of class analysis is often seen in terms of two alternatives: Marxist historical materialism versus Weberian sociology.

The Sociology of Class, Status and Power

Although Weber is often understood to argue that there are three different variables in social stratification (namely, class, status and power), it is more accurate to note that Weber analysed society in terms of the monopolization of resources by a common process of 'social closure' (Parkin, 1974). Social closure describes the action of social groups who seek to maximize their social advantages to restricting access to scarce resources (particularly economic resources) to their own members with the result that outsiders are excluded. These outsiders are often identified by reference to their physical characteristics, especially colour. For Weber, these practices of monopolization were fundamental to the economy. A rather lengthy quotation from Weber will help us to grasp his meaning more fully:

> When the number of competitors increases in relation to the profit span, the participants become interested in curbing competition. Usually one group of competitors takes some externally identifiable characteristic of another group of (actual or potential) competitors – race, language, religion, local or social origin, descent, residence, etc. – as a pretext for attempting their exclusion. It does not matter which characteristic is chosen in the individual case: whatever suggests itself most easily is seized upon ... In spite of their continued competition against one another, the jointly acting competitors now form an 'interest group' towards outsiders; there is a growing tendency to set up some kind of association with rational regulations; if the monopolistic interests persist, the time comes when the competitors, or another group whom they can influence (for example, a political community), establish a legal order that limits competition through formal monopolies ... In such a case, the interest group has developed into a 'legally privileged group' (*Rechtsgemeinschaft*) and the participants have become 'privileged members' (*Rechtsgenossen*). Such social closure, as we want to call

it, is an ever-recurring process; it is the source of property in land as of all guild and other group monopolies.

(Weber, 1968: 341–2)

Weber's notion of social closure, of course, applies not only to ethnic groups and racial orders, but to professional monopolies. It also refers to labour force divisions in terms of educational credentials (Collins, 1986: 128). The notion of social closure has a wide range, but in Weber's sociology it became closely connected with a distinction between social class and status group. In *Economy and Society*, which was published posthumously in German in 1922, Weber defined class situation as the probability of enjoying the benefits of material goods, gaining a position in life and 'inner satisfactions' as a result of a relative control over goods and skills (Weber, 1968: 302). A class merely means all those persons who share a common class situation. Weber then identified a variety of social classes, including the working class, the petty bourgeoisie, the propertyless intelligentsia, and classes privileged by property and education. Weber also recognized several different meanings of status. He defined a status group as a plurality of persons who successfully claim a special social esteem: they come into being by virtue of their life-style, through hereditary charisma or through monopolistic privilege. Weber then claimed that 'Depending on the prevailing mode of stratification, we shall speak of a "status society" or a "class society"' (Weber, 1968: 306).

The main point of these formal definitions was to provide Weber with a battery of concepts to undertake a series of historical and comparative studies of the monopolization of resources. Weber thus argued that economic wealth was not the only criterion of social power, privilege and influence. He wanted to examine societies in which prestige, through education and culture, was more significant than power, based on the ownership of the means of economic production. For example, Weber gave a particular emphasis to the historical prominence of the political and cultural status of the literati, and he noted that:

For twelve centuries social rank in China has been determined more by qualification for office than by wealth. This qualification, in turn, has been determined by education, and especially by examination. China has made literary education the yardstick of social prestige in the most exclusive fashion, far more exclusively than did Europe during the period of the humanists, or as Germany has done.

(Weber, 1951: 107)

In his comparative sociology, Weber was interested in the different patterns of monopolization and how these different formations of power did or did not contribute to social change. For example, his studies of the monopolistic powers of priests and lawyers were an important part of his general view of the dynamic nature of western cultures, and thus he shared with Marx a critical view of the Orient as a stagnant and traditional social order (Turner, 1978). In general, the tendency to stress the differences between Marx and Weber in the history of class analysis can be overdone. While Weber stressed the differences between status and class, both Marx and Weber agreed with the classical economists that capitalist society was based on class conflict, on the quest for space for 'elbow room', and on the struggle over scarce resources, a struggle which produced significant historical dynamism. Perhaps the most significant difference was that Weber did not believe that a communist society would bring about the end of class divisions or other forms of hierarchical privilege. Weber's essays (1905–1906 and 1917) on the Russian revolutions expressed his pessimistic views about the difficulties of democracy in Russian society (Weber, 1995). For Weber, systematic inequalities as a result of either class or status differences were inevitable features of all human societies, whether capitalist or communist. In general, all European sociologists were impressed by the presence of class divisions and the social significance of class conflict in the formation and development of western capitalism, and in this respect there were important differences between European and American sociology.

Social Stratification in American Sociology

Sociology in the United States was shaped by the optimistic and self-confident culture of the American community in the sense that there was a recognition of the values of democracy, equal opportunity and economic success. As a result, there was a tendency to deny the importance of class division and to assert the opportunities for social mobility, especially for immigrants to America. This optimistic perspective on the rate of social mobility in the 'new nation' can be traced back to the writings of Alexis de Tocqueville (1805–1859), especially in his *Democracy in America* of 1835–1840 (Tocqueville, 1968), where he described the 'democratic revolution' in America in terms of the impact of equality of opportunity on American culture. The rigid structures of feudal Europe were unknown in America and equality of opportunity had contained the negative consequences of capitalist economic development. A similar sentiment was expressed towards the end of the century by James Bryce who asserted confidently:

> There is no rank in America, that is to say, no external and recognised stamp, marking a man as entitled to any special privileges, or to deference or respect from others. No man is entitled to any special privileges, or to deference or respect from others. No man is entitled to think himself better than his fellows.

> (Bryce, 1899, vol. 2: 752)

In addition, the notion that America was a frontier society and indeed an empty land also created a sense of endless space and infinite opportunity for settlement and expansion. The idea that the limitation of space was a force for social change through the competition for 'elbow room' did not figure large in the social imagination. American sociology developed then in a context of social optimism and in a society where neither socialism nor Marxist theory had any significance. Early American sociology was relatively independent and 'home grown'; European sociology did not start to make an impact until the 1940s. The founders of American sociology – Lewis Morgan, Lester F. Ward, Thorstein Veblen, William G. Sumner and Charles A. Beard – produced a distinctive, 'native' sociology, which was influenced by Populism, Progressivism, the Social Science movement and the Social Gospel rather than by Marxism or European sociology (Bramson, 1961). While American sociology was not particularly shaped by Marxism, it was driven by a practical commitment to social reform through collective action and social criticism. There was a strong sense of the need for social reform in order to achieve greater social progress.

It is not surprising therefore that American sociology developed a distinctive approach to social class (Page, 1940). There was the view that one can think of social stratification as a continuum which does not have distinctive breaks or divisions. Individuals can pass relatively easily along this continuum, because social mobility is a distinctive aspect of the open nature of American society. The only negative feature of the American system of stratification was, of course, race, especially the division between white and black. A considerable amount of American research on stratification was devoted to an analysis of the problems of the black community, which was often seen in terms of caste rather than class, as for example in John Dollard's *Caste and Class in a Southern Town* (1937). American studies were also distinctive in terms of their methodology where an anthropological approach to field work was favoured in the community-studies approach. In these terms, the research of the Lynds on Middletown (Lynd and Lynd, 1929) and W. Lloyd Warner on Jonesville (1949) became famous as bench-marks for sociological investigations. American sociologists also pioneered studies into subjective attitudes towards class and status positions, as for instance in Richard Centers's *The Psychology of Social Classes* (1949).

In this early period of class and status research, there had been little attempt to produce a theory of class and definitions of class remained somewhat elementary. W. Lloyd Warner and his colleagues (Warner et al., 1949) had eventually produced a textbook on his research methodology as a guide to the research process which lay behind the 'Yankee City Series', the Middletown community studies and the research on race and community in the South. In *Social Class in America,* Warner and his fellow researchers identified two approaches to class research, namely 'evaluated participation' and 'index of status characteristics'. In evaluated participation, Warner developed six criteria by which a comparative judgement is made of an individual's standing in the community in terms of prestige, influence and rank. In the index approach, status is assigned by occupation, source of income, house type and dwelling area. We can see in this methodology that there was relatively little clear attempt to distinguish between status as a measure of prestige and class as a measure of economic location, and therefore 'social status' and 'social class' are used interchangeably. One other methodological difficulty in the research of Warner and the Lynds was that it assumed that a series of community studies would in fact produce an accurate picture of the American system of class and status as a whole.

The theory of class in American sociology was eventually enhanced by the critical debates between 'structural functionalism' and its critics in the 1940s and 1950s. Briefly, structural functionalism was a general theory of society which attempted to understand society as a system with parts or 'sub-systems', which functioned to enhance the system as a whole. For example, in *The Social System*, Talcott Parsons (1951) identified four sub-systems (the economy, the polity, the societal or value community, and the institutions of socialization) and studied their interactions or functions in relation to the total system. Functionalism attempts to understand social stratification as part of a social system, which has functional contributions to make to the functioning and survival of a system. Thus, Parsons (1949) rejected the Marxist legacy of class analysis as merely a contribution to utilitarianism, and argued that social stratification had to be seen as a general system for ranking individuals in terms of general social values. In fact, social class is the product of the 'instrumental complex' (the division of occupational skills and tasks) and 'the kinship system'. Social class, for Parsons, was the plurality of kinship units which share a common position in the hierarchy of occupations and prestige. Parsons rejected Marx's emphasis on the market in favour of an occupational analysis of class position, recognized that it is the family and its members which is classified in class and prestige terms, and claimed that stratification 'is to an important degree an integrating structure in the social system' (Parsons, 1949: 21).

The functionalist approach to class was, however, given its most decisive statement by K. Davis and W.E. Moore (1945) in 'Some principles of stratification'. They argued that in every society some tasks are more important and more difficult than others. In order that these positions can be filled by people with appropriate talent and ability, there are differential rewards (in terms of salaries, conditions of employment and prestige) attached to different positions. The training and education of individuals for these crucial tasks takes time and some sacrifice from individuals is required to undertake this training. In return, these individuals are later rewarded for their educational training in terms of higher salaries and status. Thus, social stratification functions to ensure that the most talented and highly trained people are attracted to the most difficult and important social tasks through competition and social mobility. Whereas Marx had seen class as a dynamic of social conflict in a system which was fundamentally unjust, and whereas Weber had seen class as a strategy of social closure, American structural functionalists analysed social class in terms of its positive contributions to the social differentiation of society through occupational mobility and job competition.

The so-called 'functionalist theory of social stratification' produced a long and productive debate within sociology which dominated theoretical developments in the 1950s and 1960s. Critics of Parsons argued that structural functionalism was inherently conservative in its politics, that it provided a thinly disguised justification for occupational inequalities which depended on inherited wealth and not on natural talent, and that functionalism was incoherent as a theory because it could not produce an objective measure of the function of a sub-system other than the survival of the system itself. C. Wright Mills, one of the strongest critics of Parsons, produced a series of critical studies of American society in *White Collar* (1951) and *The Power Elite* (1956), which were based on the sociology of Max Weber. With his colleague, Hans Gerth, Mills contributed to the introduction of Weberian ideas about power and conflict into American sociology as an antidote to functionalism. In *The Sociological Imagination* (Mills, 1959) he also condemned Parsons's theoretical style as 'grand theory' which he claimed was unnecessarily obscure and dense. These intellectual conflicts in sociology produced an intellectual clarification of the problems surrounding the analysis of class and broke down some of the differences between European and American perspectives. Despite Parsons's death in 1979, the intellectual conflict over critical and functionalist orientations continues in, for example, 'neo-functionalist' approaches which attempt, among other things, to build into traditional functionalism assumptions about conflict and change (Alexander, 1985).

Conclusion

In general terms, we can regard early sociology as an extended and critical commentary on classical economic theory, in particular a critique of the individualistic assumptions of economic theory. The sociological analysis of class also grew out of this engagement with economic theory via Marx's attacks on Smith and Bentham, and Weber's contribution to the debate about marginalism (Holton and Turner, 1989). In 1942, Schumpeter (1987: 13) noted in *Capitalism, Socialism and Democracy* that 'Economists had been strangely slow in recognizing the phenomenon of social classes. Of course they always classified the agents whose interplay produced the processes they dealt with. But these classes were simply individuals that displayed some common character.' The contribution of Marx and Weber was to lay bare the actual structure and coherence of classes as collective historical agents. This sociology of class also eventually produced detailed studies of what we might call the 'mentality' of different classes, of which Werner Sombart's *The Quintessence of Capitalism* (1915) is a fine example. In retrospect, sociologists have been less successful in showing systematically how cultural and economic dimensions of social stratification relate to each other in such concepts as status, caste and class.

Behind the technical discussion of class, there is an ethical issue about the nature of social inequality in capitalist democracies. Indeed for some writers there is an inevitable tension between the idea of a democracy (with its assumptions about equality) and a capitalist system (which is based on class difference). Sociologists have developed two broad approaches to this tension. They have taken the view that, while there is class inequality in capitalism, there is sufficient social mobility to prevent class divisions turning into caste divisions, that is the system remains open because people of talent can move into positions of authority. In American sociology, P. Sorokin's *Social Mobility* (1927) and P. Davidson's and H. Anderson's *Occupational Mobility in an American Community* (1937) are obvious illustrations. Alternatively, they have, following T.H. Marshall, argued that in democratic capitalism the institutions of citizenship (legal rights, political rights and welfare arrangements) work to limit the negative effects of the market and the class system. These two approaches are not incompatible, because social mobility from the working class into the middle class may depend heavily on state investment in a mass education system. The study of social class, therefore, is not only an indicator of the progress of sociology, but also a reflection on the changing nature of capitalism itself.

References

Abercrombie, N. and Urry, J. (1983) *Capital, Labour and the Middle Classes.* London: Allen & Unwin.

Alexander, J. (ed.) (1985) *Neofunctionalism.* Beverly Hills: Sage.

Berle, A.A. and Means, G.C. (1932) *The Modern Corporation and Private Property.* New York: Macmillan.

Booth, C. (1889–1891) *Life and Labour of the People in London.* London: Macmillan.

Bramson, L. (1961) *The Political Context of Sociology.* Princeton, New Jersey: Princeton University Press.

Braverman, H. (1974) *Labor and Monopoly Capitalism: The degradation of work in the twentieth century.* New York: Monthly Review Press.

Bryce, J. (1899) *The American Commonwealth.* New York: Macmillan.

Centers, R. (1949) *The Psychology of Social Classes: A study of class consciousness.* Princeton: Princeton University Press.

Cole, G.D.H. (1950) 'The conception of the middle classes', *The British Journal of Sociology,* 1: 275–90.

Collins, R. (1986) *Weberian Sociological Theory.* Cambridge: Cambridge University Press.

Crompton, R. (1996) 'Gender and class analysis', in D. Lee and B.S. Turner (eds), *Conflicts about Class. Debating Inequality in Late Industrialism.* London and New York: Longman. pp. 115–26.

Davidson, P.E. and Anderson, H.D. (1937) *Occupational Mobility in an American Community.* Stanford: Stanford University Press.

Davis, K. and Moore, W.E. (1945) 'Some principles of stratification', *American Sociological Review,* 10: 242–9.

Dollard, J. (1937) *Caste and Class in a Southern Town.* New Haven: Yale University Press.

Holton, J.H. and Turner, B.S. (1989) *Max Weber on Economy and Society.* London: Routledge.

Lee, D. and Turner, B.S. (eds) (1996) *Conflicts about Class. Debating Inequality in Late Industrialism.* London and New York: Longman.

Lockwood, D. (1958) *The Blackcoated Worker.* London: Allen & Unwin.

Lynd, R. and Lynd, H.M. (1929) *Middletown: A study in contemporary American culture.* New York: Harcourt, Brace.

Marshall, T.H. (1950) *Citizenship and Social Class and Other Essays.* London: Heinemann.

Marx, K. and Engels, F. (1968) *Manifesto of the Communist Party.* London: Lawrence & Wishart.

Marx, K. and Engels, F. (1972) *On Colonialism.* New York: International Publishers.

Mills, C.W. (1951) *White Collar: The American middle classes.* New York: Oxford University Press.

Mills, C.W. (1956) *The Power Elite.* New York: Simon & Schuster.

Mills, C.W. (1959) *The Sociological Imagination.* New York: Oxford University Press.

Page, C.H. (1940) *Class and American Sociology: From Ward to Ross.* New York: Dial Press.

Parkin, F. (1974) 'Strategies of social closure in class formation', in F. Parkin (ed.), *The Social Analysis of the Class Structure.* London: Tavistock. pp. 1–18.

Parsons, T. (1949) 'Social classes and class conflict in the light of recent sociological theory', *American Economic Review,* 39: 16–26.

Parsons, T. (1951) *The Social System.* London: Routledge & Kegan Paul.

Rex, J. and Moore, R. (1967) *Race, Community and Conflict. A Study of Sparkbroot.* Oxford: Oxford University Press.

Schumpeter, J.A. (1987) *Capitalism, Socialism and Democracy.* London: Unwin Paperbacks.

Smith, A. [1776] (1950) *An Inquiry into the Nature and Causes of the Wealth of Nations.* E. Cannan (ed.). London: Methuen.

Sombart, W. (1915) *The Quintessence of Capitalism: A study of the history and psychology of the modern business man.* London: T. Fisher Unwin Ltd.

Sorokin, P. (1927) *Social Mobility.* New York: Harper & Row.

Tocqueville, A. de (1968) *Democracy in America.* Glasgow: Collins.

Turner, B.S. (1974) 'The concept of social "stationariness": Utilitarianism and Marxism', *Science and Society,* 38: 3–18.

Turner, B.S. (1978) *Marx and the End of Orientalism.* London: Allen & Unwin.

Veblen, T. [1899] (1953) *The Theory of the Leisure Class.* New York: Mentor.

Warner, W.L. (1949) *Democracy in Jonesville. A Study of Quantity and Inequality.* New York: Harper.

Warner, W.L., Meeker, M. and Ellis, K. (1949) *Social Class in America: A manual of procedure for the measurement of social status.* Chicago: Science Research Associates.

Weber, M. (1951) *The Religion of China.* New York: Macmillan.

Weber, M. (1968) *Economy and Society.* New York: Bedminster Press.

Weber, M. (1995) *The Russian Revolutions.* Cambridge: Polity Press.

Wolin, S.S. (1961) *Politics and Vision. Continuity and Innovation in Western Political Thought.* London: George Allen & Unwin.

CHAPTER 13

THE SOCIOLOGY AND ANTHROPOLOGY OF THE FAMILY

Introduction: Defining the Family

The family, which in this chapter is employed as an abbreviation to cover the entire discussion of family organizations, kinship relations, domestic or household structures and friendship networks, is a fundamental and complex component of all human societies. The family is obviously concerned with the organization of sexual relations and the reproduction of the human species through the processes of (legitimate) mating and procreation, but its functions also extend to the organization of economic production, the social division of labour, the (re)distribution of property, the transfer of culture, the training (or socialization) of children and the provision of personal services such as the care of the elderly. The family as an institution lies at the interface of nature and culture, because it is fundamentally concerned with certain elementary biological functions (birth and death), but it is also a major vehicle for the transfer of culture. The family is also part of the apparatus of social control in human societies (Thomas, 1898).

The definition of the family is correspondingly complex and controversial. For the purpose of this introductory analysis, we may define the family as

> a group of interacting persons who recognize a relationship with each other based on common parentage, marriage and/or adoption. Some authors attempt to define 'family' in terms of function, but the functions of families vary in different societies, and there is no central function that all societies grant to the family.
>
> (Rose, 1968: 203)

The importance of this definition is that it notes that, while biological relations are important in defining family membership, the real issue is the *recognition* of a familial relationship. In the sociology of the family and kinship, we have therefore to recognize the dual significance of 'blood' and 'marriage'. While a blood relationship is formed by an act of sexual intercourse which results in off-spring, marriage is a consequence of the legal relationships which exist between people who are joined by a formal marriage ceremony or ritual; marriage is an institution which ultimately regulates and legitimizes sexual intercourse. While marriage can be terminated through separation and divorce, it is assumed that 'blood' relations cannot be so disposed of. This distinction lies behind the notion that 'blood is thicker than water', namely that the obligations of blood cannot be easily ignored, denied or neglected.

While this distinction suggests unambiguously that 'blood' and 'marriage' represent a simple dichotomy between 'nature' and 'culture', on closer inspection this distinction is more complex, because it is the recognition of a blood relationship rather than an actual relationship which is important. Thus, 'kinship is a social interpretation of natural phenomena rather than the natural phenomena themselves' (Allan, 1979: 32). In premodern societies, for example, without the assistance of DNA testing, it was almost impossible to prove fatherhood. In feudal societies, where marriage was a treaty between landholding families, the emphasis on primogeniture (inheritance by the first-born male child) resulted in endless disputes about paternity. These arrangements partly explain the importance of chastity and virginity in young brides (Duby, 1978). Here again, from a legal point of view, it was recognition of *de jure* descent rather than *de facto* biological connections which was at stake.

We might therefore provide a more elaborate account of the family by reference to a list of characteristics of the family which were outlined in Robert MacIver's famous textbook on sociology (MacIver, 1937: 197). A family involves:

1   a mating relationship;
2   a form of marriage or other institutional arrangement in accordance with which the mating relation is established and maintained;
3   a system of nomenclature, involving also a mode of reckoning descent;
4   some economic needs associated with childbearing and child rearing; and generally
5   a common habitation, home or household, which, however, may not be exclusive to the family group.

William J. Goode (1959: 188–9), one of the leading twentieth-century sociologists of the family, provides a similar but more sophisticated list of 'quasi-variables' which are:

1   fertility (which may be high or low);
2   status placement of members in stratification system (in terms of ascribed and achieved places);
3   biological maintenance or the distributive system internal to the family;
4   socialization (in terms of the degree and effectiveness of obligations towards children);
5   emotional maintenance (or the psychodynamic input–output balance of emotional security for the individual); and
6   social control (the extent of sexual control over both adults and children).

From these characteristics, we can observe that the family has important economic functions (in the production of goods and services through the household), social functions (through the reproduction of children) and political functions (in establishing, for example, legitimate patterns of inheritance). Given the importance of the family to the organization of society as a whole, we may note that political anxieties about social order and political authority are often displaced on to the family. For example, in the seventeenth century political anxiety about the authority and legitimacy of the monarchy was focused on the question of authority within the household. Sir Robert Filmer in his *Patriarcha: A Defence of the Natural Powers of the Kings against the Unnatural Liberty of the People* in 1680 expressed an anxiety about the future of the patriarchal principle of authority against the emergence of individualistic theories of social contract in a period where the stability of the kingdom was seen to be a reflection of the stability of the family (Schochet, 1975). The psychoanalytic studies which Sigmund Freud undertook of sexual repression within the family have often been interpreted by sociologists and historians as expressions of social contradiction surrounding the Jewish bourgeoisie in late nineteenth-century Vienna (Shorter, 1994). In the twentieth century, anxieties about 'the decline of the nuclear family' have disguised more general fears about male–female relationships, heterosexuality, and the reproduction of the nation as a necessary component of imperialism. The health of recruits into the army has often been taken as an indicator of the status of the family as a reproductive unit within civil society and the school as a training ground for the military. There is therefore an important nexus between family, state and empire.

The possible erosion of the nuclear family has been a persistent feature of twentieth-century social policy which has been reflected in sociology in the debate about the decline of the nuclear family. Talcott Parsons's argument about the isolation of the nuclear family (Parsons, 1943; Parsons and Bales, 1955) has been much criticized, but it is generally recognized that the modern family is small rather than extended, separate from major economic activities and specialized around the provision of intimacy and affection; as a result it is also exposed to dissolution through the availability of 'divorce on demand'. However, there is no widespread evidence to suggest that the family is disappearing from modern society, but there is ample comparative evidence of significant social change, if not crisis in kinship and familial relationships.

Universalism of the Family

Disputes about the definition of the family are not entirely productive or necessarily important. Establishing an agreement about the meaning of 'the family' may be significant where one is interested in the questions: is the family universal, or is the family peculiar to a particular type of society? The debate about the universality of the family was important in the nineteenth century when social theorists like Friedrich Engels (1942) in his *Origin of the Family, Private Property and the State* in 1884 argued, following the work of L.H. Morgan, that the nuclear or bourgeois family was a peculiar product of a capitalist economy with its emphasis on private property and individualism. The nuclear family involved systematic inequality between husband and wife, the patriarchal authority of the father; it was a form of legalized prostitution, which, for the sake of property transfers through legitimate heirs, also involved a 'double standard' whereby male respectability was based on an extensive system of mistresses and brothels. The bourgeois family would disappear with the revolutionary overthrow of bourgeois capitalism. Engels's thesis has been both criticized and admired in contemporary social theory (Barrett and McIntosh, 1991).

In 1949 George Peter Murdock, on the basis of the study of 500 societies, concluded that the family was a social group which performed essential functions in society and was based on residence, common economic activities, which involved co-operation, and biological reproduction. The family was composed of adults, with a socially approved sexual relationship, and one or more children, who could be either the natural or adopted children of the couple. Murdock concluded that no society in human history

> has succeeded in finding an adequate substitute for the nuclear family to which it might transfer these functions. It is highly doubtful whether any society will ever succeed in such an attempt, Utopian proposals for the abolition of the family to the contrary notwithstanding.
>
> (1949: 11)

Studies of Utopian experiments which attempted to replace or change the nature of the family have produced complex evidence on the nature and functions of familial relations in the Soviet Union (Geiger, 1960) and in Israeli society, where, through the development of collectivist strategies in the agricultural communes, it was assumed that the family would disappear. The kibbutz in Israel was a cooperative agricultural settlement in which the family was to be replaced by common care and protection of offspring. It has been argued that over time the collective familial structure of the kibbutz declined and was replaced by the typical nuclear family system (Spiro, 1963; Talman, 1972).

The historical evidence points to the resilience of the small family group as a 'private' institution for reproduction. However, these arguments presuppose a common and consistent definition of 'the family' across cultures and through time. Some feminist historians, by contrast, have argued that the real core of the family is in fact the mother–child relationship which is consistent across time, that the 'father' does not have to be the biological father and that the father is, in any case, typically absent from this unit. Murdock's account of the family assumed a consensus of values on the division of labour within the family and assumed considerable domestic harmony. By contrast, the modern family in industrial societies is characterized by high divorce rates, extensive involvement of women in the labour force, and significant numbers of couples who choose to live in semi-permanent relationships without a marriage ritual and who prefer to remain voluntarily childless.

In contemporary sociology, this discussion of the universality of the family is no longer regarded as important, and analysis has become more preoccupied with the relationship between the private and the public arena, the role of intimacy and affection in social relationships, the impact of reproductive technology and genetic engineering on marriage and family relationships, and the transformation of sexuality through social movements such as the women's movement and gay liberation. Sociologists are no longer concerned with evolutionary approaches to the history of the family. Their attention is turned instead to studies of changing sexual relationships in modern society and their impact on the family, for example on the consequences of transsexualism, lesbian and homosexual marriages, surrogate parenting and voluntary childlessness. In general, evolutionary paradigms are thought to be speculative and general. Contemporary family studies are more likely to be concerned with specific issues relating to fatherhood (Coltrane, 1996), childbearing (Ribbens, 1994) or family values (Stacey, 1960).

Before addressing the specific nature of twentieth-century studies of the family, I wish to outline the general dimensions of the history of family studies. I have already suggested that, given the importance of the family to the social structure as a whole, the analysis of the family has always reflected the broad debates of any given epoch. Concerns for the family and its future have followed the general contours of the debate about the rise of industrial society, which is urban, secular and capitalist. Generally speaking, the sociology of the family is concerned to understand the place (or function) of the family within the social structure of industrial society; in a more dynamic mode, sociology wants to understand the impact of processes of modernization on the family. These interests have formed the parameters within which the study of the family developed.

A History of the Anthropology and Sociology of the Family

The sociology of the family, which developed in the late nineteenth century for example with Emile Durkheim's lectures and essays on the sociology of the conjugal family in 1888 (Traugott, 1978), emerged in a context where there already existed considerable anthropological fieldwork on kinship systems in the non-western world. The study of kinship and family is a highly developed and important dimension of anthropology (Kroeber, 1909; Malinowski, 1930; Radcliffe-Brown, 1941; Tylor, 1889). However, while there is widespread agreement as to the obvious importance of the family to social structure, the founding theorists of sociology, apart from Durkheim (Davy, 1925) and W.I. Thomas (1902), strangely neglected the sociology of the family. Max Weber, Vilfredo Pareto and Georg Simmel made no direct contribution through theory or research (Goode, 1959), and it was not until Talcott Parsons's sociology of youth, ageing and the family that mainstream American sociology made a significant contribution to the theoretical analysis of the family. There were, of course, important empirical studies of family life in the United States, but empirical research on the family in the first half of the twentieth century was driven primarily by a practical focus on social problems and by a policy imperative to find solutions to family breakdown, domestic violence and single-parent households. There were a number of classics provided within this framework such as E. Groves and W. Ogburn (1928) *American Marriage and Family Relations*, M. Nimkoff (1934) *The Family* and E. Burgess and L. Cottrell (1939) *Predicting Success or Failure in Marriage*. W. Ogburn and M. Nimkoff (1955) in *Technology and the Changing Family* made an important contribution to the sociological analysis of the impact of technology, especially electronic technology, on the development of the modern family.

In Europe prior to the publication of Ferdinand Tönnies's *Gemeinschaft und Gesellschaft* (1957) in 1887, the major works of the nineteenth century on family issues were John F. McLennan's *Primitive Marriage* (1865), Pierre Frederic LePlay's *Les Ouvriers Européens* of 1855 (LePlay, 1877–9) and L.H. Morgan's 'Systems of consanguinity and affinity of the human family' (Morgan, 1871) and followed by *Ancient Society* (1877). The ethnographic, historical and anthropological study of marriage was also influenced by Edward A. Westermarck's scholarly works such as *The History of Human Marriage* (1901), *A Short History of Marriage* (1926) and *The Future of Marriage in Western Civilization* (1936).

Early theories of the family and kinship were inspired by the clash between western culture and 'primitive society' in the expansion of western colonialism and settlement, especially in the nineteenth century. In particular, cultural interaction between white settlement and aboriginal societies in North America and Australia produced the earliest theories of the family which were typically couched in an evolutionary paradigm, especially one derived from Social Darwinism. Thus, Morgan's research was strongly influenced by white encounters with the native Americans. As a lawyer in upstate New York, Morgan was interested in the Iroquois communities. From these preliminary studies, he derived a 'conjectural history' of civil society as an evolutionary progress out of the family which he divided into monogamous and group family structures. He believed that the evolution of the family from promiscuity to monogamy was driven by a moral and progressive impulse. In the late nineteenth century, studies of Australian Aboriginal family and kinship structures inspired work by F. Galton, N.W. Thomas, Carl Nicolai Starcke, Bronislaw Malinowski and many others. Evidence from studies of Aboriginal communities was thought to be useful in establishing, through contemporary fieldwork, a view of family life in 'primitive societies' from the earliest times. Starcke's *Die primitive Familie in ihrer Enstehung und Entwicklung* in 1888 and translated into English in 1889 (Starcke, 1976) was critical of the methodology and lack of genuine evidence in the work of J.F. McLennan and L.H. Morgan. McLennan's *Primitive Marriage: inquiry into the origin of the form of capture in marriage ceremonies* (1865) constructed an evolutionary picture of marriage from promiscuity through matrilineal groups, female infanticide, local exogamy, polyandry, patriliny and finally the modern family. Starcke criticized both theorists for accepting an implicit view of sexuality as an undifferentiated instinct which offered thereby a psychological explanation of social evolution. Starcke argued that concepts of blood-kinship played no part in the organization of primitive marriage and that there was no evidence for early promiscuity. He rejected the notion that incest prohibitions could be based on shared biological assumptions across cultures and history. Starcke attempted to explain early familial structures in terms of economic co-operation and organization. The study of non-western kinship structures remained an important part of both anthropological and sociological research in the development of a comparative understanding of marriage and kinship (Eggan, 1937; Mathews, 1900; Rivers, 1968).

Theories of Matriarchy

The family has been seen as a critical component of civilized life, with its emphasis on co-operation, sharing and protection of life. This idealized view of the family contrasts with militarism, the state and private property. We have already seen that in Engels's theory of the family patriarchy, property and the state were important stages in human evolution, but they also had significant negative features, when compared with (Utopian) perspectives on primitive society. The notion that the rise of military, patriarchal society destroyed an earlier, matriarchal and communal society without private property became a popular theme of early sociology.

Robert Briffault published *The Mothers* (1927) in which he argued that the mind was a social and not a biological product and that the characteristics of the human mind, which distinguishes us from animals, were the consequence of a maternal instinct. The transmission of civilization is dependent, not on biological reproduction, but on social reproduction, that is the socialization of the child, which is traditionally the responsibility of the mother. The intelligence of the human species requires a long gestation and extensive cultural socialization. Briffault assumed that education was a feminine responsibility and thus concluded that women were primarily responsible for the historical shaping of human institutions. Following the investigations of McLennan, Morgan and William Robertson Smith, Briffault argued that the principal conclusions of social anthropology were that the kinship unit is the fundamental building block of society and that women are the principal agents of the shaping of pre-historical societies. Against the prevailing theories of early society which claimed that patriarchy is the earliest principle of social arrangements, Briffault established a theory of matriarchy which claimed, not that women ruled such societies, but that feminine principles of social organization were dominant.

Although Briffault's work was criticized (Westermarck, 1934), patriarchy remained a popular conceptual framework for understanding the family in the early part of the twentieth century. The concept of matriarchy played an important ideological role in feminist and socialist criticisms of capitalism, aggression and private property. Matriarchal societies were seen to offer an important set of alternative principles for social organization. In fact these debates often repeated earlier socialist criticisms of the family since the time of the French Revolution, for example in the work of Charles Fourier and Friedrich Engels (Zaretsky, 1976). In Germany, these debates were taken up by Johann Jakob Bachofen in his theory of 'mother-right' (*Das Mutterrecht*). The idea of matriarchy was that, before capitalism, law was based, not on impersonal and abstract notions, but on the experience and tradition of community, which in turn was rooted in the family and the civilizing role of the mother. His ideas were explored by Marianne Weber and recognized as subversive by Tönnies.

Discussion of the historical role of matriarchy was also embraced by radical social movements in Germany which championed erotic love over the conformist values of the bourgeois family. Matriarchy was now associated with the idea of free love before the rise of ascetic capitalism with its emphasis on personal restraint and the family as a regulation of erotic desire. Otto Gross, building on Nietzsche, Bachofen and Freud, proclaimed the therapeutic importance of free love and his ideas were influential in the development of the bourgeois wing of the German feminist movement (Schwentker, 1987). The debate about matriarchy in the women's movement in Germany reflected anxieties about the survival of the family in a period when women were entering the labour force in increasing numbers, but it also brought into the foreground issues about female sexuality and civilization which were fundamental to Sigmund Freud's analysis of the repression of desire, the growth of neurotic illness and the internal contradictions of bourgeois family life.

A number of Freud's major works were concerned with the dynamic relationships between civilization and sexual control. Freud's 'historical' works on totemism, monotheism and civilization present an account of how the development of civilization requires the regulation and subordination of sexual drives (the id). In the life of the individual, there is a constant struggle between these biological forces (the id), culture (the super ego) and the self (ego). The role of psychoanalysis is to expose these contradictions through the process of the talking therapy, whereby the patient might learn to live with his or her past (or the unconscious). Many critics of Freud have suggested that he did not develop an adequate theory of the family, because his approach was committed to the notion of the isolated individual rather than of individuals in families (Poster, 1978).

Nevertheless, Freud generated a range of issues and ideas which have influenced the subsequent evolution of family therapy and child psychology. For example, the controversial notion of the Oedipus complex and child sexuality have become an essential component in the modern analysis of the sexual dynamics of the family. Freud argued that the child's first sexual experiences are at the mother's breast and that the mother becomes the first object of sexual attraction and jealousy, resulting in animosity towards the father. In his early work with Josef Breuer, the clinical analysis of hysteria resulted in the theory that hysteria represented submerged feelings of sexuality which were released by the patient during hysterical fits.

Freud's ideas were important in the development of the sociology of the family. For example, Parsons adopted Freud to show that the Oedipus taboo was crucial if children were to leave the home and enter into the labour force and establish their own families. The Oedipus taboo and exogamy rules were important in driving children out of the home to form new alliances through exogamous marriages.

Freud's research in general pointed to the importance of family stability for the mental health of the growing child. The conflicts and stress within the family created a poor psychological environment for the growing child. Indeed John Bowlby (1953) developed a theory of 'maternal deprivation' to explain mental illness in later life. Bowlby's investigations were used by conservative critics to argue that the absence of the working mother from the home contributed to mental instability in the child. Bowlby's strong claims about the role of the parenting for the emotional stability of the child also suggested that divorce automatically damaged the child. These notions were challenged by feminist critics on the grounds that the caring relationship is not an exclusively female function and that the mental health of the child requires stable and predictable relations with adults rather than an exclusive dependence on the mother. In fact many critics of the family have suggested that it is the over-protective and jealous mother who makes the child's entrance into adult society traumatic and difficult. Psychoanalysts attempted to demonstrate how the over-protective household might cause anorexia in the daughters who could not reconcile the demands of the parents for obedience and the pressures to leave home, to become sexually mature and independent (Bruch, 1988). Radical psychologists referred to this cloistered family as a family ghetto (Laing, 1964; 1971). In the 1960s and 1970s critical psychologists proclaimed 'the death of the family' (Cooper, 1972).

The Problems of the Twentieth-Century Family

Sociologists in the twentieth century have been preoccupied with the troubles and difficulties of the family, which are associated with the impact of industrialization, urbanization and secularization (Davis and Warner, 1937). Whereas social researchers like Charles Booth, B.S. Rowntree (1902) and the Webbs had been concerned to study the impact of poverty on the family, later sociologists came to ask more fundamental questions about the very survival of the family. William F. Ogburn (1933) suggested that the family had experienced a profound 'loss of function', because many of the economic needs of individuals were no longer serviced by the family. Parsons in his 'The kinship system of the contemporary United States' (Parsons, 1943) and 'The American family' (Parsons and Bales, 1955) agreed with Ogburn but went on to suggest that the family had been differentiated from the wider social structure to become a more specialized agency as a place of intimacy for child socialization and the nurturing of personality through socialization. The primary function of the nuclear family is the socialization of its members and the transmission of the values of the cultural system. This development was indicated by the isolation of the nuclear family, which was geographically separated in its own household and isolated in residential terms. Family members work and play outside the structures of the extended kinship system. Because the isolated nuclear family is small, this structure can place enormous emotional burdens on members of the family, especially on the mother.

Parsons's sociology of the family has been extensively criticized. It is argued that his perspective on the family failed to take family conflict and disharmony seriously, because it presents an idealized version of middle-class family life, which is far removed from the realities of the poverty-stricken families of the urban ghetto. It failed to take account of important variations in family life in the United States between, for example, black and white communities (Park, 1913). Against Parsons, many sociologists (Fletcher, 1966) have argued that the family is still a crucial institution of modern society, because it is responsible for maintaining the health and well-being of its members. It is also clear from empirical research that the nuclear family is deeply embedded in extensive kinship networks and connections (Bott, 1957). It is certainly the case that there are important social class variations in family and kinship solidarity. The traditional picture of working-class life in Britain was one of significant geographical stability and extensive kinship interaction (Stacey, 1960; Tunstall, 1962; Willmott and Young, 1967), but it is doubtful that these traditional relationships and community structures have survived urban redevelopment and city modernization (Allan, 1979). While kinship relations may be much reduced in modern suburban cultures, the middle class appear to have extensive friendship networks which may, to some extent, have replaced more conventional kinship ties. There is also some historical evidence to suggest that the extent of the traditional extended family may also have been exaggerated by sociologists (Anderson, 1975). These studies suggest that the modern family is a modified extended family in which there are important kinship networks between relatives who do not live with each other, and also a widespread dependence on non-kin relations for support. It is important to realize also that there are a great variety of household forms in modern society in which the nuclear family is not the most prevalent. The trend is towards smaller households, more people living together outside of marriage, more divorces and more people remarrying, and an increase in children born outside of marriage.

Conclusion

The principal debate about marriage and family life in the twentieth century has in retrospect revolved around the so-called romantic love complex, that is the notion of love is the basic motivation for marriage and intimacy is the foundation of marital happiness. Through the medieval period in Europe, there was a tension between passionate love and the institution of marriage (Rougemont, 1983). Marriage was essentially a contract between families, which was designed to legitimize sexual intercourse in order to guarantee the continuous ownership and distribution of property through new generations. In the tradition of courtly love (Lewis, 1936) passionate relations were driven by an irrational romantic attachment, which was the basis of a counter institution, namely adultery. Modern marriages represent a revolutionary transformation of this traditional pattern, because they attempt to base marriage on romantic attachment and to maintain marriage on the basis of reciprocal intimacy. There is an increasing social emphasis on the importance of courtship and dating behaviour in youth culture (Waller, 1937). Love rather than an economic partnership or a familial alliance becomes the sole justification for marriage, following a romantic courtship (Luhmann, 1986).

It is assumed that this emphasis on romantic love places major emotional burdens on the married couple, because they are committed to fulfilling high expectations of intimacy and sexual gratification (Thomas, 1908). This emphasis on sincerity, trust and emotional satisfaction results, paradoxically, in widespread marital unhappiness and high divorce rates, because it is difficult to achieve these norms of romantic intimacy in a period where the majority of women have entered the labour force, where the grounds for divorce are very broad and where early marriage and life expectancy combine to make multiple marriages in a single life course demographically possible. The result is a paradoxical situation of high rates of marriage, high incidence of adultery, high levels of remarriage, and extensive intra-familial conflict across generations (Davis, 1940). The complexity of modern patterns of love, intimacy and marriage has been described as 'chaotic' (Beck and Beck-Gernsheim, 1990).

This interpretation of the modern marriage as a 'transformation of intimacy' (Giddens, 1992) has been the dominant theme of contemporary sociology, where the ideal of a 'pure relationship' of love rather than calculation is seen to be the historical outcome of the rise of the romantic love complex, the quest for a democratic relationship in marriage by the women's movement, the critique of traditional double standards in marriage by feminism, and the emphasis on intimacy which is associated with gay and lesbian politics. Although these features – equality, intimacy and sincerity – are important values in modern marriage, it should be recalled that this account of the modern marriage has its antecedents in the notion of the 'companionate' marriage from an earlier period. In the United States, the companionate relationship was seen to be the emerging pattern of marriage in the 1930s. It was defined as a state of lawful wedlock, which was entered into for the sake of intimate companionship rather than for the procreation of children (Nimkoff, 1934). Such a relationship was associated with social and geographical mobility, with a leisured lifestyle referred to as 'hotel living', and with social transcience. Indeed, such a relationship was termed the 'hotel family' (Hayner, 1927). These companionate relations were assumed to be increasing, with the result that the family was evolving from an institution to companionship (Burgess and Locke, 1953).

Of course, companionate love assumes that adequate contraception is available to prevent companionate childlessness becoming a conventional family. As N.S. Hayner (1927) pointed out, the companionate relationship will become 'orthodox' in the absence of conscious and successful family limitation. The evolution of intimacy and the emphasis on sexual satisfaction in the twentieth century have followed closely on the evolution of effective contraception, the availability of legal abortion, governmental support of childcare institutions and the employment of women. The separation of economic activities and reproduction within the family is the most significant social change in family life, which is the structural basis for the companionate relationship. Where reproduction under a system of primogeniture is the principal means of economic accumulation across generations, there will be a tendency to exert close control over women to ensure security and stability of inheritance. In such a system women are expected to be virgins on marriage and the sole function of the mother is to produce a reliable lineage of males. Such a system of patriarchy is particularly important for the monarchy and hence the politics of the court was organized around such matters as marriage alliances, the production of a male heir to the throne, and the (official) fidelity of the partners. In the modern family, the nexus between economic accumulation and legitimate reproduction has been broken by the modernization of the economy, the banking system and the laws of inheritance. It is this separation, which was recognized by Parsons in his analysis of the isolation of the nuclear family, that produces the conditions under which the romantic love complex can flourish. The survival of the family in the twentieth and twenty-first centuries will depend on its place in this romantic love complex as a social arrangement for the satisfaction of sincerity, security and companionship rather than as an institution which exists to produce children and to orchestrate domestic economic activity.

References

Allan, G.A. (1979) *A Sociology of Friendship and Kinship.* London: George Allen & Unwin.

Anderson, M. (1975) *The Sociology of the Family.* Harmondsworth: Penguin Books.

Barrett, M. and McIntosh, M. (1991) *The Anti-social Family.* London: Verso.

Beck, U. and Beck-Gernsheim, E. (1990) *Das ganz normale Chaos der Liebe.* Frankfurt: Suhrkamp.

Bott, E. (1957) *Family and Social Network: Roles, norms and external relationships in ordinary urban families.* London: Tavistock.

Bowlby, J. (1953) *Child Care and the Growth of Love.* Harmondsworth: Penguin.

Briffault, R. (1927) *The Mothers.* London: George Allen & Unwin.

Bruch, H. (1988) *Conversations with Anorexics.* New York: Basic Books.

Burgess, E. and Cottrell, L.S. (1939) *Predicting Success or Failure in Marriage.* New York: Prentice-Hall.

Burgess, E.W. and Locke, H.J. (1953) *The Family: From institution to companionship.* New York: American Book Co.

Coltrane, S. (1996) *Family Man: Fatherhood, housework and gender equity.* New York: Oxford University Press.

Cooper, D. (1972) *The Death of the Family.* Penguin: Harmondsworth.

Davis, K. (1940) 'The sociology of parent–youth conflict', *American Sociological Review,* 5: 523–35.

Davis, K. and Warner, W.L. (1937) 'Structural analysis of kinship', *American Anthropologist,* 39: 291–313.

Davy, G. (1925) `Vues sociologiques sur la Famille et la Parenté d'après Durkheim', *Revue Philosophique,* 100: 79–117.

Duby, G. (1978) *Medieval Marriages. Two Models from Twelfth-century France.* Baltimore and London: The Johns Hopkins University Press.

Eggan, F. (1937) 'Historical changes in the Choctaw kinship system', *American Anthropologist,* 39: 34–52.

Engels, F. (1942) *The Origin of the Family, Private Property and the State.* New York: International Publishers.

Fletcher, R. (1966) *The Family and Marriage in Britain.* Penguin: Harmondsworth.

Geiger, H.K. (1960) 'The fate of the family in Soviet Russia 1917–1944', in N.W. Bell and E.F. Vogel (eds), *A Modern Introduction to the Family.* New York: Free Press. pp. 48–67.

Giddens, A. (1992) *The Transformation of Intimacy. Sexuality, Love and Eroticism in Modern Societies.* Cambridge: Polity Press.

Goode, W.J. (1959) 'The sociology of the family', in R.K. Merton, L. Broom and L.S. Cottrell (eds), *Sociology Today. Problems and Prospects.* New York and Evanston: Harper & Row, vol. 1. pp. 178–96.

Groves, E. and Ogburn, W.F. (1928) *American Marriage and Family Relations.* New York: Henry Holt & Co.

Hayner, N.S. (1927) `Hotel homes', *Sociology and Social Research,* 12: 124–31.

Kroeber, A.L. (1909) 'Classificatory systems of relationship', *Journal of the Royal Anthropological Institute,* 39: 77–84.

Laing, R.D. (1964) *Sanity, Madness and the Family.* London: Tavistock.

Laing, R.D. (1971) *The Politics of the Family and other Essays.* London: Tavistock.

LePlay, P.G.F. (1877–79) *Les Ouvriers Européens.* Tours: A. Maneret-Fils (second edn).

Lewis, C.S. (1936) *The Allegory of Love. A Study in Medieval Tradition.* Oxford: Oxford University Press.

Luhmann, N. (1986) *Love as Passion. The Codification of Intimacy.* Cambridge: Polity Press.

MacIver, R.M. (1937) *Society. A Textbook of Sociology.* New York: Farrar and Rhinehart.

McLennan, J.F. (1865) *Primitive Marriage.* Edinburgh: Adam & Charles Black.

Malinowski, B. (1930) 'Parenthood – the basis of social structure', in V.F. Claverton and S.D. Schmalhausen (eds), *The New Generation. The Intimate Problems of Modern Parents and Children.* London: George Allen & Unwin. pp. 113–68.

Mathews, R.H. (1900) 'Marriage and descent among the Australian Aboriginals', *Journal of the Royal Society of New South Wales,* 34: 120–35.

Morgan, L.H. (1871) 'Systems of consanguinity and affinity of the human family', *Smithsonian Institution Contribution to Knowledge,* 17: 2–570.

Morgan, L.H. (1877/1974) *Ancient Society or Researches in the Lines of Human Progress from Savagery through Barbarism to Civilization.* Glouchester, Mass.: Peter Smith.

Murdock, G.P. (1949) *Social Structure.* New York: Macmillan.

Nimkoff, M.F. (1934) *The Family.* Boston: Houghton Mifflin.

Ogburn, W.F. (1933) 'The family and its functions', *Recent Trends in the United States.* Report of President's Research Committee on Social Trends. New York and London: McGraw-Hill Book Co. pp. 661–707.

Ogburn, W.F. and Nimkoff, M. (1955) *Technology and the Changing Family.* Boston: Houghton Mifflin.

Park, R.E. (1913) 'Negro home life and standards of living', *Annals of the American Academy of Political and Social Science* (September), pp. 147–63.

Parsons, T. (1943) 'The kinship system of the contemporary United States', *American Anthropologist,* 45: 22–38.

Parsons, T. and Bales, R.F. (in association with James Old, Morris Zelditch Jr, and Philip E. Slater) (1955) *Family, Socialization and Interaction Process.* London: Routledge & Kegan Paul.

Poster, M. (1978) *Critical Theory of the Family.* London: Pluto Press.

Radcliffe-Brown, A.R. (1941) 'The study of kinship systems', *The Journal of the Royal Anthropological Institute,* 71: 1–18.

Ribbens, J. (1994) *Mothers and Their Children. A Feminist Sociology of Childbearing.* Thousand Oaks, CA: Sage.

Rivers, W.H.R. (1968) *Kinship and Social Organization.* London: Athlone Press.

Rose, A.M. (1968) *Sociology. The Study of Human Relations.* New York: Alfred A. Knopf.

Rougemont, D. de (1983) *Love in the Western World.* Princeton, New Jersey: Princeton University Press.

Rowntree, B.S. (1902) *Poverty: A study of town life.* London: Longman.

Schochet, G.J. (1975) *Patriarchalism in Political Thought.* Oxford: Oxford University Press.

Schwentker, W. (1987) 'Passion as a mode of life: Max Weber, the Otto Gross Circle and eroticism', in W.J. Mommsen and J. Osterhammel (eds), *Max Weber and His Contemporaries.* London: Allen & Unwin. pp. 483–98.

Shorter, E. (1994) *From the Mind into the Body. The Cultural Origins of Psychosomatic Symptoms.* New York: The Free Press.

Spiro, M.E. (1963) *Kibbutz. Venture in Utopia.* New York: Schochen.

Stacey, M. (1960) *Tradition and Change.* Oxford: Oxford University Press.

Starcke, C.H. (1976) *The Primitive Family in its Origin and Development.* Chicago and London: The University of Chicago Press.

Talman, Y. (1972) *Family and Community in the Kibbutz.* Harvard: Harvard University Press.

Thomas, W.I. (1898) 'The relation of sex to primitive social control', *American Journal of Sociology,* 3: 754–76.

Thomas, W.I. (1902) 'Der Ursprung der Exogamie', *Zeitschrift für Sozialwissenschaft,* 5: 1–18.

Thomas, W.I. (1908) 'The older and newer ideals of marriage', *American Magazine,* 34: 120–35.

Tönnies, F. (1957) *Community and Association.* Michigan: Michigan State University Press.

Traugott, M. (1978) *Emile Durkheim on Institutional Analysis.* Chicago and London: University of Chicago Press.

Tunstall, P. (1962) *The Fishermen.* London: MacGibbon & Kee.

Tylor, E.B. (1889) 'On a method of investigating the development of institutions: applied to laws of marriage and descent', *Journal of the Anthropological Institute,* 18: 245–74.

Waller, W. (1937) 'Rating and dating complex', *American Sociological Review,* 2: 727–34.

Westermarck, E.A. (1901) *The History of Human Marriage.* London: Macmillan.

Westermarck, E.A. (1926) *A Short History of Marriage.* London: Macmillan.

Westermarck, E.A. (1934) *Three Essays on Sex and Marriage.* London: Macmillan.

Westermarck, E.A. (1936) *The Future of Marriage in Western Civilization.* London: Macmillan.

Willmott, P. and Young, M. (1967) *Family and Class in a London Suburb.* London: Nel Mentor.

Zaretsky, E. (1976) *Capitalism, the Family and Personal Life.* London: Pluto Press.

CHAPTER 14

THE SOCIOLOGY OF GENERATIONS (WITH RON EYERMAN)

Introduction

It is generally recognized that Karl Mannheim introduced the concept of 'generation' as a viable addition to the analysis of social stratification in modern sociology in his 'The problem of generations' in an essay in the *Kölner Vierteljahrshefte für Soziologie* in 1928–9 (Mannheim, 1952). The concept was formulated as part of his broader programme for a sociology of knowledge and was an element of Mannheim's theoretical strategy to understand the 'existential basis of knowledge' by the use of concepts other than social class. It was also part of Mannheim's search for an alternative theory of social change to Marxism with its traditional epistemology, materialist definitions of interests, and narrow focus on economic class as a causal mechanism of social change (DeMartini, 1985). In particular, Mannheim employed the concept of generation to study the growth of conservative thought in modern societies (Mannheim, 1986) and the idea of generational differences subsequently worked its way into the conventional sociological lexicon. The contemporary sociological literature on generations is divided into (1) studies of generational experiences of major historical disruptions such as warfare and migration; (2) research on generational differences in cultural experience and consumerism; (3) studies of generational cohorts in terms of intellectual traditions and political perspectives; and (4) sociological analyses of specific generations such as the Lucky Generation or the Sixties. Thus the concept has been used productively to study generational differences, for example by Richard Wohl (1979) in his study of the First World War, by David Wyatt (1993) in his research on the Vietnam War and American culture, by T.M.S. Evens (1995) in a study of conflict on a kibbutz, by Anne Coombs (1996) in her study of the post-war Sydney generation, and by Jaff Schatz (1991) on the rise and fall of generational elites. Edmund Wilson (1993) in his autobiographical memories has provided a highly personal interpretation of the intellectual, political and artistic development of the Sixties. Alexander Bloom (1986) conducted a historical study of the first and second generation of New York intellectuals in terms of their accommodation to American society and the emergence of a distinctive social science tradition. The concept of generation has been routinely applied in the study of youth cultures and their impact on popular culture (Frith, 1984).

Although the notion of generational differences is widely accepted in contemporary sociology, generally speaking the fruitfulness of the concept has yet to be fully explored and appreciated in the sociological mainstream. There is little theoretical elaboration of the notion of generation and its relevance for cultural sociology. There are few significant theoretical contributions in modern sociology to the development of the theory of generations, apart from S.N. Eisenstadt's *From Generation to Generation* (1956). There is a clear awareness that generational experiences (of migration, persecution, and extermination) have been profoundly significant in the shaping of intellectual movements in for example the New York intellectuals. Daniel Bell has described the mood of three generations in *The End of Ideology* (1960) in which Jewish intellectuals in particular were shaped by the Depression, the rise of Hitler and fascism, the Nazi–Soviet Pact and the Holocaust. While ethnicity and class clearly influenced the New York Jewish intellectuals, there was also a definite sense of generational uniqueness and specificity (Podhoretz, 1967).

Although there is a literature on the sociology of generations, it is typically implicit rather than explicit. Our approach in this chapter is concerned with the cultural dimensions of generational membership rather than with the political sociology of elites and generations. This chapter provides the theoretical background to an international study of post-war generations being undertaken by the authors from the perspective of generational differences in national cultures and personal experience of traumatic events (such as conscription, peace movements and warfare).

Generation: A Working Definition

By and large the concepts which surround the idea of social class may be directly appropriated by a sociology of generations, producing a range of notions such as generational conflict, generational mobility and generational ideologies. One may conceptualize generational cultures in the same way as one now speaks about 'class cultures' or 'occupational cultures'. Generations, like social classes in Weberian sociology, are organized in terms of social closure to maximize access to resources for their members. Social closure is a strategy for controlling resources in a context of competition by defining membership by reference to some (arbitrary) principle of inclusion/exclusion such as skin colour or age (Weber, 1978: 341–3). However, one way of identifying the important differences between social class and generation would be through the problem of time and duration. In the sociology of generations, it is important to distinguish between 'contemporaries' (those who happen to be alive at the same time) and 'coevals' (those who are the same age). Thus, the issues of time, temporal identity and collective memory can be said to lie at the core of the sociological issues relating to class. A generation involves the organization of collective memory (Schwartz, 1996).

Following the work of Anthony Giddens (1984) one can also consider generations as social cohorts stretched over time. Although a generation might be arbitrarily defined in terms of years of origination, this definition of generations gains sociological substance once we direct our attention to the problem of the final termination of a generational cohort as its members evolve through a process of retirement, physical decline and death. While there are clearly social class memories, as for example in Zygmunt Bauman's *Memories of Class* (1982), our aim is to understand how generations are constituted through the institutionalization of memory through collective rituals and narratives. Intergenerational differences ('the lucky generation', 'Sixties people' or 'the generation of 1914') are identified by reference primarily to time, because it is periodization which uniquely encapsulates the strategic opportunities and difficulties that attach to specific generational cohorts. In particular, we argue that generational cultures become embodied in their cultural dispositions (dress, language and emblems) and the postures of individuals (walk, dance preferences and songs). We attempt to develop such an approach to generational embodiments of culture by the adoption and appropriation of Pierre Bourdieu's sociology of culture, and more specifically his related notions of habitus and hexis (Bourdieu, 1977; 1984; 1990).

We shall define generation initially as a cohort of persons passing through time who come to share a common habitus, hexis and culture, a function of which is to provide them with a collective memory that serves to integrate the cohort over a finite period of time. Such a definition draws special attention to the idea of a shared or collective cultural field (of emotions, attitudes, preferences and dispositions) and a set of embodied practices (of sport and leisure activities), that is, it identifies the importance of collective memory in creating a generational culture or tradition. We are also concerned with the issue of the management of generational resources over space and time. In addition to sharing a common collective culture, a generation may be conceived as a cohort which has a peculiar and strategic access to collective resources and which, through rituals of exclusion (Parkin, 1979), preserves not only its individual cultural identity, but excludes other generational cohorts from access to cultural capital and material resources generally. For example, the generation of 1945, while dispersed through social space, needs to maintain a collective access to resources, but more important, in order to sustain itself it must reflexively produce a generational memory which articulates its control over cultural capital via collective rituals and ceremonial practices. Here such recurring phenomena as the nostalgic recreation of style and the attempt to relive 'significant events' from the past, as in the recent example of the Woodstock Anniversary concerts or the revival of early Beatles songs, can be given sociological content. It can be suggested that taste in music or clothing has strategic value, even where this might be unacknowledged by both the producers and consumers of such items.

Although generations, like classes, exercise strategic exclusion, because individuals within generations may typically reproduce themselves through marriage and the creation of families, the moral issues of exchange emerge through notions of justice in terms of intergenerational exchanges, normally through patterns of inheritance. This issue of intergenerational relationships introduces the idea of the political economy of generations, as Evens's study of conflict between fathers and sons introduced a moral economy into the problem of generations (Evens, 1995). There is of course an important reciprocity between generations as, for example, parents eventually hand over the familial and collective property to new cohorts. This approach to generations would draw heavily upon existing social gerontology within which an exchange framework has been developed to account for shifts in responsibility and duties between different generational groups (Dowd, 1984; Turner, 1996). Why and how these exchanges take place between generations is still to some extent unclear but generational relations are often organized around the concept of duty and obligation whereby in exchange for their lifetime of work and social involvement, older generations may expect to receive a substantial benefit from society in terms of retirement pensions and other collective forms of security. There are of course important variations here to do with the economic framework within which different generations come into existence, integrate into society and then fragment and disappear. The 1945 generation is interesting because, arising in a period of post-war prosperity, this generation has experienced very high levels of employment and material benefit. By contrast younger generations entering the labour market in the 1980s and 1990s have been faced with a much more difficult labour market characterized by flexibility, casualization and fragmentation. Within this context of generations and resources, the current debate about retirement becomes very important. Retirement as an institution emerged as a benefit to workers who could look forward to a period of enforced leisure after a life-cycle of work provided they had an accumulation of benefits within a general system of social security. In the contemporary debate about welfare and citizenship, compulsory retirement is now often associated with ageism and with a particularistic response to age cohorts. Furthermore from the point of view of management, a fixed notion of retirement contradicts the search for more flexible modes of employment. Retirement has a very direct relationship to the level of unemployment in society, particularly unemployment amongst young workers. The struggle to remove retirement, while often couched within the discourse of human rights and social justice, may also contain an important element of intergenerational conflict and violence whereby prosperous older generations seek to maintain their control over the labour market by excluding younger groups from premature entry into full-time employment. These considerations provide us with yet another way of defining generation as a social cohort passing through time which as a result enjoys a strategic ensemble of life chances with respect to scarce resources of both a material and cultural character (Dahrendorf, 1979). We may expect therefore that intergenerational conflict will express itself in terms of a variety of resources. The struggle over labour markets, capital investments and salaries is a rather obvious feature of the political economy of generations, but there will be other struggles for cultural icons, national identity and various forms of cultural capital.

Pierre Bourdieu (1993a) treats generations and ageing as phenomena which are socially constructed by the conflict over resources (both economic and cultural) within a given field; each social field has its own specific 'laws of ageing'. What one generation has struggled to achieve may be regarded by subsequent generations as irrelevant and unimportant; this results in 'many clashes between systems of aspirations formed in different periods' (Bourdieu, 1993a: 99). Anti-youth sentiment grows out of this clash of aspirations, especially among declining social groups who see their power being overtaken by younger cohorts. Generally, old people are anti-youth for the simple reason that 'old age is also a social decline' (Bourdieu, 1993a: 100). The strategy of social closure of the older generations must be to delay the time at which they hand over power, for example by creating hurdles to success. Bourdieu has shown how these strategies work in the educational field where credentialism functions to protect the assets of senior generational cohorts. He argues, however, that the university crisis of May 1968 was in fact a crisis of academic generations not in the sense of age but in the sense of modes of generational qualifications, that is in terms of *aggregation* (Bourdieu, 1988). In the literary field, the competition for prestige is so intense that the life of an 'artistic generation' tends to be very brief as one style replaces another in a rhythm of literary fashion (Bourdieu, 1993b: 52–3). The 'neo' style replaces the 'paleo' with alarming speed as new products emerge in the literary marketplace. In these examples, we can see how Bourdieu has successfully, but implicitly, applied many of Weber's notions of social closure to cultural production, in which 'generation' is a key variable.

Cultural Dimensions of Generation

We can now offer a more complete cultural definition of generation. Following the research of David Wyatt (1993) in *Out of the Sixties*, a generation is constituted by:

1 a 'traumatic event' (such as a civil war, natural catastrophe or assassination of a political leader);
2 a set of cultural or political mentors which stands in an adversarial relation to the dominant culture and which gives articulation to the traumatic event;
3 a dramatic shift in demography which influences the distribution of resources in a society;
4 a 'privileged interval' which connects a generation into a cycle of success and failure (for example from the Progressive Era to the Depression);

5   the creation of sacred space wherein sacred places (Greenwich Village, Paris, or Woodstock) sustain a collective memory of utopia; and

6   the notion of the 'Happy Few' who provide mutual support for individuals who are accepted as bona fide members of the cohort.

Wyatt's approach captures the sociological consequences of temporal specificity or contingency, and its cultural opportunities and consequences. For example, young men born in Europe around 1894 were highly likely to experience the first mass technological war where pacificist counter-ideologies were underdeveloped and patriarchal values of unquestioned service to the nation were dominant. The First World War experience in Germany produced, through groups like the *Freikorps*, the historical and mythological foundation of European fascism; it also produced a collection of 'male fantasies' (Theweleit, 1987) which constituted the imagination of young German fascists (fear of proletarian women, hatred of women in the role of communist prostitute, fantasies of sexual and military conquest, national hygiene and purity, the dream of a male community of blood, and fear of racial impurity by rape and occupation of the homeland). By contrast, men who were born around 1907 were not available for military service and were often seen subsequently to be unmanly. Christopher Isherwood wrote of his schoolboy experiences in English public schools where his generation, by not serving in the trenches, had failed 'The Test'. And, because of a perceived lack of imaginative sensibility of a technology-fixated culture, American intellectuals of the same period felt themselves part of a 'lost' generation forced into European exile. Men born in 1945 in most European countries missed both world wars and entered life as 'a lucky generation' which experienced peace, full employment and mass consumerism.

In our approach to generations, therefore, we wish to draw attention to the modes through which a generation embodies its collective identity in response to traumatic or formative events (wars, civil conflicts and other disasters). An example of this could be a typical physical body or body image produced by generational cohorts. Just as Bourdieu has drawn attention to the body image of different classes and class fractions, so the sociology of the body could also play an interesting role in the elaboration of the theory of generations. For example, it is typically noted that men who enjoy a significant control over economic resources will form marital and sexual relations with much younger women from other generational cohorts. We could regard this strategic differential in age as part of a inter-generational struggle over sexual resources within the market-place of potential sexual partners. These strategic sexual and/or material opportunities are also expressed culturally as generational types. There were specific body images associated, for example, with proto-fascist males in the *Freikorps* culture, and Hitler came to embody the romantic images of knight on horseback as national saviour in for example 'Hitler as Flagbearer' in the painting by Hubert Lanzinger. Issues relating to sexual liberation and experimentation – the availability of the Pill, legal liberalization of divorce, and pre-marital sexual experimentation – are often seen as experiences which are constitutive of the Sixties generation (Green, 1993). It is also assumed that issues like AIDS, homosexual politics, sexual citizenship, internet sexuality and sexual tourism will shape the self-definition of generations which came to maturity in the 1980s. This consideration however leads us on to a more extended discussion of the idea of culture, habitus and generation.

A generational cohort survives by maintaining a collective memory of its origins, its historic struggles, its primary historical and political events, and its leading characters and ideologists. The Sixties generation would be therefore a classic illustration. In Australia, there is a lively discussion about the impact of warfare and post-war reconstruction on the culture and mentality of various generations, specifically with respect to their impact on national culture. For example, in *Sex and Anarchy*, Anne Coombs (1996) has described 'The Sydney Push as a generation in search of freedom' (1949–1957). Recruited from the post-war bohemian, university and fringe cultures of central Sydney, The Push expressed the oppositional values of the philosopher John Anderson and its membership included such figures as Roelof Smilde, Germaine Greer and Darcy Waters. The Push produced a series of films, plays and novels which challenged the conservatism of white, post-war Australian prosperity. Eyerman and Jamison (1995) have analysed the role of popular music in the 1960s in order to understand how social movements obtain and maintain a collective identity. A similar approach could be adopted for understanding how generations maintain themselves, that is, maintain their identity over time and space. In the modern period with improved methods of information, storage and dispersal, generations may maintain themselves more easily over both time and space by the use of electronic media such as television, film and radio. These media provide the cultural means of communication whereby shared images, shared songs and shared rituals can be enjoyed and appropriated by members of the generational cohort. These collective rituals produce an affective basis to generations, namely, an emotional substratum which is sustained by ritual practice. We may expect that in the modern period these generational cohorts still become increasingly reflexive in the sense that email and internet will be used as mechanisms whereby generational cohorts in different cultures may sustain generational conflict. With the globalization of popular culture, generations will exist more easily across social space because they will be able to share more easily a collective culture.

In terms of the recent interest in the sociology of the body (Turner, 1996), we can argue that generational cultures become inscribed upon the surfaces of bodies, producing distinctive and unique body images whereby members of a generation can identify themselves in public spaces as members of a common generational cohort. Through collectively shared notions of fashion which are embedded in a generational habitus, members of a generation, in order to enjoy the benefits of collective rituals and collective memories, will tend to adopt appropriate generational styles. The legacy of the 1960s has been the somewhat ubiquitous use of jeans, t-shirts with appropriate slogans, leather jackets and so forth. Typical for the 1970s, the Punk generations by contrast had an entirely different fashion style, and somewhat different body shape, to indicate membership. Regardless of shifts and changes in fashion, a generational habitus will tend to produce a limited and distinctive range of body style, body type and corresponding forms of fashion. The sharing of a common body image thus becomes an important index of the success of a general generational habitus in imposing particular lifestyles and life careers. The notion of 'images of aging' (Featherstone and Wernick, 1995) could be applied more generally to the question of how images of bodies become attached to cultures of generations. Obviously one answer lies in the ways in which the fashion industry creates generational bodies and types which are then attached through fashion magazines to specific generational cohorts. In Britain in the early 1980s, fashion magazine editors identified a niche market for male advertising and fashion journals for the age group around 16 to 25 years, but this group lacked a coherent image. Fashion journals came to focus on a homosexual image of strength and sensitivity (Mort, 1996).

Finally, we would suggest that with the postmodernization of culture there may be a greater fluidity in generational identity and memory. In the traditional sociology of generations, it was assumed that the history of generations as cohorts would resemble the life careers of individuals in the sense that the social history of the generation would be marked by its coming into existence, its rise to maturity, its involvement in the labour market and its final retirement and extinction. As labour markets and life-styles have become more flexible and fragmented, it may be that generational experiences become markedly different. However, these changes may in fact reinforce the importance of generational membership. As we have already noted, the generation of 1945 has enjoyed enormous material benefits in terms of full employment, access to the property markets and entrance into a mass higher educational system. In a period of high youth unemployment, it may be that the material prosperity of older generations reinforces their sense of a separate identity from younger cohorts. Youth are regarded as an unemployed, dependent and useless generation. Youth fashion emphasizes their dependency while musical groups like UB40 in the United Kingdom develop lyrics which represent the culture of the dole queue. While older generations may be successfully excluded from dominance in the area of sport and youthful leisure, they will nevertheless continue to dominate the political and economic resources in society, giving them considerable power over the cultural icons of a particular society. While many sociologists may be currently considering the decline or end of social class (Lee and Turner, 1996), it may well be that intergenerational conflicts increase with the growing uncertainty of employment and security for many sections of the population.

Habitus and Generation

Speaking generally and broadly, Bourdieu (1990: 53) defines habitus in terms of

> ... systems of durable, transposable dispositions, structured structures pre-disposed to function as structuring structures, that is, as principles which generate and organize practices and representations that can be objectively adapted to their outcomes without presupposing a conscious aiming at ends or an express mastery of the operations necessary in order to attain them.

A habitus circumscribes a set of dispositions to act and an evaluation frame of perception which are at once historical, social and individual. These dispositions are incorporated, embodied in individuals in practical interaction within an historically formed social context. Since the basic structuring structure of modern society is that of class hierarchy, the structuring structure of habitus is linked to class location. Feminist theory can be used to incorporate gender into habitus. Here gender is theorized as a social identity incorporated in relation to an objectified gender division of labour. While class identity is linked to a complex scale of social and cultural differentiation, formed in relation to a hierarchical social structure, the identity of gender is the effect of a labour of differentiation and cultural distinctions. This labour consists of numerous exclusions, oppressions and classificatory simplifications in terms of the antagonistic dichotomy of 'male' and 'female'. The body is crucial to Bourdieu's account of classification and competition, because 'the body is a mnemonic device upon and in which the very basics of culture, the practical taxonomies of the habitus, are imprinted and encoded in a socialising or learning process which commences during early childhood' (Jenkins, 1992: 76).

We would like to add another dimension to this gender classification by including generation as a mode of distinction, one based in age differentiation. These criteria of social stratification can overlap, but, as we suggested earlier, one can also think of historical circumstances where the hegemonic relations between these dimensions might shift in favour of generation, rather than class. For example, while class can be said to be the dominant structuring of collective identity formation in early modern society, gender became an important, even dominant force in modern society and generation can be said to have reached such a level of significance in late modern society. Class, gender and age (and, we might add, ethnicity in some societies), as scales of differentiation, can be thought of as different dimensions of a force field with varying degrees of significance at different historical moments.

A Generation Represents Itself

We can illustrate our more general account of generational habitus and generational identity formation with the example of the generation 1945. This generation is often identified in more popular forums as the 'baby-boomers' or the lucky generation that came before 'Generation X'. This is the cohort born at the end of the Second World War in a time when anxiety concerning peace and security in the industrialized nations co-existed with unprecedented economic expansion. In his work on the generation of 1914, Wohl recounts how the very notion of generation, as formulated most cogently in Mannheim's work, was in an essential sense a product of its time. While formulated in conjunction with Mannheim's own attempts to free himself from Marxism, the idea of a generation also expressed a more generally felt desire among the young to break with a past identified with older members of the population. The First World War was a watershed, a breaking point which clearly and cleanly divided 'youth' from 'the elders' in terms of outlook and experience, as it separated an old from a new world order. This divide helped create a self-conscious cohort whose collective identity was itself contained in the idea of 'youth', a conceptualization which cut across national and class barriers. The idea of generation, in other words, emerged as a distinctive and real social possibility in the wake of total war, and not merely as part of an intellectual discourse.

The Second World War created a similar cultural watershed. It was the same kind of 'significant event' identified by Philip Abrams (1982), following in Mannheim's path, which demarcated a social space in which biological (age) and cultural factors could interact to produce the basis for collective identity formation. In Mannheim's original formulation (Mannheim, 1952), generational unity was the last phase in a complex process where individual and collective biography interacted within a common historical context. In order for an age cohort to become a generation, something like a significant event, a war or revolution, which sorted a population not so much according to which side one was on, but more in terms of who experienced it first hand and who did not, was a clear delimiter. Of course, the more ideological or political dimensions could also prove decisive in that they could bridge gaps between age cohorts and create them amongst those of the same age group. In this case, there would be continuity rather than a change as defined by generational identity and conflict. Mannheim used the term 'generation-unit' as a means of dealing with the problem of subgroups and subdivisions within an age cohort. The Second World War created the conditions for both. Some of the old enmity which produced the war was reproduced across generations, but this was nothing compared to the sense of a new age dawning, where old antagonisms would not be the defining characteristic. It was just this sense of before and after which made for a line of demarcation of a new social space, which Mannheim called a generational location. J. Whalen and

R. Flacks (1989) have employed the idea of intra-generational differences to test the degree of identification with the Sixties Generation among its remaining members. The Vietnam War served a similar watershed function here. Their research casts doubt on the idea of a coherent and continuing generational identity; rather there were a number of distinctive groups or 'generation-units' in the Sixties.

This geographically and politically demarcated social space created the conditions for the optimism which helped produce an unprecedented upswing in the birth rates of the industrial nations. While the original idea of generational awareness was more tied to ideological factors connected to disenchantment and pessimism after the First World War, this new post-war generational awareness was as much related to the expanding numbers of young people as it was to optimism in the face of economic expansion and to what Daniel Bell (1960) identified as the desire for the end of ideology. Rapid population growth, economic expansion and a growing optimism in spite of the nuclear threat were in the background out of which a post-war generational identity took form. The new generation's primary disposition was expansionary optimism, which came to be summarized in slogans such as the Lucky Generation and the Baby Boomers. A key mechanism in coalescing this identity – as both cause and effect – were the new forms of mass media emerging out of the same context and the mass or popular culture they helped produce.

A defining characteristic of the new generation and the grounds of its distinction in Bourdieu's double-edged sense were the consumer items made available through mass media and mass production. A central aspect of the habitus of this generation-in-formation was first of all the habit of regular consumption of the commodities of popular culture. Economic expansion and optimism were in part made possible through the incredible growth of consumer industries, as well as the means to market them through mass media, and the new generation to consume them. Popular music provides an example. Recorded mass produced and distributed music had been an essential part of popular culture of the industrial nations since the early part of the century. The United States, where radio and records were available to both urban and rural populations on a mass scale since the 1920s, was perhaps the extreme, but even in the smaller nations of Europe, Sweden and The Netherlands, for example, records and radio were common consumer items, with a limited market of course, by the end of the 1930s. All this exploded in the late 1950s and early 1960s. In Sweden the idea of a specific youth culture was beginning to form just prior to the outbreak of war, but in the post-war period the notion solidified and music was one of the central components of this process. It was African-American inspired music, first jazz and then rock and roll which provided the significant symbolic keys. Both served to represent 'youth' and the 'modern', against the classical and traditional music of the elders, marking off the new generation against the old. The post-war period was the American Age and mass produced popular culture, exemplified as music, was its most visible and available form of expression. It was this that youth took as its form of representation.

In American sociology, the notion of a specific youth culture was formulated by Talcott Parsons in the 1940s. The founding father of structural functionalism was one of the first to speak of a distinct 'youth culture'. Already in 1942, Parsons referred to 'adolescence' as part of the life-cycle where 'there first begins to develop a set of patterns and behaviour phenomena which involve a highly complex combination of age grading and sex role elements ... [that] may be referred to together as the phenomena of the "youth culture"' (Parsons, 1964: 91). In the context of discussing emerging gender differences among American adolescents, Parsons characterized the period of youth as one of considerable 'strain and insecurity' in American society, at the same time as he warned against the 'tendency to the romantic idealization of youth patterns' by adults who, because of similar 'strains', look back upon childhood and adolescence as a period of carefree existence which contrasted greatly with their present work and family-related responsibilities.

Parsons was also one of the first to notice the potential emergence of the great cultural shift which occurred in the 1960s: when youth and youth culture became a model and ideal for the rest of society. It should also be noted that in this essay Parsons is very much aware of the differences related to social class. The 'youth culture' he is concerned to identify in the 1940s is that of the urban middle and upper class. In the 1960s, when Parsons (1962) returned to the theme in 'Social change and youth in America', the idea of youth and youth culture had become more general and universal, reflecting shifts not only in American social structure but in the rest of the industrially developed world as well. By the late 1950s and early 1960s, the 'privilege' of youth had spread to a much wider segment of the population. These circumstances led social scientists like Flacks (1971) and Kenneth Keniston (1968) to speak of youth as a social movement and as a source of radical social change.

While social scientists pondered the meaning and effects of youth culture on post-war society, young people were themselves forming their own particular frames of reference and identity, their own generational habitus. With money to spend and age-specialized consumer items becoming more available, regular visits to the record shop, cinema, and clothing store began to produce an outward generational style and an inward framework of evaluation or taste. What was good was noisy, fast and colourful; what was bad was mundane and mediocre, the colourless grey-flannel suit of the new men of power that C. Wright Mills and other theorists of mass society were analysing in the early post-war period. Marlon Brando's 'The Wild One' (1950) helped crystallize the black-leather jacket, the motorcycle and the tough-guy posturing that Elvis Presley later put to music, and which James Dean would modify. These mass projected image-styles which, along with the hip existentialism of the Beats, were formative seeds from which the social movements of the 1960s would flower. It was these movements however which were the real catalysts to the identity formation of the generation of 1945.

From the perspective of generational habitus, the social movements of the 1960s, the student movements, anti-war and peace movements, the radicalism in support of third-world national liberation, the women's movement and gay liberation movements, and the cultural avant garde in theatre and the arts, can be seen as part of the social space in which the generation of 1945 could define its collective identity. If we view social movements as forces which open up social spaces where new forms of knowledge, as well as collective identity, can emerge, then the social movements of the 1960s were constitutive of a generational consciousness (Eyerman and Jamison, 1994). Within their sphere the marks of generational distinction were realized. That is to say, the social movements of the 1960s were as much social and cultural as they were political in the instrumental and strategic sense. The forms of music, the electric rock which evolved out of the rock and roll of the 1950s, the revived and rejuvenated forms of diverse 'folk' music, and the associated life-styles, clothing, sexual attitudes and practices, and so on, were constitutive of the social movements of the 1960s and the generation of 1945 (Gitlin, 1987; Cantwell, 1996; Eyerman and Barretta, 1996; Eyerman and Jamison, 1998). While the movements provided space for the self-production of a generational identity, the commercial mass media amplified and, at the same time, commodified it. In this sense, the culture industry played an important role in the social movements of the 1960s, in helping to solidify and magnify a generational identity. This role was neither entirely unintended nor strategically planned; rather one can say the interests of industry and the needs and desires of actors coincided for a time.

The specific details of this aspect of generational habitus are too well known to bear much elaboration here. What we would point out however is that to the extent that these social movements can be considered 'youth' or 'new' social movements, they can be studied as both cause and effect of generational identity-formation. At least as a hypothesis one could view these movements as expressing strivings for generational distinction, as well as being a formative aspect of that distinction. As this generation has matured, the romanticism of youth may have declined, being replaced increasingly by negative images of youth. This negative image of youth may now be associated with dependency, as unemployment, alcoholism and high suicide rates are characteristic of youth in a period of globalization of labour markets, and a decline in mass employment (Cote and Allahar, 1995). In economies which have embraced Thatcherite social policies and abandoned post-war commitments to mass education and full employment, many of the institutional conditions which fuelled youthful rebelliousness and radical politics have been eroded, leaving behind a more alienated but compliant youth population.

Conclusion

The principal conclusion of this chapter is that generational consciousness, when it is forged by a major traumatic event such as mass warfare, can overcome and transcend the barriers of social class to produce a powerful, solidaristic force in social relationships. These solidaristic ties can, of course, often assume a romantic or nostalgic aura, but they remain no less powerful. British Second World War films such as *Dam Busters* have a powerful message of social nostalgia in which class divisions did not stand in the way of heroic co-operation between men and women of different class backgrounds. These war films and classic actors such as Jack Hawkins probably help to compensate for Britain's monumental post-war failures. In general, wartime experiences have in the 20th century produced an influential and emotionally powerful source of social identity and imagery. However, the Sixties generation, which in most societies grew up in a period of peace and prosperity, was held together more by novel experiences of consumerism than by warfare. For this generation, war, the Second World War and the Vietnam War, formed part of the Other against which it distinguished itself.

As economic class has declined in significance as the primary form of social stratification, life-style and generational differences have increased as indicators of status variations. In a mass cultural market, 'there is also the persistent reassertion of hierarchy and distinction, as elite groups and privileged consumers attempt to distance themselves from the vulgar world of the masses' (Turner, 1988: 71). Generational conflicts over positional goods and the symbols of cultural distinction will increase. At least the 'strong idiom' of class analysis (Lee and Turner, 1996) has receded, creating social opportunities where cultural capital can function as the basis of social membership and identity. In the late 20th century, generational differences are increasing in importance as the foundation of the life-style attributes of status.

In conceptual terms, generation can provide a useful dimension for the analysis of changing life-cycles in modern society, especially in terms of intergenerational conflicts over scarce resources. As youth unemployment increases with technological change, and as compulsory retirement has been made questionable by legislation relating to ageism, there are significant political conflicts around the generational dimensions of ageing, the life-course and resource allocation. Because the Sixties generation was brought up with an ideology of perpetual youthfulness, it may be difficult for this generation to withdraw from a leadership role in cultural and social terms. The 1990s have seen a more or less permanent 'revival' of nostalgic interest in the music and life-style of the Beatles, the Rolling Stones, the Doors and Elton John, who have become the icons of the century. A sociological understanding of the 20th century requires a better understanding of the distinctive generational movements which have shaped its history, politics and culture.

References

Abrams, P. (1982) *Historical Sociology*. Ithaca, NY: Cornell University Press.

Bauman, Z. (1982) *Memories of Class: The pre-history and after-life of class*. London: Routledge & Kegan Paul.

Bell, D. (1960) *The End of Ideology*. New York: Collier.

Bloom, A. (1986) *Prodigal Sons. The New York Intellectuals and Their World*. New York: Oxford University Press.

Bourdieu, P. (1977) *Outline of a Theory of Practice*. Cambridge: Cambridge University Press.

Bourdieu, P. (1984) *Distinction. A Social Critique of the Judgement of Taste*. London: Routledge & Kegan Paul.

Bourdieu, P. (1988) *Homo Academicus*. Stanford, CA: University of Stanford Press.

Bourdieu, P. (1990) *The Logic of Practice*. Cambridge: Polity Press.

Bourdieu, P. (1993a) *Sociology in Question*. London: Sage.

Bourdieu, P. (1993b) *The Field of Cultural Production*. Cambridge: Polity Press.

Cantwell, R. (1996) *When We Were Good*. Cambridge, MA: Harvard University Press.

Coombs, A. (1996) *Sex and Anarchy. The Life and Death of the Sydney Push*. Ringwood: Viking Press.

Cote, J.E. and Allahar, A.L. (1995) *Generation on Hold: Coming of age in the late twentieth century*. New York: New York University Press.

Dahrendorf, R. (1979) *Life Chances*. London: Weidenfeld & Nicolson.

DeMartini, J. (1985) 'Change agents and generational relations: a reevaluation of Mannheim's problem of generation', *Social Forces*, 64: 1–15.

Dowd, J.J. (1984) 'Benefices and the aged', *Journal of Gerontology*, 30: 102–8.

Eisenstadt, S.N. (1956) *From Generation to Generation*. Glencoe, IL: Free Press.

Evens, T.M.S. (1995) *Two Kinds of Rationality. Kibbutz Democracy and Generational Conflict*. Minneapolis: University of Minnesota Press.

Eyerman, R. and Barretta, S. (1996) 'From the 30s to the 60s: the folk music revival in the United States', *Theory and Society*, 25: 501–43.

Eyerman, R. and Jamison, A. (1994) *Social Movements. A Cognitive Approach*. Cambridge: Polity Press.

Eyerman, R. and Jamison, A. (1995) 'Social movements and cultural transformation: popular music in the 1960s', *Media, Culture & Society*, 17(3): 449–68.

Eyerman, R. and Jamison, A. (1998) *Music and Social Movements: Mobilizing tradition in the twentieth century*. Cambridge: Cambridge University Press.

Featherstone, M. and Wernick, A. (eds) (1995) *Images of Aging: Cultural representation of later life*. London: Routledge.

Flacks, R. (1971) *Youth and Social Change*. Chicago: Markham.

Frith, S. (1984) *The Sociology of Youth*. Ormskirk: Causeway Press.

Giddens, A. (1984) *The Constitution of Society*. Cambridge: Polity Press.

Gitlin, T. (1987) *The Sixties*. New York: Bantam.

Green, J. (1993) *It: Sex since the Sixties*. London: Secker & Warburg.

Jenkins, R. (1992) *Pierre Bourdieu*. London: Routledge.

Keniston, K. (1968) *Young Radicals: Notes on committed youth*. New York: Harcourt, Brace and Jovanovich.

Lee, D. and Turner, B.S. (eds) (1996) *Conflicts about Class. Debating Inequality in late Industrialism*. London: Longman.

Mannheim, K. (1952) 'The problem of generations', in *Essays on the Sociology of Knowledge*. London: Routledge & Kegan Paul. pp. 276–320.

Mannheim, K. (1986) *Conservatism: A contribution to the sociology of knowledge*. London: Routledge & Kegan Paul.

Mort, F. (1996) *Cultures of Consumption, Masculinities and Social Space in Late Twentieth-Century Britain*. London: Routledge.

Parkin, F. (1979) *Marxism and Class Theory. A Bourgeois Critique*. London: Tavistock.

Parsons, T. (1962) 'Youth in the context of American society', *Daedalus* (Winter): 97–123.

Parsons, T. (1964) *Essays in Sociological Theory.* New York: Free Press.

Podhoretz, N. (1967) *Making it.* New York: Harper & Row.

Schatz, J. (1991) *The Generation: The rise and fall of the Jewish community of Poland.* Berkeley: University of California Press.

Schwartz, B. (1996) 'Memory as a cultural system', *American Sociological Review*, 61: 908–27.

Theweleit, K. (1987) *Male Fantasies.* Cambridge: Polity Press, 2 volumes.

Turner, B.S. (1988) *Status.* Buckingham: Open University Press.

Turner, B.S. (1996) *The Body & Society.* London: Sage.

Weber, M. (1978) *Economy and Society.* Berkeley and Los Angeles: University of California Press, 2 volumes.

Whalen, J. and Flacks, R. (1989) *Beyond the Barricades.* Philadelphia, PA: Temple University Press.

Wilson, E. (1993) *The Sixties. The Last Journal 1960–1972.* New York: Farrar Straus Giroux.

Wohl, R. (1979) *The Generation of 1914.* Cambridge, MA: Harvard University Press.

Wyatt, D. (1993) *Out of the Sixties: Storytelling and the Vietnam generation.* Cambridge: Cambridge University Press.

CHAPTER 15

THE SOCIOLOGY OF CITIZENSHIP

Introduction

Societies face two contradictory principles. They are organized around issues of scarcity, which result in exclusionary structures such as gender divisions, social classes and status groups, but they must also secure social solidarity. In social science, these contradictory principles are characteristically referred to as the allocative and integrative requirements. In a secular society, especially where social inequality is intensified by economic rationalism, citizenship functions as a major foundation of social solidarity. The article also explores the scope of citizenship studies through an examination of identity, civic virtue and community. In concludes with an extensive critique of the legacy of T.H. Marshall, pointing to the future of citizenship studies around the theme of globalization and human rights.

This chapter on citizenship provides an overview of the contemporary literature and development of social science approaches to social and human rights. It is in part an extended commentary on the legacy of T.H. Marshall (1893–1981), although I argue that an adequate understanding of the issues surrounding citizenship in modern societies must go well beyond the Marshallian framework. I treat citizenship as a particular case of social rights and indicate some of the tensions between social and human rights. Marshall developed a theory of post-war societies through an analysis of the relationships between social class, welfare and citizenship; his approach to the citizenship debate proved to be seminal (Andrews, 1991; Beiner, 1995; Blumer and Rees, 1996; Roche, 1992; Turner and Hamilton, 1994). The aim of this chapter is both to provide a composite picture of his ideas and some fundamental criticisms of his approach, and thus to suggest a variety of approaches and issues beyond the Marshallian tradition.

To start with, one may define citizenship as a collection of rights and obligations which give individuals a formal legal identity; these legal rights and obligations have been put together historically as sets of social institutions such as the jury system, parliaments and welfare states. Citizenship has traditionally been a fundamental topic of philosophy and politics, but, from a sociological point of view, we are interested in those institutions in society that embody or give expression to the formal rights and obligations of individuals as members of a political community. Figure 15.1 provides us with a summary of the key components of citizenship in modern societies.

I refer to this approach as 'sociological', because its main concern is with the institutions of citizenship, social identity, the nature of inequality

Figure 15.1   A Sociological Model of Citizenship

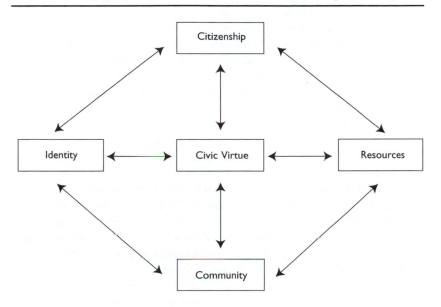

and access to socio-economic resources. 'Political' models of citizenship typically have a sharper focus on political rights, the state and the individual. Thus, the history of political ideas about citizenship starts with J.-J. Rousseau's theory of social contract and Johann Gottlieb Fichte's science of rights rather than with Marshall's 'citizenship and social class' (Marshall, 1950). Sociologists have been concerned to understand how the institutions of citizenship protect individuals and groups from the negative outcomes and unintended vagaries of the market in a capitalist society. This focus on the re-distributive potential of citizenship institutions (the allocative function) provided the basis for sociological approaches to questions about justice and equality. Thus, citizenship controls the access of individuals and groups to scarce resources in society. These legal rights and obligations, once they are institutionalized as formal status positions, give people formal entitlements to scarce resources in society and by 'resources' I mean primarily economic resources such as social security, health-care entitlements, subsidized housing, retirement packages, or taxation concessions. 'Resources', however, also include access to culturally desirable resources or 'goods' such as, within a traditional liberal framework, rights to speak your own language in the public arena or rights relating to religious freedoms. These resources therefore include not only the traditional economic resources of housing, health, income, and employment, but also cultural resources such as education, knowledge, religion and language. These rights to cultural resources can be conceptualized within the paradigm of cultural capital via the sociological theories of

Pierre Bourdieu, especially in his *Distinction* (1984). There are also political resources which are related to access to sources of power in society, rights to vote, rights to participate politically and so forth.

It is conceptually parsimonious to think of three types of resource: economic, cultural and political. Alongside these resources, we typically find three forms of rights: economic rights which are related to basic needs for food and shelter; cultural rights which include both access to welfare and access to education; and finally, political rights which cover the conventional area of liberal concern such as individual freedoms, and rights to expression through political means such as parliaments. These rights may be collectively referred to as 'social' rights as distinct from human rights, because they typically presuppose membership of a nation-state.

The first thing to emphasize about citizenship is that it controls access to the scarce resources of society and hence this allocative function is the basis of a profound conflict in modern societies over citizenship membership criteria. The process of and conditions for naturalization and de-naturalization tell us a great deal about the character of democracy in society because these processes relate fundamentally to the basic values of inclusion and exclusion (Brubaker, 1992). French colonialism typically involved a notion of a *mission civilisatrice* in which the metropolitan culture attempted to impose a uniform identity on its dependent regions and in the nineteenth century colonization required cultural assimilation (Aldrich and Connell, 1992), but these inclusionary/exclusionary processes are obviously not merely about cultural identity. Take, for example, in contemporary Britain the anxiety about granting unconditionally comprehensive citizenship rights to the denizens of Hong Kong. In societies like Australia and Canada limitations on migration are historically related to attempts to control access to resources by selective control of migration and naturalization. The 'white-Australia policy' is a typical illustration of citizenship as a form of social closure, to use the terminology of Max Weber's political sociology (Parkin, 1979). Social closure is an elementary form of group solidarity, producing an inevitable alienation and stigmatization of 'outsiders'. This 'fear of diversity' which underlines social closure is in many respects the social driving force behind political theory as such (Saxonhouse, 1992). The boundaries of the state produce an enduring crisis of belonging for marginal communities in ethnically plural society and in this negative sense citizenship is about the policing of borders (Connolly, 1995). The status of aboriginal membership within the political community of the 'white-settler societies' and post-colonial societies is probably the most difficult legal and political problem of contemporary states. Any bench-mark of citizenship would have to include some notion of egalitarian openness to difference and otherness and an essential ingredient of liberal democracy. Who gets citizenship clearly indicates the prevailing formal criteria of inclusion/exclusion within a political community and how these resources following citizenship membership are allocated and administered largely determines the economic fate of individuals and families. These economic dimensions of citizenship are a crucial feature of citizenship entitlement and there are various overt measures of government policy which impinge directly on the enjoyment of these citizenship privileges; taxation policy is a particularly good example. However, there are many disguised or covert economic conditions or processes which influence citizenship. Thus we can regard inflation as a negative and largely unintended erosion of citizenship, while systematic corruption in public life is a major negative indicator of the condition of citizenship in a modern society. I attempt to analyse these issues in a subsequent discussion of solidarity and scarcity.

The next important aspect of citizenship is that it confers, in addition to a legal status, a particular cultural identity on individuals and groups. The notion of the 'politics of identity' indicates an important change in the nature of contemporary politics. Whereas much of the struggle over citizenship in the early stages of industrialization was about class membership and class struggle in the labour market, citizenship struggles in late twentieth-century society are often about claims to cultural identity and cultural history. These struggles have been about sexual identity, gay rights, gender equality, and aboriginality. Most debates about citizenship in contemporary political theory are as a result about the question of contested collective identity in a context of radical pluralization (Mouffe, 1992). When political scientists therefore refer to 'citizenship', they are not merely thinking about access to scarce economic and political resources, they are concerned ultimately with questions about identity in civil society and civic culture. In formal political philosophy, the notion of citizenship contains a clear notion of the civic virtues which are regarded as necessary for the functioning of a democracy. The word 'citizenship' (*cité/zein*) itself indicates a connection with the rise of bourgeois society and in particular with the tradition of civil society (*die bürgerliche Gesellschaft*). For the Scottish political economists such as Adam Smith and Adam Ferguson, civil society was contrasted with the barbarism of primitive society; citizenship was seen to be connected with *civilitas* (Bobbio, 1989). In Germany, the idealists merged the idea of the Greek polis with the tradition of independent German towns with their distinctive educational cultures (in the virtues of the *Bildung* tradition) to produce a defence of individual rights against both the militarized aristocracy and proletarian vulgarity. The high point of this tradition was in Fichte's Kantian statement of the intersubjectivity of rights (Ferry, 1990). The values of citizenship were merged with those of civilization and hence Weber was to argue that citizenship as a uniquely western institution had its origin in the peculiar structures of the Occidental city. However, for Weber the basis of 'democratization is ever where purely military in character; it lies in the rise of disciplined infantry' (Weber, 1981: 324).

The decline of the noble cavalry marks the rise of the urban militia, the autonomous city, civil society and citizenship. The status of citizenship was part of the process of civilization wherein the virtues of the knight-at-arms were transferred to the arena of the royal court with its effeminate courtiers and its ideology of courtesy, and later to the disciplined asceticism of the bourgeois household. These social conditions also indicate the rootedness of the concept of obligation as the cornerstone of bourgeois responsibility (to family and occupation), bourgeois morality with respect to the public/private division, and bourgeois versions of civil republicanism (Selbourne, 1994). This politico-moral configuration was also the origin of Karl Marx's hostility to the 'possessive individualism' of the English utilitarians such as Bentham and Mill, and to the narrow, undimensional development of the 'political' in classical liberalism. With the rise of economic rationalism in the twentieth century, interest has once more returned to the analysis of the market in relation to possessive individualism, indifference to strangers and hostility to welfare-dependency among the economically marginalized. Citizenship and civic virtues are once more seen to be an essential ingredient of a civilized and pluralistic democracy. This concern for the political threat to civic culture in a market society has been associated with a re-appraisal of Mill's liberalism (Bobbio, 1987), the importance of pluralism (Hirst, 1989) and the role of voluntary associations in democracy (Cohen and Rogers, 1995). The cultural dimension of citizenship is now an essential component of citizenship studies, especially in a context where there is political ambiguity around the analysis of cultural fragmentation and simulation brought about by postmodernization.

The final component of this sociological model of citizenship is the idea of a political community as the basis of citizenship: this political community is typically the nation-state. When individuals become citizens, they not only enter into a set of institutions that confers upon them rights and obligations, they not only acquire an identity, they are not only socialized into civic virtues, but they also become members of a political community with a particular territory and history. In order to have citizenship one has to be, at least in most modern societies, a bona fide member of a political community. Generally speaking, it is rather unusual for people to acquire citizenship if they are not simultaneously members of a political community, that is a nation-state. One should notice here an important difference between human rights and citizenship. Human rights are typically conferred upon people as humans irrespective of whether they are Australian, British, Chinese, Indonesian or whatever, but, because human rights legislation has been accepted by the nations of the world, people can claim human rights, even where they are stateless people or dispossessed refugees. In general, citizenship is a set of rights and obligations that attach to members of formally recognized nation-states within the system of nations and hence citizenship corresponds to legal membership of a nation-state. Citizenship identities and citizenship cultures are national identities and national cultures. Since nations are imaginary communities (Anderson, 1983) and since nations are created (James, 1996), the communal basis of citizenship has to be constantly renewed within the collective memory by nostalgic festivals, public ceremonies of national struggle and effervescent collective experience. National culture has all the characteristics of a civil religion, and hence modern citizenship is a form of social solidarity.

The next section of this chapter deals with my main theme which is the difference between solidarity and scarcity. From a sociological perspective, citizenship provides modern society with an important ingredient of solidarity. This argument concerns the idea of citizenship as social solidarity, namely that citizenship is an answer to the question 'how is society possible, given the significant differences that exist between different social groups and different communities within the nation-state?' To some extent, one could argue that industrial societies have passed through a long period of secularization in which there has been a major decline in general religious values, at least if we confine our attention to western Christian societies or societies which have a legacy of Christianity. In a secular society, public debates are neither couched in the language of religion nor are they resolved by religious institutions. In this social context, citizenship functions or plays the role of a secular religion. With the decline of formal religion, citizenship provides us with a common national culture, common set of identities, and a common value system. What holds secular societies together is a common citizenship as a foundational basis for society in a multicultural environment. In political terms, multiculturalism can be successful where it is based on an overt policy of expanding citizenship participation. A common foundation of citizenship gives different ethnic groups access to scarce resources and makes their cultural diversity possible. Citizenship provides a form of solidarity, if you like a kind of social glue, that holds societies together which are divided by social class, by gender, by ethnicity and by age groups. The solidarity of the political community of modern societies is provided by citizenship which works as a form of civic religion. This 'sociological argument' is taken directly from J.-J. Rousseau's account of the social contract and it is associated with various theories regarding the role of education in creating civic virtues.

One can conceptualize all human societies as divided or organized along two contradictory principles, namely solidarity and scarcity. All human societies, in order to exist, have to find some common basis, some form of solidarity, which will not overcome but at least cope with the problems of difference, diversity and conflict. All human societies must have some basis in solidarity in order to exist, but all human societies, precisely because they are human societies, are also characterized by scarcity. What do I mean by scarcity? The resources of society can never be wholly or systematically distributed in an egalitarian fashion to everybody because there are fundamental scarcities of an economic, cultural and political nature. Scarcity is a very difficult notion to define. It is the basis of all economic theory; economics is about the management of scarce resources in matching means to ends, but it is wrong to think that scarcity exists in only primitive or simple societies. Indeed Marshall Sahlins (1974) has argued in his economic anthropology that scarcity is institutionalized in modern economies, whereas so-called primitive economies were ones of abundance. One can easily imagine a hunter-gatherer society where access to food was limited by the actual difficulties of hunting wild animals and gathering natural produce, but scarcity is always relative to demand as well as to need, and thus scarcity is a fundamental element of the most advanced and prosperous societies. This argument is brilliantly analysed in Nicholas Xenos's *Scarcity and Modernity* (1989). Scarcity in wealthy societies is a function of the growth of expectations about assets, wealth and success, and hence it is possible to date this form of scarcity to the rise of mass consumerism, for example to the Crystal Palace and the Great Exhibition of 1851 (Richards, 1991). Scarcity is a function as much of prosperity and wealth as it is of poverty. Scarcity is manifest in social inequality and the typical forms of social inequality that we experience in modern societies are, obviously, differences of social class or access to wealth. However, scarcity also follows the contours of gender, age and ethnicity. This tension between scarcity of perceived means to desired ends and the need for social solidarity in a context of pluralism is the focal point of citizenship.

In the third part of this chapter, I want to return to the work of T.H. Marshall. In *Citizenship and Social Class*, Marshall (1950) took citizenship and class as fundamental features of modern capitalist societies. Referring primarily to the UK (see Table 15.1), Marshall said that in the seventeenth and eighteenth centuries legal rights were acquired in relation to the jury system, the right to a trial, the right to a fair hearing, and access to legal resources. Marshall claimed that in the seventeenth and eighteenth centuries, it is possible to perceive a growth of legal rights as the first form of elementary citizenship and these legal rights are best expressed or institutionalized in the jury system. In the eighteenth and nineteenth century, there was a growth in political rights and these political rights were eventually institutionalized in parliamentary institutions. Finally, in the nineteenth and twentieth centuries, citizenship expanded further to include social rights. These social rights were institutionalized in the welfare state, and Marshall then went on to argue that citizenship mitigates the inequalities created in the market-place. Citizenship overcomes, mitigates and reduces the impact of economic inequalities that have their origin in the market-place. To put this claim more directly, citizenship tends to resolve or minimize the antagonisms between social classes which are characteristic of the rise of capitalist economies and the capitalist market-place. Marshall had in mind the fact that in the late nineteenth century many European societies went through a significant period of class antagonism and class conflict. Rather than this class conflict spilling over into major revolutionary confrontations, he argued that citizenship reduced the level of class struggle and class antagonism because it redistributed some of the resources, which had become available as a consequence of economic growth.

Table 15.1   Marshall's Model of Citizenship

Period	Rights	Institutions
17–18th centuries	Legal rights	Jury system
18–19th centuries	Political rights	Parliaments
19–20th centuries	Social rights	Welfare state

Through retirement schemes, social security schemes, family benefits, general education and the welfare state, class conflict is contained. While inequality remains a fundamental feature of modern industrial capitalist societies, it is mitigated or regulated by the growth of citizenship entitlements. Marshall argued in effect that citizenship redistributes some of the scarce resources of a capitalist society in order to lessen the revolutionary conflict between classes by creating a common form of solidarity in a political community. This debate about welfare, class and capitalism can be located within a traditional Marxist framework in which the collapse of capitalism is contained by political reformism, which leaves the fundamental structure of class exploitation unchanged (Turner, 1986).

Finally, Marshall went on to argue in *The Right to Welfare and other Essays* (1981) that modern industrialist capitalist societies should be called 'hyphenated societies' because we refer to them as democratic-welfare capitalist societies or societies which have some democratic redistribution of wealth (however minimal) through the institutions of citizenship. He called it a 'hyphenated society' because it combines some element of democratic egalitarianism and inequality of capitalist relations in the capitalist market-place and the capitalist economy. Marshall laid the foundation for much subsequent writing and analysis of the role of citizenship in contemporary societies.

In this section of my argument, some critical objections to Marshall's work are examined. The first criticism is that his notion of citizenship is incomplete. For example, many writers argue that in the twentieth century there was the growth of various forms of economic citizenship and these took the form of workers' participation and workers' councils, economic democracy or industrial democracy. In many western societies, often influenced by Swedish models of industrial relations, there were various attempts to create citizenship in the work place. One of the criticisms of Marshall is that, if a society does not have basic economic citizenship, then the other rights (the legal, political and social welfare rights), tend to be relatively unimportant; for example, citizenship is only minimal, if people do not have some control over their work situation. If there is no redistribution of shares and profits, and if there is no workers' democracy or workers' councils, then citizenship is limited. In many European economies, there were various attempts to set up workers' discussion groups, workers' participation, and consultative relations which gave expression to the idea of economic citizenship. In Yugoslavia, there were extensive experiments in workers' self-management programs (Pateman, 1970: 85–102).

Other writers suggested that Marshall's model was also incomplete because there has been a significant development in the twentieth century of cultural rights. For example, many societies in the nineteenth century developed repressive language policies that made the use of minority languages illegal or at least socially stigmatized in public places. In various societies, the growth of national citizenship in the nineteenth century resulted in nationalistic attempts to regulate and control what languages could be spoken publicly. With the growth of multiculturalism in the twentieth century, there is a greater willingness to tolerate the use of minority languages in the public arena. In many European societies, legislation has been developed to protect these minority languages. There is, at least from the formal legal perspective, a greater public tolerance of cultural difference.

Another illustration of the expansion of cultural citizenship in terms of rights to education would be the great explosion of universities in the middle of the twentieth century. Karl Mannheim (1992) pointed to a number of major educational changes in European societies which were indicative of a more general democratization of culture. He argued that there had been important changes of value with democratization: these included the principle of the ontological equality of human beings, individual autonomy, and equality of opportunity. These changes of value in the field of education included: an optimistic pedagogy which assumed that all children were capable of educational development; a rejection of conservative ideologies of privilege; a scepticism about the authority and privilege of expert knowledge; a criticism of privileged recruitment to elite social office; and the erosion of the barrier between elite and popular culture. Following Marshall, Parsons (1971) also developed the view that the educational revolution which created a mass education system after the Second World War was an important component of modernization; the 'educational revolution' has the same sociological status as the 'industrial revolution', and for Parsons the university was the institutionalization of cultural citizenship. Because the American higher education system had produced a more effective mass education system, it was less characterized by elitism and privilege than the traditional European model with its rigid principles of selectivity.

The first criticism of Marshall's theory of citizenship is that it is an incomplete description of some of the key features of rights in the twentieth century. The second problem with his treatment of citizenship is that he regarded the community basis of citizenship as homogenous. That is, in Marshall's account of citizenship, it is taken for granted that modern societies are homogenous in ethnic, cultural and other terms. Marshall nowhere addressed the issue of ethnic diversity; he showed no understanding of linguistic, religious and cultural differentiation. The only divisions that Marshall's theory recognized in the community are social class divisions. The whole point of his theory was directed to the assumption that the only diversity in the community is social classes and that governments can overcome that class diversity by creating a common basis of citizenship (Turner, 1986). It is very obvious in the twentieth century that the majority of societies are heterogeneous; they are multicultural and highly diverse. As a result partly of twentieth-century labour mobility and general post-war migration, industrial societies have multiple ethnic communities and they have a whole series of religious and cultural divisions. One crucial issue for twentieth-century societies is the political management of difference and diversity – aboriginal, cultural, linguistic and religious. For example, Marshall's 'British' view of citizenship had nothing to say about ethnic diversity, but it quite significantly had nothing to say about one of the major problems of modern society which is: how do states adequately respond to the claims to rights by the aboriginal communities that occupied the land prior to white invasion and settlement? In many white-settler societies, there is a prevailing official history which takes the view that the land was empty prior to white 'settlement' – a term which is obviously preferred to 'invasion'. There is an established debate in Australia over the original constitutional arrangements which assumed that the Australian colony was an empty land. Alexis de Tocqueville also propounded the notion that the North American nomadic communities were not actually there, at least as occupants of the land. De Tocqueville said it is because native Americans did not create property, that they were not actually present in North America (Connolly, 1995). There is a similar Zionist view in the settlement of Israel where the early constitution of Israel assumes an empty space. Palestine was an empty territory to be settled and cultivated by European Jews who were returning to the land (Said, 1994: 34–5). One of the problems about the idea of citizenship is whether it can deal with the question, not only of ethnic diversity, but of aboriginal dispersal and denial. Another way of expressing that is to say that Marshall took identity for granted; it is somehow totally unproblematic for Marshall. In Australia, for example, there are many people who have dual citizenship and in a sense they have a dual identity. Marshall's theory does not provide any guidance for understanding citizenship in a multicultural environment, where there are systematic contradictions of identity.

Marshall's theory has also been challenged by feminist political theory which notes that his account of citizenship depends upon Fordist assumptions within which men go to work to generate an income to sustain their own domestic arrangements and also to produce through superannuation care for the future of their household. Women were assumed to be domestic labourers who serviced their men and reproduced society through childbearing within the nuclear family. Social contract theory reproduced the dominant assumptions of patriarchy which reproduced the public/private division (Pateman, 1988). Marshall's theory assumed an almost perfect division within the public realm (of citizens) and the private world (of women and children). Women's unpaid domestic labour was thus essential to the maintenance of the external political structures of citizenship. These Fordist assumptions have been transformed by changes in the labour market such as flexibilization, by the increase in female employment, by changes to the family which have often been associated with the feminization of poverty with the growth in single-parent families, and by changes to retirement legislation. The conventional and simplistic division between the private and public realms has been transformed by changes to both, which have generally rendered Marshall's underlying assumptions invalid or at least dated. For feminist political theory, the historical relegation of women to the private domain of the nuclear family creates permanent dependency (Pateman, 1989).

Another critical issue in Marshall's theory is that it assumed that these rights are evolutionary and cumulative. Because he argued that the rights of citizenship are cumulative, he also assumed that once you have legal rights and have won the political battles of parliamentary democracy and, once you have won your social welfare rights, then these rights are not eroded by subsequent social struggles. Marshall claimed that each of these historical stages is a successful accumulation of citizenship. This is a very optimistic picture of the historical evolution of rights. One of the important debates emerging in contemporary democracies is whether previous rights can be sustained in a society which is more and more dominated by the needs of the market-place under the rhetoric of economic rationalism. In a market driven society, young people find it very difficult to enter the labour market and get access to resources because of the nature of the modern economy. If we regard full employment as an entitlement, it may be the case that social rights are obliterated or at least weakened as a consequence of economic rationalism. It is quite clear that one can identify many societies that have highly developed social and economic rights but they do not have adequate legal and political rights. In traditional debates about communism versus capitalism, one criticism of the communist regimes of Eastern Europe was that, while they had institutionalized social and economic forms of citizenship, these societies were often weak in terms of legal and political rights. They had economic rights without a comprehensive civil society, because they had achieved industrialization without a liberal-bourgeois revolution against feudal privilege.

The final criticism of Marshall's theory is that it had a one-dimensional view of citizenship. In the literature on citizenship, there is a conventional division between active versus passive citizenship. Table 15.2 summarizes the idea of active versus passive citizenship.

This criticism of Marshall indicates that there are different types of citizenships, which embrace different levels of active involvement in the public domain (Turner, 1989). This distinction involves an historical model

Table 15.2 Summary Response to Critiques of Marshall

Below	Above	
Active	Mixed active/passive	
Revolutionary	Constitutional	Public
France	Monarchy Britain	
Mixed active/passive	Passive	
Liberalism	Plebiscitary	Private
USA	Germany	

(Mann, 1993). Some types of citizenship may be revolutionary; for example, in the French Revolution, there developed a form of citizenship which was grasped from below by popular struggle and by popular social movements. In the French Revolution, there was a clear sense of the public arena as a place where citizens could act as political agents and secure new social rights. This model of citizenship attempts to make a distinction between active or revolutionary citizenship which is the product of social struggles and within which there is a clear and decisive notion of the value of the public over the private. By contrast, consider the use of the plebiscite as simply a mechanism for selecting leaders. Having conducted an election and appointed a government, a leader once in power can rule arbitrarily because the leader does not have to confer or consult with political supporters. In Weber's political sociology, a plebiscite is simply a way of installing a type of leadership which is not immediately answerable to its clients. The French Revolution created an active sense of citizenship in a European revolutionary tradition and by contrast Germany had a passive notion of citizenship. In Weber's analysis of German politics, he advocated the importance of what he called plebiscitary democracy, that is a democracy based upon strong leadership and passive forms of citizenship. In Germany, Lutheranism created a weak sense of the public arena, because it assumed that good citizens were people who accepted moral values appropriate to ethical actions in the private domain of the home. Lutheranism created a sense of the public arena as a dangerous and negative place. By contrast, consider individualistic liberalism and the revolutionary struggle to create America as an independent nation. It created a constitution with a strong sense of democracy from below, where congregationalism and Protestant asceticism favoured trust in self-government and participatory citizenship. However, this sense of republican virtue has been converted into private 'habits of the heart' (Bellah et al., 1985) and American democracy is weakened by the emphasis on the private in liberalism which, in granting individual rights (freedom of speech, and freedom of association), has a weak sense of the public domain. England is a top-down democracy in which, because of the monarchical settlement, one has a patriarchal idea of the parliament and the monarchy. Nevertheless there is a sense of the public arena being morally acceptable. In English culture, Lutheranism was not particularly strong and Anglicanism provided a model of public

Table 15.3   A Revised Model of Citizenship

Period	Person	Rights
City-state	Denizen	Legal rights
Nation-state	Citizens	Political rights
Welfare-state	Social citizen	Social rights
Global capitalism	Human being	Human rights

events which was not privatized. The revolutionary settlement of 1688 provided a parliamentary system which was top-down but institutionalized a mode of relatively active citizenship. What I want to suggest finally is a historical view of this process (see Table 15.3).

Citizenship emerged with the city-state and created an idea of the denizen, where nation-states created a primitive notion of citizenship based upon political rights. This form was followed by the welfare state where we have social citizenship based upon social rights. In this historical model, the question is: what might come next? One answer may be found in global capitalism, where there is an emerging notion of human rights. As the world economy becomes more and more globalized, more workers will travel between economies in search of employment; there will be increasing conflict in the labour market over access to global resources. The sovereignty of the nation-state is eroded by global market trends so that more and more of the national economy is owned by international corporations and it may be that traditional forms of citizenship cannot express or do not correspond to the idea of an increasingly global market.

This model of the history of citizenship can either have an optimistic or pessimistic conclusion. The optimistic one is that through the United Nations, and through agreements about human rights, we can manage the problem of interstate violence, terrorism and conflict. The other model is that in fact we do not have cumulative citizenship; what we have is a breakdown of citizenship. Nation-states no longer adequately provide citizenship for their members and instead we have a growing war of mega-cities and mega-economies against each other. Human rights will not be protected because the so-called 'new world order' operates in the interests of a small number of powerful economies through the mechanism of the World Bank, the International Monetary Fund and the General Agreement on Tariffs and Trade (Muzaffar, 1993). The pessimistic view of the future is that societies like China will break down into mega-cities warring with each other and that the international links in the economy will undermine traditional notions of citizenship and that the political future will be a much more insecure and uncertain environment. Regardless of these historical changes, the idea of citizenship is a central aspect of the modern struggle for democracy and an essential concept for the analysis of international conflict over scarce resources within a world economy.

References

Aldrich, R. and Connell, J. (1992) *France's Overseas Frontier.* Cambridge: Cambridge University Press.

Anderson, B. (1983) *Imagined Communities. Reflections on the Origin and Spread of Nationalism.* London: Verso.

Andrews, G. (ed.) (1991) *Citizenship.* London: Lawrence & Wishart.

Beiner, R. (ed.) (1995) *Theorizing Citizenship.* Albany: State University of New York Press.

Bellah, R., Madsen, F., Sullivan, W.M., Swidler, A. and Tipton, S.W. (1985) *Habits of the Heart.* New York: Harper & Row.

Blumer, M. and Rees, A.M. (1996) *Citizenship Today. The Contemporary Relevance of T.H. Marshall.* London: UCL Press.

Bobbio, N. (1987) *The Future of Democracy.* Minneapolis: University of Minneapolis Press.

Bobbio, N. (1989) *Democracy and Dictatorship. The Nature and Limits of State Power.* Cambridge: Polity Press.

Bourdieu, P. (1984) *Distinction. A Social Critique of the Judgement of Taste.* London: Routledge & Kegan Paul.

Brubaker, R. (1992) *Citizenship and Nationhood in France and Germany.* Cambridge, MA: Harvard University Press.

Cohen, J. and Rogers, J. (eds) (1995) *Associations and Democracy.* London: Verso.

Connolly, W.E. (1995) *The Ethos of Pluralisation.* Minneapolis: University of Minnesota Press.

Ferry, L. (1990) *Rights – the New Quarrel between the Ancients and the Moderns.* Chicago: University of Chicago Press.

Hirst, P.Q. (1989) *The Pluralist Theory of the State.* London: Routledge.

James, P. (1996) *Nation Formation.* London: Sage.

Mann, M. (1993) *The Sources of Social Power. The Rise of Classes and Nation-States 1760–1914,* vol. 2. Cambridge: Cambridge University Press.

Mannheim, K. (1992) *Essays on the Sociology of Culture.* London: Routledge & Kegan Paul.

Marshall, T.H. (1950) *Citizenship and Social Class and Other Essays.* Cambridge: Cambridge University Press.

Marshall, T.H. (1981) *The Right to Welfare and Other Essays.* London: Heinemann.

Mouffe, C. (ed.) (1992) *Dimensions of Radical Democracy.* London: Verso.

Muzaffar, C. (1993) *Human Rights and the New World Order.* Penang: Just World Trust.

Parkin, F. (1979) *Marxism and Class Theory: A bourgeois critique.* London: Tavistock.

Parsons, T. (1971) *The System of Modern Societies.* Englewood Cliffs, NJ: Prentice-Hall.

Pateman, C. (1970) *Participation and Democratic Theory.* Cambridge: Cambridge University Press.

Pateman, C. (1988) *The Sexual Contract.* Cambridge: Polity Press.

Pateman, C. (1989) *The Disorder of Women.* Cambridge: Polity Press.

Richards, T. (1991) *The Commodity Culture of Victorian England.* London: Verso.

Roche, M. (1992) *Rethinking Citizenship. Welfare, Ideology and Change in Modern Society.* Cambridge: Polity Press.

Sahlins, M. (1974) *Stone Age Economics.* London: Tavistock.

Said, E. (1994) *The Politics of Dispossession. The Struggle for Palestinian Self-Determination 1969–1994.* London: Chatto & Windus.

Saxonhouse, A.W. (1992) *Fear of Diversity. The Birth of Political Science in Ancient Greek Thought.* Chicago: University of Chicago Press.

Selbourne, D. (1994) *The Principle of Duty.* London: Sinclair-Stevenson.

Turner, B.S. (1986) *Citizenship and Capitalism. The Debate over Reformism.* London: Allen & Unwin.

Turner, B.S. (1989) 'Outline of a theory of citizenship', *Sociology,* 24: 189–217.

Turner, B.S. and Hamilton, P. (eds) (1994) *Citizenship, Critical Concepts.* 2 vols, London: Routledge.

Weber, M. (1981) *The City.* New York: Free Press.

Xenos, N. (1989) *Scarcity and Modernity.* London: Routledge.

CHAPTER 16

CONCLUSION: COHERENCE AND RUPTURE IN THE DISCIPLINE OF SOCIOLOGY

In western cultures, the concept of 'discipline' has an inevitably religious ambiance. Within a traditional sense, a discipline may be defined as an organized perspective on phenomena which is sustained by the academic training or disciplining of the mind. Like the related notions of cultivation and culture, a discipline requires disciplinary practices, if a certain type of mentality is to be sustained over time among a community of scholars. Disciplines of mind and body within a monastic context were, in Michel Foucault's sense, technologies of the soul. Some disciplines appear to be less concerned with the transmission of a body of knowledge than within a set of methodological practices, such as an ethnographic imagination. In some cultures, such as Buddhism, these intellectual or spiritual disciplines more explicitly involve the disciplining of bodies. A fundamental discpline is one which provides the basis for a cluster of applied or interdisciplinary fields. Following Pierre Bourdieu, these practices of knowledge are constituted by power relationships and social structures within the academy. The rise and fall of disciplinary regimes are consequences of powerful alliances which marshall the distribution of rewards within a field of academic practice. Disciplines are periodically fragmented and dispersed by internal intellectual struggles and by external conflicts with adjacent disciplines. Some disciplines – homoeopathy or astrology – never get fully accepted into the academy, while certain area studies – Soviet studies – may disappear. Disciplines through internal specialization – human and physical geography – may fragment and divide, and as a consequence disciplines which are held together by the requirements of an external professional body may be more resistant to internal fragmentation. In the twentieth century, sociology has neither enjoyed the professional benefits (and limitations) of external regulation, nor the comfort of internal disciplinary coherence.

Disciplines are obviously artificial constructs; they are not naturally occurring intellectual divisions which refer to divisions of the mind. They are socially constructed perspectives constituting a particular slice of reality and as such they can always be either reconstructed or deconstructed. Disciplines can also be merged or integrated with related fields to construct, for example, interdisciplinary studies. As I have just indicated, while Soviet studies have largely disappeared from the university system,

European studies are a growing area of teaching and research. Women's studies, while often claimed by radical feminists to be a discipline, are in fact multidisciplinary studies rather like the social sciences. Talcott Parsons's analysis of the four sub-systems of the social system (the famous AGIL formulation) was an attempt to provide an intellectual justification for the particular configuration of disciplines in the Harvard interdisciplinary programme on social institutions (Parsons, 1951). It attempted to show how economics, sociology, social psychology and politics could be complementary disciplines in the social sciences. A cluster of related disciplines traditionally forms a faculty, of which historically there are only two – the arts and science. Finally a set of faculties forms a university as an institution which seeks to offer a universal education in human knowledge of the world through the enforcement of discipline.

The rise and fall of disciplines, and the formation and erosion of faculties, and the changing role of the university are interconnected social effects of a complex web of social and intellectual causes. The sociology of science typically divides these causal factors into internal causes (the ways in which disciplines may respond to internal intellectual problems in the discipline) and external causes (the ways in which disciplines are shaped by the environment of the broader society). One influential account of the external circumstances in the rise of sociology (Nisbet, 1956) argued that sociology emerged primarily as a conservative reaction to the social consequences of the French and industrial revolutions. Its principal concepts – anomie, alienation, authority, community, the sacred and so forth – were designed to understand the disruption to social order which was arising from urbanization and industrialization. The etymological roots of the term 'sociology' suggest a conservative origin. In the 1830s Comte began to replace the notion of 'social physic' with a neologism 'sociology'. The new term indicated that sociology was the study of community, or more literally companionship (*socius*), by the methods of a positivist science. This notion that sociology was the science of a social body or organism, which is held together by notions of the sacred and ritual practices, became the dominant image of sociology in the French tradition. For Durkheim, sociology was the scientific study of institutions by a positivistic methodology and he established sociology in the university around the turn of the century through a classic argument that sociology is a discipline which explains social life by 'social facts'. In this respect, sociology may be regarded as an academic discipline which came into existence as a conservative response to the growing instability of the social structure following the impact of industrial capitalism.

Of course, the story is more complex. The metaphors which were used to understand these changes also played an important role in the sociological imagination, and thus functioned as a source of mental pictures or vocabulary for these changes. One important notion – the so-called organic analogy – was taken from Darwinistic evolutionary biology. Biological sciences and medical metaphors were to be an important feature of sociological thought in the late nineteenth and twentieth centuries. Within this Darwinistic paradigm, social order was paradoxically the outcome of violent struggles of species to adapt successfully to their environments. Therefore, government intervention to influence these 'natural' processes could only result, according to the ideology of the survival of the fittest, in social disaster, for example by protecting degenerate individuals.

In England, Herbert Spencer attempted to integrate a commitment to liberal individualism and social Darwinism, and developed a version of structural functionalism in which societies as systems adapt to their environment through a process of structural differentiation. In Germany, Marx and Engels also recognized the influence of Darwin and to some extent one can regard the class struggle as a social mechanism by which revolutionary, as opposed to evolutionary, change takes place. In this case, 'historical materialism' was the Marxist equivalent of 'evolutionary change'. Weber was also partially influenced by Darwinistic metaphors in his Freiburg inaugural address when he referred to the struggle for space ('elbow room') in eastern Germany in terms of a struggle between species. In France, Durkheim's notions about positivistic sociology were influenced by his reading of medical positivism.

How far these medical and biological perspectives influenced Parsons's own version of structural functionalism has remained controversial (Haines, 1987). Parsons's functionalism was certainly influenced by medical and biological theories of organic systems. For example, medical theories which studied the human body as a functional system proved to be significant in Parsons's early understanding of how social systems adapt to their environment. However, his later work on social systems theory was more directly influenced by cybernetics and he came to understand social systems as organizations of media of communication. Contemporary social systems theory, for example in the work of Niklas Luhmann (1995) has followed a similar route in which social systems are essentially communications systems whose functions are about the management of meaning and the simplification of complexity.

In this collection of essays, I have however been more interested in the specific relationship between Marx's political economy, the sociology of Weber and the legacy of that intellectual encounter. My perspective on sociology argues that there is a continuous, internal intellectual thread to sociology as a discipline, namely the debate with economic theories of society. If we regard Marx's political economy as a response to classical economics (such as Adam Smith and Ricardo) and utilitarian theory (Jeremy Bentham), then Weber's sociology was a response to Marx's economic theory of social class and social change. Weber's primary concern, at least in his comparative sociology, was to understand the economic ethics of the world religions in order to develop a view of social change (especially rationalization) as a response to the Marxian legacy. Although the work was a posthumous publication, the title of *Economy and Society* (Weber, 1978) is significant as an indication of the general orientation of his research. In a similar fashion, Durkheim's writing on suicide, professional ethics and the division of labour was a response to the limitations and negative effects of the hedonistic component of utilitarian economics. Mannheim's works on culture and knowledge were a critical response to the weakness of economic reductionism in Marx's economic analysis of class. Simmel's sociology of money attempted to provide an analysis of money as a symbolic system of exchange, the consequences of which increase alienation. Parsons's sociology, especially in *The Structure of Social Action* (1937), was an extended criticism of the limitations of rationalist positivism in economic theory insofar as they cannot respond effectively to the Hobbesian problem of order.

We can argue therefore that classical sociology emerged as an intellectual response to economic theories of society, and that its early formulation of class analysis, its development of theories of social change and its understanding of cultural phenomena were responses to the limitations of economic theory. In particular, sociology denied that marginal utility theory was an adequate explanation of human motivation or an adequate account of value. Early studies of religion were for example attempts to understand magic and religion without assuming that they represented faulty versions of utilitarian rationality. Sociology emerged as the study of companionship (*socius*), and companionship indicates the importance of sharing resources such as bread (*pan*) if fellowship is to be sustained. Sociology's preoccupation with the symbolic realm of human culture, namely religion in its broadest significance, has been based on a concern to understand how social bonds are formed and sustained, despite rather than because of economic exchange. Sociology was 'conservative' only in the sense that it regarded industrial capitalism as a threat to the possibility of community.

Sociology as a discipline has been concerned with the relationship between two dimensions of human collectivities, namely scarcity and solidarity. It recognizes that scarcities, which are predominantly economic and political aspects of society, are inescapable features of all human existence, and that somehow societies have to cope with and respond to scarcity. Scarcity does not disappear with increasing economic prosperity, because paradoxically it exists amongst plenty. As prosperity increases new goods become desirable, and hence they become scarce. The development of social arrangements to cope with scarcity are mundane and ubiquitous. For example, the formation of a queue is a basic response to scarcity, because it sets up an orderly method of managing the limitation of a desirable good. However, the precise nature of the queue has important cultural components: is the principle first in first served, or the elderly and the needy to the front, or the strongest to the front? How do we get people to accept and enforce queueing as a legitimate solution for scarcity?

Alongside the fact of scarcity, sociologists have argued that society needs some level of social order if it is to survive. The question of solidarity has been a specifically sociological interest, and it is this analysis of social order which has driven sociologists into an exploration of the functions of language, symbolic systems, communication and values, namely culture.

It is important for sociology to retain a concern for the dynamic tensions between both scarcity and solidarity. An emphasis on questions relating to scarcity often leads to an accusation of 'economic reductionism', whereas the opposite emphasis on solidarity raises objections about a conservative bias or even 'idealism'. Sociology as a discipline can function effectively as the scientific study of society when it is concerned to probe the contradictions, ambiguities and tensions between scarcity and solidarity, that is between patterns of inequality and relations of co-operation. The Marx–Weber dialogue was beneficial to the rise of sociology because it endlessly explored these paradoxes of social struggle and co-operation in the period of the development of European industrial capitalism. The debates about status and class, religion and capitalism, ideology and knowledge, intellectuals and hegemony, and sociology and political economy can in retrospect be seen as explorations of the scarcity/solidarity dichotomy. In this respect, the analysis of social citizenship can be seen as at least one outcome of this legacy, because in T.H. Marshall's formulation citizenship mediates between scarcity (in the form of class inequalities) and the need for solidarity (in the redistribution of resources to contain class conflict and promote social solidarity). The result of those debates was to produce a rich legacy of theories, concepts, methodologies and empirical findings which constituted sociology as a discipline.

Parsons's structural functionalism has often been criticized for its conservative bias, as a sociology which explained social order by reference to shared values and as a result neglected issues relating to scarcity. This criticism is somewhat misleading and exaggerated, because in fact Parsons's account of the social system was an attempt to understand two crucial dimensions of any society, namely the dimensions of allocation and integration. The allocative function required an analysis of how scarce resources are distributed; the integrative function, of how social integration is secured. In the allocative functions, there were political decisions about the ends or goals of society, and economic decisions about how, within the political framework, society can produce goods and services. In the integrative function, there is the motivation of individuals to achieve necessary goals and objectives, and finally there is the need to maintain values and norms to resolve social conflicts and tensions. This scheme was intended both to produce an interdisciplinary programme and to defend sociology as a discipline within the action frame of reference. Parsons's model of political, economic, cultural and psychological inputs to the four sub-systems (of goal-attainment, adaptation, integration and latency) was originally developed in the context of the emerging interdisciplinary programme at Harvard, namely the Department and Laboratory of Social

Relations (Parsons, 1973). The specific task of sociology within social systems theory was to understand how values contribute to maintaining social solidarity through an analysis of action. According to Parsons's principle of voluntary action, people make choices between different courses of action with respect to scarce resources in terms of values and norms.

The Parsonian solution to the relationship between scarcity and solidarity was never entirely successful for reasons which have been addressed in Chapter 9 on Parsons and the social system. The Parsonian paradigm was heavily attacked by so-called conflict theory which claimed that Parsons's sociology neglected issues to do with scarcity such as class structures and inequality. With the breakup of the influence of Parsonian sociology after his death in 1979, no paradigm has emerged as dominant and in the post-war period there have been various trends in sociology (symbolic interactionism, ethnomethodology, conflict sociology, rational choice theory and so forth) which have sought to correct the (alleged) problems of the Parsonian paradigm. There have also been attempts to restore a Parsonian approach in the form of neo-functionalism (Alexander, 1985). The failure of sociology to resolve these intellectual disagreements has produced further fragmentation and uncertainty. Indeed with the rise of postmodernism and cultural studies, there have been arguments to suggest that the very concept of 'the social' was historically limited.

The implication is that the end of 'the social' is also the end of sociology. The growth of cultural studies was initially not related to the intellectual fragmentation of sociology but to the crisis in departments of English literature. Cultural studies proved to be a successful response to the institutional and ideological crises of English literature. The challenge to the English canon from decolonization literature, multiculturalism and feminism was crucial in the transformation of the study of English literature into literary studies. However, cultural studies eventually grew out of literary studies and cultural studies has continued to be a literary study of texts. As a result, society is simply read as a cultural text in which it is deconstructed or undone. Studies of cultural hyper-reality attempt to analyse the boundary between the real and the unreal in the age of global television without any commitment to systematic empirical research into social relationships. Textual analysis has no clear sense of the need to assess empirically the effects of texts, or signs, or images. It has little sense of the phenomenological concreteness of the experiences of cultural objects in particular times and places. The underlying common theme of both cultural studies and postmodern theory is the impact of information technology on education, social stratification, political struggles and cultural representation. The erosion of English literature by literary studies, and the incursions on literary studies made by cultural studies, redoubled the tendency to subsume the social under the cultural.

In some respects, the crisis of English literary studies in American universities has been far more profound than in British and Commonwealth universities. In America during the cold war, a unified curriculum for literary studies was important to differentiate western from Soviet culture. With the collapse of the 'communist menace', American literary studies as a coherent university programme began to fall apart. The emphasis on multiculturalism and the recognition of difference ruled out any normative or canonical curriculum. The impossibility of a unitary programme of literary studies created an academic vacuum which was quickly and effectively filled by cultural studies. The study of media, communication and culture became dominated by a power/knowledge problematic which, with one or two notable exceptions, was explored almost exclusively first at a textual level and later at a digital level. These disciplinary changes need to be also seen within the context of a growth in the corporatization and commercialization of the university system. Literary studies does not sit easily within a university system which needs to generate significant injections of investment funding from private industry. By contrast, cultural studies can claim to have some relevance to the growth of the communications and consumer industries.

In a period of state intervention in the regulation of the economy and the creation of a welfare state, the discipline of sociology could legitimately claim to have relevance to the creation and professional development of policy analysts, civil servants and professional workers in the service sector. During the 1960s Marshall's theory of social citizenship provided an intellectual framework for both social policy and social work. It was an obvious bridge between Weberian sociology and applied social science. With the erosion of a centralized welfare state and the growth of neo-liberalism, there has been a marked departure from social Keynesian policies with the result that the traditional place of sociology with respect to training in social policy has been undermined. With the spread of cultural studies and the decline of centralized welfare policies, sociology has often become subsumed under either 'social theory' and/or 'cultural studies' as a general or liberal education.

This co-optation of sociology is unsatisfactory because 'reading' all social relations as cultural relations, apart from its other difficulties, leaves out the tensions between scarcity and solidarity as the intellectual terrain within which the social sciences function. Cultural studies has not only marginalized the questions traditionally addressed by Marxist political economy, but also Weberian sociology as a general framework for the analysis of patterns of scarcity and solidarity. We can define Weber's principal analytical interests as the problem of scarcity (especially a scarcity of meaning with secularization), the political scarcity of resources (which underlies the division between class, status and power), the sources of social solidarity in common religious systems, and finally the problem of social change within a dynamic of scarcity and solidarity. Rationalization can be interpreted as a process which attempts to resolve the historical problem of scarcity and solidarity through secular regulation. These political-economy dimensions in both Marx and Weber are lost in cultural studies which we can criticize as apolitical culturalism.

There is a case for defending the legacy of Marx and Weber in classical sociology, and further a need to defend the idea of theoretical cumulation. The principal political component of cultural studies is the idea of difference, which is borrowed from postmodernism. Because in modern societies, culture is diversified through multiculturalism there is a greater sense of the hybridity of modern cultural forms. Because there cannot be an authoritative or unified culture, we need to protect and celebrate different cultures. This argument in its own terms is perfectly valid, but by implication it also argues that morality is also fragmented and relativized. In short, cultural relativism is equated with moral relativism. Because postmodern cultural studies assumes moral relativism, it cannot produce, let alone accept, a unified moral criticism of modern societies. It is intellectually unlikely that cultural studies could develop an equivalent to Weber's notion of rationalization or Marx's concept of alienation. Postmodern cultural studies finds it difficult to promote a political vision of the modern world apart from an implicit injunction to enjoy diversity. This lack of politico-moral direction exists in a context of increasing alienation of intellectuals from McUniversity and increasing rationalization of educational systems. Cultural studies, despite claims to a connection with critical theory, are not adequate as a contemporary response to politics and ethics.

In a period where multidisciplinary cultural studies have flourished, arguments in favour of disciplinary training must appear (and are) inherently conservative. I suggest there are at least three important responses to contemporary multidisciplinarity. The first is that multidisciplinarity has to presuppose strong disciplines as the foundation for cross-disciplinarity co-operation. The second is that multidisciplinarity is in fact weak interdisciplinarity, because it makes no assumptions about what might be appropriate combinations of study. Thirdly, multidisciplinarity is perfectly compatible with the McDonaldization of the university curriculum, because it is very compatible with departmental and faculty closures on the grounds that in a perfect world of borderless multidisciplinarity everything is compatible with everything else. The disciplinary basis of the social sciences is worth defending on the grounds of depth and progression through a body of knowledge. Finally, sociology makes an important contribution to the study of scarcity and solidarity in modern societies, but to remain a discipline it requires an awareness of and commitment to the peculiarities of its own historical tradition: Marx and Weber are major aspects of that historical specificity.

References

Alexander, J.C. (ed.) (1985) *Neofunctionalism*. Beverly Hills: Sage.
Haines, V.A. (1987) 'Biology and social theory: Parsons's evolutionary theme', *Sociology*, 21(1): 19–39.
Luhmann, N. (1995) *Social Systems*. Stanford: Stanford University Press.
Nisbet, R. (1956) *The Sociological Tradition*. New York: Basic Books.

Parsons, T. (1937) *The Structure of Social Action.* New York: McGraw-Hill.

Parsons, T. (1951) *The Social System.* London: Routledge & Kegan Paul.

Parsons, T. (1973) 'Clyde Kluckhohn and the integration of the social sciences', in W.W. Taylor, J.L. Fischer and E.Z. Vogt (eds), *Culture and Life. Essays in Memory of Clyde Kluckhohn.* Carbondale and Edwardsville: Southern Illinois University Press. pp. 30–57.

Weber, M. (1978) *Economy and Society.* Berkeley: University of California Press, 2 volumes.

Index